Ethnicity and Empire in Kenya

From India to Africa, British imperial rule was built upon the service of "martial races." The label described subject peoples with an apparent aptitude for warfare, who provided military support for the empire in its colonies, and indeed further afield. This book is about the creation and development of ethnic identity among East Africa's premier martial race – the Kamba – who comprise approximately one-eighth of Kenya's population today. From the British perspective, the Kamba were a simplistically "martial" and "loyal" people they recruited in large numbers as soldiers and police during the colonial era. But this understanding hid a more complex truth. Since 1800, men and women, young and old, Christians and non-Christians, and the elite and poor had fought over the virtues they considered worthy of honor in their communities, and which of their visions should constitute "Kamba." This process of "making Kamba" frequently intersected with the colonial state: Chiefs and war veterans, for instance, demonstrated skill in leveraging their martial reputation for financial benefits from the government in Kenya. But ultimately, women's arguments about the importance of community came to the fore as the Kamba role in Kenya's military declined in the 1960s. The book ends by reflecting on Kamba ethnicity in twenty-first-century Kenya, especially following the post-election violence of 2007 and 2008.

Based on extensive archival research and more than 150 interviews on several continents, Myles Osborne's *Ethnicity and Empire* is one of the first books to analyze the complex process of building and shaping "tribe" over more than two centuries. It reveals new ways to think about several themes central to the history of European empires and their colonies: soldiering, "loyalty," martial race, and the very nature of imperial control.

Ethnicity and Empire in Kenya

Loyalty and Martial Race among the Kamba,
c. 1800 to the Present

MYLES OSBORNE

CAMBRIDGE
UNIVERSITY PRESS

CAMBRIDGE
UNIVERSITY PRESS

32 Avenue of the Americas, New York NY 10013-2473, USA

Cambridge University Press is part of the University of Cambridge.

It furthers the University's mission by disseminating knowledge in the pursuit of education, learning and research at the highest international levels of excellence.

www.cambridge.org
Information on this title: www.cambridge.org/9781107680524

© 2014

First published 2014
First paperback edition 2015

A catalogue record for this publication is available from the British Library

Library of Congress Cataloguing in Publication data
Osborne, Myles, author.
Ethnicity and empire in Kenya : loyalty and martial race among the Kamba, c. 1800 to the present / Myles Osborne.
pages cm
Includes bibliographical references.
ISBN 978-1-107-06104-0 (Hardback)   1. Kamba (African people)–History.
2. Ethnicity–Political aspects–Kenya.   3. Kenya–Politics and government–To 1963.
4. Great Britain–Colonies–Africa–Administration.   5. Allegiance–Kenya.   I. Title.
DT433.545.K36083 2014
305.8963953–dc23
2014004591

ISBN 978-1-107-06104-0 Hardback
ISBN 978-1-107-68052-4 Paperback

For my parents

Contents

Acknowledgments

As I was putting the finishing touches on this book, I discovered two old passports tucked away in a cardboard box at the bottom of my closet. A quick flip through revealed visa after visa – and an overwhelming variety of entry and exit stamps – from Kenya over the past decade. Some simple calculations disclosed that I had traveled to the country seven times, and spent close to two years living there.

After the predictable flash of concern that I should, perhaps, have more to show for these research trips, my next thought was of the vast number of debts I had incurred along the way. They were not, of course, restricted to people in Kenya, but many others in the United States and United Kingdom who provided academic counsel, research assistance, or simply a friendly face in an unfamiliar place. This book would never have been concocted, written, or published without the help of the people mentioned below, though they bear no responsibility for any errors that appear in its text.

This final product has been written, shredded, and rewritten more times than I care to remember since its first manifestation as a doctoral thesis in 2008. But I hope that it retains the attention to detail, nuances of social history, and clear argumentation that I learned at Harvard University under the guidance of Emmanuel Akyeampong and Caroline Elkins. During each stage of the dissertation they were generous and encouraging, and have continued to play a role in my career as mentors. Similarly, John Lonsdale has helped guide this project since 2006, with the characteristic thoughtfulness that has inspired many junior scholars. This book derives, in many ways, from arguments put forth in his classic essay "The Moral Economy of Mau Mau," published in 1992.

His encouragement to think deeply about the cultural basis for ethnic identity was vital in my own learning about Africa, and in the production of this book.

In Kenya, Mwendwa Musyimi accompanied me on innumerable trips around the country to conduct interviews. He is one of the most hard-working and good-humored people I know, and the quality of my oral interviews owes much to his personality and acumen. I doubt whether there exists any pertinent political or social question about Kenyan society that we have not debated on some hillside during the course of a multi-hour walk. Many of those conversations concerned the men and women who were the sources for our interviews, and often our hosts: I can certainly never repay the countless cups of tea, plates of *mūthokoi* (de-husked maize), or beds we were offered, nor will I forget the hours people took to sit with us and patiently discuss Kamba history.

In Nairobi, John Nottingham has been a good friend and source of wisdom on Kenyan history (not to mention England's cricket team) since 2004. During the same period, Frederick Iraki of the United States International University has been a constant presence, always sharing local knowledge and sage counsel. And a group of Kenyanists provided academic stimulation and excellent company: They include Brian Casady, Dave Eaton, Lynsey Farrell, Sunil Lakhani, Julie MacArthur, Daniel Ostendorff, and Suraj Shah. Sana Aiyar's copious and typically hilarious responses to questions about Kenya's Indian community were gratefully received, as were Kelly Jo Bahry's offers of couch space, floor space, or company in a *matatu* (public minibus) on the way to an interview.

In the Kenya National Archives, Peterson Kithuka and Evanson Kiiru were generous with their time and expertise, while Richard Ambani discovered "lost" files with a panache that has proved the savior for several generations of Kenyanist historians. Archivists at many other repositories have provided invaluable assistance. These include the staff at the National Archives, Imperial War Museum, University of Birmingham, British Library, and Rhodes House Library in the United Kingdom; McMillan Library, the University of Nairobi Library, and Africa Inland Mission Archives in Nairobi; and the Billy Graham Center and Wheaton College Archives and Special Collections at Wheaton in the United States. Lucy McCann of Rhodes House, Brian Arensen of the Africa Inland Mission, and the staff of the Imperial War Museum went above and beyond the call of duty to help a rushed researcher. Each helped me to procure permissions to cite from restricted documents, for which I thank both them and the copyright holders of these pieces.

I owe intellectual debts to a number of scholars who have encouraged me to question and analyze my material in new and varied ways through their critical readings of my articles or chapters. In this, I am grateful to Huw Bennett, Jeremiah Kitunda, Joanna Lewis, Kate Luongo, Greg Mann, Tom Metcalf, Maarten Onneweer, Tim Parsons, Ed Steinhart, Heather Streets-Salter, and Richard Waller. John Catton and his colleagues at the King's African Rifles and East African Forces Association provided quick and detailed information about several military photographs from the Kenya National Archives.

Chuck Ambler and Derek Peterson both read the "final" draft of this book and provided extraordinarily perceptive, prompt, and helpful comments. They then proceeded to read the "final final" draft with similar attention. Whatever merits the "final final final" version owes much to their willingness to devote the time and energy to help me improve, clarify, and tighten my thinking and writing.

In Colorado, a faculty writing group including Lucy Chester, Sanjay Gautam, Mithi Mukherjee, John Willis, and especially Marjorie McIntosh helped me to refine my chapters and ideas. Scott Bruce, Susan Kent, and Anne Lester provided the friendship and mentorship that have enabled me to progress along my chosen career path with far less bumping and jarring than I experienced on the road in eastern Kenya. In addition, Reg Carlyon and her team at the Interlibrary Loan Office patiently fulfilled the most obscure of requests, while Eric Lovell drew the maps that illustrate the text, graciously tolerating repeated entreaties for increasingly minor alterations.

I am also grateful to the publishers of the following journals for permission to reproduce sections from several previous articles. Parts of Chapters 6 and 7 first appeared in the *International Journal of African Historical Studies* as "The Kamba and Mau Mau: Ethnicity, Development, and Chiefship, 1952–1960" (2010) and in the *Journal of Imperial and Commonwealth History* as "Controlling Development: 'Martial Race' and Empire in Kenya, 1945–59" (2014). Several pages of information on the politician Paul Ngei (in Chapters 7 and 8) first appeared in "'The Cat With Nine Lives': Paul Ngei and the Making of Modern Kenya," in the *Journal of Eastern African Studies* (2012).

Various organizations and committees at Harvard University and the University of Colorado Boulder provided funding to facilitate this research. At Harvard I received grants from the Department of History, Committee on African Studies, Frederick K. Sheldon fund, Graduate Society, and Project on Justice, Welfare, and Economics at the

Weatherhead Center for International Affairs. At the University of Colorado Boulder, grants from the Graduate Committee on Arts and Humanities, Dean's Fund for Excellence, and Eugene M. Kayden fund allowed me to continue my research in Kenya and the United Kingdom. An international research program established through the generosity of Hazel Barnes and Doris Schwalbe permitted me to spend several weeks in London working at the National Archives at a crucial time in this project.

As this book neared its final stages, a number of people with Cambridge University Press hauled it toward – and then shoved it across – the finish line. They include Britto Fleming Joe, Will Hammell, Dave Morris, and Sarika Narula. Lila Stromer copyedited the entire draft with patience and great attention to detail, and Linda Woods brought the same talents to her proofreading and editing of the very last version (once I could no longer tolerate its presence in my house).

Over the past five years, Jessica Leigh has provided encouragement at the most difficult stages of this project. I first met Jess when she was in the midst of a somewhat discouraging diatribe about professors at the University of Colorado Boulder. I doubt whether she imagined then that she would end up engaged to one some years later, or know as much about the process of academic book production or the tenure system as she now does.

But finally, and most importantly: This book is dedicated to my parents. Almost nothing I have achieved – and certainly not this book – would have come to pass without the endless time, support, and inspiration they have given me over the years.

Boulder, Colorado
April 22, 2014

Maps

FIGURE 1: Map of Machakos and Kitui districts ("Ukambani") as they existed during the majority of the twentieth century.

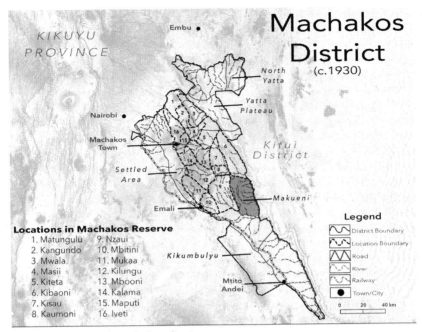

Machakos District (c.1930)

KIKUYU PROVINCE

Embu •

North Yatta

Yatta Plateau

Nairobi •

Machakos Town

Settled Area

Kitui District

Emali

Makueni

Kikumbulyu

Mtito Andei

Locations in Machakos Reserve

1. Matungulu	9. Nzaui
2. Kangundo	10. Mbitini
3. Mwala	11. Mukaa
4. Masii	12. Kilungu
5. Kiteta	13. Mbooni
6. Kibaoni	14. Kalama
7. Kisau	15. Maputi
8. Kaumoni	16. Iveti

Legend
- District Boundary
- Location Boundary
- Road
- River
- Railway
- Town/City

0   20   40 km

FIGURE 2: Map of Machakos district, *c.* 1930.

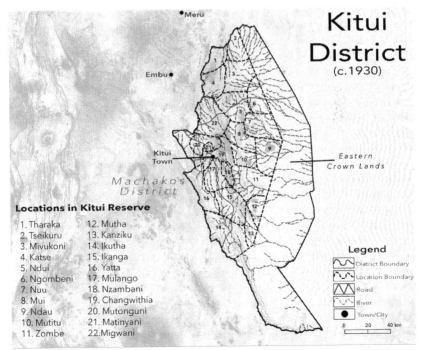

Kitui District (c.1930)

• Meru

Embu •

Kitui Town

Machakos District

Eastern Crown Lands

Locations in Kitui Reserve

1. Tharaka	12. Mutha
2. Tseikuru	13. Kanziku
3. Mivukoni	14. Ikutha
4. Katse	15. Ikanga
5. Ndui	16. Yatta
6. Ngombeni	17. Mulango
7. Nuu	18. Nzambani
8. Mui	19. Changwithia
9. Ndau	20. Mutonguni
10. Mutitu	21. Matinyani
11. Zombe	22. Migwani

Legend
- District Boundary
- Location Boundary
- Road
- River
- Town/City

0   20   40 km

FIGURE 3: Map of Kitui district, *c.* 1930.

Introduction

On January 11, 1945, a young British lieutenant serving in the King's
African Rifles was given the responsibility of transporting a small group
of Kamba chiefs from the shores of Lake Victoria – in Uganda – to
Nairobi, the capital of Kenya Colony. The chiefs had just carried out an
important undertaking in the war effort: They had visited a barracks at
Jinja and given speeches to boost the morale of the rank-and-file soldiers
there. They had then taken pains to meet with the troops individually, and
assured them that their families back at home were being looked after
while they served in foreign lands. British military officials considered
these sorts of visits vital for the overall prosecution of the war: for a large
proportion of the rank-and-file were also Kamba, and because the "tribe"
was considered East Africa's premier martial race[1] – a people who supposedly possessed an in-born aptitude for military service – ensuring their
satisfaction was paramount in the midst of conflict.
  The lieutenant piloted his lorry without issue through much of the
wasteland that is northern Kenya. It is easy to imagine how the chiefs
experienced the journey. They would have worn their old uniforms,
carefully mended where the inevitable tears had appeared over time,
and their medals would have shone brightly on their chests: for practically
all of them had extensive military backgrounds and had served in the First
World War in the East African Campaign. It was for this reason that
British officials had chosen them – and not any other chiefs – to go to Jinja.

---

[1] During the nineteenth and twentieth centuries, the term "race" – in the context of "martial
race" – was used to describe any ethnic, religious, or other group with "warlike" characteristics. Streets, *Martial Races*, 6–10.

1

As war veterans – and deeply proud of their service – they would have borne the bumping and jarring of the rough roads stoically, without complaint. They would have conversed amongst themselves in Kikamba;[2] when it came to chatting with the lieutenant, some would have stuttered in stilted English, and others spoken more fluently.

To the north of Nairobi, the lieutenant pulled his lorry over at one of the checkpoints that dotted the colony during its wartime footing. He handed his papers to the British officer on duty, and exchanged small talk: "I have half the Wakamba reserve on board!" he joked, perhaps gesturing toward the back of the vehicle.

The lieutenant's comment caused uproar. Documentary evidence does not allow us to understand precisely what upset the chiefs. Possibly they disliked being lumped together with the common men and women from the villages, or took umbrage at words they considered flippant or disrespectful. Perhaps there were other reasons. But the issue caused by one off-hand remark quickly escalated.

The following day, the lieutenant penned a groveling apology to the district commissioner of Kitui, the eastern of the two Kamba districts, from which several of the chiefs hailed. "[My] remark, I admit unreservedly, was foolish and in the poorest of taste," he wrote, "I . . . realise that my conduct was both ill-considered and undiplomatic." Not only had the lieutenant embarrassed himself, but also those above him in the military hierarchy. He continued: "I would be grateful . . . Sir, if you would assure the Chiefs, should they mention the incident, that I, and my superiors, are unreservedly apologetic for this breach of manners."[3] It is difficult to imagine that a note about the incident did not end up in the young man's personnel file.[4]

The incident encapsulates the relationship between Kamba leaders and the state in Kenya during the later colonial period. The Kamba – a Bantu-speaking people living in modern-day central and eastern Kenya, in

[2] This is correctly "Kĩkamba" but appears without the accent for ease of reading. Similarly, Gĩkũyũ – referring to the language or people of central Kenya – is rendered "Kikuyu." All other Kikamba words – with the exception of the names of informants or historical figures – are produced in standard (accented) orthography.

[3] Kenya National Archives [hereafter KNA], DC/KTI/7/5, Holt to DC [District Commissioner] Kitui, January 12, 1945.

[4] The recollection of one former district officer – and later district commissioner – is instructive here. When I mentioned Kamba chiefs to him, he laughed loudly, and said: "Junior officers used to get practically slapped on the head and told these [the chiefs] are the bosses," he told me. "They're the ones that keep the tribe straight!" Personal communication, April 4, 2011.

an area usually called "Ukambani"[5] – possessed a reputation for sterling military service and loyalty. Colonial and military officials leaned heavily on them to fill the ranks of the police and soldiery. Kamba soldiers were proud of that reputation: They recalled decades of war against "the Maasai" in the nineteenth century as having hardened them into a fighting "tribe" whose courage and abilities in battle had no peer, and who always gladly volunteered in large numbers for military duties. British officers and colonial officials, therefore, came to view the Kamba as they did the Sikhs of India, Gurkhas of Nepal, or Scottish Highlanders: as a "race" of soldiers who "naturally" made good fighting auxiliaries.[6]

But this simplistic understanding conceals a more complex truth. First, few thought of themselves as "Kamba" before the 1940s, when daily life was oriented in a profoundly local way. And second, this apparently all-encompassing martial identity was only a thin veneer: Beneath its surface, old and young, Christian and non-Christian, elite and non-elite, men and women, educated and not fiercely contested and debated what was "Kamba." Each had their own conceptions of what virtues, values, and practices constituted "proper" behavior in their communities, and by extension, should constitute the basis of "Kamba" culture.

Ethnicity and Empire explores this process of "making Kamba" over the past 200 years of East Africa's history. Its central theme intersects with a number of broader issues that have concerned historians of empire and colonialism. First, it takes the imperial label of "martial race" – a nineteenth-century British construct applied to peoples from India to West Africa, and beyond – and recasts it as a contested space that encompassed local debates about martial service. Thus when British officials defined the Kamba in martial terms, it meant that local leaders could use that military reputation to pressure the colonial government in Kenya for benefits, and also attempt to solidify positions of authority at home by bolstering their social standing.

Second, this book addresses the hoary notion of "loyalty." The term appears throughout colonial history, used in plain fashion: Some peoples were "loyal" and others "disloyal" depending on their relationship to the colonial power. But this work suggests that "loyalty" was a far richer

---

[5] This is an informal and commonly used term. Until the 1990s, Kamba lived in Machakos district – in the west – and Kitui district in the east. Since the 1990s, the Kenyan government has created, erased, or altered a variety of different locations and districts. This book typically refers to Machakos and Kitui because these districts were in existence for the majority of the period under study.

[6] Enloe, *Ethnic Soldiers.*

concept with deeper meanings. On one level, it was the arena in which
Kamba and colonial officials negotiated their relationship; colonial propaganda demanded Kamba remain "loyal" to the government, as befitted a
people with a history of martial service, and Kamba reminded officials of
that service to procure advantages. But "loyalty" – rendered in Kikamba
as *ĩwi* – came to mean much more: by the 1940s, veterans argued that it
described a set of shared values that constituted the core cultural material
in Kamba communities; others – women in particular – disagreed.

Third, this work contributes to a new wave of research on development in
Africa by bringing ethnicity into dialogue with the colonial development
agenda. After the Second World War, Britain instituted new programs
of "development" and "welfare" in an effort to create new, visible manifest-
ations of its trusteeship in Africa. This was an effort to assuage pressure from
the United States and the Soviet Union – as well as intellectuals in Africa,
India, and the Caribbean – that Britain grant independence to its colonies.
In Kenya and elsewhere, however, these new programs were actually
methods of imperial control. During the 1940s and 1950s, officials diverted
enormous chunks of the colony's development monies to the Kamba in
an effort to maintain political calm, as well as to ensure the "loyalty" of
Kamba soldiers and police (the proportion rose from 39 to 53 percent of the
colony's overall funding, while Kamba comprised one-eighth of Kenya's
population). Aware of officials' worry, leaders leveraged their martial
reputation to press for greater and greater benefits from these programs.

Finally, this book provides the first comprehensive history of the
Kamba. Due to the relative political insignificance of the Kamba in postcolonial Kenya, scholars have perhaps assumed a similar trend in the
preceding years. This study weaves the Kamba into a revisionist approach
to Kenya's history, arguing that our understanding of the country has
been greatly compromised by their absence.

No analysis of this book's topics relating to colonialism or imperialism is
possible without understanding the process of "making Kamba." If "the
Kamba" did not exist in common consciousness (as opposed to – say – in
the minds of missionaries or district administrators), then any discussion
about "them" (or "the Sikhs," or "the Gurkhas") cannot proceed with
validity.[7] It is, in fact, almost impossible to separate "making Kamba"
from any discussion of martial race, loyalty, or empire.

[7] Lonsdale, "Gusii."

Much of the research on the creation of ethnicity in sub-Saharan Africa analyzes the role played by colonialism in this process. During the 1980s, Leroy Vail produced arguably the most direct statement of colonialism's impact in his now-classic edited volume, *The Creation of Tribalism in Southern Africa*. Basing his argument on a series of case studies drawn from the region, Vail suggested that severe famine and drought, combined with the presence of the all-encompassing migrant labor system of the gold mines, led chiefs and commoners to seize upon ethnicity as a way to negotiate these challenging circumstances.[8]

Charles Ambler's excellent work on central Kenya in the late nineteenth century – which addressed Kikamba-speaking peoples[9] in part – reflected this approach. For Ambler, the commencement of colonial rule led to the promulgation of ethnic boundaries that are recognizable today, and removed the flexibility that previously existed (an argument made more broadly by Mahmood Mamdani).[10] The two existing studies that address geographically and chronologically limited periods of "Kamba" history reflect a less nuanced approach. Arriving before the publication of Vail's work and that of Terence Ranger,[11] both Robert Tignor and J. Forbes Munro assumed the existence of a coherent "Kamba" tribe by the late nineteenth century, which they used as a baseline for their studies.[12]

But these works overemphasize the impact of colonial rule.[13] From the perspective of the quiet reading rooms of the National Archives of the United Kingdom, colonial bureaucracy seems neat and clear in its delineation of Africans into "tribes." But the colonial state was rarely some behemoth that shaped the day-to-day aspects of African lives in the early twentieth century. It was more analogous to the "thin white line" described by Anthony Kirk-Greene: a handful of youthful administrators, stumblingly trying to make sense of a world that bore little resemblance to Winchester or Eton.[14] In Sara Berry's succinct summation, this was

---

[8] Vail (ed.), *Creation of Tribalism*.
[9] This term is used instead of "the Kamba" to avoid implying a sense of ethnic unity that did not exist until around the time of the Second World War (see Chapter 1).
[10] Ambler, *Kenyan Communities*; Mamdani, *Citizen and Subject*; Mamdani, "Making Sense."
[11] Ranger, "Invention of Tradition."
[12] Munro, *Colonial Rule*; Tignor, *Colonial Transformation*. A similar criticism may be leveled at Kennell Jackson's work, the most well-known example of which is Jackson, "Dimensions."
[13] Spear, "Neo-Traditionalism."   [14] Kirk-Greene, "Thin White Line."

"hegemony on a shoestring."[15] Some parts of Kitui never received a visit
from an administrator or missionary before the 1920s, and in many areas
life continued as it always had: As late as 1929, approximately 30,000
"Kamba" trekked west and "became" "Kikuyu." Women had a particular ability to slide between "tribes" without difficulty, causing disquiet for
many British administrators who cherished neatness and order.

This is not, of course, to argue that the colonial emphasis on tribes was
irrelevant. It provided African peoples with an extraordinary opportunity: They could – in John Iliffe's words – "*create* [my emphasis] tribes to
function within the colonial framework."[16] The system catalyzed the
discourse between peoples in central and eastern Kenya as they sought
to create "Kamba" around their own – frequently competing – visions.
Intellectuals and others attempted to use the weight and authority
conveyed by tribe to increase their own personal power and to accrue
benefits for their people. It was Africans alone who could give the "tribal"
units genuine meaning, and they worked hard to fill these "empty
boxes."[17] This effort was successful when it built upon the shared history,
experiences, and values that had developed among many Kikamba-
speaking peoples during the eighteenth and nineteenth centuries: These
were the buried commonalities, the "roots of ethnicity," that could be
molded into "Kamba."[18]

. John Lonsdale provided the most coherent and comprehensive treatment of this process in a seminal essay on the Kikuyu. For Lonsdale,
ethnicity was an arena of debate in which Kikuyu people argued over
virtue and morality. This "moral ethnicity" was a set of standards of
behavior that sustained Kikuyu communities, and was often at odds
with – or contrary to – the external manifestation of ethnicity ("political
tribalism") that African intellectuals presented to the colonial state.[19]

Matthew Carotenuto's and Julie MacArthur's work – in the cases of
the Luo and Luyia, respectively – are in significant part inspired by this
approach. But there are important distinctions between these examples
and that of the Kamba. In the cases of the Kikuyu, Luo, and Luyia,
intellectuals did extensive linguistic work as they sought to define and

[15] Berry, *No Condition is Permanent*, 22–42.
[16] Iliffe, *Modern History of Tanganyika*, 318.
[17] Ranger, "Invention of Tradition Revisited," 84.
[18] I am grateful to Richard Waller for helping me to clarify my thinking on this point. The
phrasing "roots of ethnicity" is borrowed from Atkinson, *Roots*.
[19] Lonsdale, "Moral Economy."

redefine their communities.[20] In each case, they wrote histories of their "tribes." In Kikuyu and Luo areas, the pages of newspapers and newsletters like *Muigwithania*, *Mumenyereri*, and *Ramogi* were important sites for these discussions.[21] In Luyialand, the Luyia Language Committee was active from 1941 in such work, though the magazine *Muluyia* does not seem to have gained the importance of the others.[22]

Yet unlike these communities, the development of a Kamba ethnic identity – and the desire of a majority of people to ascribe to it – came late, in the 1940s. Uniquely, it was driven by powerful war veterans and chiefs who successfully pulled together a series of disparate strands of cultural argument. This process is all the more difficult to identify because no Kamba intellectuals published newsletters or histories: There is an almost complete absence of non-government publications written in Kikamba before 1963 (and few after). Nor did any easily visible ceremony of circumcision – as in the Kikuyu case – clearly convey "tribal" membership in Kamba communities.[23]

Ethnicity and Empire resolves these difficulties in two ways. First, it places the colonial period in the context of the past 200 years of East Africa's history, unlike almost all other contemporary works on ethnicity in sub-Saharan Africa. This enables all-important arguments and discussions among nineteenth-century Kikamba-speakers to elucidate later debates under colonial rule. Only with this deeper reaching into the past – and toward the present – does the opacity of Kamba history lighten.[24] Second, it relies on more marginal sources for studying Africa's history, which take on tremendous import.

In this regard, historians are fortunate that Ukambani was a frequent stop for a variety of missionaries, anthropologists, travelers, and others during the late nineteenth and early twentieth centuries. They include the Swedish anthropologist Gerhard Lindblom, who undertook field research in 1911 and 1912, and published extensive findings. The publications of several early colonial administrators assigned to Ukambani are also of great value. Men such as Charles Hobley and Charles Dundas were semi-professional anthropologists – "anthro-administrators," in Kate Luongo's phrase – whose works are important sites for revealing

---

[20] In the Kikuyu case, see especially Peterson, *Creative Writing.*
[21] Carotenuto, *"Riwruok E Teko"*; Lonsdale, "Moral Economy."
[22] MacArthur, "Making and Unmaking."   [23] Thomas, *Politics of the Womb.*
[24] This approach owes much to scholarly work on precolonial Africa. See Atkinson, *Roots*; Greene, *Gender.*

arguments between Kikamba-speaking peoples about "custom" and
"tradition."[25] The worldview of early Christians is revealed through their
translations of biblical passages;[26] proverbs and folk tales published
during the early twentieth century speak to virtues people considered
important at the time; and vocabularies help unpack how people
conceived of the "tribe" to which they supposedly belonged. These kinds
of sources are complemented by information drawn from more than 150
in-person interviews with people living in central and eastern Kenya – as
well as with former British administrators and settlers – in addition to
the more "standard" records of the British government, colonial administration, missionaries, and the military.[27]

Scholars have argued that the experience of serving under British officers
during the Second World War caused African veterans to view themselves
as a separate, privileged *caste* after 1945.[28] But among Kamba, the war
was the crucial event from which a wide sense of *ethnic* identification
spread. The experience of war meant that this ethnic identity was
conceived initially in martial terms, though this was quickly contested.
To British officials, the war simply provided confirmation for something
they had "known all along": The Kamba were a "martial race."

The term "martial race" came into common parlance during the
consolidation of British rule in India in the mid nineteenth century.[29]
It was developed in large part following the Indian Uprising of 1857,
which caused a crisis of confidence for liberal British administrators. They
came to classify Indians into "martial" and "non-martial" groups, basing
their assertions on the colonial science of ethnography.[30]

The majority of scholarship on martial races approaches the topic in
a similar fashion. It typically stems from the logic that because the term
was a British one, then the concept barely involved the Africans or Indians
who were labeled "martial." But this is a highly problematic perspective.
As scholars such as Antoinette Burton and Mrinalini Sinha have
demonstrated, the relationship between colony and metropole was one
of two-way exchange.[31] The categories of "colonized" and "colonizer"
constantly shifted, and most importantly, happenings in the empire

[25] Luongo, *Witchcraft*.
[26] An approach inspired by Peterson's work. Peterson, *Creative Writing*.
[27] For more details about sources and methods, see *Bibliography*.
[28] Killingray, *Fighting for Britain*; Parsons, *African Rank-and-File*, 53–103.
[29] The foundational work on India's "martial races" is MacMunn, *Armies*.
[30] Dirks, *Castes of Mind*.   [31] Burton, *Heart of the Empire*; Sinha, *Colonial Masculinity*.

resulted in important ideological shifts back in Britain. In a recent monograph, Heather Streets has shown specifically how the ideology of martial race impacted British ideas at home.[32]

Taking its lead from these scholars, this work seeks to expand the notion of martial race, arguing that current understandings pay little heed to the role played by colonized peoples in creating, accentuating, and projecting a martial nature, and the degree to which this reflected preexisting values.[33] In the majority of work on India, scholars note vaguely that precolonial culture was probably important in some fashion in the process of becoming "martial," but that categories like "Gurkha" and "Sikh" were as much the "product of imperial imaginations as they were the result of indigenous development."[34] This seriously minimizes the efforts of colonized peoples to shape their own destinies under British rule.

Few studies genuinely attempt to decipher the motivations of colonized peoples for joining martial service. There are partial exceptions: In his work on the Singh/Sikh peoples of India, Richard Fox considers the role played by class, religion, and occupation in creating a Singh/Sikh identity.[35] And David Omissi goes further in his *The Sepoy and the Raj*. For Omissi, economic considerations were certainly important for young men who joined colonial forces. But he pushes his analysis beyond the purely economic by addressing how male considerations of *izzat* (honor) and status led men to enter martial service.[36]

The study of martial races in Africa has never reached anything close to the level in Indian historiography.[37] The major area where it has received attention concerns the relationship between precolonial background and the likelihood of peoples joining the colonial military. Thus Tim Parsons and Risto Marjomaa – writing about the Kamba and Yao of Nyasaland – have argued that service in the early colonial military was minimally related to any precolonial characteristics, instead emphasizing the relevance of economic factors and the location of army recruiting offices (respectively) in the process of becoming "martial."[38]

But these materialistic arguments do not reflect the rich diversity of reason and motive that guide human experience; nor do they reflect

[32] Streets, *Martial Races*.   [33] For instance, Caplan, *Warrior Gentleman*.
[34] Peers, "Martial Races."   [35] Fox, *Lions of the Punjab.*
[36] Omissi, *Sepoy and the Raj*, especially 76–112. For an earlier rendering, see MacMunn, *Armies*.
[37] Kirk-Greene, "*Damnosa Hereditas*."
[38] Marjomaa, "Martial Spirit"; Parsons, "Wakamba Warriors."

the role that martial service played in communities in central and eastern Kenya, and surely the remainder of Africa. To understand "martial race," it is vital to understand communities more deeply, and to reflect on fault lines including gender, generation, class, religion, and more. What sort of status in their communities did young men believe that they might win by joining martial occupations before, during, and after colonial rule? What did colonial chiefs think of this sort of recruitment? What community values did young men claim to possess through soldiering? How did young men use their service to challenge their elders and ostensible betters? What advantages came from widely projecting a martial identity? It is essential here to blur the apparent divisions between military, cultural, and social history: The bonds and dissonances between these disciplinary lines reveal a more profound understanding of martial races, colonial militaries, and soldiering in Africa.

Finally, the historiography on martial races has utterly ignored women, viewing them as irrelevant in such "manly" and "masculine" occupations. Yet women played a central role: At a simplistic level, they conveyed respect for the demonstration of male virtues. But more importantly, they labeled what behavior and standards constituted the cultural material that became "Kamba," and what role martial identity played in that process. By the late 1950s, women had successfully argued that martial virtue was irrelevant without a strong record of supporting community interests; it was *community*, they stated, that constituted the true meaning of "Kamba."

Male leaders proved more adept at negotiating with British officials than with their wives, sisters, and daughters. They "sold" the Kamba as a plainly martial "tribe" – with a history and reputation for soldiering – that deserved respect and benefits. The situation was similar to the experience of the *Tirailleurs Sénégalais* in French West Africa. As Gregory Mann shows, these men believed that France had incurred a "blood debt" to them for the military service they had provided during much of the twentieth century.[39] But unlike West African veterans, Kamba leaders tried to make gains based on ethnic identity, not caste.

Almost every discussion or debate between Kamba leaders and British officials during the later colonial period circulated around the idea of "loyalty." Leaders claimed that they possessed the quality and should be

---

[39] Mann, *Native Sons.*

respected for it; British officials reminded them of the quality to try to calm political dissent. The term "loyalty" is one that historians – as well as scholars in other disciplines – have been wary of confronting, despite the fact that colonial history in Africa and India is riddled with its use.[40] In part, this is because it raises the specter of "collaboration." From the 1960s onward – with most African colonies independent – it seemed to refer to those who had acted against the best interests of their own people by serving in colonial military forces. This was especially true in Kenya, where "loyalists" – a clearly related and similar word – referred to those Kikuyu who sided with the British during Mau Mau.[41] Despite scholarship on the concept of "collaboration" – which rejects its binary opposition with "resistance," and which provides a more nuanced understanding of the term – the concept of "loyalty" has escaped such treatment.[42]

Collaboration

Loyalty was never such a simplistic term for Kamba, nor did they usually render it in English. The philosopher Andrew Oldenquist neatly sums up the crux of the problem concerning the utility of the term itself:

> If I say that I ought to defend my country, I have ... loyalty. But if I am willing to replace "my country" with, e.g., "a democratic country" or "a Christian country," I have not a loyalty but an ideal.[43]

For Kamba, "loyalty" connoted far more than a simplistic bond to the colonial military. In the early 1940s, people began to use ĩwi to translate the term, a word that had previously meant simply "obedient." Returning veterans argued that ĩwi represented a conglomeration of virtues shared by prominent men that constituted their moral community, and ensured that society would function in an ordered way.[44] They attempted to suggest that "proper" women, too – who did not travel far from home, and who listened to their husbands – were ĩwi, using the word's original meaning of "obedient."

But women rejected these assertions. While men were absent during the war, they had traveled extensively, established businesses, and built networks that allowed them to survive the difficult war years. They denied that any index of respectability could be focused on men alone. Instead, they argued, the maintenance of the family and community sat at the

---

[40] Consider recent work such as Stapleton, *African Police*.
[41] Branch, *Defeating Mau Mau*.
[42] Atieno Odhiambo, *Paradox of Collaboration*; Steinhart, *Conflict and Collaboration*.
[43] Oldenquist, "Loyalties," 175.
[44] For a useful comparison, see Mottahedeh, *Loyalty and Leadership*.

heart of what was "Kamba." They contended that martial service meant nothing without the all-important community sustenance beneath it. Ultimately, they won.

British officials were unaware of many of these debates that raged between different sections of Kamba society. From their perspective, the fact that the Kamba comprised the majority of the army and police was the only factor of note. And it was this knowledge that spurred officials to harness the new colonial agenda of "development" and "welfare" to try to secure political calm in Ukambani after the Second World War.

Scholars have written a variety of detailed empirical analyses of development over the past several decades, notably David Morgan's comprehensive five-volume collection.[45] More recently, the subject has been treated in a more nuanced and Afrocentric manner, as social historians have turned to consider the subtleties of the institution.[46] But they have ignored two vital factors: how development funding was distributed among different ethnic groups, and how ethnicity appeared in the debates over development. This is, indeed, surprising, given the importance of ethnicity to our understanding of African history. The Kamba example demonstrates how officials used development programs as bargaining chips to prevent uprisings in Kamba areas. Ukambani received approximately half of the colony's funds in the decade following the war. This "deal of development" was an effort to use the new post-war agenda to keep political calm.

In practice, though, these programs functioned as anything *but* neat, rhetorically advantageous methods of imperial control that experts had in mind. At each step, Kamba chiefs pressed for more and more funding from officials. Chiefs demonstrated a great ability to negotiate the terms on which development funding was given and implemented.[47] They used "loyalty" as a tool to frame their demands, enjoying the privileged status they commanded as East Africa's premier martial race.

[45] Morgan, *Official History.* See also Havinden and Meredith, *Colonial Development*; Lee and Petter, *Colonial Office.*
[46] See, for instance, Frederick Cooper's introduction to a special issue of the *Journal of Modern European History.* Cooper, "Writing the History of Development."
[47] For a similar process in French West Africa, see van Beusekom, *Negotiating Development.*

LAYOUT

Ethnicity and Empire is organized in eight chronological chapters. Chapter 1 explores the world of central-eastern Kenya during the nineteenth century. Despite the convictions of European explorers, hunters, and missionaries, no Kamba "tribe" as such existed. Inhabitants' lives were typically organized around the family, village, or clan. Though they shared no "ethnic" bond, these peoples did share various common experiences and values, which were later shaped into the basis for a broader union. Most were linked to the experience of mobility and movement: All communities participated in trading, hunting, and raiding, and people often resorted to temporary or permanent migration in order to negotiate frequently arid conditions. *Andũ anene* ("big men" or "prominent individuals") and *athiani* (war and hunting leaders, though the terms often overlapped) stood at the heart of these communities. These men had built their reputations through hunting and raiding. Their occupations required a core set of virtues that were respected by a majority of peoples in the region: bravery; secret knowledge relating to war and the hunt; experience of the wider world; and skillful martial service. They held their communities together, and received honor for their abilities to pilot their dependents safely through difficult conditions. Women played a central role in confirming these virtues, but also earned honor themselves in the domestic sphere, which they would later argue constituted core cultural material for "Kamba" peoples.

Chapter 2 opens with the devastating famines that swept through much of East Africa at the end of the nineteenth century. Reflecting the local orientation of communities in the region, people moved to areas where they could survive, easily crossing boundaries between apparent "tribes" as best suited their circumstances. The period of famine coincided with the arrival of the Imperial British East Africa Company, and a series of skirmishes with various athiani followed. The conflict offered confirmation to the British that "the Kamba" were a "warlike" people, and they soon began recruiting youths to serve as auxiliaries and police in the colonial forces. For young men, this service permitted the expression of virtues they considered important, and was therefore attractive, unlike waged labor.

But the British presence brought difficulties in the ordering of communities. Officials needed local leaders to aid in tax collection and labor recruitment, and so implemented a system of headmen and chiefs. People viewed these appointees as useless puppets, as they were rarely men of any status, who in any case quickly resorted to corruption. But these new appointees did not sit back and accept these slights, but attempted to rework conceptions of virtue in their communities. Those who deserved respect according to "Kamba custom," they informed British administrators, were those who possessed wealth in cattle and could dispense good judgment.

Chapter 3 is about the First World War and its aftermath. Youths joined the British forces in large numbers, though the war was ultimately devastating for many communities. The experience made the positions of chiefs untenable; on the one hand, people held them responsible for sending thousands of young men to their deaths. Those who returned home from war, on the other hand, gained respect and honor like the athiani of the previous generation, and moreover had money to buy cattle and become wealthy.

At the same time, a series of movements appeared that expressed alternative visions of community for the poor and disenfranchised of the region. Prophets led two of these movements, and American missionaries – who had started to gather small pockets of Christians at their mission stations – the third. Women, in particular, found these new communities attractive because they provided them a greater degree of freedom; many were overburdened with work as a result of absent men, and harassed by chiefs and elders. Each movement had its own competing conceptions of what virtues were worthy of honor, none of which were related to martial occupations or wealth. Demonstrating how little ethnicity organized people's lives, at the end of the 1920s, 30,000 men, women, and children fled west during the famine of *Nzalukanje* and "became" Kikuyu.

From this kernel of Christian possibility sprung a political organization called the Ukamba Members Association (UMA), around which Chapter 4 is pinned. The UMA – founded in 1938 – produced the first genuine effort to bring "the Kamba" together, and even built firm links with Kikuyu politicians. It was led by youthful intellectuals – almost all of whom possessed a military or police background – who organized a march and "sit-in" in Nairobi to protest a government-enforced confiscation of cattle from northern Machakos. Despite contemporary memories, though, the protest was as much about land as it was about cattle, and more complex than a unified front against government oppression. It eventually split across gender and generational lines as young men and women attacked their purported seniors.

The protest carried tremendous import because by 1938, the Kamba were considered the foremost martial race of East Africa, and constituted almost a quarter of the colonial military and Kenya Police. Conflict with the Axis powers was imminent. Fully aware of this, UMA leaders used a tactic that Kamba leaders would deploy through the end of the colonial period. They played on their martial reputation and the "loyalty" they had demonstrated as police and soldiers since the First World War to exert pressure on the Kenyan government. They warned that Kamba might refuse to serve in the armed forces if war broke out. They were attempting to procure advantages that came from *being Kamba*. The administration was forced to back down, especially as it believed the UMA was involved in the Mombasa strikes that commenced in 1939.

Chapter 5 describes how a sense of Kamba ethnic ascription became widespread during the 1940s. The transformation was spearheaded by the experience of the Second World War, both at home and abroad, combined with an Ukambani that was – by 1945 – far more closely connected to the wider workings of the colony with roads and schools. War veterans were lauded in the villages because they had demonstrated virtues that all could agree were worthy of leadership positions: They had fought in other parts of the world and shown their bravery; they had sustained people back at home through their wage remittances; and many were, by 1945, educated and often Christian, which attracted them to those constituents. By the late 1940s, they had taken over the majority of chiefly positions, comprised a large proportion of African representatives on government councils, and formed their own political groups. With power concentrated in their hands, veterans drove home martial virtue (rendered through the term ĩwi), as the central characteristic of what it was to be "Kamba," temporarily sweeping away dissenting views. Kamba ethnic identity became seemingly gendered as masculine, with a series of expectations related to agriculture deemed the domain of women. The ability of women to move between tribes – which they had always enjoyed, far more so than men – receded.

The position of strength Kamba veterans occupied was a potential problem for the colonial government. Chapter 6 demonstrates how officials provided new post-war development and welfare funding programs to Kamba areas to try to ensure political calm. In most cases, chiefs successfully negotiated the terms on which funding was received and programs implemented. They phrased their demands in terms of their loyal service in the colonial military, and enjoyed the privileged status to which they were becoming used as East Africa's premier martial race.

Chiefs acted to try to restrict many of the freedoms in trading, travel, and business that women had developed during the war years.

Yet women refused to relinquish their hard-won gains. They rejected īwi as a gendered index of respectability, arguing that maintaining the extended family and community – which they had managed almost single-handedly during the war – was the core virtue for Kamba. Women and chiefs also found themselves challenged by elders, who seized the opportunity presented by a colonial effort to reconstitute "traditional" councils and customs to bring social life closer to a vision they espoused. They tried to bring young men, too, under their authority, and acted to clip the wings of the fledgling African Brotherhood Church.

Chapter 7 is about the Mau Mau conflict. It describes the limited participation of the Kamba, and details those participants' experiences in the "Pipeline" system of detention camps. Mau Mau represented the zenith of the process of "controlling development." The largest post-war development plan in British Africa – the Swynnerton Plan – was aimed at Ukambani during the 1950s, due to the importance of ensuring the continued good service of Kamba troops and police. The Swynnerton Plan went some distance toward removing the social concerns that were so fundamental to Mau Mau's expansion in Kikuyuland. It also provided women with the opportunity to solidify their networks of commerce and trading through welfare groups, and continue to contest chiefs' powerful efforts to equate "Kambaness" with soldiering.

Chapter 8 pivots from the advantageous position occupied by Kamba in the colony during the 1950s to Ukambani's decline into something of a backwater fifteen years later. By the late 1950s, Kamba leaders had publicly hammered home martial service as the crux of ethnic identity, relegating all other possibilities. This "martial bloc" was a tremendous threat to Kenya's first president, Jomo Kenyatta, who excised Kamba (and Kalenjin) from the Kenyan Army in large numbers. Kenyatta's actions removed the major avenue of access to the politics of the state that Kamba had enjoyed.

This simplified version of Kamba ethnic identity, though, little reflected life in the villages of Ukambani. By the late 1950s, women had spent two decades arguing for the centrality of community sustenance as the primary way to derive respect and honor. This was reflected as Kamba politicians sought votes as independence approached; Paul Ngei (in Machakos) and Ngala Mwendwa (in Kitui) not only had to heed masculine assertions about martial service – in Ngei's case, citing his own military background, and for both, arguing for Kamba jobs in the military – but also to demonstrate to female voters that they had the interests of the community at heart. By the 1960s, women played an arguably greater role in Kamba politics than men.

The marginalization of the Kamba in recent decades is in great part responsible for the fact that Kamba communities today are relatively impoverished compared to others in Kenya. Thus when the post-election violence began in late 2007 – a contest over the spoils of political office, and the nation's precious resources, notably land – the Kamba were the one major ethnic group that remained outside the scrum. Yet the long history of martial service and ideas of loyalty have not disappeared entirely. Both are commonly evident in the political arena, and loyalty has come to encompass values like honesty and dependability – which either men or women can possess – that people commonly describe as "Kamba" attributes.

Chapter 1

Traders, warriors, and hunters

Above all, engaging in trade with the coast as well as the interior . . . [is how]
they have attained considerable opulence, as the commerce in ivory is
chiefly in their hands.[1]

Since the days of the Roman Empire, trading towns on the East African
coast participated in a vibrant system of commerce that linked the coast
with Arabia and India. Ships from far-flung ports of the Indian Ocean
arrived to trade their goods with local merchants, always timing their
arrivals and departures with the ocean's cyclical monsoon winds. By the
mid nineteenth century, the cosmopolitan city of Mombasa had risen
to prominence as one of the major entrepôts in the trade, under the
stewardship of the Omani sultan in Zanzibar, Seyyid Said. Ships arrived
in Mombasa to buy goods like ivory from Swahili middlemen who,
in turn, had purchased their products from the Africans of the interior.[2]

One witness to this system of trade was a German missionary in the
employ of the Anglican Church Missionary Society (CMS) named Johann
Ludwig Krapf. Krapf was no stranger to the African continent: He had
lived and worked in Ethiopia for five years – and then got married in
Alexandria – before his arrival in Mombasa in 1844. During his tenure
in East Africa, Krapf came into frequent contact with the various communities of the interior. He was struck, in particular, by the important
role Kikamba-speaking peoples (or as he referred to them, "the Kamba")

---

[1] Krapf, *Travels*, 353.
[2] For an exposition of early trade between the Swahili coast and the Indian Ocean world,
see Pearson, *Port Cities and Intruders*.

played in the trade. In 1849, he noted that "above all, engaging in trade with the coast as well as the interior ... [is how] they have attained considerable opulence, as the commerce in ivory is chiefly in their hands."[3] The missionary's observations, indeed, spurred him to journey to the interior in the final months of that year, and then again two years later. Krapf encountered these communities of Kikamba-speaking traders while their domination of East Africa's northern trade routes was at its peak. Moving from central Kenya to the coast – and aided by communities living within a short distance of Mombasa, with whom they shared linguistic affinity – caravans of as many as 300 to 400 people traversed the country. They made immense profits, and traded in items ranging from arrow poison, to wire, to ivory.

Trading over a variety of distances was one aspect of the mobility and movement that characterized life for many peoples living in central-eastern Kenya during the eighteenth and nineteenth centuries. With the exception of central Machakos, where the tall hills and adequate rainfall made agriculture viable, the region was largely arid. Pastoralism was common to the south and east, and men often traveled for days or weeks at a time to graze their cattle. Others raided widely for the beasts from other Kikamba- or Maa-speaking peoples, and still more hunted for elephant. Perhaps most importantly, frequent famine meant that it was not rare for families or whole communities to resort to temporary or permanent migration in order to find better circumstances for survival, often among new peoples far from their former homes.

The experience of movement – and the various mobile occupations that people undertook to negotiate their trying circumstances – led to the expression of a series of virtues that were respected – and expected – in these communities, particularly among their leaders. At the pinnacle of these small social groupings were the *andũ anene* ("big men" or "prominent individuals"). In these so-called "chiefless" societies, these men possessed higher social status than any others.[4] Their control over the trade in ivory permitted them to build large herds of cattle, gather retinues of followers, and build wealth. Yet these factors were not the root cause of their prestige. Initially, they had earned respect from their communities from their successes as warriors or hunters. It was only over time that they had come to lead raiding and hunting parties, and sometimes head trading caravans, which enabled them to expand their wealth.

---

[3] Krapf, *Travels*, 353.   [4] Tignor, "Colonial Chiefs."

Andũ anene exhibited virtues that were most highly prized: bravery in battle or the hunt; specialized or secret knowledge about the martial disciplines and the wider world beyond their home villages; and the ability to maintain and defend their communities.[5] If elites demonstrated these virtues, they were accorded respect and honor. But the poor, too, could access honor through this system, as could women. For the latter, it resulted from their abilities to produce children and sustain their communities, something that was so vital as men were often absent. Decades later, women would argue that this cultural material was the core of "Kambaness."

The fact that members of these widely dispersed communities shared a common language (though its dialects varied tremendously), as well as experiences, occupations, and values, does not, however, reveal anything about ethnicity. Few members of Kikamba-speaking communities identified themselves as "Kamba," as opposed to members of a homestead, family, village, or clan. The majority of communities were oriented in a profoundly local way, and there was little evidence of any effort to mobilize a wider ethnic identity. Yet these older commonalities (the "roots of ethnicity") would become particularly important during the twentieth century when such a process *did* occur. Intellectuals, chiefs, soldiers, and others would pick over this shared past to gather the cultural material that they argued constituted the history of the Kamba "tribe." Their efforts were usually successful when the values and history they evoked resonated deeply with a majority of people.

MIGRATION AND TRADE

The first European missionaries, explorers, and soldiers who arrived in East Africa – as well as later scholars – all noted that "Kamba" peoples dominated trade between the continent's interior and the coast during the middle decades of the nineteenth century. Trading over long, middle, and short distances was, however, part of a longer history of mobility that had characterized much of the past several hundred years of the region's historical record.

Oral traditions collected during the twentieth century – though they should be treated with some caution – suggest that peoples speaking an early version of Kikamba first settled on the eastern fringe of Kenya's

[5] de Luna, "Hunting Reputations."

highlands – in what would become central and southern Machakos – some time around 1600.[6] Initial migrations from this heartland were over short distances and largely restricted to the hills in and around Mbooni, which – running north to south for approximately 60 miles, and exceeding 7,000 feet in altitude – are excellent locations for practicing agriculture. By the mid eighteenth century, pioneers dispersed from these hills in all directions, settling central Kitui, and in the following century made their final migrations into the drier northern Kitui – including Migwani and Mumoni, in modern-day Mwingi – as well as Iveti, Matungulu, and Kangundo in northern Machakos.

Environmental pressures inspired these constant migrations; for the area that became known as "Ukamba" or "Ukambani" by the late nineteenth century is a place where famine and drought have always been common. The defining experience of *yūa* (famine) for many older men and women was the first thing of which I became utterly convinced during my first summer undertaking field research in Kenya. As a fresh-faced graduate student, I spent three months hiking through the red hills of northern Machakos learning the more practical aspects of my chosen discipline, and asking naïve questions that would cause great embarrass- ment as I read over my field notes years later. I always began interviews by asking my subjects when they were born. Most did not know the exact date, explaining that, "education had not yet arrived then." They would then pick the name of the famine closest to the time of their birth, to provide a sense of chronology. This was frequently *Mūvunga* ("rice" – so named because people ate rice to survive, in 1898–1899), or Nzalukanje (the term refers to the way people fluttered their eyelids in embarrassment when friends or relatives approached them for food during the famine, in 1928–1929). Several could even repeat the names and dates of famines stretching back to *Ngovo* ("disappointment") in 1836.

The prevalence of famine meant that entire communities would move locations if their home areas became overly hostile.[7] Some headed for the coast (to Rabai during Ngovo, for instance) or to northern Tanzania,

---

[6] Linguistic and archaeological evidence, however, suggests that this initial migration possibly took place earlier. Information about early Kamba migrations is from Ambler, "Population Movement"; Jackson, "Dimensions"; Munro, *Colonial Rule*, 8–14; Spear, *Kenya's Past*.

[7] Likely famine periods of 1790–1791, 1803, and 1822–1825 align with migration stories found in oral traditions. Cummings, "Development," 86; Low, "Northern Interior," 315. See also Kimambo, "Economic History."

often moving to areas inhabited by previous generations of their families. Migration and travel were defining experiences for these communities.[8] One author even suggests that the name "Kamba" may derive from the Bantu (though not Swahili or Kikamba) verb *hamba*, meaning "to travel, journey about." He suggests that a likely explanation of *Wakamba* is therefore "travelers."[9]

These histories of migration and movement, combined with a recalcitrant environment and the presence of Kikamba-speaking communities near the coast, were tremendous spurs for the formation of long-distance trade. These factors explain why people seized upon such trading before almost all others in the region.[10] While Krapf suggests that this began in 1836, Kennell Jackson, using oral traditions to reconstruct the past, suggests that the 1770s is more likely. In his discussions with Kamba of the older generations during the late 1960s, Jackson noted "an immediacy, a tangible quality that cannot be detected in any other phase" as his informants discussed the stories they were told by their older relatives about trade between 1775 and 1850.[11]

While Jackson's dating is certainly open to question, that long-distance trade existed some decades before 1836 makes sense: Without preexisting trade networks, it is difficult to imagine the complex, long-distance trade in ivory suddenly appearing. More likely, long-distance trade was a natural expansion of the smaller-scale system that existed by the late eighteenth century.[12] This system of bartering for food across short and medium distances was called *kūthūūa*, and was an essential tactic for survival in famine-prone lands.[13] Through this kinship-based system, small groups of men and women – often numbering fewer than ten – traversed the land in order to find or trade for food.

The first European to write about the traders of the interior confirms that long-distance trading was established by the 1820s, and seemingly

[8] A series of strict taboos banned sexual contact during these kinds of journeys. Dundas, "Native Laws," 243.
[9] Hildebrandt, "Ethnographische," 348.
[10] For obvious reasons, Kamba assigned particular importance to rain-making, and believed that Krapf might possess such powers. Archives of the Church Missionary Society, Birmingham [hereafter CMS], CA5M2, Krapf's Journal, April 15–19, 1846; CMS, CA5O16, Krapf's Journal, November 17 and 20, 1849; Krapf, *Travels*, 169, 290.
[11] Jackson, "Dimensions," 178; Jackson, "Ethnohistorical Study," 224–240.
[12] Krapf, *Travels*, 256–257. See also Lamphear, "Kamba."
[13] Cummings, "Aspects," 213–269; Cummings, "Development," 87–89.

had been for some time. Thomas Boteler – a lieutenant on a Royal Navy surveying expedition to the coast of East Africa between 1822 and 1826 – wrote a journal during his service, which was published posthumously. Boteler noted:

At the small village of Jof, situated a few miles from Mombas [*sic*], an annual fair is held in the month of August, at which ivory and cattle are the principal articles for sale, being brought from the interior by a tribe termed Meric Mungoans [Kamba], who purchase them from the elephant hunters for beads and brass wire.[14]

Similarly in 1833, another naval officer stationed in Mombasa referred to the Meric Mungoans, reporting their trade in "ivory, skins, [and] rhinoceros' horn."[15] The etymology of the term "Meric Mungoans" is unknown, but it was certainly a term used in reference to Kikamba-speaking peoples (though the implication that the "tribe" carried out this trading was certainly incorrect, as is explained below). In 1846, Krapf provided the first recorded use of the term "Kamba" by confirming that "Wakamba ... are called Mericmungoans in the interior."[16]

It is clear, however, that from the 1840s onward, long-distance trading – especially in ivory – reached a new level. One contemporary observer – Charles Guillain, a Frenchman residing in Mombasa during the 1840s – described one caravan that brought in between 300 and 400 frasillas (10,800 to 14,400 pounds) of ivory. Some reports suggest that "Kamba" caravans like this arrived weekly in Mombasa during this decade.[17] The prevalence of ivory trading is also demonstrated by one Swahili trading party – numbering 200 – that came to Kitui during the 1850s. The party's members dispersed throughout Machakos and Kitui to trade, and during this time, one merchant – described as a "*small* [my emphasis] merchant" – was able to gather almost 1,500 pounds of ivory.[18] Thus when Krapf arrived in November 1849, he reported a complex trading network that existed between peoples he neatly labeled as "Kamba," "Swahili," and "Nyika." Kikamba-speaking peoples typically sold cattle and ivory to coastal peoples (including the Swahili), as well as sheep, goats, and grease. In return, they received "cotton fabrics (Americano), blue calico [cloth], glass beads, copper

[14] Boteler, *Narrative of a Voyage*, Vol. II, 205.　　[15] Emery, "Short Account," 283.
[16] CMS, CA5M2, Krapf's Journal, July 14, 1846.
[17] Guillain, *Documents sur l'histoire*, Vol. II, Part II, 211–217.
[18] Burton and Speke, "Coasting Voyage," 194.

and brass wire, ruddle [a type of red ocher], black pepper, salt, luaha, [and] blue vitriol (zinc)."[19]

A trading caravan was an impressive sight as it moved through Machakos or Kitui on its way to Kikuyu, Kisii, Lake Baringo, Embu, or Mberre. It is easy to imagine villagers running from their homes to catch sight of one, perhaps drawn by the singing that often accompanied its passage. A caravan would pass across the plains, below the hills and gently descending ridges where villages clung precariously, and around the valleys that dot that part of East Africa. It might be spread out across a quarter of a mile, and include several hundred men, moving swiftly. It would bristle with elephant tusks and weapons if a successful raid, hunt, or trading bazaar had taken place. Likely too, some captives or slaves could be spotted in its midst. In the hot season, men wore sandals, otherwise the footwear hung from their belts, dangling and knocking together with the calabashes of food that adorned their shoulders. Each night, when the caravan stopped to rest, men would remove flints from their belts to light fires and cook dinner. A caravan was always prepared for any eventuality: Weapons were ready for battle, and ropes and strong swimmers if a river crossing were necessary.[20]

Caravans carried a wide variety of goods, but none was more significant than ivory. (One European woman who wrote vocabularies of Kikamba and Kikuyu in 1904 even claimed that Kikamba-speaking peoples did not distinguish between the elephant, as an animal, and ivory, its prize. She translated both as *(u)nzoo*, implying that the totality of the elephant's existence was as a producer of ivory.[21]) In East Africa, the ivory trade reached its peak during the nineteenth century, though its existence was recorded almost 2,000 years earlier. It was driven by demand in Europe and America, where the soft (and therefore easily carvable) African ivory was greatly prized, particularly compared to the more brittle Asian ivory. In Kenya, the majority of ivory trade occurred through Kitui, due to its proximity to both the coastal markets and larger herds of elephant. People from Kikuyu and Embu came to Kitui to sell ivory, and traders from Kitui traveled to these areas – as well as Meru – to engage in this trade.[22]

[19] Krapf, *Travels*, 353.
[20] This description is compiled from Krapf, *Travels*, 300–310; Lindblom, *Akamba*, 345–346.
[21] Hinde, *Vocabularies*, 20–21, 34–35.
[22] For more on the ivory trade in nineteenth-century East Africa, see Alpers, *Ivory and Slaves*; Beachey, "East African Ivory Trade."

It was in central Kitui that Krapf met the famed "merchant prince" and ivory trader Kivui wa Mwendwa. Kivui is probably the most well-known "Kamba" figure from the nineteenth century, and was one of the foremost andũ anene. Like other powerful men in the region, he was no leader of "the Kamba" or "Kamba people," but rather a Kikamba-speaker who had gathered a series of clients and dependents around him. One of Jackson's informants described him as "endowed with wealth in cattle, kin, and in people." Kivui garnered fame for his trading exploits and prowess through the region. In later life, he dispensed judgment and settled disputes in areas as far away as central Machakos.[23]

One of Krapf's main objectives for traveling to Kitui during the final two months of 1849 was to find Kivui. He had heard reports about Kivui while in Mombasa, which described him as a great trader who was respected by – and personally known to – Arabs there. Krapf also considered that he might be able to convert Kivui to Christianity. Both Krapf and his companion, Johannes Rebmann, strongly believed that "the Kamba" occupied a crucial position for the potential spread of the Word. If they could successfully preach their teachings there, the religion's dispersal throughout central Kenya would face little opposition.[24] (Krapf had gone so far as to translate St. Mark's Gospel into Kikamba in preparation, several years before setting foot in Ukambani.[25]) As the most influential figure in the interior, Kivui was an essential component of this project. Although Krapf was unsuccessful in convincing Kivui about the merits of Christianity, he was nevertheless impressed by him, and stayed with him for several weeks. Kivui presented Krapf with valuable goods he had earned through trade, including beads and calico. And at the moment of Krapf's departure, Kivui's speech was significant in demonstrating the wide range of movement he undertook in his business, and indeed the influence he wanted Krapf to know he possessed: "I wished to bestow upon him [Krapf] one elephant's tusk four feet long, another three feet and a half in length ... but here I have no

---

[23] Jackson, "Ethnohistorical Study," 251–260. Low uses the term "merchant prince" to describe Kivui. Low, "Northern Interior," 314.

[24] CMS, CA5M2, "Dr. Krapf's Journal Description of a Journey to Ukambani in November and December 1849," 253–254. In Rebmann's underlined words – practically the only ones in his journal to receive such emphasis – "the importance of that people for this part of Eastern Africa is so great." CMS, CA5M2, Rebmann's Journal, February 12, 1848.

[25] KNA, MSS/23/3, Papers of T. H. R. Cashmore, *Church Missionary Society in Kenya: Beginnings in East Africa, 1844–1944* (unpublished typescript, n.d.), 7.

Kikamba-speakers displaced in trade [handwritten marginal note, rotated]

ivory, it is at Kikuyu. I will go and fetch it, and then I will travel to the coast [to meet Krapf]."[26]

But the domination that Kikamba-speaking peoples enjoyed over these trade routes was relatively short-lived, and disappeared due to the encroachment of outsiders from the coast. Though Swahili traders had arrived in Kikuyu areas via Machakos and Kitui in the late 1840s, they were initially unable to impact the cross-country trading system. Yet over the following decades, and certainly by 1870, the Swahili came to control the majority of trade in East Africa. Their caravans looped north from Mount Kilimanjaro directly into Kikuyu country, thereby circumventing the trading centers of Machakos and Kitui. Coastal traders were aided by tax conditions that favored them over the majority of ivory traders working in the interior. Many prominent traders in Machakos and Kitui were reduced to serving as agents for Swahili caravans as they journeyed past their villages. In some areas, the system of "legitimate" trade was replaced by that involving robbery, violence, and the taking of slaves. Wars against Galla-, Nyika-, Maa-, or other Kikamba-speaking peoples caused further disruptions to the trading system.[27]

PEOPLE OF THE BOW

Scholars have focused mainly on trade in their studies of Kikamba-speaking communities in the nineteenth century, as well as the significance of this trade for the economy of East Africa. But they have largely ignored how the social organization of communities in Machakos and Kitui was inextricably linked to these wider systems. At the heart of the ivory trade was the requirement for skilled warriors, who permitted the product's safe transport and protected their communities from raiders. But protecting the ivory trade was one thing; the ivory itself had to be procured from elephants, which required extraordinary talent in hunting. Where smaller, non-ivory trade occurred, parties at the very least had to defend themselves against wild animals, and hunt for food on their journeys. These occupations were linked together through skilled use of the bow and arrow. Thus virtues connected to raiding and hunting formed core cultural material in communities of the region, with knowledge of the wider countryside highly prized.

---

[26] Krapf, *Travels*, 297.
[27] Jackson, "Ethnohistorical Study," 220; Lamphear, "Kamba," 98–99; Low, "Northern Interior," 316–317.

The link between trade and these martial occupations was abundantly clear; indeed, separating "trade" from "hunting" and "warfare" is almost impossible. During the earlier days of migration and settlement, it was war and hunting leaders – who traded extensively as they moved – that led mobile groups to new locations. Around the turn of the nineteenth century, for instance, a series of all-male bands of traders and hunters moved south into what is today northeastern Tanzania. They moved initially to trade and hunt, but another important objective was to prepare the way for more extensive settlement. Once the men had established themselves in a suitable area, they then sent word home for the women and children to follow.[28] Contemporary informants are quick to add that these types of men were those who commanded authority in the past. As one noted, leaders "had to know hunting routes and trails in the country."[29] This was an essential prerequisite for leaders of peoples whose history was a litany of stories of migration, and meant that they headed their communities above potential competitors like *athani* (prophets), or those who could predict the rain.

These links are especially visible among the leaders of communities in Machakos and Kitui. Kivui, for instance, was arguably the greatest trader in the region's history. But he was also the head of a large group of hunters and warriors, as these men were responsible for protecting his trading caravans. Kivui himself had first earned his reputation as a result of his ability to carry out raids and to hunt. Edward Steinhart notes that although Kivui was respected for his wealth, the fact that he had procured it as a leader of vast hunting parties was important: "respect and awe … [were] attached to successful hunting leaders."[30] Nor was Kivui the first: A warrior-trader named Sila wa Kata from Mwala predated Kivui by almost a century.[31]

Another such leader was Nzambu wa Ndove, who lived in Migwani. Like Kivui, Nzambu was a trader and hunter of some repute. These occupations meant that Nzambu had spent much of his life traveling long distances from Migwani. Therefore, in 1898, with the famine of Mŭvunga in its first year and devastating much of Ukambani, it was Nzambu who rounded up starving families and took them eighty miles north to Mwimbe – on the eastern slopes of Mount Kenya – where they survived.

---

[28] Lamphear, "Kamba," 82.
[29] Interview 101, Kanziku, June 27, 2009. This book is shaped in large part by evidence from more than 150 interviews. For details on the interview process, see *Bibliography*.
[30] Steinhart, "Elephant Hunting," 337, 342. [31] Cummings, "Development," 89.

Nzambu's knowledge of the routes used in trading and hunting meant that he was the man who could lead these people to safety.[32]

The centrality of war and hunting in these communities is perhaps most clearly demonstrated through the figure of the *mūthiani* (plural: *athiani*). Athiani were married men, who were initially leaders of trading parties. By the nineteenth century, however, they had become respected leaders of both hunting and war parties, and played a central role in the organization of society. (The parties themselves would switch from war or raiding to trade and vice versa with ease, depending on what was required.) When athiani reached sufficient age or status they were usually described as andū anene, though in many areas the terms were used somewhat interchangeably. Crucially, there was no distinction in terminology between athiani as hunting or war leaders, as the occupations were so similar. It was common, indeed, for hunters to serve as long-range scouts for warriors: When they traveled in search of antelope and larger game, they often encountered enemies and their herds of cattle. They then passed along this intelligence to the athiani, who prepared for defense, or organized raids on enemy cattle.[33]

It is unlikely that members of these communities distinguished greatly between war and hunting. One informant told the anthropologist Lindblom in 1911 or 1912, "Is it not war to hunt such animals as the elephant, the rhinoceros, the buffalo and the lion?" The view of the highly capable Swedish scholar was that "rites connected with entering upon such a hunt show great resemblances to the precautions taken on entering upon military and plundering expeditions."[34] These types of reactions were common among my own interviewees. As one noted, "the mūthiani used to command the young hunters ... He was like a major general in a war."[35] Another waxed lyrically about the Kamba history of hunting and war, stating that strategies were the same in both: "A Kamba would know how to encircle the enemy. Kambas would divide themselves into several groups during fights to try to surround their opponents ... That way, they could defeat the enemy. They learned that through hunting."[36] It is important, however, to treat these latter recollections critically. Many informants aged around eighty today were raised listening to stories about Kamba hunting prowess; they were young when Kamba comprised almost 40 percent of Kenya's armed forces during the 1940s and 1950s,

[32] Ambler, *Kenyan Communities*, 2–3.   [33] Macdonald, *Soldiering*, 41.
[34] Lindblom, *Akamba*, 465.   [35] Interview 90, Kanziku, June 24, 2009.
[36] Interview 84, Ikutha, June 22, 2009.

and Kamba communities earned great rewards from the colonial government based on their service (see Chapter 6). The past can come across as
uncomplicated and idyllic; thus Lindblom's confirmation is important.

In Machakos, athiani more commonly functioned as war leaders.
Trading success during the first half of the century meant that by 1850,
a significant concentration of wealthy cattle-owners had appeared.
Requiring more grazing land, these men moved south and west, toward
the Kapiti Plains. Here, at altitudes between 2,000 and 4,000 feet, there
was rarely enough rain for agriculture, but conditions were ideal for
pastoralism. This newfound wealth certainly caught the attention of not
only other Kikamba-speakers, but also several groups of Maa-speakers,
who were undergoing their own great expansions in an easterly direction.
Quite why the latter movements occurred is still a subject of some debate;
they were possibly the result of a lack of resources, which produced
competition for those necessary to maintain a pastoralist lifestyle.
This period of conflict – known as the Iloikop Wars, and described by
scholars as a period of "civil crisis" or civil war – led to an increased level
of conflict with Kikamba-speaking peoples. It is important here to sound
a word of caution, however: Reading European sources, secure in their
identification of neat "tribes" – or listening to contemporary informants –
the nineteenth century was a running battle between "the Kamba" and
"the Maasai" for control of cattle. More likely, those with greater wealth
caught the attention of those with less, irrespective of "tribe," which as
explained below, held little relevance for the peoples of the region.[37]

In Kitui, hunting was especially prominent, though it was common in
Machakos too. This was in part due to a greater distance separating the
peoples of Kitui from the period of conflict involving Maa-speakers, and a
lower population density that reduced the likelihood of conflict over
resources among Kikamba-speaking groups. In addition, Kitui had a far
higher concentration of elephants, the source of valuable ivory, and its
dryness meant that agriculture was difficult: The majority of the district is
below 2,000 feet in altitude, and rain is in short supply, making even
pastoralism problematic in places.

In his study of hunting in Kenya, Steinhart notes that hunting was
"seen as embodying ... and enhancing community values." Steinhart
compares hunting with baseball in the United States or soccer in Europe
to illustrate its significance; for hunting was widespread among the

---

[37] Galaty, "Maasai Expansion"; Unomah and Webster, "East Africa," 278; Waller, "Economic and Social Relations"; Waller, "Lords," 327.

peoples of nineteenth-century Kenya, and played a central role in social life.[38] Yet among some peoples of eastern Kenya – including a significant proportion of those living in Kitui – hunting with the bow and arrow, which had taken place for centuries, was first tied into the practices and values of the modern era.[39]

While most peoples in Kenya hunted to at least some degree, inhabitants of Kitui were the only ones to hunt for elephant. Indeed, people specifically distinguished between common hunting and elephant hunting, which required the maximum degree of martial skill. It was a skill that certainly required the ability to shoot well, but the best athiani could call on spirits to assist them in guiding their arrows. One informant recalled that athiani could even "kill an elephant with one shot" (though this was surely aided by the poison they used).[40] To shoot with accuracy and success was the mark of an excellent hunter. After all, anyone who missed his target during the hunt was dishonored by being prohibited from taking meat from the kill.[41]

Oral testimony is remarkably consistent in detailing the specialized knowledge athiani possessed, which distinguished them from everyone else. Before departing on a hunt or to war, a mūthiani had to remain celibate the night before his departure, while he was strengthened with charms (*mūthea*) from a medicine man.[42] The charms gave the mūthiani a range of advantages: They protected him from injury from his enemies, and ensured that wild animals would not bother the party at night. Certain charms allowed him to better track cattle raiders, and "freeze" them in their tracks so they might be caught. Some charms required that the mūthiani blow powder in the direction of an elephant to slow it down (which presumably also served as a way to gauge the direction and strength of the wind). But perhaps the most important skill he could possess was the ability to control the elephant:

As the elephant was coming towards a group of hunters and its mūthiani, if the mūthiani sensed that his team was preparing to run away out of fear, he personally left them and went to meet the elephant. He then placed his bow down on the ground in front of it, and the elephant could not cross the bow.

---

[38] Even CMS missionaries were aware of – and referred to – the semi-mythical Kamba hunters of eras past. KNA, TC 11/81, *Taveta Chronicle* (Easter 1895), 7.

[39] Steinhart, *Black Poachers*, 23.   [40] Interview 100, Kanziku, June 27, 2009.

[41] Steinhart, *Black Poachers*, 19–23, 42–58; Steinhart, "Elephant Hunting," 346. See also Dundas, "History of Kitui," 524.

[42] Hobley, *Bantu Beliefs*, 193.

It then returned in the direction from which it came. The mūthiani used traditional charms to do this.[43]

A mūthiani's status was bolstered by the variety of rare products (or "prestige goods") he could acquire from his travels throughout the land. Wearing items like a leopard skin distinguished him; few could procure something so exotic.

Women did not take part in the hunt, and indeed there were certain taboos against this. Although the evidence is sparse, it is clear that women played a role in war. Jackson identifies a female mūthiani named Kalekye Nzelele. She appears "prominently" in oral traditions on conflict with Galla peoples during the mid nineteenth century. Nzelele hailed from Endau in eastern Kitui, and was possibly responsible for a new set of raiding tactics that produced great success for her charges.[44] Unfortunately, however, little more evidence exists on female athiani from the period, and it is unlikely that more will be discovered at this juncture.

In his important study of honor in Africa, John Iliffe finds affinity with a simple definition of the concept: that it is a "right to respect."[45] Yet that right was never one that elites could demand out-of-hand from members of their communities.[46] Honor had to be earned, and thus non-elites played a central role in articulating what was acceptable and what *virtues* were worthy of celebrating. Athiani had to carry out certain tasks: Together with young men (*anake*) they recruited, they were responsible for defending their villages from any incursions and for organizing raids for cattle. Looking after these young men was especially important: Their safety was paramount, as was instructing them in the ways of hunting and war if they proved adequately skilled. Together with their charges, athiani led hunts for valuable elephant meat, which could sustain a village for weeks once it was dried and hauled home. And they knew the all-important routes through the wider countryside to get food – or even shift their communities – during times of famine, demonstrating an ability to move and interact in a wider world that was unfamiliar to the majority of people in their home communities. Athiani faced danger, food deprivation, and strenuous exertion on a daily basis in order to sustain their dependents, and possessed the specialized knowledge required to carry

[43] Interview 84, Ikutha, June 22, 2009.
[44] Hobley, *Ethnology*, 70; Jackson, "Dimensions," 211; Jackson, "Ethnohistorical Study," 245.
[45] A definition provided by Frank Henderson Stewart. Iliffe, *Honour*, 4.
[46] See also Lynch, *I Say To You*.

out their duties; in this, they reflected the virtues that held together the communities of the region.

If the athiani fulfilled their part of the bargain, their communities conveyed honor upon them. This commenced immediately with their return to the villages following a successful expedition: A mũthiani and his warriors were publicly welcomed, sometimes with the accompaniment of "solemn" playing of wind instruments made from the horn of the kudu or oryx.[47] They might return with small children or women they had captured, who then grew up with their own families or relations, adding to the strength of the community. (The children were sometimes described with humor as "my children which I produced with my bow."[48]) Lindblom reported that there was no greater achievement for a warrior than to return home from battle with the spear of a Maasai warrior whom he had dispatched. In such an instance, he was given an honorific title – which replaced his given name – for the remainder of his days.[49] Demonstrating the importance of his achievements for the wider community, a successful warrior or hunter would tour his relations' homes, and indeed the homes of his clan members, from whom he received the reward of several goats. In some cases, admirers would bring him beer for a week.[50] There is even some suggestion that men in certain areas were not allowed to marry until they had killed an enemy.[51]

Women played a vital role in bolstering and reinforcing values considered important in their communities. This was expressed most clearly through the institutions that surrounded hunting and raiding. Women typically prepared food to give the men strength before they departed on these expeditions. When a successful hunter returned, he was smeared with fat by his mother to purify him. At the celebration that followed a successful raid or hunt, women ululated and sang songs of praise for the returning warriors, lauding their achievements.[52] Of utmost importance in this process was dancing, which typically accompanied an event like a feast, or followed a hunt or raid.

Charles Dundas witnessed a variety of dances in the first years of British administration, and while it is important not to assume that such practices had remained static since the mid nineteenth century, his descriptions are nevertheless revealing. Dundas described that in the past, men had always come to dances armed, which they still did on occasion

---

[47] Lindblom, *Akamba*, 405.   [48] Lamphear, "Kamba," 90–91.
[49] Lindblom, *Akamba*, 197.   [50] Decle, *Three Years*, 488–489.
[51] Hobley, *Ethnology*, 45.   [52] Lindblom, *Akamba*, 198.

under British rule. At all dances Dundas viewed, the man's role was to demonstrate his bravery and courage.[53] He boasted of his achievements to the women present, calling "I am a lion" or "I am a leopard."[54] In one song, a youth exhorts his fellow anake to find women for themselves, and raises his own prestige by singing of the wider country he knows: "I have drank from the waters of many rivers. On Kilimandjaro I have sung." The song leader continues by evoking martial service: "Young men, draw near to the women's breasts ... Take one step to the front, like soldiers!"[55] If a woman deemed that a man was worthy of honor, she chose him as a partner in the dance.[56] But if a man had exhibited cowardly behavior, he received a wide spread of insults, and was unlikely to find a wife.[57]

A deeper consideration of how members of Kikamba-speaking communities discoursed about honor – or what constituted appropriate leadership in their communities – is difficult, but perhaps possible on some level. First, there is oral testimony: Informants are quick to describe "ideal Kamba men" as those who were "sharpshooters" who could "shoot without missing." Just as a skilled hunter could quickly finish his kill, a skilled warrior had his shooting ability to thank for his success. As one elder noted, "Kambas used to win against the Maasai because they had bows and arrows which were poisoned ... they could shoot the Maasai from quite a distance, and the Maasai only had spears and swords."[58] Yet using oral interviews in this fashion is fraught with problems. It is impossible to distill community values from testimony provided some 150 years later, even if "old stories" are constantly told and retold. Such tales have been constantly rethought, reworked, and re-created over time to reflect values considered important at particular moments in history. (Thus stories of age-old conflict with "the Maasai" likely reflect more recent historical events, and ignore conflict between different communities of Kikamba-speakers.)

---

[53] The Kikamba word for "hero" (*gumbau*, rendered in the older orthography) was also used to mean "bravery" or "valiant." Some contemporary informants describe that community leaders were simply called *ngŭmbaŭ* in the past. Interview 18, Mitaboni, July 23, 2004; Krapf, *Vocabulary*, 20, 57; Shaw, *Pocket Vocabulary*, 23.
[54] Dundas, "History of Kitui," 506–507.   [55] Lindblom, "Kamba Folklore III," 54–55.
[56] Lindblom concurs with Dundas's description. Lindblom, *Akamba*, 407–416.
[57] Lindblom, *Akamba*, 199–200.
[58] Interview 90, Kanziku, June 24, 2009; Interview 100, Kanziku, June 27, 2009; Interview 114, Mwingi, June 30, 2009.

It is fortunate, however, that a series of Kikamba texts exist that were published during the nineteenth century, which provide hints about how men and women conceived of leadership. It is clear that a word for "king" existed in Kikamba – Krapf used *zumbe*, and later translators provide similar words (today: *mūsumbī*). Yet these societies had nothing approaching kings, and in his translation of St. Mark's Gospel, Krapf used the term only to refer to the powerful and foreign King Herod, and never to other prominent men. When it came to rendering "lords" or "chief men," Krapf chose andu anene and *andu a mbe* ("ancestors"; literally, "before men").[59] The implication is clear: Leaders were normal men who distinguished themselves by exhibiting community virtues in situations of hardship and danger.

Slaves or the poor living on the Swahili coast during the nineteenth century could gain status via *ustaarabu* ("becoming Arab") – as their masters did – despite the wishes of the latter.[60] The poor of Ukambani had a similar ability: If they demonstrated bravery and valiance then their family origins mattered little. Proverbs demonstrate that merit warranted respect, not birth: One stated "The guineafowl bears a francolin," a version of the well-known Nandi expression, "The lion gives birth to a hyena."[61] It acknowledged how a respected man or woman did not necessarily produce a child with similar characteristics. Thus those at the economic or social fringes of their communities could rise to positions of leadership if they possessed sufficient acumen and ability.

It is important, too, to recognize that honor was not solely a masculine attribute, and women's role was more important than offering plain confirmation of male character. Women also earned honor that gave them status in their communities. Certainly, this was not unique to the Kamba case: In southern Africa, in particular, "heroic and householder honour" coexisted comfortably at the time.[62]

Women received honor for their reproductive abilities, which were highly valued in these sorts of small-scale societies. Large kin groups possessed advantages: Undertaking agriculture and looking after cattle – as well as activities like raiding or trading in a difficult environment – required willing workers.[63] Thus women who produced large numbers of children were lauded in proverbs. One ran, "The clans of the wilderness

---

[59] Krapf's translation is from Krapf (trans.), *Evangelio*, 23 (Mark 6:21).
[60] Glassman, *Feasts and Riot.*   [61] Lindblom, "Kamba Folklore III," 29.
[62] Iliffe, *Honour*, 140.   [63] Guyer and Belinga, "Wealth in People."

are two, withered trees and fresh trees."[64] The two clans are men and women, and the men are "withered" because they cannot produce children. The importance of childbearing was reflected in marriage practices: One of the few acceptable reasons for divorcing a wife was because she could not produce children. In such a case, the brideprice – a sum given by a man's family to that of his prospective wife – was returned and the marriage annulled.

Women's abilities to sustain their families were just as important as in the case of men. The responsibility of looking after the home – both physically and regarding much of the social education of children – fell on their shoulders when men were absent. Maintaining gardens to produce food was a central part of this, as was dancing skillfully (see above). Proverbs recognized that men could not act independently of women. One explained, "If two persons are travelling together and one gets pricked, the latter can not travel as fast as the other." As Lindblom reveals, people used the saying when a man's wife had "deserted" him, and he was left trying to fend for himself. Another saying concerned an unfortunate, orphaned child who had no mother to raise him. This "calf" would have to "lick himself" as he tried to become an adult: The odds were stacked against him as he went about trying to raise funds for his brideprice payment.[65]

Thus although male virtues were more prominent in these communities during the nineteenth century – based largely on the needs of survival – female input was integral in determining community values.[66] Decades later, women argued that community and family sustenance formed the core of what was "Kamba": Their efforts resonated because of this historical background.

LOCAL BONDS

Early European observers believed that Africans lived in neat, discrete "tribes." Those who wrote about "the Kamba" in the nineteenth century – men like Boteler, Guillain, Krapf, and Rebmann – therefore believed that they could easily identify the Kamba "tribe" and the approximate boundaries of the area "it" occupied. Thus missionaries confidently wrote "Ukambani" in careful Gothic letters on their maps by the mid nineteenth century. Missionaries like Krapf, explorers like Frederick Lugard,

---

[64] Lindblom, "Kamba Folklore III," 32.   [65] Lindblom, "Kamba Folklore III," 31–33.
[66] As in the case of the Asante in West Africa. Allman, "Be(com)ing Asante," 104.

and administrators like Charles Hobley wrote copiously on "the Kamba," each detailing traditional "Kamba" practices that had supposedly existed in unchanging fashion since some distant point in the vaguely defined past.

The traders and athiani with whom Europeans interacted probably played a role in accentuating the latter's beliefs about the nature of tribes. It is worth remembering here that these sorts of men (and occasionally women) were unrepresentative of the majority of peoples of the region. They were elites, and certainly not naïve when it came to interacting with ostensibly different cultures. Kivui, for instance, made a point of donning Swahili garb when in Mombasa to fit in with the local traders, from whom he presumably expected a better reaction.[67] Andŭ anene played on "tribal" stereotypes to gain advantages in trade by spreading rumors about "Maasai" raids in order to dissuade others from encroaching on their territory.[68] There is little reason that leaders would not have played on European beliefs about "tribes" and their reputations if they believed it would protect their industries or improve their positions. Thus leaders may have described themselves as heading vast "tribes" or united "armies" of Kamba to serve their own purposes.

In actuality, though, the organization of societies in central and eastern Kenya was profoundly local, and few identified themselves – or thought of themselves – as "Kamba."[69] The smallest territorial unit in which people lived was the *ŭtŭi* (plural: *motŭi*). An ŭtŭi was based around some natural feature of the environment – such as a hilltop or ridge – and comprised several *mĩsyĩ* (homesteads), each of which was inhabited by an extended family. Trading caravans, indeed, were typically organized by ŭtŭi in the eighteenth century.[70] The families undertook joint tasks with their neighbors (known as *mwethya*), and often intermarried. This joint work brooked no distinction of gender or age, and was essential for maintaining the small communities. One Kikamba proverb ran *makani kuti nganga ngu* – "In the fields there are no old guineafowl" – meaning that everyone was expected to work to prepare the fields for the rains.[71] When some kind of larger cooperation was required – such as when an area needed to resist a raid, or perhaps organize an offensive one – several motŭi joined together to form a *kĩvalo* (plural: *ivalo*), the largest unit of community organization.

[67] Lamphear, "Kamba," 89.   [68] Unomah and Webster, "East Africa," 286.
[69] Ambler, *Kenyan Communities*.   [70] Cummings, "Development," 95–96.
[71] Lindblom, "Kamba Folklore III," 32.

Overlaying this system were *mbaĩ* (clans), which could claim the loyalty or affiliation of a member at certain times. (The term likely developed initially from meaning something close to "extended family," and in some areas was perhaps used in this manner.[72]) Hunting parties, for instance, might comprise members of multiple different clans, brought together by the personality and acumen of the mũthiani. Clans practiced exogamy; members married outside their own clans in order to build bonds with wider communities (although given the expansion of clans over the past 150 years, the practice no longer exists). In Ukambani today, it is common to find members of the largest clans like the Atangwa separated by distances of several hundred miles; this was not the case during the nineteenth century, when clans were much more geographically restricted. (One author suggests that seventeenth- or eighteenth-century clan origins can be traced to communities living in areas surrounding a particular hill or mountain, which was often given the same name as the clan, before later dispersals took place.[73]) Clan members often marked items they considered valuable – such as arrows, cattle, or beehives – with clan symbols.[74]

Studying Kikamba vocabularies from the nineteenth century reveals much about how people conceived of the world around them. Most important is that Kikamba had no word for "tribe," nor any collectivity of any size beyond the kĩvalo or mbaĩ (with the exception of *nthĩ*, meaning a broad, geographical area usually translated as "country"). Krapf simply used the word *mbai* to mean "tribe" in his vocabulary of 1850, as did the missionary Archibald Shaw in 1885.[75] Thus Krapf's translation of St. Mark's Gospel – in which Jesus recounts how "nation shall rise against nation" – was rendered as *mbai ikaumama ulu wa mbai* (literally, "clan shall rise against clan").[76] In 1904, the Leipzig Lutheran missionary Ernst Brutzer rendered the twelve tribes of Israel as *mbai ikumi na yili*.[77] Today, Kamba use the word *ũko* to mean "tribe," but its usage dates from the time of the Second World War.

Attention to linguistic detail is vital for another reason too. Throughout this chapter, I have used the phrases "Kikamba-speakers" and "Kikamba-speaking peoples" rather than "Kamba" or "the Kamba,"

[72] See, for instance, Middleton, *Central Tribes*, 80.
[73] Muthiani, *Akamba from Within*, 12.
[74] Hobley, *Ethnology*, 46; Lindblom, *Akamba*, 129–138.
[75] Krapf, *Vocabulary*, 55; Shaw, *Pocket Vocabulary*, 181.
[76] Krapf (trans.), *Evangelio*, 53 (Mark 13:8).
[77] Brutzer (trans.), *Meka ma Atume*, 73 (Acts 26:7).

in order to avoid implying any sense of ethnic unity that simply did not exist in the nineteenth century. Yet even the phrase "Kikamba-speakers" is of limited use because seemingly distinct languages like "Kikamba" or "Kikuyu" can insinuate a strong delineation between peoples. This apparent distinction must be challenged.

During the nineteenth century, it is likely that Kikamba and Kikuyu speakers shared closer linguistic affinity than they do today, especially in areas where they lived in close proximity.[78] There, at the margins, it may well have been difficult to classify one language as "Kikuyu" and one "Kamba"; more likely, they blurred together. Lindblom, an expert on Kikamba, noted that residents of Mumoni, Kilungu, and far eastern Kitui spoke a form of Kikamba with significant linguistic differences from central Machakos, in dialect, phonology, and vocabulary. He went so far as to describe the Mumoni dialect of "Kikamba" as "transitional to ... Kikuyu."[79] Kikamba spoken in some of these western areas was possibly more similar to Kikuyu than it was to Kikamba spoken in far-flung parts of Kitui. Thus people living further west referred to the Supreme Being as *Ngai*, as did Kikuyu speakers; but those in Kitui used *Mūlungu*, close to the Taita *Mlungu*.

If people lived in such a "local" way, then where did the term "Kamba" itself originate, and what did it mean? Possible explanations evoke the central practices in the lives of people in the region. As noted above, Hildebrandt suggests that the term "Kamba" was related to travel; yet one competing theory derives from the Swahili word *kamba*. *Kamba* translates most simply as "rope" or "string," and was possibly used in the past to refer to the strings of a bow. Given the importance of the bow and arrow in Kamba life, this is certainly a plausible explanation; possibly the actual answer is a combination of the two theories.[80] What is more significant is that Kamba elders interviewed in 1911 and 1912 provided little useful information on this question to Lindblom. Despite his efforts, the Swede admitted defeat, confessing in frustration that, "Of at least a

---

[78] Both languages derive from Thagicu, which was spoken approximately 1,000 years ago near the upper parts of the Athi and Tana rivers. Spear, *Kenya's Past*, 38–40.

[79] Lindblom, *Notes*, 18.

[80] A long conversation with Jeremiah Kitunda has convinced me that the explanations presented here barely scratch the surface of a complex problem; I eagerly anticipate his future work on the subject. *Kamba* in Swahili also means "honeycomb." The Kamba were expert beekeepers from at least as early as the nineteenth century, giving a third possible explanation. Jeremiah Kitunda, personal communication, 2011; Lindblom, *Akamba*, 14–15, 349.

hundred of the older men questioned, none seem to have so much as thought of the matter." His criticism was, in fact, even broader: "It is quite futile to try to get any insight into the history of the tribe through the Akamba themselves."[81] The fact was that elders considered themselves members of an mbaĩ or kĩvalo and not "Kamba," and thus had little interest in the question. This is in striking contrast to a series of oral histories carried out in 1977 by Raphael Sungi and Musyoka Muliungi, and Jeremiah Kitunda in the 1990s. By then, elders were quick to arrive at complex stories of origin for the name. In the highly ethnicized political world of late colonial and independent Kenya, explaining tribal histories and origins was vital.[82]

The term "ethnicity," then, is unhelpful in understanding the peoples of Machakos and Kitui in the nineteenth century and earlier. It is more productive to think of common experiences and *occupations*, and the *virtues* related to them, in order to understand the history of the region. There are strong similarities between the histories of the peoples of central and eastern Kenya: Kikuyu-speakers were the "people of the digging stick" – brought together by the need to clear the thick forests to carve out space for agriculture. These people who lived in the country's more central regions – which were wetter, higher in altitude, and better for agriculture – frowned upon war as something less than honorable, and respected those who worked hard and made the land productive.[83] To the east, where the environment forced a different set of occupations like trading, hunting, and raiding, community values were connected to these occupations that provided a different way for people to negotiate their own environmental circumstances.[84] Thus by the nineteenth century, some majority of the people who spoke Kikamba or Kikuyu did share certain values that were distinct from others, which would eventually

[81] Lindblom, *Akamba*, 14, 349.

[82] Unfortunately, these documents are currently untraceable in the Kenya National Archives. I have relied on Jeremiah Kitunda's generous information about their contents. Jeremiah Kitunda, personal communication, 2011.

[83] Lonsdale, "Moral Economy," 334, 342.

[84] Waller, "Ecology." Stories of origin reflect the ecological differences between the two regions. One tale describes how in a bygone era some peoples moved into a land dominated by baobab trees (*myamba*) and therefore took the name "Kamba." Others from the same group went to live in another area with fig trees (*mĩkũyũ*), and became "Kikuyu." Other tales describe two children from the same mother, one of whom was named Kamba, the other Kikuyu. Burton, *Zanzibar*, Vol. II, 63–64; Interview 66, Tala, November 14, 2006; Jeremiah Kitunda, personal communication, 2011.

be seized upon and molded into constituting "Kamba" and "Kikuyu" ethnic material during the twentieth century.

CONCLUSION

A significant proportion of communities in Machakos and Kitui shared common experiences and occupations during the nineteenth century. During this period, a series of values and virtues came to constitute important cultural material. They were related – in the main – to war and hunting, and derived from the mobility and movement that were a central part of life. Community leaders had to demonstrate specialized knowledge, bravery, and skill in the face of danger, as well as exceptional abilities in using the bow and arrow. Through these occupations, leaders maintained and protected their communities, and their success in these fields was celebrated. But this was no uniquely male situation; women, too, earned honor for their own roles in community sustenance.

The hostile interior of East Africa was the stage for the development of core beliefs, but demanded that those at the tribe's exterior – either geographically or materially – discard them when necessary. In the words of Lonsdale, "a narrow ethnic loyalty could invite destitution."[85] In the insecure environmental conditions of nineteenth-century Kenya, the line between members of each "tribe" was often blurred by simple need, and people moved between regions without difficulty. In some cases, lineage groups married their women to men in "Embu" or "Kikuyu" areas to facilitate the exchange of food to ensure the rest of the group's survival. The process also worked in reverse, and was emphasized because periods of famine in eastern Kenya often did not coincide with those in more central regions.[86] Women who were unable to provide food for their families – often in the absence of men who were away trading or hunting for food – often became migrants, and were easily integrated into other ethnic groups, far more so than men. One boy from Mumoni was adopted by an Embu household during the late 1890s, where he had fled as a result of famine. Ambler notes that, "In 1900, when hordes of raiders from Mumoni and Migwani attacked Embu communities, neither this boy nor his neighbors questioned his loyalty to his new family and community."[87]

---

[85] Lonsdale, "Moral Economy," 329.
[86] Muriuki provides dates for famines in Kikuyu areas. Muriuki, *History*, 49.
[87] Ambler, *Kenyan Communities*, 44–45.

Communities in Ukambani always accepted needy strangers from other areas, requiring only that they pledge loyalty to the local "settlement."[88]

During the course of my research in Ukambani, I sometimes discovered that my informants could sum up a notion better than I or my fellow scholars. This was emphatically true when I asked one aging gentleman in Kitui about the nineteenth century. He began by explaining that today it was easy to tell who was a Kikuyu and who was Kamba. But, he said:

In the old days, Kikuyu men might come here to look for food, and perhaps for a wife. Sometimes they might find one. Then she would go back to Kikuyuland with him. Now she is Kikuyu *kabisa* [Swahili: completely]. But not now – that was in the early times.[89]

[88] Dundas, "Native Laws," 273 n. 1.   [89] Interview 101, Kanziku, June 27, 2009.

Chapter 2

Red dirt, red strangers

Riddle: [What] is here, and at Mombasa?
Answer: The famine.[1]

Oral traditions describe that when representatives of the Imperial British East Africa Company (IBEAC) arrived in central Kenya in the late 1880s, their appearance caused little surprise. For during the latter decades of the nineteenth century, various seers in the country had already predicted the British arrival. In Kikuyuland, these prophecies were made by the famous Cege wa Kibiru. In Ukambani, the prophet Masaku – after whom Machakos was named – was reputed to have predicted the European coming, as did the seer Syokimau. Syokimau had stated that, "A serpent was coming with people inside it ... who would dominate the country."[2] The serpent, of course, was the railway line that by 1901 stretched more than 600 miles across the countryside, linking the Indian Ocean with Lake Victoria via Nairobi and paving the way for the imposition of British colonial rule in East Africa.

It is easy to think of the British arrival as the most important – or even only – factor in shaping the lives of Kikamba-speaking peoples around the turn of the twentieth century. To some degree, this is a result of record keeping: The long, detailed testimonies of railway surveyors, travelers, and colonial administrators seem to connote a high level of influence in the

---

[1] Lindblom, "Kamba Folklore III," 10.
[2] Njau and Mulaki, *Kenya Women Heroes*, 55–59; Somba, *Akamba Mirror*, 2. Prophecies about the impending European arrival are common in Kenyan (and African) literature. Consider, for example, Thiong'o, *Weep Not, Child*, 29.

day-to-day lives of Africans. But the fact that significant social reordering took place did not mean that it was always caused by the "red strangers."[3] Certainly, the new British presence had an impact; but just as significant was its coincidence with a decade of unrelenting natural disasters that included disease, famine, and drought.

Members of communities spread throughout Machakos and Kitui undertook a wide range of actions to survive the period. Some – women in particular – migrated away and entered new kin groups in Kikuyu, Embu, or Taita areas. Others pawned their children to Kikuyu or Indian traders in exchange for food. Many men chose to serve as military auxiliaries, police, or hunters for the British, work that they found attractive. And on their part, British officials eagerly recruited those they viewed unproblematically as "Kamba," believing them to be a people suited for martial occupations based on the earlier accounts of travelers, explorers, and missionaries. Famine conditions forced men and women to make stark choices: They had to decide which social bonds they most prized and cherished. Links of clan and extended family frequently fell by the wayside because fathers and mothers had only enough food to sustain themselves and their sons and daughters. Many families relied on cattle for survival; indeed, some only escaped starvation as a result of the beasts.

The most prominent aspect of British administration imposed upon the newly titled East Africa Protectorate was the establishment of a system of chiefs. Concerned to govern as cheaply and easily as possible, British officials installed chiefs to run the day-to-day lives of African peoples. In Ukambani, the chiefs were rarely men of prominence; younger or less respected men took the new government positions, and the athiani were passed over. Because these chiefs had not exhibited virtue – nor possessed honor – to any degree, they were disobeyed or simply disregarded. But the chiefs were unwilling to accept these slights; they attempted to redefine what constituted virtue in their communities to place themselves at the center of social life.

ECOLOGICAL DISASTER

During the 1880s and 1890s, central-eastern Kenya was one of many regions in sub-Saharan Africa assaulted by an extraordinary confluence of disease and famine, in the wake of which colonialism followed. Rinderpest – a viral cattle disease – was one of the most significant

---

[3] The title of one of Elspeth Huxley's best-known novels. Huxley, *Red Strangers*.

environmental threats. African cattle had no natural defenses against it, and it was fatal for almost all it infected, typically within one to two weeks of first symptoms. Before 1864, rinderpest was found only in Egypt on the African continent. But when the Italians invaded northeastern Africa – establishing a colony in Eritrea in 1890 and trying to do the same in Abyssinia (Ethiopia) – they brought infected cattle from Aden and India to supply their forces. By the end of 1890, rinderpest had spread to the shores of Lake Tanganyika, and continued to move south. Helge Kjekshus has documented the number and effect of cattle deaths throughout East Africa, which resulted in the loss of 95 percent of cattle in some areas. In Ukambani, outbreaks of rinderpest (nicknamed *Ulaya*, meaning "Europe") occurred in 1890 and 1891, as well as in 1897 and 1898.[4] The peoples of central and eastern Kenya battled for control of the stock left unharmed by the ravages of the disease.[5]

Locust swarms also swept through both Machakos and Kitui in 1894 and 1895, followed by smallpox and influenza in 1897. Dry conditions exacerbated the spread of the two diseases: As people left their home areas in search of better living conditions – or hunters and traders moved across the countryside – they often succeeded in spreading the viruses. The effect of smallpox, in particular, was debilitating because few had any natural immunity to it. Alfred Arkell-Hardwick – a European hunter and ivory merchant – described the situation that faced one band of refugees who tried to head north across the Athi river:

They were extremely emaciated ... Suddenly the Maranga [people from central Kikuyuland] who were watching them raised the shrill cry of "Ndui! Ndui!" (smallpox), and rushing at those of the Wakamba who had already landed, then drove them into the water and across the river again.[6]

Maa-speaking peoples, on the other hand, viewed smallpox as a "White Illness," and became wary of approaching Europeans, whom they believed carried it.

Famine, though, was perhaps most damaging to these communities. The 1870s, 1880s, and especially 1890s produced arguably the greatest series of famines the region had ever known.[7] The most serious was

---

[4] For more information on local names given to various diseases in Ukambani, see KNA, DC/MKS.4/6, Machakos District Political Record Book, Vol. IV (1914–1920).
[5] Kjekshus, *Ecology*, 126–132; Mettam, "Short History," 22.
[6] Arkell-Hardwick, *Ivory Trader*, 354. See also Ambler, *Kenyan Communities*, 142–143.
[7] The most prominent famines in the 1870s and 1880s were *Ngeetele* (*c.* 1870–1871) and *Ndata* (1882–1883). The explorer Joseph Thomson witnessed Ndata.

Mũvunga, which occurred in 1898 and 1899. Years later, a colonial officer used this "Great Famine" as a dating device: For Charles Dundas, it was the central event in the past several decades around which his discussion of Kamba law and custom could center, rather than, say, the British arrival.[8] Mũvunga means "rice" in Kikamba: The famine was so-named because people procured rice from missionaries and the colonial government as the famine reached its height. In Kitui, the famine is often labeled *Ngomanisye* (more proper *Yũa ya Ngomanisye*) – "the famine of everywhere." It is difficult to overestimate its demographic and physical impact. As one American missionary described:

Would God I could dip my pen in blacker ink and sketch for Christendom's perusal the daily procession of human skeletons that pass our door, so thin, poor souls, that one almost fancies he hears the clatter of the bones in those fearfully emaciated bodies.[9]

Stuart and Rachel Watt, who established the second mission station in Ukambani in 1893 (much to the disdain of IBEAC administrators), were horrified. As Rachel Watt described:

The scenes around our Mission Station were appalling. Skeletons were tottering hither and thither with every bone and joint in their body exposed to view. No matter where one went, corpses strewed the tracks. Little skeleton babies were found crying by the dead bodies of their mothers ... my husband [often] dragged the naked bodies of men and women and hid them away from sight in the holes and crevices of the earth.[10]

For one of Watt's sons, aged only four years old, images of the famine were etched into his mind. They were the first memories he could recall from childhood: "I remember seeing the half eaten corpse of an African woman, that had fallen down dead or dying near our home ... [it] had been partly devoured by hyenas."[11] Old men recall that hyenas grew so bold as to attack living children or weakened adults.[12]

As a result of the famine, the missionaries of the Africa Inland Mission, who had only arrived in December 1895, closed down two of their mission stations in Ukambani (at Nzaui and Mukaa) leaving only two

---

[8] Dundas, "Organisation and Laws," 265.   [9] *Hearing and Doing* 3, 5 (1899), 4.
[10] Watt, *Heart of Savagedom*, 358.
[11] Bodleian Library of Commonwealth and African Studies at Rhodes House [hereafter RHL], Mss. Afr. s. 391, Papers of J. A. Stuart Watt, Untitled (handwritten notes, n.d.).
[12] RHL, Mss. Afr. s. 1770, Papers of Tom Askwith, *Memoirs of Kenya, 1936–61* (unpublished typescript, n.d.), Vol. I, Chapter 1, 9–11. See also RHL, Mss. Afr. s. 54–57, Papers of Francis George Hall, October 17, 1899.

functioning (at Kangundo and Kilungu).[13] One British official estimated that 25 percent of Kamba died during the famine.[14] Others suggested that the figure was perhaps as high as 50 percent.[15] Some who were able fled to the coast or to Kikuyuland. Yet many parents could not travel the long distances with small children, and whole families died.

Stories about Mũvunga are still told today. Perhaps the oldest woman I interviewed for this project grew quiet and thoughtful when I asked her about the famine. She was a child when Mũvunga occurred, she said, and looking at the deeply set lines that covered every part of her visage, it was difficult to be skeptical. The abiding sense she conveyed was of the utter hopelessness of the situation that faced the people of Ukambani: in her words, "People couldn't do much farming ... they ate the reserve food, then the next thing to do was wait and die ... in a home like this one of mine, people died completely, completely, completely."[16]

In reference to this disastrous period, H. R. Tate – initially a district officer and later provincial commissioner of Nyanza during the 1920s – noted that, "The Akamba ... will not part with their treasured herds [of cattle] ... Many of them died of starvation, leaving their livestock to their children, sooner than kill what would have saved their lives." Tate continued to emphasize that simply selling or eating cattle would have alleviated some of the conditions brought about by famine.[17] Tate's words provide an important point of entry into a consideration of cattle, which gained increased significance in this new, uniquely insecure environment.[18]

In 1898 and 1899, cattle were frequently all that stood between life and death for families in Ukambani. Their importance was magnified because more people owned the beasts than at any point before. This was in large part because the risk of owning the animals had diminished by the 1880s. The hold of Maa-speaking peoples on the grazing lands in southwestern Machakos had declined, and by the 1890s, they had temporarily abandoned much of eastern Kajiado.[19] Without having to constantly protect their beasts from raiders – something that required the assistance of the andũ anene – families in central and southern Machakos took on cattle ownership, often adding it as another option to agriculture.

---

[13] On the early activities of the mission in Ukambani, see Anderson, *Grasshoppers*, 20–28.
[14] Munro, *Colonial Rule*, 48.　　[15] Tate, "Notes," 135.
[16] Interview 20, Mitaboni, July 27, 2004.　　[17] Tate, "Notes," 135.
[18] See also Herskovits, "Cattle Complex."
[19] I am grateful to Richard Waller for his input on these migrations.

And when Mūvunga struck, it came at a time when other environmental factors had already heaped pressure upon crop production. Locust swarms, plus the deaths of family members from disease, meant that communities had not grown adequate food reserves that might have enabled them to survive the famine. In addition, increasing Zanzibari domination – and British restriction – of trade meant that recourse to this type of activity was no longer easily possible. Colonial regulations banned the sale of cattle outside Ukambani due to an outbreak of rinderpest, much to the horror of Protestant missionaries.[20]

Cattle permitted families to survive for several reasons. First and foremost, they could "bleed" their beasts, a process in which a blunt arrow was used to open the animal's neck to produce blood, which contained vital nutrients. In addition, families needed a way to eat after the end of the famine, as it would take at least one season to grow more crops. Thus keeping cattle alive was essential to survival. While thousands of cattle certainly died, some families survived solely as a direct result of these animals, something reflected in oral accounts. As one informant recalled, "[At that time] the blood of cows was given as food."[21] Another remembered that people killed and ate all their cattle except for two, which they saved to continue to obtain blood.[22] This experience under Mūvunga is part of the reason why Kamba today – and particularly those of the older generations – say *Masyaiwe na ng'ombe* – "They [Kamba] were born with cattle."[23]

The type of cattle owned by communities in Machakos and Kitui were extraordinarily resilient in times of drought. Cattle in East Africa around the turn of the twentieth century – before the situation became more complicated with the introduction of European cattle – fell into two groups: humped zebu and sanga. Both are members of the *Bos indicus* group, although Kamba cattle are – and were then – entirely humped zebu. Humped zebu are typically smaller than sanga cattle and are particularly hardy. And smallness is a tremendous advantage: as Philip Raikes explains, "[T]he smaller an animal the greater is the proportion of hide surface to weight and volume and thus the greater is its ability to withstand heat." Humped zebu were up to 70 kilograms (approximately 154 pounds) *lighter* than cattle belonging to Maa-speaking groups, as a result of the latter procuring cattle from Boran stock for breeding during

[20] KNA, TC 11/81, *Taveta Chronicle* (October 1899).
[21] Interview 15, Ngelani, July 21, 2004.   [22] Interview 22, Mitaboni, July 28, 2004.
[23] Interview 14, Mitaboni, July 20, 2004. See also O'Leary, *Kitui Akamba*, 24.

the nineteenth century; their smaller size was therefore an advantage. In addition, some evidence postulates a connection between smallness of size and resistance to disease.[24]

Ownership of cattle – a relatively recent import in many areas – had now provided a vital means of survival. Certain cultural practices related to cattle suggest a new moral architecture surrounding the beasts, and reveal much about the way communities were organized. Famine forced families to tighten their social circles; because food was scarce, providing for any extended family was out of the question. Thus rather than the imposition of colonial rule bringing broader *ethnic* definition, families in Ukambani experienced the opposite: Wider bonds of clan or kivalo fell by the wayside, a process exacerbated by migration. Where families could create links to external communities – perhaps by marrying a young man or woman into another group – they were of immense value, and had to be protected at all costs. Thus a new custom appeared, on which a variety of administrators commented in the first decade of the twentieth century: Cattle given as bridewealth payment were never slaughtered, but instead cherished and protected in all but the direst circumstances. They were the only cattle people branded – a relatively new practice – along with those gained in blood money payment.[25] The cattle symbolized the bond between two families, and the bond permitted survival during famine.

Charles Dundas extends the importance of cattle still further. Dundas was one of a series of capable "anthro-administrators" who worked in Ukambani during the first years of company and colonial rule. These men were expected to have a genuine understanding of anthropology, which was deemed essential for their duties. Dundas came to the conclusion that Kamba inscribed their family histories onto cattle. As one man he met explained:

Every day I look at my cattle and I say these I inherited from my father, those are their increase, those were paid for my brother who was killed, and these I got for my daughters, but if I slaughter or sell them, who shall remind me of all this [?][26]

If the man had destroyed or sold his animals, several generations of his family – and the collective memory of respected ancestors – would cease to exist. As a result, people gave each of their cows a distinct name to remember them better.[27]

[24] Raikes, *Livestock Policy*, 54–57.   [25] Hobley, *Ethnology*, 22.
[26] Dundas, "History of Kitui," 501.   [27] Lindblom, *Notes*, 90.

For those without access to cattle, migration was one of the most common solutions to famine conditions. This was more difficult for men than women, whose reproductive capabilities were highly valued. Often women chose to leave their home areas after becoming convinced that their husbands – absent for long periods trying to trade or hunt for food – would never return. Discourse among Kikamba-speaking peoples reveals conflict over this process: One well-known famine song lamented, "When it rains very little, we are deprived of the wives [who leave]." Men asserted that they had neither abandoned their families, nor abdicated their responsibilities: A proverb argued, "If in the dry season a man leaves his dwelling, he is likely to return with the rainy season."[28]

Throughout African history, the ability of senior lineage members to choose which people "their" women married has had a great bearing on social dynamics. In her study of the Anlo-Ewe, Sandra Greene demonstrates how ethnicity and gender intersected in the eighteenth and nineteenth centuries: Strategic marriage enabled certain clans to maintain "insider" status in communities where refugees and migrants were common.[29] In Ukambani, the opposite was true. Lineage elders were quick to marry women to Embu or Kikuyu families, or even Indians working on the Uganda Railway. These hastily formed bonds could produce vital food from their new kin. In other cases, women or children were "pawned" – or given in temporary exchange – in return for food.[30] Those who remained at home sung that these women had "gone to wash 'lesos' and 'dig with their bottoms'" – to wash cloth typically worn by Swahilis, and have sex with them.[31]

Areas across the Athi and Tana rivers were little affected by Mūvunga, and thus the process of migration was exacerbated. Kikuyu areas had plentiful supplies of food; and to the southeast, the people of Taita country were free of famine. Migration occurred to such a degree that one missionary told a British official that he thought the practice of polygamy in Ukambani might end due to a shortage of available women once the famine was over.[32] Women and children had usually migrated as a temporary measure, but in many cases, "became" Embu or Kikuyu, and never returned to Ukambani. British officials in the 1950s even wondered

---

[28] Lindblom, "Kamba Folklore III," 36, 42.   [29] Greene, *Gender*, 1–135.

[30] The concept of "pawnship" was the source of frequent misunderstandings between different peoples. Eliot, *East Africa Protectorate*, 125; O'Leary, *Kitui Akamba*, 24. On pawnship more broadly, see Falola and Lovejoy (eds.), *Pawnship in Africa*.

[31] Lindblom, "Kamba Folklore III," 44–45.   [32] Hobley, *Ethnology*, 14.

whether Kenya's first president – Jomo Kenyatta – was actually born in
Ukambani, and his mother had moved to Kikuyuland during the 1890s as
a way to survive famine.[33]

Others turned to trading as a way to negotiate their difficult circumstances. Some men and women joined the Swahili and European caravans –
which had become a common sight in Ukambani – and worked as porters
for wages. A few recommenced the practically defunct ivory trade, and
slave trading expanded in scope.[34] But the majority sold their wares in less
formally organized fashion: Little groups of men and women, often
numbering ten or fewer, spread out from their homes to trade small
volumes of goods across the country.

Perhaps the most vivid oral testimony I collected for this book was
stories about these "famine travelers." Every man or woman in Machakos
can recall a story from these times, when his or her grandmother or
great-grandfather journeyed from some far-flung part of the region to
Nairobi or the coast. They traveled there to sell chickens or gourds, which
they had carried on their heads for sometimes upward of 100 miles. The
sheer numbers of people that moved between Machakos and Nairobi
caught the attention of District Commissioner R. G. Stone some years
later, who put it best when he wrote: "[F]rom the numbers of people one
sees taking chickens and eggs to Nairobi it would seem that they supply
the greater part of those articles of food consumed in the whole of Nairobi
and its environs."[35] The traders then turned around and came home to
their families, from whom they had been absent for sometimes as long as
a month. Men and women participated in this trade as equals: They
journeyed together – often along old trading and hunting routes that were
used decades earlier – and took the same risks. As one man explained,
"We couldn't go alone because of animals and snakes. We went in parties
of ten, twelve, sometimes twenty, and everyone had their own hens,
fifteen or twenty, as many as could be carried."[36] Some bands comprised

---

[33] Luongo, *Witchcraft*, 34.
[34] Ainsworth, "Journey," 409–412. The explorer Höhnel stated that entire districts had
emptied due to the threat of Kamba slave traders. Höhnel, *Discovery*, Vol. I, 331.
[35] KNA, DC/MKS.1/1/10, Machakos District Annual Report, 1920. Jackson's work illumin-
ates the presence of this trade in the late nineteenth century. Jackson, "Dimensions."
[36] The Jeremy Newman Papers [hereafter JNP], Interview with Ishmael Mwendwa, Tala,
June 16, 1973. JNP contains a series of interviews carried out by Jeremy Newman in
Ukambani in 1973 and 1974. I am grateful to John Lonsdale for bringing these papers to
my attention and Jeremy Newman for his permission to cite them. They are archived
online. Osborne, "Jeremy Newman Papers."

all women, some all men, and some were mixed. It seems that all-women trading groups enjoyed an advantage over men: They were afforded a degree of immunity from harassment.[37]

The actions of these men and women are lauded throughout Ukambani today, and stories of their achievements told and retold. There is a powerful degree of consistency and pride in these tales. This is clear, for instance, in comparison with stories about wars with "the Maasai." Stories of "Kamba" and "Maasai" conflict are often clichéd, and difficult to genuinely believe; they perhaps owe more to a series of conflicts from the 1960s than some vaguely defined past. In contrast, stories of the famine travelers are packed with detail, from the names of the men and women themselves, to the precise routes they traversed, to the items they traded.

These famine travelers were honored for their service. On one level, this is because they represented community virtues to a high degree: They journeyed in unknown lands, faced danger from bandits and wild animals, hunted for their food, and allowed those at home to survive. But perhaps more importantly, the attachment of these travelers to their families was the real, defining reason for travel; the bonds of family reflected the way communities were organized during these times. Men and women earned respect that brooked no distinction of gender.

RED STRANGERS

Along with sweeping environmental changes came the British, represented by the newly created IBEAC.[38] The company had become the official representative of the Crown in East Africa following the receipt of a royal charter from Queen Victoria in September 1888. It aimed to administer large swathes of land contiguous with the territories now known as Kenya and Uganda, though they were ill-defined at the time. It also loftily planned to end the slave trade that existed between the East African interior and the coast, thereby justifying its motto of "Light and Liberty." The British government viewed company control as a favorable option in East Africa (and in other parts of the continent) because such an arrangement absolved it from responsibility – both financial and administrative – for areas whose value and viability were largely unknown.

[37] Robertson, "Gender and Trade."
[38] On the history of the IBEAC, see Kiewiet Hemphill, "British Sphere."

The company's officers were consumed with building the "Uganda Railway," which first required extensive surveying to determine the ideal location for the line.[39] The first expeditionary force proceeded inland in 1889, establishing a government station at Machakos, which became the first capital of British East Africa (preceding Mombasa and then Nairobi). The Machakos station (or *boma*) was little more than a guardhouse, though stoutly defended. It had a thatched roof perched above its walls on wooden supports, and flew the Union Jack from a flagpole. The station was situated on low ground, close to a water source, and was overlooked by the village in which Masaku had lived until his death during the late 1880s. Machakos was already an established trading center, and became the most important post in the interior for the IBEAC before the railway line was completed. The line that eventually followed passed along the southern border of Ukambani, across the dry Athi Plains, and on to Nairobi.

On August 4, 1889, the IBEAC established its first formal relationship with a *mũndũ mũnene* (singular of andũ anene). Expedition leader Frederick Jackson signed a treaty with Mboli – a leader in Iveti, a hilly region of northern Machakos – whom he described as a "first-class ruffian."[40] The treaty was written in Arabic and English; Mboli could not read its contents, and because he could not write either, signed with an "X." In doing so, Mboli agreed to put himself and "all his territories, countries, peoples, and subjects under the protection, rule, and government of the Imperial British East Africa Company," and "ceded to the said Company all his sovereign rights and rights of government."[41] It is likely that Mboli was a man of significance, but little more; "territories," "countries," and "subjects" was certainly absurdly highfalutin language. One company official even admitted this years later; but for Jackson, the more authority Mboli claimed to have, the greater Jackson's influence borne via the treaty.[42] The treaty reflected a vast misunderstanding of the organization of Kikamba-speaking peoples: For Jackson, he had made an agreement with "the Kamba"; in fact, it was with one personage in one small region of the wider countryside.

The 1889 expedition laid the groundwork for the railway survey that followed two years later. The survey team ultimately decided on a route

[39] Despite its name, the Uganda Railway did not actually enter Uganda at any point, running westward as far as the shore of Lake Victoria at Kisumu.

[40] Jackson, *Early Days*, 168.   [41] Great Britain, *Mombasa Railway Survey*, 15.

[42] As the district commissioner of Machakos later noted, "Whether Mboli was a genuine chief is doubtful, but at any rate he has sunk to a very inferior position since those days." KNA, DC/MKS.4/2, Machakos District Political Record Book, Vol. I (Part I) (-1910), 1.

FIGURE 4: Kamba *askaris* (soldiers) at Fort Machakos after it was rebuilt, *c.* 1911. KNA: 725.18 PER [998369]. Reproduced here with permission from the Kenya National Archives.

via Tsavo and Kibwezi that passed close to the southern limits of where Kikamba-speaking peoples lived (though some remained beyond the line further to the south). Yet while the survey was a success, the ability of the company to build the line was in grave doubt, in large part due to its appalling financial situation. Thus the British government assumed responsibility for the territory of British East Africa in 1895 (the year after it claimed Uganda from the company), renaming it the East Africa Protectorate. On the ground – in some ways – little changed initially; many of the company's officials continued their work as before, just under a new master. But the transfer ushered in the era of formal colonial rule, which would eventually transform the landscape of Kenya and the lives of those inhabiting it.

One of the first requirements for officials of the IBEAC (and later colonial government) was to procure soldiers who could help first to "pacify" – and then control – newly acquired territories in East Africa. "Native auxiliaries" were significantly cheaper than British soldiers, an important consideration in the imperial exercise of frugality. When it came to finding soldiers to serve in the protectorate, administrators initially favored Sudanese – who had served effectively in Uganda – and Swahili. But their numbers were insufficient, so auxiliaries drawn from the protectorate itself were also required.

An official of the IBEAC – or later colonial administration – had two sources from which he could glean information to guide his choices. The first was books and articles published by earlier travelers to the area in which he found himself working, and the second, personal experience and the advice of his superiors. Regarding the former, it is possible to state with some authority that European visitors to East Africa – and certainly explorers – all read one another's work before departing from their home countries. Considering the atmosphere of excitement in Europe – especially in London – about the exploration of Africa during the mid to late nineteenth century, European presses typically published one another's work. Krapf's *Travels* appeared in London in 1860 in English translation and quickly sold out several print runs, as did Karl Peters's *New Light on Dark Africa* in 1891. While the books of Germans J. M. Hildebrandt and Baron von der Decken were never translated into English, bulletins summarizing their travel experiences were published in the journal of the Royal Geographical Society of London.[43]

Officials little understood the complex web of values shared by many Kikamba-speakers who were associated with hunting and war. They were more concerned with whether peoples they encountered were "peaceful" or "warlike," in order to know first whether they would likely require "pacification" – in the parlance of the times – and related, whether they might make good auxiliaries. And the available information seemed to show that "the Kamba" were a "fighting" people, something that was seemingly confirmed by the experiences of Europeans who encountered "them."

The first port of call for a company employee or administrator wishing to learn about the interior of East Africa was the writings of the German missionary Krapf. In his work, Krapf described the Kamba "tribe" as "celebrated," and praised the way warriors handled themselves in several skirmishes he witnessed. On the German's second journey to Ukambani in 1851, he found himself the recipient of aggression. Near the Tana river, a band of robbers attacked Krapf, Kivui, and their party. Kivui and one of his wives were killed, but Krapf escaped. When he finally returned to Kivui's men, Krapf realized that they held him responsible for the

---

[43] Rigby, "Hildebrandt"; Thornton, "Notes on a Journey."

trader's death. The missionary wrote, "I had little doubt of some homicidal attempt [on my life] and, therefore, resolved to escape." He was kept hostage until he took his chance to flee in the early hours of one morning, finally achieving safety after several more days on the run.[44] Krapf himself never again traveled to Ukambani during his remaining residence in East Africa.

Those who followed Krapf received a similar reception. A number of communities – especially those involved with trading – viewed Krapf as directly responsible for causing Kivui's death, and associated other Europeans with the German. When Hildebrandt entered Kitui more than two decades later, some athiani passed a sentence of death upon him, and one of Kivui's sons tried to kill him in hand-to-hand combat. They also attempted to poison him, then fired arrows at him.[45] Count Samuel Teleki – a keen hunter of aristocratic Hungarian descent – and his guide Ludwig von Höhnel had a similar experience. They were threatened in the notorious Kilungu in southern Machakos, where later explorers and company officials including James Macdonald and Frederick Lugard faced difficulties.[46] Karl Peters noted how Kamba harassed others around them, especially Galla, also believed to be a "warlike tribe."[47] Some Galla apparently resorted to living on an island in the middle of the Tana river because it afforded good protection from raids.[48] Several IBEAC employees also noted how Kamba had driven other peoples out of their lands and claimed them.[49]

Expertise with the bow and arrow, that most central skill for men, also caught European attention. During his time with the railway survey, Macdonald witnessed conflict between "the Kamba" and "the Maasai." Though he rated the former little in open battle, their tactic of using poisoned arrows fired from positions affording cover – especially in the hills of central Machakos – to defeat their enemy earned his respect. The bow, he explained, was "death-dealing" in their hands, and indeed, he found himself on the receiving end of several poisoned arrows in Kilungu.[50] The American William Astor Chanler, accompanied by Höhnel on the Austrian's second African expedition between 1892 and 1894, stated, "With bow and arrow they [the Kamba] are excellent shots,"

[44] Krapf, *Travels*, 284, 305, 318–351.   [45] Rigby, "Hildebrandt," 451–453.
[46] Höhnel, *Discovery*, Vol. II, 307–312.   [47] Peters, *New Light*, 127, 169.
[48] Ravenstein, "Ormerod's Journeys," 287.
[49] Pigott, "Pigott's Journey," 132–133; Ravenstein, "Jackson and Gedge's Journey," 193.
[50] Macdonald, *Soldiering*, 39–44.

and suggested that, "After the British become better acquainted with the capabilities of this tribe, they will make use of its members as troops ... there is not a race in East Africa like them for undergoing privations, or fighting."[51] European observers also rated their hunters highly.[52]

Explorers and missionaries encountered Kikamba-speaking peoples at a particularly significant moment. The second half of the nineteenth century featured an increased level of conflict between the peoples of Machakos, but also between them and Maa-speaking groups to the southwest. The latter were decimated by cholera (in 1869), and smallpox in 1883 and 1884, as well as pleuro-pneumonia – a bacterial disease deadly to cattle – around the same time. Raiders from Machakos harassed these communities almost at will, building enormous herds of cattle, and expanding the frontiers of settlement to the south and west.[53] Among Europeans in the second half of the nineteenth century, "the Maasai" had a reputation for savagery and violence that was unmatched, though with hindsight, somewhat undeserved. Thus Europeans deemed the fact that "the Kamba" persistently won success against "the Maasai" particularly notable. The explorers Richard Burton and John Hanning Speke, for instance, were surprised at this, and drew attention in somewhat admiring tones to Kamba bravery.[54] The first officials of the IBEAC who arrived in East Africa echoed similar sentiments, including George Leith, the first company administrator at Machakos.[55] Similarly, that most ardent imperialist and creator of "indirect rule," Frederick Lugard, held the Kamba in the highest regard. He observed that the Kamba were at "constant war" with the Maasai, noting approvingly that, "[T]hey make it pretty hot [for them]."[56]

Lugard reserved a special place for Kamba peoples in his writings. In 1891, Charles Latrobe-Bateman – the second IBEAC administrator at Machakos – asked Lugard to punish several villages close to the Machakos boma for a perceived wrong. Rather than taking Latrobe-Bateman's side, Lugard assumed that the villagers could never have committed such an offense: "There must be some cause for this with a people like the Kamba," he wrote, an extraordinary reaction at the time and in that

[51] Chanler, *Through Jungle and Desert*, 408. See also Hobley, *Ethnology*, 44.
[52] Hobley, *From Chartered Company*, 163; RHL, Mss. Afr. s. 380, Papers of John Ainsworth, *Reminiscences of East Africa* (unpublished typescript, n.d.), 1.
[53] Low, "Northern Interior," 308.   [54] Burton and Speke, "Coasting Voyage," 193–195.
[55] RHL, Mss. Brit. Emp. s. 22/G/5, George Leith, "Report of a Journey to Machakos," August 11, 1890.
[56] Lugard, *Rise*, Vol. I, 283. See also Perham (ed.), *Diaries*, Vol. I, 150.

context, "and I want to get to the bottom of it and hear *their* side." For Lugard had noted earlier in his diary that he was "unwilling to have a row with the Wakamba of all people!" By that point, Lugard had made blood-brotherhood with one group near the boma (on October 2, 1890) in an attempt to secure peaceful relations with them. He was devastated on his return from Uganda in 1892 to find the IBEAC engaged in war, which seemingly caused him to question the imperial project itself (importantly, in his private diary, which he never expected to be published): "[T]he Company [is] fighting in Kikuyu ... [and] among the ... Wakamba ... Such is our vaunted 'peace for Africa!'"[57]

One of the main aims of early IBEAC administrators stationed at the Machakos boma was to ensure stability and security in the surrounding area. But the first two men – Leith and Latrobe-Bateman – were of poor quality, and unable to effectively interact with the local andũ anene (Leith earned the nickname *Kĩkombe* – meaning "cup" – a reference to his fondness for liquor).[58] In 1891, Leith cut down a tree that formed part of a shrine (*kĩthembeo*), in order to make a flagpole. As a result, warriors from Iveti took up arms against the company, though Leith was able to neutralize their threat through the use of rifle fire and burning down some of their huts.[59] The state of affairs calmed in early 1892, however, with the arrival of John Ainsworth at Machakos. Ainsworth, an extremely capable administrator, was able to make peace with those around Iveti, establishing far better relations than typically existed between other

[57] Perham (ed.), *Diaries*, Vol. I, 126, 288–290, 301; Vol. III, 388. This was probably one of the major reasons for Lugard's bad relationship with John Ainsworth. See also Maxon, *John Ainsworth*, 1–16. The opinions that men like Krapf, Burton, and Speke held about the Kamba is perhaps related to a belief that the Kamba were part of a more advanced "race" than other Bantu-speaking groups in Kenya. This was in large part based on Krapf's assertion in his journal – following his first visit to Ukambani – that, "The Wakamba ... in no way ... belong to the negro-race." Precisely *how* he "classified" the Kamba was surprisingly unclear; he seemed unable to decide more than the fact that they were all descended from "father Ham." Krapf's theories appeared in a piece in the *Journal of the Royal Geographical Society* the following year in 1850, which was based on information gathered from Krapf and several other explorers. As the author explained, the Kamba were "not negroes," and this "great people" possibly had very "fair" skin. "This should come as little surprise," noted the author, because "That there are white people in the interior of Africa has often been asserted." CMS, CA5M2, "Dr. Krapf's Journal Description of a Journey to Ukambani in November and December 1849," 292; MacQueen, "Notes," 246.

[58] Munro, *Colonial Rule*, 35.

[59] Maxon, *John Ainsworth*, 6–7; Munro, *Colonial Rule*, 35–36.

peoples and their administrators. The fact that he married – or at least cohabited with – a local woman was in part responsible for this.[60]

But Ainsworth soon faced trouble from more distant areas, and found himself in need of auxiliaries. Based on his experiences and readings, he quickly turned to the warriors of Iveti, using them on assignment in 1893. In January of that year, he received a message from W. P. Purkiss, the superintendent of Kikuyu Province. Purkiss was temporarily in charge of Fort Smith – the company's center of operations in Kikuyuland – following the departure of Major Eric Smith. Purkiss asked for help because he was in "a lot of trouble . . . and the Fort was practically invested [under siege]." Anxious to assist, Ainsworth engaged 100 bowmen from Machakos and formed a raiding party. The party marched over thirty miles the following day to Fort Smith, where he and his men quickly dispersed the Kikuyu warriors.[61] Nor, indeed, was this the first time: Two years earlier, Wilson had collected an "insignificant force" of volunteers to "teach the Kikuyu a lesson," which they promptly did.[62]

Presumably impressed by their service, Ainsworth formed a formal "militia" of young men from Iveti the following year. He needed to defend western Machakos and the company's caravans against Maasai raiders, who began an especially aggressive (and somewhat desperate) series of incursions in the region during the early 1890s. That Ainsworth would choose a relatively small force to ward off Maasai warriors, who supposedly inspired such terror throughout East Africa, clearly reflected the high regard in which he held his soldiers. The force comprised 100 men to serve as guards manning a series of watchtowers, plus 6 companies of 11 men each, trained in the use of firearms.[63]

But in 1895, when officials placed Ukambani into the newly created Athi district (naming Machakos "Ulu" and Kitui "Nengia"), Ainsworth's control existed little outside Iveti. In early 1895, Ainsworth made his first extensive journey east, from Machakos to Kitui. On that journey he viewed much of the countryside for the first time, and came into contact with communities living far from Machakos. He sent a dispatch back to the Royal Geographical Society describing his journey, detailing a

---

[60] Maxon, *John Ainsworth*, 45, 85. Elijah Mutambuuki – born at the very end of the nineteenth century – recalled the following about Ainsworth: "He was very popular because he married an African girl called Mukulu. This woman gave birth to a child but the woman died and Nzueni [Ainsworth] kept the child." JNP, Interview with Elijah Mutambuuki, Tala, July 1, 1973.

[61] Goldsmith (ed.), *John Ainsworth*, 19–20.   [62] Lugard, *Rise*, Vol. II, 536.

[63] Maxon, *John Ainsworth*, 31.

"system of continual raids" that existed between "Mala" (Mwala, in central Machakos) and Kitui.[64] This state of violence in the remainder of Ukambani was quickly evident as Ainsworth's recently built police post at Mukuyuni was destroyed, and the entire garrison except six killed. Then, a different group of warriors attacked his post at Kyaana. Andū anene in these outlying regions were particularly opposed to Ainsworth's efforts to reduce slave trading, from which they made great profits. They had not entered into the reciprocal relationship of trade with the IBEAC like those near the Machakos boma.

As Ainsworth tried to bring an end to slave trading in Ukambani in 1894 and 1895, he used his levies drawn from Iveti – on whom he had come to rely – against the powerful Mwatu wa Ngoma of Mwala. Ainsworth had initially established good relations with Mwatu, who perceived that a solid relationship with Ainsworth could only assist in his development as a military leader. Mwatu, indeed, allowed Ainsworth to establish a police post in Mwala. Yet the peace did not last. Between 1895 and 1897, Ainsworth carried out "punitive expeditions" against Mwatu, as well as some allies with whom Mwatu had made peace in order to fight Ainsworth. Ainsworth then moved against the athiani of Kathome and Kyaana, to the east of Machakos, before turning on those of Kiteta, Katuma, and Kibaoni in 1895 and 1896, and then Kilungu in 1897, confiscating cattle and goats as he went.[65]

Opposition to Ainsworth's forces mirrored nineteenth-century conflict in the interior of East Africa. There was, of course, no united "Kamba" front against him. More likely, Ainsworth was viewed as simply another mūthiani from Iveti who had gathered warriors and attempted to increase his influence and wealth. For in the 1890s, none of the more restrictive aspects of British rule had yet appeared: There was no taxation, nor was land use restricted in any way. From the British perspective, while "resistance" to the implementation of rule was troubling, it was expected from a people they considered "warlike." As a later administrator summarized: "[T]he Akamba gave a good account of themselves and compared with other African tribes proved themselves no mean opponents, but on the contrary quite highly skilled in the art of warfare."[66] The British certainly

---

[64] Ainsworth, "Journey," 407–408.
[65] KNA, DC/MKS.4/2, Machakos District Political Record Book, Vol. I (Part I) (-1910). Ainsworth frequently noted the loyalty of his Iveti auxiliaries. See, for instance, RHL, Mss. Brit. Emp. s. 22/G/5, Ainsworth to Administrator, January 31, 1894.
[66] KNA, DC/MKS.4/2, Machakos District Political Record Book, Vol. I (Part I) (-1910), 33.

wanted to remove the possibility of the athiani and their charges main-taining any independence as military leaders, but were happy to engage them as auxiliaries.

Serving in the martial disciplines under British authority was attractive work for young men. In addressing this topic, it is imperative to remove any artificial distinctions between work as auxiliaries, soldiers, police, or hunting guides. From the perspective of most youth at the time, separating these categories would have made little sense, for several reasons. First, there were, of course, no categories of "soldiers" and "police" in nineteenth-century Ukambani; even hunting and war were considered practically the same occupations. Second, there was little distinction between the army and police in the early days of colonial rule: Police carried out missions just as arduous – and often more so – than the army, and the two served together on occasion. Third, the King's African Rifles – the formal colonial military – was hardly a crack force during the first decade of the twentieth century, and was in many ways inferior to the police. Its African soldiers carried barely functional weapons and were commanded by poor-quality officers who were rejects from British regi-ments. The police were – in the words of Lonsdale – "better educated and expected to have a real measure of knowledge of law and police duties."[67] Perhaps Major General Joe Ndolo, the head of the Kenyan Army after independence, put it best when he stated: "[When I enlisted] I did not know the difference between the Army and the police."[68]

But most importantly, police and military service, as well as hunting, all permitted the expression of male virtue in social life. All required bravery, the ability to shoot well with a gun or bow and arrow, and the knowledge of the wider countryside commoners did not possess. Wages from this service – and sometimes meat from hunting expeditions – sustained communities in Ukambani, allowing these men to continue to provide for their families. The transition between the ways they won honor before – and after – the British arrival was minimal. In writing about the Iveti levies, Munro goes so far as to state that Ainsworth was "assuming some of the functions of a *mūthiani* ... replacing the trad-itional spoils of war by payment for turning out in the militia force."[69] Ainsworth easily slotted into the world of nineteenth-century Ukambani. In 1850, Krapf made no distinction in his translations of the words

[67] Lonsdale, "Conquest State," 10.   [68] Parsons, *1964 Army Mutinies*, 51.
[69] Munro, *Colonial Rule*, 38-39.

"warrior" and "soldier," rendering both *mundu wa kau* (literally, "man of war"); in 1958, John Mbiti used *mũsikalĩ* for both.[70]

As well as serving as auxiliaries, young men joined the British East Africa Police – formed in 1902 – in large numbers, and joined explorers and officials in their hunting parties as scouts and trackers.[71] From evidence collected from a series of hunting accounts for his social history of hunting in Kenya, Steinhart concludes that Kamba peoples were "important actors in the rise of colonial hunting."[72] Others continued to hunt outside the colonial sphere. Though the Game Ordinance of 1906 provided the legal backing for restricting hunting (now called "poaching") – by requiring game licenses – implementation was scattered, at best. Athiani-led expeditions to hunt elephant and procure valuable ivory continued, and a wide ring of ivory smuggling appeared.[73] Officials' difficulties were compounded by the fact that chiefs were often complicit in the hunting of elephant and sale of the resultant ivory.[74] In his analysis of poaching in Kitui between 1900 and 1960, Michael Stone argues that illegal hunting continued throughout the colonial period: District officials were unable to prevent or control poaching for the entire span of these years.[75]

It is important not to divorce Mũvunga from these changes. In the years following the famine, men took on any and all jobs to procure food or money. Yet once the economy rebounded, youths jettisoned jobs working on the railways as porters, or on European farms, yet employment levels in the police, or as hunters and auxiliaries, increased. District officials were utterly bemused; as one noted in 1908:

[70] Krapf, *Vocabulary*, 46, 58; Mbiti, *English–Kamba Vocabulary*, 43, 50.

[71] Clayton and Killingray, *Khaki and Blue*, 109–110; KNA, DC/MKS.1/1/2, Machakos District Annual Report, 1910–1911; Ward and Milligan, *Handbook*, 178. See also Wolf, "Asian and African Recruitment." Unfortunately some of the materials Wolf references are no longer available in the Kenya National Archives.

[72] Steinhart, *Black Poachers*, 55–58. Perhaps the most famous hunting expedition ever mounted – that of the former president of the United States, Theodore Roosevelt, in 1909 and 1910 – specifically trained Kamba skinners to prepare hides for shipment back to the United States. RHL, Mss. Afr. s. 771, Papers of Robert Foran, *Memories of Roosevelt* (unpublished typescript, n.d.), 130.

[73] Hunter, *Hunter*, 200; Steinhart, *Black Poachers*, 152–153.

[74] Consider Mwandau of Migwani, who administered oaths to his hunters to ensure their loyalty to him. KNA, DC/KTI.7/4, Dundas, "Districts of Kitui," 1. Similar suspicions about chiefly complicity existed in Mumoni. KNA, DC/KTI/1/1.1, Kitui District Annual Report, 1910–1911.

[75] Stone, "Organized Poaching."

People will not work even in the parts of the district where there is no food. I induced 225 men to go to work on the Railway for a white contractor and 140 ran away in 3 days [*sic*] time ... Everything was excellent, good houses and fair pay, and as much ready cooked food as a man could eat, no limit being put on the amount.[76]

Young men chose martial occupations despite the fact that they had little overwhelming financial requirement to earn money to pay tax: They did not own huts, and therefore had no tax burden before the Hut and Poll Tax Ordinance of 1910 (though tax on dwellings began in 1902 – see below). Martial service provided them with a way to earn prestige and respect, which was especially important once raiding ended with the firm imposition of colonial rule. The new system fitted onto existing ways of life very easily: Officials worried that service in the police was viewed simply as government-sanctioned raiding.[77] Initially, athiani had resisted Ainsworth's attempts to restrict their autonomy, but they quickly decided to work alongside "Nzueni" to maintain their positions, and thus remained prosperous into the twentieth century as a result.

CHIEFS AND CATTLE, ATHIANI AND AUTHORITY

New land policies and restrictions were some of the most tangible effects of British rule in Africa. By 1905 – when the Colonial Office took over the administration of the protectorate from the Foreign Office – it was believed that European settlement was the most likely method for balancing Kenya's books. By 1906, almost 2,000 settlers had moved to the protectorate, including several hundred farmers from South Africa. Settlers received large amounts of land at first 21- and then 99-year leases in the Highlands (soon known as the "White Highlands") at low or no cost. This "alienated land" was ideal for European settlement because it was the most agriculturally productive in the protectorate, and situated close to the railway line.[78]

In 1902, Machakos (known as Ulu until 1922) and Kitui were gazetted as districts in Ukamba Province. Yet any strict determination of the land that residents could occupy was initially undecided. This changed with the establishment of the two "native reserves" in 1906. Reserves were areas of low agricultural potential in which Africans were permitted to

[76] KNA, DC/MKS.1/1/1, Machakos District Annual Report, 1908.
[77] KNA, DC/MKS.1/1/1, Machakos District Annual Report, 1908.
[78] Wolff, *Economics*, 47–67; Zeleza, "Establishment of Colonial Rule," 35–70.

live, in contrast to Crown or alienated land that was reserved for the use of the government or settlers. In Machakos, the boundaries of the reserve excluded the fertile land from the Mua Hills across the Athi Plains to Ol Donyo Sabuk, which was set aside for white settlement.[79] In addition, the Kapiti Plains to the west were outside the reserve, as was the Yatta Plateau to the northeast. Approximately half of Machakos district became a reserve area: It comprised 2,204 square miles, from a total of 5,414. In Kitui, a district of 18,281 square miles, the reserve included only 5,016.[80]

On one level, officials created reserves to aid administrative order. But perhaps the major reason was to force Africans out of these marginal (and usually overcrowded) areas to find work as laborers on European farms. While European settlement in Ukambani never approached the levels of Kikuyuland, the hills of western Machakos were excellent areas for agriculture, and settlers quickly moved in, especially after 1910 (though villagers continued to plant their crops in European areas, despite all entreaties).[81] The reserve boundaries – especially in the vicinity of the Mua Hills – gave Kikuyu political parties common ground to join with Kamba in resisting the state decades later.

These large, sparsely populated European farms – with their brick or wooden farmhouses – drew a stark contrast to the villages of Ukambani. Here, residents lived in conical huts, with thatched roofs, and a low door through which one entered. Usually a fireplace with three stones occupied the center of the room. Each family's huts were set close together, protected from wild animals by circles of thorny branches (often from the acacia tree). During the night, goats and chickens stayed in the huts for warmth and protection, but cattle were outside, within a larger enclosure. Granaries were built outside the huts, and sometimes in the fields. A special place called *thome* (see Chapter 6 for more details) – where men and occasionally women gathered to tell stories, educate the youth, or play *bao* (a mancala board game) – was shared by several homesteads.

---

[79] In 1906, the Mua Hills were gazetted within the reserve, but four years later they were excised by officials who changed the boundaries to permit white settlement there. KNA, DC/MKS.4/2, Machakos District Political Record Book, Vol. I (Part I) (-1910), 191.

[80] On the exact boundaries of Ukamba Province, see KNA, DC/MKS.4/5, Machakos District Political Record Book, Vol. III (1911–1914), 18–19; on Machakos: KNA, DC/KTI.1/2/1, Ukamba Province Annual Report, 1915–1916; on Kikumbulyu, a sparsely inhabited region of southern Machakos: KNA, DC/MKS.4/2, Machakos District Political Record Book, Vol. III (1911–1914), 229–230; on Kitui: KNA, DC/KTI/1/1.1, Kitui District Annual Report, 1914–1915.

[81] For the reminiscences of these early settlers, see Hill, *Early Memories*.

Dress and comportment also differed greatly from European fashions. Men and women wore skins or blankets – with the latter becoming more and more popular at the time – though they were often discarded while at work in the fields. Ornaments reflected decades of trading: Both sexes wore beads strung on brass or copper wire around their necks, hips, or arms. Bracelets and rings were common, and European products like umbrellas were greatly desired as prestige goods. Perhaps the most notable bodily modification was sharpened teeth. Men and women chiseled several of their front teeth into points, though the specific number of teeth chipped – and the style in which it was done – varied widely throughout Ukambani, and was only later considered an "ethnic" marker. The practice itself seems to have appeared during the mid nineteenth century – warriors, certainly, exhibited such style – and was one of the first practices deemed "non-Christian" during the early twentieth century (see Chapter 3).[82]

This village life was certainly impacted by land delineation, but colonial rule brought two other major changes: first, the imposition of tax, and second, new systems of governance. Taxation appeared via the Hut Tax on African Dwellings in 1902, and was initially set at 3 Rs (rupees) per year. On one level, the purpose of taxation was to provide funds for the running of the protectorate – something a recalcitrant London was unwilling to do – but it also aimed to force Africans to work as laborers, occupations they would have to undertake in order to procure funds for the tax payments. This was initially a relatively minor imposition for many: A month's wages as a laborer were roughly 3 to 5 Rs.[83] Officials anticipated that the new tax would force men in Machakos into work on European farms. But they had underestimated the robustness of the economy. In the years following Mūvunga, it had rebounded with great vigor. Machakos, for instance, had become a major trading center, supplemented by the historical centers of trade in the interior. And people demonstrated their ability to adapt: In 1909, for instance – a year in which officials banned cattle trading in Ukambani because of an outbreak of the tick-borne East Coast fever – they instead exported more than 63,000 sheep and goat skins.[84]

[82] This description is based on Dundas, "History of Kitui," 492–498, and Lindblom, *Akamba*, 371–397, 431–448.
[83] Wolff, *Economics*, 96.
[84] KNA, DC/MKS.1/1/1, Machakos District Annual Report, 1908–1909; KNA, DC/MKS.1/1/2, Machakos District Annual Reports, 1909–1911.

Men also demonstrated the ability to sidestep Hut Tax, much to the chagrin of officials. Hut Tax was imposed on each individual hut, and therefore each family living inside it. Thus one man with three wives, each of whom lived in her own hut, had to pay tax on three dwellings. In Machakos, men responded by enlarging their huts, and moving in all their wives, thereby circumventing the majority of the required tax payment. In Kibwezi, 100 men simply moved their huts to Taita to avoid the tax.[85] One angry official noted, "By passive resistance they obtain their own way while they pretend to be only anxious to do as they are told."[86]

Tax collection was one of the main duties of newly appointed chiefs and headmen, the day-to-day faces of the new administration. The central principle at the heart of this system was that African "traditional" leaders continue to rule as before, simply under the new aegis of Great Britain. Administrators assumed that Africans lived in tribes governed by chiefs, and therefore imposed this system on the Kamba. Few administrators realized that Kamba societies were historically "chiefless." The new system was based on the kĩvalo. Administrators simply took the ivalo and turned them into "locations," each of which was administered by a chief or headman. The result was – if not a disaster – then something close, and officials constantly lamented the fact that chiefs seemed to have no control over their people.

In nineteenth-century Ukambani, the words and actions of the *atumĩa* (elders) – typically former athiani who had reached old age – carried the most weight. Yet officials passed over them for chiefly appointments and instead favored younger men – or older men who had rarely achieved prominent positions – who were willing to better serve the needs of the state. In Machakos, these men were nearly always labor recruiters, as officials saw the procurement of labor as so vital to the state's financial interests. They were quick to use their positions to gain property or favors over their enemies or competing lineages, and were supported in this by the administration. Almost universally hated, they were referred to as *manyenyambatwa* – so greedy that when they finished eating roasted meat, even licked the stick clean.[87] One informant interviewed in 1973 by Jeremy Newman described Musau – Ainsworth's former interpreter – as "chosen by the D. C." He was "friendly to the Europeans," the man continued, "[and] was chosen to collect people for work." Musau became

---

[85] KNA, DC/MKS.1/1/1, Machakos District Annual Report, 1908.
[86] KNA, DC/KTI/1/1.1, Kitui District Annual Report, 1913.   [87] Mutiso, *Kenya*, 216.

"almost like a ruler of Ukambani," the man remembered, leveraging his association with the Europeans to gain power.[88]

The resolution of disputes – an essential aspect of small-scale societies – was also transformed. In the nineteenth century, older men and women had sat on councils (*nzama*) that judged disagreements.[89] But colonial changes produced a crisis in the management of disputes: Instead of respected elders passing judgment after restricted consultation in the nzama (the word itself meant "secret" at the time), younger chiefs and headmen – all male – now headed publicly accessible "native tribunals."[90] In 1911, one official vented his frustration at this system of governance and mediation: "We became saddled with a large number of persons of no importance and possessed of no authority."[91]

The fact of the matter was that chiefs and headmen paled in comparison to the athiani. In Kitui during the early years of the twentieth century, most athiani simply continued to operate as before – something that was possible in the far-flung district – although some played a part in the colonial system.[92] They stood in contrast to the chiefs who were widely viewed as irrelevant. Athiani were accountable to their communities, and expected to put community interests first; chiefs, on the other hand, were not, as they were appointed by the government, and had not proved themselves worthy of respect as had the prominent individuals of Ukambani for decades. Moreover, they were universally regarded as corrupt, and having little interest in those they supposedly "served": The district commissioner of Machakos, for example, had permitted chiefs to fine any individual several head of livestock if they believed that individual had "abused" them, and many chiefs built up large herds of animals.[93] In previous decades, a man could not gain vast herds without having succeeded in raiding and hunting; now, chiefship was another avenue to these gains. A mũthiani gathered people for war or the hunt via his personal status and bond to his community; a chief, on the other hand, had no such tie to his people. Thus when one administrator questioned

---

[88] JNP, Interview with David Kaindi, Mbooni, February 13, 1974.
[89] KNA, DC/MKS/8/14, "Discussion Paper," 1949.
[90] Today the word "nzama" means a meeting or deliberation, but in 1850 Krapf translated *ndeto jia nsama* as "secrecy." Krapf, *Vocabulary*, 43.
[91] KNA, DC/MKS.1/1/2, Machakos District Annual Report, 1910. See also Dundas, "Organisation and Laws," 241–250, and KNA, W. E. H. Stanner, *The Kitui Kamba: A Critical Study of British Administration* (unpublished typescript, c. 1940), 4-6.
[92] O'Leary, *Kitui Akamba*, 28.
[93] KNA, DC/MKS.1/1/2, Machakos District Annual Report, 1909.

a young man as to why he did not obey his chief, he replied, "He is not my father."[94] Commoners rejected the chiefs who failed to demonstrate virtuous behavior.

Chiefs were certainly aware of their weak positions. Yet theirs was no passive acceptance of their status; instead, they fought to gain prestige. This process was common throughout sub-Saharan Africa at the dawn of colonial rule; as Iliffe shows, traditional ways of earning honor "fragment[ed]" at the time.[95] Some – like youth and women in Ukambani – continued to earn it in essentially the same way. Others – like the chiefs – sought to create new avenues to respect.

Chiefs attempted to rework concepts of virtue in their communities, especially relating to cattle. In previous decades, ownership of cattle came about as the result of a lifetime of success in raiding, hunting, and the related system of trading. As Lonsdale wrote in reference to Kikuyu societies during the nineteenth century, "[W]ealth rewarded virtue."[96] Here, chiefs argued, "wealth *was* virtue." Chiefs could do nothing about their lack of a history of proven leadership or failure to gain status as hunters or warriors; but they proved adept at gathering resources, and in particular, cattle. They controlled native tribunals, for instance, where the payment of cattle to file a case (or as bribes) was commonplace. In their discussions with administrators, chiefs described the values that were required for men to take positions at the pinnacles of their communities. Gone was any mention of war, hunting, or martial occupations. Now, as chiefs informed the administrator Charles Hobley, those who achieved positions in the top levels of their communities merited them for two reasons: first, their skill in dispensing judgment, and second, their ability to pay to join higher councils of elders.[97] This was Ukambani's "country club": Newly minted chiefs could do nothing about their lack of "class," but could instead pay extortionate membership fees to enter.

Cattle were certainly important in a variety of communities in the nineteenth century. Prominent men had gathered large herds, which signified their wealth, and enabled them to bond followers to themselves. But in many parts of Ukambani, cattle ownership was a recent phenomenon. Particularly along the hillsides of central Machakos, and in central Kitui, the climate and soil were more suitable for cultivation, which villagers living there practiced extensively. (As far back as the mid nineteenth century, Krapf had noted rice, Indian corn, and cassava under

---

[94] Dundas, "History of Kitui," 487.   [95] Iliffe, *Honour*, 227.
[96] Lonsdale, "Moral Economy," 343.   [97] Hobley, *Bantu Beliefs*, 220–222.

cultivation, and learned that maize, millet, beans, and peas were also commonly grown.[98]) People in Ukambani were far from being "men of cattle," a term they used to describe Maasai in battle songs.[99]

Now, chiefs forced a transformation: They argued that it was a *Kamba* virtue to own cattle. Cattle came to denote status: As the owner of a small farm north of Machakos Town once told me – tidily summing up the assertions of many others – "Having more cattle visible made you famous, a big man. It was like having a big, visible bank."[100] The importance of cattle was magnified at the turn of the twentieth century because fewer beasts were available – due to disease and famine – and the fact that the animals had permitted many families to survive this difficult period. The chiefs' successful effort is, indeed, still in evidence today: Walking through Ukambani, only the poorest homes are without at least one of the beasts. Over the past century, men and women have created a series of historical assertions about the possession of cattle, and sayings about them: Any interview question about how long Kamba have owned cattle receives the response *mũno tene* – "since time immemorial."

This effort to center cattle as part of the "Kamba" cultural package occurred at the same time that administrators were attempting to gather facts and assertions about "tribal customs." This repository of information was constructed from discussions between administrators and chiefs and elders who – one must assume – worked under the government umbrella. In these discussions, chiefs evoked the notion of "tribe": They described "Kamba" customs, despite the fact that practices ranging from marriage to circumcision to land ownership were undertaken in vastly different ways throughout Machakos and Kitui. British administrators, themselves convinced that Africans had practiced various customs in an unchanging fashion for centuries, were persuaded by the chiefs' efforts to call on the distant past to authenticate their claims.[101]

Chiefly assertions about the prominence of cattle are quite extraordinary. Chiefs and elders told Dundas, for instance, that any new settler to a district had to give a bull to the elders. They explained that compensation for a wrong had to be paid exclusively in cattle, unlike in Tharaka or Kikuyu, or, indeed, the Kamba past, when goats were commonly used.[102] The same occurred for bridewealth: Now, payment was said to be between

---

[98] Krapf, *Travels*, 169.   [99] Lindblom, *Akamba*, 199.
[100] Interview 4, Mutituni, July 9, 2004.
[101] For a comparable example, see Moore and Vaughan, *Cutting Down Trees*, 1–19.
[102] Dundas, "Organisation and Laws," 279, 291.

two and five cows, and involved no other animals or payments (interviews disagree: People insist goats were and are still used).[103] And a series of beliefs appeared that specifically related to cattle.[104] That chiefs and headmen molded older stories and custom is neatly demonstrated by new stories of origin that were recorded by administrators: The older tale of the two children "Mkamba" and "Mkikuyu" – born to the same parents, and who had moved away to establish themselves and their descendants – was reworked to include a third child, "Mzungu" (European).[105]

These changes meant that chiefs could associate themselves with the institutions that formed the core of social life. They described how circumcision – the ceremony young people underwent to achieve adulthood – could not take place without the payment of cattle.[106] Migrants had to pay to move to new communities, and payment of cattle as a part of bridewealth was now essential (see above). As chiefs were the ones who controlled these resources, they were able to gain status, and force commoners to become their dependents.

The process of naming was sometimes used to solidify this transformation. In the nineteenth century, only a warrior could have his name replaced, after some daring feat or accomplishment. When Lindblom published his work on Kamba nomenclature, a second instance arose. Lindblom stated that any person who experienced a "considerable change of social position" could be renamed, and the old name discarded. Therefore, he explained, one "old man ... was called *Nzioka* as a boy, and *Iata* at the dances. Later he came to own a great herd of cattle and received the name *Malata* ('footprints of animals') ... which replaced the other two and became exclusively used."[107] One can almost picture one of the nouveau riche whispering these facts in the Swede's ear: an unimpressive past forgotten, replaced by a new, prestigious present. When Lindblom published a later work, he revealed the name of his assistant: Kioko wa Malata (Kioko – the name given to a boy born in the morning – son of Malata).[108] Kioko was clearly the son of a wealthy, elite leader, the type of man who provided information on supposed "customs" to anthropologists and administrators. Ainsworth's second interpreter, Musau – little respected by his people – named his son Mūthiani, probably in an effort to evoke older forms of prestige.[109]

[103] Dundas, "Native Laws," 253.   [104] Hobley, *Bantu Beliefs*, 140, 159.
[105] Dundas, "History of Kitui," 534.   [106] Lindblom, *Akamba*, 51.
[107] Lindblom, *Notes*, 87.   [108] Lindblom, "Kamba Folklore I," vi.
[109] JNP, Interview with Elijah Mutambuuki, Tala, July 1, 1973.

Stories reflected the transition: Agriculture became less prestigious, and cattle worthy of honor. One story told to Hobley in the first decade of the twentieth century – the first heard in Ukambani and recorded by a European – directly juxtaposes agriculture against cattle ownership. In the story, a hare is frustrated because he is poor. To solve his problem, he steals some cattle from a Kamba man. When the man begins to search for his missing animals, the hare cuts the tails from the cattle and buries them. Thus when the man arrives to see the tails protruding from the earth, it seems to him that the earth has swallowed the cattle. The man then takes a digging stick – the tool used to perform agriculture, and especially common among the Kikuyu – and digs for his cattle until he is exhausted. The story highlights two important themes: first, that anyone without cattle is poor; and second, that digging (agriculture) is hard work, and ultimately fruitless.[110]

Cattle appear prominently in stories collected by Lindblom throughout Ukambani in 1911 and 1912. Lindblom grouped the tales into five sections: Tales about Animals, Tales about Ogres and Giants, Episodes from the Life of the Natives, Myths and Legends, and Imported Stories. Unfortunately, only the first two categories exist in published form today; yet in his introduction to the series, Lindblom discussed Episodes from the Life of the Natives. The most common stories were those about boys living in poverty who through some feat or cunning become immensely rich. They then took many wives, and came to own a large number of cattle. Lindblom states that this was the most popular subject for stories. The sayings with which a storyteller finished his recounting also stressed the centrality of cattle: "May you become rich in goats and I in cattle!" he might cry, or "May your cattle eat earth and mud, but mine the good grass!"[111]

CONCLUSION

Both Jackson and Munro view the famine of Mũvunga as the point at which "Kamba resistance" to British rule ended. Yet reading the history of the region in terms of the colonial presence obscures much about the process of social identification that was the result of famine and drought. Communities faced a dramatic reordering: Men and women struggled to reshape their lives following the extraordinary period of dislocation, and seized on closer bonds of family to negotiate the difficult period.

---

[110] Hobley, *Ethnology*, 111–114.   [111] Lindblom, "Kamba Folklore I," ix–xi.

With the British arrival, newly minted chiefs used the opportunity to seize power and try to consolidate their gains. For the first time, they described "Kamba" practices as a way to try to cement their authority, evoking the supposed history of the tribe to authenticate their claims. In this process, cattle – the banknotes of the nouveau riche – took on immense prominence. On one level, they had provided the means for survival for many families during famine; but they were also a resource through which new chiefs could solidify their hold on power. The chiefs listed "customs" about the possession of cattle, and associated themselves with central rituals in social life.

For young men, service as auxiliaries, hunters, and police was attractive, and continued to be an important facet of their lives. These occupations provided the opportunities for distinction in their communities, as previous methods for achieving this were now fewer: Independent hunting was somewhat restricted, and raiding extremely difficult after 1900 with a stronger British presence. European explorers and British administrators, of course, missed the complex array of virtues related to war and hunting, instead arriving at the simpler conclusion that "the Kamba" were a warlike and martial people that they should press into service as auxiliaries.

Chapter 3

Of volunteers and conscripts

If you happened to meet a German, and said that you were Kamba, he would hate you.[1]

In late 2006, I found myself searching for a small village called Sengani, near Tala market, a little more than an hour's *matatu* (public minibus) ride to the northeast of Nairobi. Although this was the third consecutive year I had walked Ukambani's hills carrying out interviews, I was particularly looking forward to this one. My subject was Stephen Savono Maveke, a man whose resume alone predicted a fascinating conversation. Maveke was once a signalman in the King's African Rifles (KAR), detained during Mau Mau, played top-flight football in Kenya, and became the only paramount chief in Machakos's history after independence. He was an associate of men from the prominent Kamba politician Paul Ngei to Kenya's second president, Daniel arap Moi. And having met Maveke, I could attest that he was indeed a fascinating man. Maveke had a story to tell about the First World War:

At that time, Tanganyika was ruled by the Germans. They fought all the way to Mombasa, to Voi, and in Taita-Taveta. The British government had sent white and Kamba soldiers to fight against the Germans. Whenever the Germans killed a black soldier, they checked his teeth and saw that they had been sharpened. Then they asked, "Who are these people who sharpen their teeth?" And they were told that they were Kambas ... If you happened to meet a German, and said that you were Kamba, he would hate you ... They said that they were

---

[1] Interview with Stephen Savono Maveke, Tala, November 14, 2006.

72

fought and defeated by a people with sharpened teeth. We used to meet Germans in Nairobi when they came to visit the city.[2]

Maveke asserted that the Kamba earned a reputation throughout the British Empire for their fighting skills during the First World War. Others concur with the stiff-backed 91-year-old, agreeing that the Kamba single-handedly enabled the British to drive out the Germans. In actuality, neither declaration is accurate. But the experience of the war did become a foundational part of Kamba lore. It was used as an important building block in constructing the history of the "tribe" during the 1930s and 1940s.

Contemporary recollections are at odds with history. In actuality, the war thrust the British administration of Ukambani into chaos. Various groups – including young men, women, elders, and religious figures – all challenged chiefs and headmen, whom they believed were not supporting community interests, as was their duty. Each group had its own conflicting visions of what virtues and practices were worthy of respect among its members. Christians, in particular, came to form distinct populations in the villages of Ukambani: Christianity drew father against son, and clan member against clan elder, as differing conceptions of social order were frequently incompatible. These undercurrents swirled powerfully beneath the calm surface created in the written work of missionaries, anthropologists, and administrators, who wrote neat descriptions of Kamba custom and social life.

During and after the First World War, there is little convincing evidence of any rigid or widespread ethnic affiliation. Social life was extraordinarily diverse. People throughout Ukambani lived vastly different lives in practically every way. Many communities were still mobile at certain points, especially during times of famine, and discarded "tribal" identity without issue. Ukambani was a maelstrom of constantly shifting social ordering, and it was only during the 1930s that this fluidity began to change.

THE "WAR OF THE QUIVERS"

The First World War broke out in 1914, while colonial rule in the protectorate was in its infancy. As the war began, most in Europe believed it would be over "by Christmas." In East Africa, there was little hint as to the tremendous toll it would take on the region. As one scholar noted, "[I]t seemed impossible that war would break out ... neither colony

---

[2] Interview with Stephen Savono Maveke, Tala, November 14, 2006.

[the British East Africa Protectorate nor German East Africa] appeared to have the prerequisite resources for a fight."[3] Yet these notions quickly proved false. Britain moved thousands of troops into East Africa in the hope of a rapid victory, but they failed in their objective: Colonel Paul von Lettow-Vorbeck (nicknamed "von Lettow-Fallback" by the Allied forces) led them on a merry dance around eastern and southern Africa for the better part of four years.

At the commencement of hostilities, the Colonial Office and War Office conceived of the conflict as a "White Man's War," one which might require some African manpower for logistical support, but certainly not as part of the actual soldiery. Yet as in the South African War (1899–1902), these notions quickly came under debate as death tolls rose. The example of the French – who used troops from West Africa on the Western Front with success from the outset of the war – was frequently discussed. Winston Churchill, in particular, was a strong advocate of African recruitment, speaking powerfully on the subject in the House of Commons.[4] But while the Colonial Office successfully resisted calls to recruit a "million black army" for fighting in Europe, in Africa itself, the situation was entirely different. African soldiers were cheaper than British regulars, and possessed a degree of resistance to diseases such as malaria and yellow fever from which European troops suffered greatly.[5]

South African forces operating on the Allied side in German South-West Africa could use vehicles or animal power to move artillery and supplies; however, in East Africa, humans had to bear the brunt of this labor. This was a result of the lack of good quality roads, combined with the presence of endemic trypanosomiasis. The disease – carried by the tsetse fly – is fatal to oxen, cattle, horses, and donkeys, so humans had to serve as substitutes for these beasts of burden.[6] During the course of the war, therefore, the British and Germans mobilized over a million Africans in East Africa. On the British side, the majority served as "porters" in the Carrier Corps. They went where oxen and vehicles could not, carrying loads on their backs, and ·frequently surviving on fewer than 1,000 calories per day.[7] Yet for these men – who were not involved in the

---

[3] Paice, *Tip and Run*, 14.

[4] See, for instance, Great Britain, *House of Commons Debates*, Vol. 92, Cols. 1387–1389, April 4, 1917.

[5] For more on the debate in Britain over recruiting Africans troops, see Killingray, "British Imperial African Army."

[6] Savage and Munro, "Carrier Corps Recruitment," 314. See also Ford, *Trypanosomiases.*

[7] Killingray, "Labour Exploitation," 493.

physical fighting – the war was no less dangerous. Disease, poor rations, and backbreaking labor meant that Africans died in extraordinary numbers. The official count stated that 45,000 African soldiers and porters drawn from the East Africa Protectorate and Uganda Protectorate died during the conflict, but the actual number was likely far over 100,000.[8]

In an ideal world, the British would have recruited all the men required for the conflict from the official armed forces of East Africa, the KAR. The KAR was formed in 1902 from an amalgamation of the Uganda Rifles, Central Africa Rifles, and East Africa Rifles. Sudanese, Yao (who were predominantly Muslim), Zanzibaris, and Indians made up the majority of the KAR's fighting strength.[9] W. Lloyd-Jones, a major in the KAR, reflected the thinking of the time with regard to what made "good" soldiers in East Africa. He explained that, "Nilotic Sudanese and the tribes of northern Uganda show signs of the effects of former Asiatic invasions, to which they owe their warlike characteristics." The Sudanese had demonstrated their loyalty by remaining with the stranded Emin Pasha in Equatoria Province for several years (despite some British misgivings following their 1897 mutiny), and had served under Lugard in many campaigns. The "aboriginal tribes of Kenya," Lloyd-Jones continued, "have not proved themselves suitable for enlistment in the KAR," although Kamba made "excellent police."[10] Colonial conceptions of the Kamba as a fighting people did not mesh with imperial conceptions of what made suitable soldiers.[11]

Thus with the commencement of the war, the British recruited Africans from what they considered "martial" groups for the KAR, where they took part in the actual fighting, and the majority for the Carrier Corps, where they worked as porters. Typically, men from Ukambani served in the Corps. In the early months of the war, volunteers were common. At one point, for instance – in just one week – Kiteta and Mbooni locations provided 600 men for the Carrier Corps. Officials found men in both Machakos and Kitui willing to join up, and recruiters encountered little

---

[8] Hodges, "Military Labour," 148; Paice, *Tip and Run*, 3.

[9] Parsons, *African Rank-and-File*, 14–16.

[10] Lloyd-Jones, *K.A.R.*, 138, 229. Lloyd-Jones also provides details about troops recruited for service in East Africa between 1888 and 1902. Almost none were drawn from the East Africa Protectorate.

[11] Distinguishing the "imperial" from the "colonial" is important; too often the terms are used interchangeably. For a useful and nuanced exposition of this separation, see Mukherjee, "Justice, War."

opposition as they went about their work. Relatively few deserted, and recruiting officers rejected only 6 percent of men from Machakos for service.[12]

But the flow of men quickly dried up once stories about the harsh conditions of service filtered back to the reserves. A declining number of applicants for service in the Corps resulted in the Native Followers' Ordinance of 1915, which led to what Parsons describes as "informal conscription."[13] With the new ordinance, chiefs became responsible for recruitment quotas. Sources attest to men resorting to bribery to avoid conscription, and the settling of personal scores. In some cases, recruiters passed ropes through the earlobes of young men and literally dragged them off to fight.[14] Many deserted from the Carrier Corps, and others fled whenever rumors surfaced that a recruiting officer had arrived in the vicinity of their homes. Men's initial excitement about the possibility of becoming soldiers was quickly tempered. Desertion was common, particularly following the "Grand Levy" of 1917.

COMMUNITIES IN CRISIS

The social dislocation brought by the war is clear from a simple glance at the numbers of men involved. At the beginning of the conflict, officials had corresponded with one another to ascertain the potential numbers of recruits in each district. In Machakos, the district commissioner reckoned – at the end of 1914 – that approximately 6,000 youths were available.[15] In Kitui, officials calculated that 7,420 could be summoned.[16] By the time recruitment ended in July 1917, officials had recruited 3,900 and 3,885 men from Machakos and Kitui, respectively.[17] This number did not include an extra 1,728 workers from Kitui employed outside the district on farms and the railway, and probably a higher number from Machakos. The lack of young men in various locations was striking: In many, more than 50 percent were absent, and in one sub-location – under the control of Headman Kasioka, in Kitui – the proportion was as high as

---

[12] KNA, DC/MKS.1/1/2, Machakos District Annual Report, 1915–1916.
[13] Parsons, *African Rank-and-File*, 63.
[14] Hodges, *Carrier Corps*, 100. For an excellent treatment of African recruitment during the First World War, see Savage and Munro, "Carrier Corps Recruitment."
[15] KNA, DC/MKS.10B/6/1, DC Machakos to PC [Provincial Commissioner] Nairobi, December 23, 1914.
[16] KNA, DC/KTI/1/1.1, Kitui District Annual Report, 1914–1915.
[17] KNA, DC/KTI.1/2/1, Ukamba Province Annual Report, 1917–1918.

74.1 percent (132 out of 178).[18] Such was the impact of the conflict that the population of Machakos actually decreased in the war's final years. Even once the difficult war years had passed, respite was elusive: The Spanish Flu swept through Kenya in 1918, and famine in the early 1920s followed hard on its heels.

While the imposition of colonial administration had already caused social tensions, they now burst into the open. Chiefs, in particular, were implicated. The responses of commoners to the chiefs' "easy tyranny" (as one official described their rule) varied: Young men fresh from the war challenged them, as did women and religious figures.[19]

Young men had experienced a high degree of excitement to serve in the forces, especially in 1914 and 1915. One subject interviewed by Munro noted that in Machakos, young men called the First World War the "War of the Quivers." As he explained, "Here in Ukambani *anake* were collected and told to carry bows and arrows ... This was how Kamba soldiers were called up."[20] The chance to take up traditional weaponry against a new enemy was surely exciting for many young men. Nor were their options entirely restricted to the Carrier Corps: Those who fought bravely could receive transfers from the Corps to the KAR.[21]

Martial service provided a long-established way to gain honor in many communities of the region, and officials noted that while young men were unwilling to serve as laborers, they quickly came forward to serve in the military.[22] As noted in Chapter 2, chiefs had tried to minimize the importance of this service: They had argued that wealth *was* virtue – irrespective of how it was procured – and justified their positions based in large part on the ownership of cattle. But now, young men stood on a more equal footing with their chiefs: Wages from service in the war allowed them, too, to purchase cattle. Moreover, they had gained their rewards from brave service far away. They had become worldly men. And when they returned to their homes, the young men emphatically rejected their government-appointed leaders, who had not earned honor in the way they had. One district official worried that "returned carriers and KAR have lost a great deal of any respect which they had for the chiefs."[23]

[18] KNA, DC/KTI/1/1.1, Kitui District Annual Reports, 1916–1918.
[19] KNA, DC/KTI/1/1.1, Kitui District Annual Report, 1910–1911.
[20] Joseph Munyao, Interview with Munro. Hodges, *Carrier Corps*, 99.
[21] Moyse-Bartlett, *King's African Rifles*, 301.
[22] KNA, DC/MKS.4/6, Machakos District Political Record Book, Vol. IV (1914–1920), "Economic – Native Labour – Carrier Corps," n.d.
[23] KNA, DC/MKS.1/1/1, Machakos District Annual Report, 1918–1919.

Chiefs' constituents blamed them for the deaths of young men during the war. When recruitment had taken place, chiefs and headmen were responsible for bringing forward youths who were not essential to the working of their village or location. This standard was often broken: Some who did not want to fight were able to bribe figures in positions of authority, while some older men – perhaps out of favor with a certain chief – were forced to go to war. Officials noted that chiefs rarely sent their own sons away. One man interviewed by Newman in 1974 worked as a "conscriptor" during the First World War. He remembered it well: "Not all people went off to fight freely, and I know because I was one of those going round forcing people to go ... I was paid ten rupees a month in this job which I could use for cattle and goats." By the end of the war, the man owned approximately 300 cattle.[24]

Chiefly corruption – which extended to some proportion of elders – was rife. Chiefs and elders sat together on nzama that regulated matters of dispute or conflict. District officials described that the institution of this system "was the signal for the commencement of robbery and extortion," and that "many thousand head of cattle changed hands."[25] The system not only enriched these men, but gave them a level of social control: If cattle were essential for bridewealth payments – and they controlled cattle – they also therefore controlled marriage. British officials constantly pressed for bridewealth to be paid in rupees and later shillings instead of cattle, but – the district commissioner of Kitui noted – the idea "met with a flat and determined refusal." Elders and chiefs played on "tradition" to reject the suggestions, explaining that it was "not the custom of *zamani* [long ago]."[26]

Efforts to use "custom" in this fashion became more and more common. Reading the accounts and testimonies of district officials from the first quarter of the twentieth century, one is struck by the almost constant lamentations recorded by chiefs about the state of society. They railed, in particular, against young men drinking and women traveling outside the reserves. For while colonialism had brought chiefs power, it also provided more secure conditions in the colony: Women could travel more easily outside their home areas to trade and sell goods, due to improved security. Officials noted that more and more women were applying for divorces under the colonial system, and other cases of litigation increased annually.

[24] JNP, Interview with Mukonzo, Kee, January 4, 1974.
[25] KNA, DC/MKS.4/2, Machakos District Political Record Book, Vol. I (Part I) (–1910), 11.
[26] KNA, DC/KTI/1/1/.2, Kitui District Annual Report, 1925.

Circumstances after the end of the war seemed to show that the world was in disorder. The Spanish Flu struck Ukambani at the end of 1918. Ironically, the disease was transferred to the reserves by soldiers returning from an awards ceremony in Nairobi. Over the following year, 7,591 died in Machakos, a number mostly comprised of young men. In some districts, as many as 15 percent of people died.[27] In Kitui, the district commissioner described that the flu and war losses caused "havoc."[28] And on the tail of the flu came famine. In Machakos – where agriculture was more common than in Kitui, and the land more crowded – the rains were sub-standard for at least six years in the 1920s. And to compound matters, the whole region was beset by the economic depression that followed the war.

The role of community leaders in the years before the institution of colonial rule was to maintain security and prosperity in their communities. Male leaders sustained their communities with wealth they won from hunting, war, or trade. But chiefs had emphatically failed in this responsibility: They had never earned respect in war or by hunting, and moreover typically put their personal agendas before those of their charges. They had accumulated vast wealth while the majority of villagers fell on hard times. Proverbs described that this type of behavior was unacceptable. One read: "The people ... [who] cooked porcupine quill ... [said] it tasted like cattle."[29] It criticized the behavior of those who refused to share their wealth with others. Beliefs appeared that supported such notions: People in some areas stated that if you drank tea while others watched you – and therefore you did not share your tea with them – then you would get ringworm.[30] Athiani had been dependent on their communities to achieve respect and honor; now, chiefs' constituents rejected them.

Two outbreaks of what officials termed "anti-government hysteria" provide a fascinating window into considering how women and older men without political or judicial authority challenged the rule of their government-appointed leaders during the early twentieth century. They had their own visions of what virtues were worthy of honor in their communities, and rejected the assertions of chiefs – and indeed young men – that status was based on wealth and martial service, respectively.

[27] KNA, DC/MKS.1/1/1, Machakos District Annual Report, 1918–1919.
[28] KNA, DC/KTI/1/1.2, Kitui District Annual Report, 1919–1920.
[29] Lindblom, "Kamba Folklore III," 29.   [30] Interview 55, Miu, October 19, 2006.

Scholars have viewed the episodes of 1911 and 1922 as directed against the colonial administration, though in actuality, they more reflected social tensions in certain communities in Machakos.[31] In 1911, the district commissioner described that "an epidemic of hysterical mania" had broken out.[32] It centered on a woman named Siotune wa Kathuke and a man, Kiamba wa Mutuaovio. Both lived in close proximity to Machakos Town, and the movement was geographically restricted to that area. It was focused around an evil spirit who appeared in the form of an "unmarried girl," and was led by witchdoctors.[33] Certain aspects seemed directed against the government: Men and women drove cattle into the Mua Hills, which the government had recently removed from the Kamba land unit and earmarked for European settlement. Troops were sent to resolve the problem. One of the most interesting facts about the movement was that Kiamba commanded an army, said to resemble the police, but with one important difference: It was comprised entirely of women.[34]

The painstaking care with which officials investigated the second outbreak enables some connections to be drawn between the two. In 1922, Ndonye wa Kauti led a movement that the government again labeled "anti-colonial" in aim.[35] Ndonye lived on the side of a hill near Kilungu, and began preaching to those in the immediate vicinity. He claimed he could drive the Europeans out of the colony, and therefore end the requirement to pay tax. Within weeks, people had gathered at his home from towns throughout the region, and between April and September, more and more arrived every day. It was particularly notable that large numbers of women followed both Ndonye and Kiamba. In the case of Ndonye, women from Kilungu bucked the supposed control of their husbands and chiefs, and flocked to Ndonye's home month after month. There they danced, and worked in his gardens. Chiefs complained that they were powerless to do anything: "[A]ll our womenfolk [had] gone," one worried.

These facts, combined with the existence of Kiamba's "army" of women, were significant contraventions of apparent customs.[36] By forming an

---

[31] Mwanzi, "African Initiatives," 80; Tignor, *Colonial Transformation*, 333–336.
[32] Mahone, "Psychology of Rebellion."
[33] KNA, DC/MKS.1/1/2, Machakos District Annual Report, 1911–1912; KNA, DC/MKS.4/2, Machakos District Political Record Book, Vol. I (Part I) (-1910), 25.
[34] Tignor, *Colonial Transformation*, 333.
[35] Information on Ndonye presented here is from KNA, PC/CP.8/2/4, Administration – Native Deportees, 1922–1928.
[36] Luongo demonstrates how these moments were also important sites for contesting the nature of power through possession and prophecy. Luongo, "Prophecy."

army, women were copying a typically male occupation: Though women sometimes fought in raids during the nineteenth century, there is no evidence whatsoever of all-female raiding parties. Women took men in their communities to task for failing to provide adequately as was expected of them, by playing on these older forms of masculine honor. A song they sang in 1911 reflected this theme. By chance, Lindblom was on hand to record it: "I am seeing the things of God," they sang, "who is coming to the earth to purify men. Listen to the drum of God!"[37]

Though difficult to prove comprehensively from the archival record, women's displeasure was surely tied to their own ever-increasing burdens. By the early 1920s, some villages were practically devoid of men, as a result of war, disease, and famine. Women were saddled with a huge variety of tasks: They bore responsibility for physical and social reproduction, as well as care of the household, and agricultural work; even the care of cattle was sometimes added to their lists, something they raised in songs.[38] As they struggled, chiefs and other men in their communities became wealthy, while they remained poor despite working harder and harder. They drew themselves in contrast to these rich, prosperous men:

At Kitilli's there are many servants, male as well as female, herdmen for goats and herdmen for sheep, and also herdmen for the cattle ... I, [am] a poor person, who has neither a family of my own nor a mother, indeed, nor even any other relatives to speak to. Death – I will give him neither food nor water – death has not let me retain my father and others that were near to me. Now there is nothing else for me to do than lying here (on my knees) grinding flour ... How forlorn I am! ... I do not possess even the most trifling thing I can call my own.[39]

Documents also reveal that a large number of male elders arrived at Ndonye's home. Like women, many elders formerly in positions of authority had been ignored for roles in the new colonial administrative system. At Ndonye's home, the elders undertook an extraordinary job: They built Ndonye a new home within a matter of weeks. Building the home was considered women's work, and *absolutely not* the work of older men. As these elders demonstrated their displeasure, they were dramatically breaking supposedly established customs.

The actions of these men and women seem to represent visions of community virtues that were tied neither to martial service nor the possession of cattle, as young men and chiefs had argued. By tending gardens,

[37] Lindblom, "Kamba Folklore III," 57–58.
[38] Lindblom, "Kamba Folklore III," 48–49.
[39] Lindblom, "Kamba Folklore III," 50–51.

building homes, and complaining about the standards of leadership in their communities, these men and women argued that the sustenance of the community was paramount, and wealth or martial service irrelevant if this was not achieved. Ndonye's community presented an opportunity for social reordering, and women there worked hard to earn honor: They tended gardens, produced food, and danced. In the case of older men, it is possible that Ndonye won their admiration in another way: There is some suggestion that he possessed the authority of athani from years past whose influence had been subsumed to those of traders, hunters, and warriors during the later nineteenth century.

British officials were oblivious to the significance of many of the events that took place during 1922: Their major concern was whether Ndonye was insane enough to be committed to a lunatic asylum, or simply deported as a normal prisoner. They therefore missed a rather fascinating aspect of the episode: Ndonye's actions seemed to demonstrate a calculated effort to mobilize *Kamba* – as opposed to villages, clans, or anything else – and in fact spread his ideas far beyond Kilungu and its surrounding areas. In this, he was evoking a similar breadth of protest as had chiefs in their own discussions of custom. Ndonye ordered people to construct a road from his home to the top of the hill on which he lived, and they had begun building the road when the district commissioner came to visit. Ndonye explained to the district commissioner that the road would go first to Heaven, and then the remaining parts of Ukambani. "All ... will come [here]," he claimed. Ndonye received emissaries from Kisau, eager to hear his message, and traveled to Nzaui and Nziu to preach. Interestingly, he preached only in Swahili – a rather unusual practice, considering that the majority of people around him would have spoken only Kikamba – which presumably reflected his desire to spread his message widely and probably added to his mystique.

The episode of 1922 was a microcosm of the crisis facing a variety of communities in Ukambani. There was no proper leadership: Chiefs and headmen had failed to earn honor, and had sacrificed the interests of their communities, all the time taking liberties to enrich themselves. Colonial officials had erred drastically in the way they had implemented control: Dundas described how the nzama had accidentally excluded senior elders, who were "indignant" at the offense.[40] There was no option but for transformative action: In 1925, all judicial powers were removed from

---

[40] Dundas, "Organisation and Laws," 242, 248–250.

the chiefs. Only newly appointed, senior elders were allowed to adjudicate significant disputes. Each location in Machakos had twenty "special constables" appointed, called athiani. They served below headmen; in this, officials were playing on the respect conveyed by the office of the athiani.[41] The situation in Kitui was less severe: The appointment of elders to positions of power had been carried out with a greater degree of success, though officials noted that chiefs constantly tried to usurp them. But the chiefs here had far less power: In 1916, the district commissioner had noted that when headmen gave orders, they were ignored unless they transmitted them to elders, who then passed them on to the people.[42]

"REJECTS" AND "MAN-EATERS"

Today, any visitor who arrives in a town in Ukambani on a Sunday morning is greeted by the sound of hymns. They emanate from a variety of churches of many different denominations. Some are well funded, and have high brick walls topped with peaked rafters, under which 1,000 people can congregate. Others are small concrete boxes – that serve as shops during the week – into which a seemingly impossible number of plastic chairs or improvised seats are forced. Perhaps 90 percent of Kamba – or more – are Christian today, but during the 1910s and 1920s they were a distinct, tiny minority.

The arrival of Christianity in Ukambani further rearranged an already unstable social order. Missionaries – and the small communities of Christian converts who gathered around them – espoused vastly different visions of daily life. In Christian communities, virtuous behavior had nothing to do with war or the possession of cattle. The former was deemed entirely un-Christian, and the latter usually a remote possibility for those who came to the mission stations, as they were usually close to destitute.

The Church of Scotland established the first mission station at Kibwezi, but the prevalence of malaria and drought meant that it was short-lived.[43] The independent missionary Stuart Watt – who came to East Africa with his wife and four children – followed the Scottish mission, building in Ngelani – near Machakos Town – in 1893.[44] That year, the German

---

[41] KNA, DC/MKS.4/8, Machakos District Political Record Book, Vol. VI (1925–1930), Note by Silvester, "Division of Functions of Government," October 29, 1927.
[42] KNA, DC/KTI/1/1.1, Kitui District Annual Reports, 1913, 1915.
[43] On the Church of Scotland Mission, see Macpherson, *Presbyterian Church.*
[44] See also RHL, Mss. Afr. s. 391, Papers of J. A. Stuart Watt.

Lutheran Leipzig mission opened a station in Ikutha, in southern Kitui. They opened four more stations in the district during the next decade, largely sticking to areas visited by Krapf. But despite these early incursions, Ukambani soon came to be dominated by the Africa Inland Mission (AIM). Staffed largely by American missionaries, the AIM had four stations by the time of the First World War: at Kangundo, Machakos, Mbooni, and Mukaa. The AIM's presence in Ukambani was further solidified when the Leipzig missions closed due to the deportation of Germans from the colony in 1914. This transferred their three remaining missions (at Ikutha, Mulango, and Miambani) into AIM hands. The Holy Ghost Fathers, a Roman Catholic denomination, also had a station in Kabaa.[45]

The AIM missionaries – who frequently numbered fewer than ten in total in Ukambani before the 1920s – faced enormous challenges in these early years. Famine and disease were common, and the deaths of missionaries not rare. Their faith was sorely tested, and success hard-won: Bernice Davis, stationed in Mukaa in 1911 with her husband Elwood, described in her letters how she was "becoming discouraged."[46] Efforts to spread the Gospel to several small outstations in the surrounding countryside had met with little success: "It makes me sad to see and hear it all," she lamented.[47] And the work was hard: A typical day in the life of Elwood Davis began at 5.30 a.m. with "private devotions," and consisted of a variety of tasks ranging from language study to organizing African workers before bed at 9 p.m.[48]

At Mukaa, the number of boys and girls attending school was abysmally low. Missionaries struggled to convince the children's parents of the merits of education, and few permitted them to attend lessons. In 1906, Mr. and Mrs. Burness had approximately eighteen boys each day in the school, but no girls. They reported that duties "in connexion with the charge of the cattle" – herding – kept children away.[49] Only after the mission opened a separate school for girls were some allowed to

---

[45] Onneweer, "Redeeming Ukamba Word." For more on the AIM, see Anderson, *Grasshoppers*. Information on the locations and histories of mission stations in Ukambani is largely drawn from district reports between 1908 and 1916. A more general introduction is found in Oliver, *Missionary Factor*.

[46] Archives of the Africa Inland Mission, Nairobi [hereafter AIM], Box 2, File 22, Bernice Davis to Downing, December 30, 1911.

[47] AIM, Box 2, File 22, Elwood Davis to Downing, January 11, 1912.

[48] AIM, Box 2, File 22, Elwood Davis, "Schedule of Day's Work," 1911.

[49] Church Missionary Society, *Proceedings*, 62.

FIGURE 5: The original Africa Inland Mission building at Mukaa. Its date of construction – 1903 – is just visible below the peak of the roof. It is no longer in use. (Photo: Author.)

attend: fifteen did so in 1911.[50] In 1908, only one man at the mission requested baptism, then withdrew his request.[51]

Mission education seemed to offer little to wealthy families. Chiefs and headmen, therefore, largely refused to send their children to school, preferring that they remain at home to help there or in the fields. One woman interviewed in 1974 remembered, "[O]nly the children of the poor went to school"; because her father was fairly well off – with thirty-five cattle and forty goats – there was no reason for her to go.[52] Those who attended school were usually the children of poor families. Several missionaries took advantage of this by giving sugar or salt to children who attended, items that certainly must have been attractive. Other children who arrived at the mission stations were orphans: The missions took many in after the famine of Mũvunga because their families were unable to care for them.

[50] AIM, Box 10, File 5, Report for Mukaa Station: January–May 1911.
[51] Church Missionary Society, *Proceedings*, 52.
[52] JNP, Interview with Mary Muendi, Okia, March 5, 1974.

Men and women today recall a series of stereotypes and fears that accompanied education, particularly that of girls. One man I interviewed in 2004 was at least 100 years old when we spoke. He summed up the assertions of many: "It was said when we were young, if a girl went to school, she would become a prostitute." He himself had received no education, and lived in a poor household. His small garden was empty of animals, and he was dressed in rags. He was very sick at the time, though he insisted on being interviewed; indeed, he died soon after we met. Though they had believed these rumors in the old days, he explained, he had realized his error: Time had shown that the educated were "leaders and guides of the rest."[53]

Boys and girls who attended mission schools often faced ridicule from their age-mates. One lady called Tabitha Kyai remembered, "We were laughed at." This was due, in large part, to certain distinct practices Christian missions demanded of their adherents. Missions banned young women from attending dances, where many spent a large part of their time. I asked Tabitha whether she was disappointed to miss all the dances, the source of such excitement for young people. "Did you sneak in sometimes?" I said. She laughed. "I didn't sneak in, but I might come close and watch a bit!" At the dances, women met young men and socialized with them, which was a way for women to earn respect; those who danced well were celebrated by their age-mates. But missionaries considered this inappropriate. Tabitha remembered that older women told them, "You will not give birth because you don't attend dances." In this statement, older women linked dancing and the female ability to bear children, two central ways to earn respect for women.[54]

Physical attributes often made it clear who was a Christian and who not. Missionaries banned several typical bodily modifications that usually accompanied the passage into adulthood. The two most common were teeth-chipping and removal, and puncturing of the earlobe. These dental practices involved the removal of the two central incisors in the lower jaw and the sharpening of the central and lateral incisors – and sometimes two cuspids – in the upper. In the upper jaw, these modifications were made for aesthetic benefits, but the removal of the lower teeth was more practical: Medicine and food could be passed through the hole formed

---

[53] Interview 4, Ngelani, September 9, 2004.   [54] Interview 146, Mukaa, May 14, 2012.

by the removal of the lower teeth (thus tetanus – which frequently includes lockjaw – might be circumvented). Along with this came the puncturing of the earlobe and the insertion of thick thorns or other objects to increase the diameter of the hole. These marks brought respect: Informants remembered that in their youth, if you did not get these treatments, when you went to perform work with other members of the community, the meal at the end of the day was humiliating. "[Y]ou could not eat from a nice gourd (*nzele*) ... you would be given food on a broken piece (*kĩseleũ*)," said one.[55]

The circumcision of girls was another practice that missionaries strongly frowned upon. The operation itself was less significant in a variety of ways in Ukambani than in Kikuyu areas. But it brought Christian youths and the missionaries who supported them into direct conflict with their families. One man described the conflict as *ngusanĩso* – a "tug of war."[56] Another lady – the daughter of one of Mbooni's first Christian converts – recalled that her father expressly forbade that she be circumcised. And it caused tremendous problems in the family:

My grandfather and grandmother brought troubles to try to make us refuse the Gospel. For example, circumcision. My grandfather was very tough on this issue. But my father said his children were his own and they would not be circumcised. He refused. My grandfather used to say that if his granddaughters were not circumcised, their children would die at birth.[57]

The issue concerned not just the family, but the clan as well. Another man remembered an incident from his youth:

One lady was beaten by her husband to the extent of him gouging out her eye and knocking her teeth out of her jaw. The wife was born-again [Christian] and she was refusing to allow her daughters to be circumcised. The clan was called up and came and beat her up.[58]

Another action by two boys concerned the district commissioner of Kitui so greatly that he included it in his annual report. The boys removed an offering made by their stepmother at a sacred grove where she believed important spirits lived. The boys threatened to cut down the grove itself, an event that had precipitated full-on war in 1891.[59]

---

[55] Interviews 55, 56, and 57, Miu, October 19–20, 2006.
[56] Interview 145, Mukaa, May 14, 2012.   [57] Interview 148, Mbooni, May 16, 2012.
[58] Interview 149, Mbooni, May 16, 2012.
[59] KNA, DC/KTI/1/1.2, Kitui District Annual Report, 1924.

These issues reflected a wider problem from the perspective of elders, chiefs, senior clan members, and family patriarchs: They were losing control over women in their communities. Like many women across sub-Saharan Africa, women in Machakos and Kitui seized upon Christianity in large numbers because it permitted them to resist subjugation to men.[60] Male control was also threatened by European missionaries, who had no fear of taking on chiefs and elders to prevent their flocks from being forced into "dark" ways.

No missionary in perhaps the entirety of the protectorate had as much personality, power, and drive as George Rhoad. Rhoad was a stocky, strong man of medium height, who sported a gold tooth in the center of his mouth. He drove a Harley-Davidson motorcycle with a sidecar. "Bwana Loosi" is remembered with a mixture of awe and respect; in the pulpit, one man remembered, "He was shouting while he was preaching." Everyone knew that under Rhoad's protection, chiefs could do nothing about "troublesome" Christian girls. "Chiefs feared him," said one man, "he might also fight them [physically]." People remember that chiefs had no option of circumventing Rhoad: He was not afraid to use the law courts or his association with the district commissioner to achieve his goals.[61] Rhoad was close with the district commissioner, Campbell: In 1924, Rhoad's son Gordon noted in his diary that his father often traveled with the district commissioner, and the two men regularly played tennis together. Rhoad senior struggled to cope with Campbell's powerful serve and groundstrokes.[62]

Rhoad's station was Mbooni, where he achieved more success than almost any other missionary, turning the station (which still stands) into his own mini-kingdom. Harmon Nixon, who later became the AIM's field director for East Africa, remembered that, "Mr. Rhoad had practically his own government. He had his own tribal retainers who went on his errands ... [He] built many miles of good roads."[63] It seems that Rhoad worried little about how precisely he procured labor for these sorts of projects, and some remember forcible "persuasion." But there was little doubt that Rhoad was driven to spread Christianity by almost any means necessary.

[60] See, for instance, Paul Landau's work on the Tswana. Landau, *Realm of the Word*.
[61] Interview 151, Mbooni, May 16, 2012.
[62] Wheaton College Archives and Special Collections, SC/165, Diary of Gordon Rhoad, February 7, 1924.
[63] Billy Graham Center Archives [hereafter BGC], Collection 81, Box 12, Folder 45, Interview with Harmon Nixon, April 26, 1971.

Perhaps Rhoad's greatest obsession was promoting the education of girls. In this, he was somewhat exceptional: The AIM subscribed to the mantra "preach not teach" and saw education as a somewhat secondary consideration in their mission (Rhoad, indeed, left the AIM during the 1920s in part as a result of a disagreement over this issue). Rhoad gave sugar and salt to children who were willing to come to school, and pressed hard to attract more girls, building a separate boarding house for them. In 1912, resistance to his agenda appeared. Male elders, in consultation with Rhoad, had allowed him to begin a class for girls. But the community's women refused to accept it. One medicine woman called Syoivuku gathered 300 women to protest Rhoad's actions. They surrounded his house, chanting, "We are not willing to give up our children." The standoff lasted for four days. Rhoad finally threatened to bring the district commissioner, and then they dispersed.[64]

Over the hills of central Machakos, in Mukaa, was another long-serving missionary, who would remain in Ukambani for twenty-five years before his death in 1944. LeRoy Farnsworth was of similar build to Rhoad, though he perhaps did not possess quite the same fire. He served with his wife Emma, a talented linguist and capable pianist. Farnsworth shared Rhoad's desire to educate girls and protect them from marriage to non-Christians. Elderly men and women remember Farnsworth and Rhoad acting in concert if they believed girls were threatened by the forces of "darkness": Farnsworth commonly sent girls to Rhoad if they came under threat in their communities, knowing that chiefs or elders could not reach the girls there. Today, men and women from Mukaa deny the suggestion that chiefs had any authority in such situations when missionaries challenged them: "Chiefs were not powerful," laughed one man when I asked him about the situation, shaking his head in amusement. "Missionaries were very powerful," he said, "A chief could be jailed."[65]

The most prominent case involving Farnsworth came in 1938, and extensive reports on the matter enable a close look into a common issue facing communities of Christians. A girl was betrothed to an "old heathen," but because of her Christian convictions did not want to marry him. Her father, however – a non-Christian – did not want to relinquish the brideprice he had gained for his daughter, and thus refused to intervene to stop the wedding. The girl fled with her brother, who was also

[64] AIM, Box 3, File 46, Downing to Hurlburt, August 15, 1912.
[65] Interview 144, Mukaa, May 14, 2012.

a Christian, to the district commissioner's office in Machakos, where a district officer heard her case. He sent the girl back to her father, but she soon fled again, this time without her brother. Elders – some from the same clan – tied up the brother for two days in an effort to discover the girl's whereabouts, but without success. She had fled to another village to a Christian family, where a different district officer heard her case again. Ultimately, she was allowed to remain in that village, where she married a man of her choice.[66]

The case of Ndonye wa Kauti – described above – similarly threatened the authority of chiefs and elders. Ndonye used Christianity – and certain trappings of European society – as a way to bring adherents to his side. As he described, "I am to build a school in which to teach all people ... I shall bring trousers, and I shall teach you." He told his followers how God would help them build a cart road from Heaven to his house, along which a telegraph line would run. At his home, God would provide "pencils, books and other European articles." He took aspects of Christian teaching, and altered them: Ndonye told how God had made the world in four days, rather than seven. He used imagery from the Trinity, but the third manifestation of God – rather than the Holy Ghost – was a spirit called "Simiti," possibly taken from the English word "cement" (from which his house was built). And like Jesus at the Last Supper, Ndonye told his followers that he would be arrested, but then returned to them. Perhaps threatened by the influence Ndonye held, chiefs and headmen kept the movement quiet from administrators until it had progressed significantly.[67]

Episodes like these threatened not just chiefly control, but were cause for concern amongst administrative officers: for missionaries were unafraid to direct their attacks against the government if it failed to treat Christian converts fairly. In 1909, government soldiers used excessive force in collecting tax from some Christians near a mission station. Rhoad complained on their behalf, and publicized the matter in the AIM's magazine, *Hearing and Doing*. His advocacy was so successful that several headmen in the region started building roads toward Rhoad's station in order to benefit from his aura and influence.[68] In 1924, Rhoad went one step further, writing a petition to the Colonial Office on behalf of a group of elders who were concerned by the upcoming East African Commission.

[66] KNA, DC/MKS/15/2, Farnsworth to DC Machakos, February 21, 1938.
[67] KNA, PC/CP.8/2/4, Administration – Native Deportees, 1922–1928.
[68] Rhoad to the Editor, *Hearing and Doing* 15, 1 (1909), 12–13.

Though he noted that he was only serving as their amanuensis, Rhoad explained that he "largely shar[ed] their apprehensions."[69] Administrators looked on with disapproval. Different district commissioners in Machakos considered Rhoad and his compatriots' efforts in female education "foolish," which could bring nothing but trouble.[70] "A missionary who does not come up to a very high standard ... [is] a positive menace to the peace and good order of the whole district," noted one.[71]

Early Christians came to form separate communities in Ukambani, with interests and practices that drew a line between them and the remainder of people in their villages. Because they were usually poor and possessed little authority, they were called *milisũ* – "rejects" – signifying their separateness from the mainstream of village life. Near the Catholic Holy Ghost Mission at Kabaa, Christians were *malyandũ* – "man-eaters" – a reference to the Catholic sacrament of taking the body of Christ at communion.[72] And Christians had their own words for non-believers: They called them *alei* (literally, "refusers" [of the Gospel]) or *asenzi* ("idiots"). Missionaries encouraged their charges to have nothing to do with non-Christians. One man who first attended school in 1922 remembered that he was "told to break off relations" with alei: They were supposed to live separate lives.[73]

Avoidance of teeth-chipping, ear-piercing, or circumcision further marked off believers from non-believers. Young Christian men and women married amongst themselves; as late as 1939, administrators noted that an uncircumcised woman could not find a husband outside the missions.[74] Non-Christians thought such women might even "move [have sexual intercourse] with dogs."[75] The strict stipulation that Christians take one wife – and avoid alcohol and tobacco – further distinguished them. Even

---

[69] The National Archives of the United Kingdom [hereafter TNA], CO 533/329, George Rhoad, "Memorandum Presented to the East African Commission on Behalf of the Kamba People," November 5, 1924.

[70] KNA, DC/MKS.1/1/2, Machakos District Annual Report, 1912–1913.

[71] KNA, DC/MKS.4/2, Machakos District Political Record Book, Vol. I (Part I) (-1910), 162.

[72] At the Roman Catholic Mission near Kabaa, one man recalled the following: "Some people said these Catholics are man-eaters. They eat the body. One [Catholic] father went to Kombe, having baptized his child. The child later died [while he was absent]. The child was buried by the locals [in a non-Christian ceremony]. When the father returned, he said the child must be exhumed and buried in the Christian way ... They thought he was going to eat the child." Interview 147, Kabaa, May 15, 2012.

[73] JNP, Interview with John Muiya Kivati, Tala, December 10, 1973.

[74] KNA, DC/MKS/7/2, "Convictions of Adultery with a Married Woman," *c.* January 1939.

[75] Interview 39, Mulala, July 26, 2005.

on a day-to-day basis, Christians greeted one another differently: Instead of the usual "*Wakya?*" or "*Avai!*,"[76] they asked "*N'uvoo?*" meaning, "Is it peace [with you]?"[77]

Christians had their own competing versions of what they considered virtuous behavior. These ran in contrast to ideals related to war or the ownership of cattle: for neither were attributes possessed by the majority of early Christians. Martial notions of honor, indeed, were anathema to many of them. One convert directly contrasted these occupations with his newfound religion: "Before I heard the Words of God I was very bad and used to raid the Masai[78] and steal their cattle and kill their men," he explained.[79] Among Christian women, chastity was greatly valued: This, of course, was in striking contrast to most communities where the production of many children at a young age was encouraged, and few taboos existed against premarital sexual intercourse.[80] And moreover, Christian women did not attend dances, those central locations for the procurement of female honor, and venues for social interaction.

One of the most important sources in trying to learn how early Christians understood the world around them is through studying biblical translations in the vernacular. In his landmark *Creative Writing*, Derek Peterson demonstrates how these translations can provide an important window into African societies.[81] Focusing his work on Kikuyu in Nyeri, Peterson shows how early biblical translations were far from being the work of missionaries alone: African catechumens who assisted them worded translations to reflect values *they* considered significant.

Missionaries stationed in Ukambani had moved on in leaps and bounds since Elmer Bartolomew's anguished letter written from Kangundo in 1900. When forty-three women and eighteen men arrived at his station

[76] "Wakya" is a greeting often used by older people addressing those younger than them, and "avai" by younger people addressing their elders. However, this accounting is somewhat inadequate: In practice, the gender and clan of the person speaking and the person being addressed must be taken into account in determining the propriety of the greeting. Women, for instance, would never address one another with "avai" irrespective of age. I am again grateful to Jeremiah Kitunda for his assistance here.
[77] Farnsworth, *Kamba Grammar*, 126.
[78] Today the spelling "Maasai" is commonly used, but during the colonial era the word was typically rendered "Masai."
[79] BGC, Collection 81, Box 1, Folder 41, J. W. Stauffacher, *History of the Africa Inland Mission* (unpublished typescript, c. 1915), 18.
[80] Interview 68, Yathui, November 15, 2006.   [81] Peterson, *Creative Writing*.

to look for work following famine, he enthused that it was, "A most blessed opportunity to preach the gospel." But, he continued, "neither of us [he nor his wife] were able to do so. Oh, for a tongue to make known unto them the way of life!"[82] During the first decade of the 1900s, it was common for AIM missionaries to study Kikamba for two to three hours per day. Indeed, they firmly believed that they should not teach English to their charges. And the Leipzig missionaries Brutzer, Hofmann, and Pfitzinger were similarly active: They published a translation of St. Luke's Gospel and a collection of biblical histories in 1898, as well as Acts of the Apostles (*Meka ma Atume*) in 1904.[83] Nor were the AIM missionaries resting on their laurels in translation work: Rhoad was active, as was Emma Farnsworth later. Rhoad rendered the Gospels of St. Mark and St. John in Kikamba in 1915 and 1916, respectively, and then the entire New Testament by 1920.[84] This was the first AIM version of this part of the bible in any African language in Kenya.[85]

In *Creative Writing*, Peterson reveals much about Kikuyu society by comparing biblical translations in Kikuyu with extensive dictionaries written in the language and published in Kenya and Britain. Thus he could translate the Kikuyu word *irĩ* as "livestock" as well as "gardens," but also uncover more complex and revealing meanings including "sustenance," "substance," and "prosperity" from using T. G. Benson's monstrous Kikuyu–English dictionary. Benson's 1964 offering ran to 562 pages of dense print, with each page containing two columns of words; his entry on irĩ alone was 126 words.[86] Nor was Benson's dictionary unique; he was following in the footsteps of Archbishop Beecher and his wife, and Arthur Barlow.[87]

The AIM missionaries published a Kikamba–English dictionary in 1939, the only such work in existence before John Harun Mwau's 2006 offering.[88] The AIM dictionary was a hugely important publication, rendering approximately 6,000 Kikamba words into English.[89] It is exceptional: beyond it, only simple vocabularies exist. These other works

---

[82] *Hearing and Doing* 4, 6 (1900), 5.   [83] Struck, "Collections," 398–399.

[84] Rhoad (trans.), *Maliko* (St. Mark's Gospel); Rhoad (trans.), *Yoana* (St. John's Gospel).

[85] Rhoad and AIM (trans.), *Ũtianĩo Mweũ wa Mwĩaĩi* (New Testament).

[86] Benson, *Kikuyu–English Dictionary*, 189–190; Peterson, *Creative Writing*, 11.

[87] Barlow, *Tentative Studies*; Beecher and Beecher, *Kikuyu–English Dictionary*.

[88] Mwau, *Kikamba Dictionary*.

[89] Africa Inland Mission Language Committee in Ukamba [hereafter AIMLCU], *Kikamba–English Dictionary*. It is important to note that neither the second edition (1949) nor third (1970) were revised in any way from the initial 1939 production.

typically include only several hundred words in translation, since Krapf first published his own in 1850. All translate a small number of English words into Kikamba, and none attempt the reverse translation. Bleek included approximately 50 Kamba nouns in his *Comparative Grammar* published during the 1860s, and Last included 250 in his *Polyglotta* of 1885.[90] Archibald Shaw provided translations for approximately 2,000 English words into 5 different African languages in 1885, but had little expertise in Kikamba, providing plain, one-word translations.[91] A similar criticism may be lodged against Hildegarde Hinde's 1904 publication, and even John Mbiti's short English–Kikamba dictionary of 1959, which itself ran to little over 2,000 words.[92]

The dictionaries of Krapf and the AIM provide a window into how Christians in Ukambani conceived of the concept of honor (*ndaĩa*) in their communities. When Krapf produced vocabularies of a variety of East African languages in 1850 – including Kikamba, Kikuyu, and Swahili – he rendered the verb "to honor" as *zonokea*.[93] Thus in his published translation of St. Mark's Gospel of that year (though it was actually written at least several years earlier), he rendered "honor thy father and mother" as *uzonoke au na inia wagu*.[94] No other source translates "honor" as anything close to *zonokea*, even accounting for changes in Kikamba orthography. Rhoad used *taya* in his own 1915 translation,[95] and the word is still in use today (*taĩa/ndaĩa*).

Yet there is tantalizing evidence of something more: Today, *nzonoko* means "shame," perhaps the closest *opposite* of "honor." In another part of St. Mark's Gospel, Krapf used *makkia* to translate "honor," which he later realized actually meant "pity" or "commiserate" in Kikamba (today: *makkĩa*).[96] This is surely too much of a coincidence: It seems clear that the idea of honor was a target for mischief in the translation, but unfortunately there is insufficient information to reveal more.

The AIM dictionary is more revealing, however, and demonstrates how early Christians disagreed with "standard" conceptions of honor in their communities. Missionaries rendered "(to) honor" as (*ku*) *taia*, its plain translation. But the adjectival form was not "honorable," as one would

[90] Bleek, *Comparative Grammar*, 184–186; Last, *Polyglotta*. See also Wakefield and Johnson, "Routes of Native Caravans," 311.
[91] Shaw, *Pocket Vocabulary*.
[92] Hinde, *Vocabularies*; Mbiti, *English–Kamba Vocabulary*.   [93] Krapf, *Vocabulary*, 20.
[94] Krapf (trans.), *Evangelio*, 40 (Mark 10:19).
[95] Rhoad (trans.), *Maliko*, 33 (Mark 10:19).
[96] Krapf (trans.), *Evangelio*, 27 (Mark 7:10); Krapf, *Vocabulary*, 7, 34.

expect; instead, it was "proud." Nor was the sample reflexive verb "honor oneself." Missionaries believed that *itaia kw-* was better rendered as "praise" or "exalt" oneself – hardly the same thing, and implying negative attributes.[97]

For these Christian communities, education was a central part of their value system. Thus the translation of a section of St. Matthew's Gospel that referred to "the poor" was rendered as *andū-ndja (ndia)* – "foolish men."[98] Christians viewed the poorest people as those who lacked knowledge, not goods: They, after all, had the former, but rarely the latter. The word *wui*, meaning "wisdom" or "wise" (as in the case of King Solomon, *wui wa Tsolomo*, and today rendered *w'ūĩ*) also meant "clever" or "sharp."[99] In these ways, Christians demonstrated their disapproval with "standard" conceptions of what constituted important virtues, and highlighted those that resonated for them.

AN ETHNIC BOND?

In 1922, political unrest and protest swept through parts of central Kenya. It was focused on a Kikuyu named Harry Thuku, a telephone operator at the Treasury, whose political platform was the East African Association (EAA). Though the membership of the EAA was predominantly Kikuyu, Thuku claimed that it represented all Africans in the colony (known officially as the "Colony and Protectorate of Kenya" – or simply "Kenya" – after 1920). During 1920 and 1921, Thuku travelled throughout central Kenya holding mass meetings in which he railed against taxation and various labor regulations, and argued that the government should grant Africans the right to own private property. His opposition to the administration led to his arrest on March 14, 1922. What followed was a scene well known to all those familiar with Kenya's history: A crowd gathered outside the police station in Nairobi where Thuku was detained. By March 16, it had grown to approximately 8,000 people. When some began to throw stones at the police lined up outside the station, they responded with gunfire: At least 21 Africans died in the shooting.[100]

---

[97] AIMLCU, *Kikamba–English Dictionary*, 179.
[98] AIMLCU, *Kikamba–English Dictionary*, 145; Pfitzinger (trans.), *Mataio*, 67 (Matt. 26:9).
[99] AIMLCU, *Kikamba–English Dictionary*, 203; Pfitzinger (trans.), *Mataio*, 30 (Matt. 12:42).
[100] Rosberg and Nottingham, *Myth*, 47–55.

Before his detention, Thuku had made an effort to spread his message in Ukambani (as well as areas inhabited by Kenya's other ethnic groups), believing the EAA would have a "great voice" if it spoke for all Kenya's peoples. He had contacts there; his sister, Mwihaki, was married to a man from Machakos, and he often visited her there. Thuku was also close friends with James Mwanthi – a powerful speaker of some influence, who later became a politician and chief – who was himself involved in the leadership of the EAA.[101]

Thuku met with Chief Mathendu and the Machakos District Council during the early months of 1922. He tried to win their support for his organization, asking them to sign membership papers for the EAA, which the leaders said they would consider. This was apparently "tantamount to a refusal," and members of the council said that they considered the Kikuyu "foolish."[102] At the end of the year, the provincial commissioner of Ukamba Province summed up the reaction to Thuku in his territory: "[I]t is gratifying to be able to record that the Thuku riots … made little impression … all attempts made by Thuku previously to enlist the support of the Akamba in his propaganda, proved quite abortive."[103] Thuku never made an effort to move to other parts of Ukambani, and Kitui district reports do not even mention him, simply noting that everything was quiet "as usual."[104]

When leaders in Machakos rejected Thuku, they suggested, rather interestingly, that he return to the Kikuyu, a people with whom "the Akamba had little in common."[105] This sort of statement provides a point of entry into considering whether "the Kamba" constituted a unified "tribe" of any description by the 1920s. Such statements imply its existence, and certainly chiefs would have wanted people to believe that they represented "the Kamba."

European-authored texts published at the time give the impression that missionaries, anthropologists, and administrators oversaw a system of neatly organized tribes. Administrative decrees built and bolstered such order: Male migrant laborers were issued with identity cards (*kipande*) after the war that identified them as "Kamba." And the provincial system

[101] Thuku, *Autobiography*, 11–34.
[102] KNA, DC/MKS.5/1/2, Minutes of a Meeting of the Machakos District Council, March 22, 1922.
[103] KNA, PC/CP.4/2/2, Ukamba Province Annual Report, 1922.
[104] KNA, DC/KTI/1/1.2, Kitui District Annual Report, 1922.
[105] KNA, DC/MKS.5/1/2, Minutes of a Meeting of the Machakos District Council, March 22, 1922.

was altered in December 1919 to produce neater ethnic lines: Kikuyu living in Kiambu were removed from Ukamba Province, which became a province inhabited by "Kamba" alone.

At face value, the Kamba example seems to provide proof for Leroy Vail's well-known assertion about the central role of missionaries and anthropologists in "creating" rigid ethnic groups in early twentieth-century Africa. Vail describes these two groups of Europeans as "culture brokers."[106] They carefully recorded and standardized tribal customs, supposedly in existence since time immemorial. In the case of missionaries, these customs and tribal histories were often taught to young people in schools. Thus, following Vail's argument, they contributed to many African peoples at the beginning of the twentieth century starting to think of themselves as members of "tribes."

Certainly, missionaries were prominent in Ukambani before much of the rest of Kenya. But Ukambani was peculiar in receiving a significant amount of study from both anthropologists and ethnologists. Its early administrators published extensively on the Kamba, and could lay claim to being semi-professional in this regard (hence the term "anthro-administrators"). Charles Hobley, for instance, who became sub-commissioner in Ukamba Province in 1906, published a significant number of books and articles on the ethnology of East Africa's peoples, including two books – *Ethnology of Akamba* and *Bantu Beliefs and Magic* – which dealt in large part with the Kamba.[107] Similarly, Charles Dundas – who began his service as a district officer in 1908, and ended up serving in both Kitui and Kiambu – wrote extensively in the *Journal of the Royal Anthropological Institute of Great Britain and Ireland.*[108] Others were pure academics: Lindblom – a gifted ethnographer and still a recognized authority on Ukambani – lived there during his doctoral dissertation research, and even participated in a hunt in 1911 and 1912.[109] Like the missionaries, these men all carefully attempted to distinguish Kamba "customs," and define what made the Kamba different from other ethnic groups.[110]

Any student of African history can access the voluminous papers left by missionaries, administrators, and anthropologists from the early twentieth century. Missionaries wrote letters, notes, magazine articles,

---

[106] Vail (ed.), *Creation of Tribalism*, 1–19.
[107] For more on the approximately 100 articles written by Hobley, see Matson and Ofcansky, "Bio-Bibliography."
[108] See, for instance, Dundas, "History of Kitui" or "Native Laws."
[109] Lindblom, *Akamba*, 469.   [110] See also Tate, "Notes."

and biblical translations; anthropologists and administrators published books, chapters, and articles, and left their own extensive and wide-ranging correspondence. But though these sources are immensely valuable, they also carry a danger: A clearly written, typed, and dated letter can provide a feeling of security in reconstructing history. It is easy to attach excessive weight and authority to the written word, simply by virtue of the medium, and therefore allow European preconceptions about African tribes to work into one's own view.

In actuality, the impact of these few Europeans was far less significant than their writings imply. First, consider the numbers: During the 1920s and even into the 1930s, the AIM was delighted if it had ten healthy European missionaries in service in Ukambani. In 1938 in Kitui, it had only three in the entirety of the district.[111] There, only Mulango station plus a few pathetic outschools functioned, and the organization even considered closing its oldest stations in Mbooni and Mukaa.[112] As late as 1935, missionary W. J. Guilding believed that he could sell only 100 copies of the New Testament to people in the environs of his station in the course of a year, which he believed was far better than he could have hoped for in the past.[113]

Similarly, administrators' influence was restricted to major centers like Kangundo, Machakos Town, Kitui Town, and Mulango. These men little touched the lives of the majority of Ukambani's residents. The government system of education was little better than the missionary: As late as 1945, only 12 percent of children attended elementary school in Machakos, and the numbers were lower in Kitui.[114] These were minor influences in a region where the population was around 250,000.

Possibly the greatest evidence that the colonial impact on ethnic identification was lightly felt came with the great famine of Nzalukanje in 1929. When I carried out interviews in Machakos and Kitui during the 2000s, a good number of the oldest generation could still recall the events of the 1920s with clarity. Nzalukanje (1928–1929) was first and foremost in their minds.[115] They recalled it in vivid detail, but perhaps the most

[111] BGC, Collection 81, Box 23, Folder 13, Report for Ukamba District, August 1938.
[112] AIM, Box 4, File 3, Guilding to Downing, July 10, 1935; Guilding to Downing, July 22, 1936.
[113] AIM, Box 4, File 3, Guilding to Downing, July 10, 1935.
[114] KNA, DC/MKS/1/1/29, Machakos District Annual Report, 1945.
[115] Nzalukanje was also known as Kīthii (ground meal) or Kakuti (a type of dance performed by women before they received food) in some areas. O'Leary, "Responses to Drought," 319–321.

telling account came from an elder who had lost several close family members during the event. He found himself unable to talk about the famine, simply repeating – over and over – "[It] was terrible," and sadly shaking his head.[116]

With little government help forthcoming, families resorted to older methods of famine survival. They hunted for elephant, rhinoceros, and other game; they traded cattle across the Tana river in exchange for grain; and much to the consternation of officials, concerned with neat administrative order, 35,000 men, women, and children fled Kitui district: 30,000 headed to Kikuyu Province and 5,000 toward the coast.[117] The majority of these famine-travelers "became" Kikuyu, and never again returned to Ukambani. The famine showed the tenuousness of administrative order, and demonstrated that as late as 1929, movement across tribal boundaries was simple.

While external forces had done little to shape a fixed form of ethnic identification, neither had internal forces. The fact that chiefs in Machakos chose to speak for "the Kamba" during the Thuku episode belied the fact that they had little ground on which to claim such power. These men struggled to maintain control in their own communities; speaking for "the Kamba" was laughable.

Moreover, there was not yet common cultural material that could unify disparate communities in Ukambani. Widely dispersed communities throughout the region shared different values. Christians respected those who were educated and practiced their religion properly. Young men who had gained warrior status used it to contest chiefly assertions about their right to be in charge. Chiefs commonly recalled "custom" from some vague past, and stressed the ownership of cattle, to try to give their rule legitimacy. It seems that in Kitui, elders frequently operated outside the chiefly system, earning respect for the wise judgment they had demonstrated for many years.

Any process of building a genuine "Kamba" ethnic affiliation was, therefore, yet to take place by the 1920s. This was in stark contrast to the goings-on in Kikuyu areas. In Kikuyu Province, a cadre of young intellectuals including James Beauttah and Joseph Kang'ethe formed the Kikuyu Central Association (KCA) in 1924. In Lonsdale's words, the KCA "conjured up a tribe."[118] They wrote petitions, held meetings, and took

---

[116] Interview 14, Mitaboni, July 20, 2004.
[117] KNA, DC/KTI/1/1.2, Kitui District Annual Report, 1929.
[118] Lonsdale, "Moral Economy," 371.

oaths to bond themselves together. This new community allowed them to press their demands from the government, and indeed resist members of the older generation who tried to control them. Kikuyu intellectuals wrote five histories of the "tribe" during the interwar period, in an effort to build a shared history and thus a more concrete, stable political community.[119]

In contrast, Ukambani had produced no cliques of intellectuals by the 1920s, and the first political organization of any significance did not appear until 1938. Practically no literature in Kikamba was written before 1963, and certainly nothing resembling a history of the "tribe." It is possible to argue, indeed, that a comprehensive history of the Kamba people has never been written, though this book is perhaps the closest effort thus far. Ukambani's communities were still organized in a profoundly local way.

The famine of Nzalukanje marked the beginning of the end of a degree of independence that the residents of Ukambani had enjoyed in participating in the colonial economy. Before the 1920s, they had interacted selectively with it: Few worked outside their home districts on settler farms, or as porters or railway workers, leading the British to believe that they were simply "lazy." The situation was dramatically different in Kikuyuland; in 1921, 36 percent of men worked for wages within the European economy, compared to only 7 percent in Ukambani.[120] The 1920s, however, saw the beginnings of great changes. The ease of movement to Nairobi increased, with better transport available, and more and more men from Machakos and Kitui became migrant laborers.

This process was exacerbated by the world depression of 1929, and the famine of Nzalukanje. These factors meant that people were unable to sell their cattle for any reasonable profit. This was particularly jarring because survival depended on these sales (residents of Machakos sold 60,000 cattle during the famine, approximately one-third of the total in the reserve). Informants remember bitterly how they had to accept extremely low prices offered by Kikuyu for their stock. Locust swarms exacerbated difficulties for agriculturalists.[121]

This period of difficulty was partially responsible for an increase in the numbers of Kamba in the KAR. In 1927, they made up only 7.3 percent of its soldiers; the upward shift began in 1929, when the percentage rose to 13.9 percent, and continued throughout the 1930s as more troops were

---

[119] Lonsdale, "Moral Economy," 375.   [120] Munro, *Colonial Rule*, 95.
[121] KNA, DC/MKS.1/1/22, Machakos District Annual Report, 1930.

required.[122] But it would be wrong to see the difficult environmental conditions of this period as entirely responsible for the increase. Many young men wanted these jobs from the early 1920s but there was simply no demand after the war. The district commissioner of Kitui noted in 1921 that the number of applicants for service in the KAR was "more numerous than could be suited."[123] In short, the work was always desirable, but the government was not always hiring.

Policemen, however, were always essential to the working of the colony, and therefore recruitment for this occupation continued at a high rate throughout the 1920s. The police is, therefore, perhaps a better location to gauge the degree to which youth were attracted to martial service. The proportion of Kamba in the police was already high from the 1910s. In 1927, Kamba comprised 25 percent of the force's African policemen. Enlistment figures for the Kavirondo – a colonial label encompassing such groups as the Kisii, Luyia, and Luo – reveal that they made up 26.8 percent of the total, therefore only just outstripping the number of Kamba, despite the fact that their population numbers dwarfed the latter.[124]

Many of the youth desired jobs as soldiers and in the police because the occupations permitted the expression of important virtues, and the chance to win honor and gain status in their communities. Migrant labor or waged employment never had the same level of attraction; certainly, they involved traveling far from home and sustaining their communities, but never the bravery or specialized knowledge that came from the martial occupations.

But by 1930, administrators' concern regarding Ukambani was focused on one factor, and one alone: land. They regarded its degraded state with a mixture of sadness and frustration. They were convinced that something drastic needed to be done – indeed, that it was their *responsibility* to do something.[125] And thus for the first time, Ukambani became fully drawn into the orbit of the colonial system, and the first significant effort to pull disparate groups of Kamba together appeared in response.

[122] Parsons, *African Rank-and-File*, 68.
[123] KNA, DC/KTI/1/1.2, Kitui District Annual Report, 1921.
[124] TNA, CO 533/380/10, Kenya Police Annual Report, 1927.
[125] KNA, DC/MKS.1/1/22, Machakos District Annual Report, 1930.

Chapter 4

The destocking episode

Between 2,000 and 3,000 natives, including women and babies, have arrived in Nairobi.[1]

On February 19, 1938, Air Marshal Sir Robert Brooke-Popham – governor and commander-in-chief of Kenya Colony – sent a telegram to William Ormsby-Gore, the Conservative colonial secretary in London. "The drastic action has begun," he stated, "I feel strongly that it would be criminal to wait any longer." The "drastic action" was a carefully planned program of destocking and reconditioning in the Machakos reserve. Its most visible manifestation, which had just commenced, was the forced removal of large numbers of cattle from the northern locations of the district. Officials believed that an excessive amount of stock was responsible for the overcrowded reserve's poor soil fertility and overall "degraded" land condition, and therefore acted decisively – though with little foresight – to solve the problem.[2]

Colonial administrators had failed to anticipate any response to their new policy, which was a serious error. The recently formed Ukamba Members Association (UMA) – led by the fiery Samuel Muindi Mbingu – quickly demonstrated that it was unwilling to accept the government's actions. Three thousand men, women, and children marched from northern Machakos to Nairobi and began a "sit-in" protest near the racecourse. In addition to organizing the march, the UMA – working hand-in-hand

---

[1] *The Times*, "Destocking in Kenya Native Reserve: 3,000 Protest Marchers," July 30, 1938.
[2] TNA, CO 533/492/1, Brooke-Popham to Ormsby-Gore, February 19, 1938.

with Kikuyu political parties, as well as contacts in London – was able to exert significant pressure on the colonial administration. News about the sit-in created a mountain of negative publicity for Nairobi – especially in Great Britain – and the governor was forced to back down and rescind the destocking policy. The march was a unique kind of protest in colonial African history: Men, women, and children from one "tribe" challenged the government and won, without a drop of blood shed on either side.

The march to Nairobi has become perhaps the defining moment in Kamba history. Kamba hold it up as an example of united, tribal action, an odyssey undertaken to resist unfair treatment from the British. They assert – now, as then – that the ownership of cattle was a fundamental and essential part of Kamba life and identity *mũno tene* – since time immemorial – and thus they had to resist such encroachments powerfully. No one put it better than Dorothy Uswii, a tiny, wizened relic of a bygone era, who informed me that she was 107 years old when I interviewed her in 2004. She lived in Kavaa, a tiny hamlet in Ngelani, where the destocking episode was focused. To hear the lady speak about the past was clearly an honor for many in her village: People gathered throughout the day to listen to our conversation. When it came to the topic of cattle, she became very quiet. "[Kamba] were given cattle *by God*," she stressed, pausing to let the import of her statement sink in.[3]

The destocking incident is practically the only one in Kamba history on which scholars have focused a significant amount of attention. They have depicted it in similarly neat fashion: as a government versus Kamba confrontation about cattle. But the reality was more complex: First, genuine "Kamba" unity in 1938 was fleeting. Certainly, young intellectuals claimed it: They declared that they spoke for "the Kamba" via the UMA, as a way to gain authority in their negotiations with the British. But they also used the moment to issue a powerful challenge against chiefs, headmen, and elders.

Second, the movement was just as much about land as it was about cattle. An increase in individualized land tenure in northern Machakos meant that many young men had simply no prospect of owning land. The UMA, indeed, was formed as an organization to protest colonial land policies before the destocking began. Once the cattle were returned in late 1938, the UMA turned back to its original agenda. And here, the young

---

[3] Interview 12, Ngelani, July 17, 2004.

men – and indeed women – disagreed with the "senior" men in their communities, most of whom had secure access to large portions of land.

The moment also showcased a clear expression of a tactic that Kamba leaders used for the remainder of the colonial period: playing on their martial reputation to win advantages from their opponents. Young men had used the same technique after the First World War; they had evoked their military service and bravery to demand respect, and contest the authority of their chiefs and elders. In 1938, the same thing happened again, but this time they also leveled their sights at the colonial authorities. Their efforts to exert pressure on the government carried weight: By 1938, there were more Kamba soldiers in the KAR than from any other ethnic group, and with a new Italian presence in Abyssinia, and the stirrings of Germany in Europe, there was a high likelihood that large numbers of African troops would be required imminently. UMA leaders described how they were a "loyal" and "martial" people, and warned administrators that they would be unable to recruit Kamba soldiers if their demands were not met.

A REASSESSMENT IN UKAMBANI

The Colonial Development Act of 1929 represented an important change-of-heart in the way the Colonial Office thought about development in the colonies. The act initially provided relatively little funding for Kenya, which was in the midst of a titanic struggle against the results of the Depression, and its impact was therefore limited. But it represented an increased level of attention to African agriculture, and the way Africans used their land.[4] These changes came about for four reasons, neatly summarized by David Anderson:

Economic reassessments brought about in the colonies, as elsewhere, by the Depression of the early 1930s; the international alarm generated by the cata-strophic experience of the southern plains of America in the Dust Bowl, at its height in 1935; the recognition during the 1930s that rapid increase in the human and stock populations of the African Reserves was creating serious pressure on the land; and, finally, the fear that the apparently increasing incidence of drought conditions in many parts of East Africa over the period 1926 to 1935 indicated that the region was becoming progressively more arid.[5]

[4] The most comprehensive empirical study on colonial development is Morgan, *Official History*.
[5] Anderson, "Depression," 322–323.

In Kenya, officials wrote dire warnings that many districts could barely feed themselves, and would surely end up relying on the government for food. At the forefront of this new imperial and colonial concern was Ukambani, an area that officials believed was most urgently in need of assistance. This new attention resulted in a significant change in the level of interaction between the government and people of Machakos, and to a lesser extent, Kitui. The relative isolation of Ukambani's reserves disappeared as agricultural experts and colonial officials now descended upon them.

Officials made all sorts of recommendations about the rehabilitation, reconditioning, and development of land in the reserves. They variously suggested building dams and terraces (steps cut into a hillside to prevent the top-soil from being washed away in heavy rain), afforestation, and new farming techniques, all the while fiercely debating the root cause of the land's degradation. One of the most enduring beliefs was that soil in the reserves was becoming progressively more infertile as a result of excessive numbers of African cattle and goats living there. Experts believed that each area of land had a certain "carrying capacity" of stock, and throughout Ukambani, came to view cattle and goats as the problem.

The 1930s was not the first time that officials – and settlers – in Kenya had discussed the perceived overpopulation of African stock. They had broached the topic as early as the first decade of the twentieth century, and it had received official attention in the Ormsby-Gore Commission of 1924. The commission's report had specifically warned the government that "new attitudes and techniques of livestock control" were essential to restrict potential damage in reserves where land was limited and populations rising.[6] In 1926, the government passed the Crop Production and Livestock Ordinance, which gave it legal authority to cull stock where necessary. The ordinance remained unused, until following a severe drought in Ukambani during the mid 1930s, its potential resurfaced.[7]

In 1937, colonial officials' opinions about land in the Kamba reserves received backing from a series of high profile experts. Sir Frank Stockdale visited Machakos on his tour of East Africa, and published a report about his journey for the Colonial Advisory Council of Agriculture and Animal Health.[8] Sir Edward Ruggles Brise, chairman of the Agricultural Committee of the House of Commons, also toured Machakos. But without

---

[6] KNA, DC/MKS/1/1/27, Machakos District Annual Report, 1938.
[7] TNA, CO 533/372/9, Crop Production and Livestock Ordinance, 1926.
[8] See also Kenya, *Meat and Live Stock*.

question the most highly qualified agricultural expert, whose voice carried the most weight, was the one without a knighthood. Described years later by Sir Roger Swynnerton as "the real hot-gospeller on anti-erosion work," Colin Maher was a prominent member of the Department of Agriculture in Kenya, and an expert on soil conservation.[9] He spent several months doing research in both Machakos and Kitui, and produced extensive reports – totaling hundreds of pages – on the districts. While he did not view Kitui as particularly overstocked, or the pressure on land so severe, his indictment of Machakos was damning:

> The causes are wrong use of land; wrong methods of farming, wrong densities of population and stock, settlement in wrong situations. The outward and visible signs of soil erosion are merely the tokens of man in a state of unbalance with his environment ... The Machakos Reserve is an appalling example of a large area of land ... which has been subject to un-co-ordinated and practically uncontrolled development by natives whose multiplication and the increase of whose stock has been permitted, free from the checks of war and largely from those of disease, under the benevolent British rule.

He advocated a strict program of reconditioning and destocking, focusing especially on cattle:

> The only way out of this vicious circle of overstocking and decreasing carrying capacity seems to be systematic culling and destruction of the unwanted animals by Government, with or without compensation to their owners, under the powers which exist for culling native stock, but which have never been utilised hitherto on any scale.

Maher believed that the reserve had a "carrying capacity" of only 20,000 cattle, which could perhaps rise to 100,000 after "years of major reconditioning." The number of cattle in the Machakos reserve in 1938 was approximately 250,000.[10]

Based on these opinions, Brooke-Popham applied to the Colonial Development Fund for an initial grant of £10,000 – with a later addition

---

[9] RHL, Mss. Afr. s. 1426, Sir Roger Swynnerton, Interview with Geoffrey Masefield, November 5, 1970.

[10] RHL, Mss. Afr. s. 755, Papers of Colin Maher, Colin Maher, "Soil Erosion and Land Utilisation in the Ukamba Reserve (Machakos)," February 1937, 3–5. R. O. Barnes produced a useful set of black-and-white aerial photographs showing the extent of erosion in Machakos. KNA, DC/MKS/10A/29/1, R. O. Barnes, "Memorandum on Soil Erosion, Ukamba Reserve," 1937. See also KNA, DC/KTI.5/1/1, Colin Maher, "A Soil Erosion and Land Utilisation Survey of the Ukamba (Kitui) Reserve," Part I, 1937; KNA, DC/KTI.5/1/2, Colin Maher, "A Soil Erosion and Land Utilisation Survey of the Ukamba (Kitui) Reserve," Parts II and III, 1937.

of a further £24,000 – to institute the destocking program. He wrote to the colonial secretary confirming that, "Cattle must be the principal target of the administrative weapons employed in this campaign."[11] Brooke-Popham hoped that the destocking campaign in Ukambani would serve as a model for addressing the problems of soil erosion in the rest of Kenya. Indeed, its significance was even broader: Southern Rhodesia also implemented a destocking campaign in 1938, and later attempts to do the same throughout the colonies continually referenced the Kenya administration's efforts in Ukambani.[12]

The increased concern with African land was no simple, benevolent move to assist Africans and their food production. It also reflected the colonial state's desire to bolster the settler economy, which was inextricably linked to levels of government revenue. The settler economy had prospered during the 1920s following a boom period caused by the war, but had collapsed after the Wall Street crash. World market prices for crops (especially coffee and maize) had dropped precipitously, and the economic disarray resulted in one-fifth of settlers leaving the colony. By the mid 1930s, few signs of improvement were visible. Settlers had long depended on the state for assistance; they paid no income tax, for instance, and the state had always shown itself quick to enforce labor ordinances on Africans to guarantee them cheap workers. Now, the state again stepped in to help settler farmers, many of whom had taken up cattle ranching in the 1930s.

One of the major difficulties facing settler producers was that they could not compete with African farmers, who were undercutting them. African producers had weathered the economic depression of the early 1930s with relative success, and provided approximately three-quarters of the maize and beef sold in the colony's markets. Rather than trying to restrict African production, "The trick needed," as Lonsdale points out, "was some control that could release but restrain the tide of African supply, so that it floated settler production rather than swamped it." In the case of beef production, this centered on a scheme that would involve a company from Southern Rhodesia called Liebig's, of which Brooke-Popham was a great advocate. The plan was simple: The state would compel Africans to sell their large numbers of cattle to the company's new factory at Athi River. By fixing low prices for the sale of African

[11] TNA, CO 533/483/7, Brooke-Popham to Ormsby-Gore, September 18, 1937.
[12] On destocking more widely (and the example of Kenya) see, for instance, Shutt, "Settlers' Cattle Complex."

cattle, Liebig's could make enough profit to build a facility to chill settler beef for export, which was where the real money could be made.[13] As one European settler – whose family raised cattle in Machakos at the time – put it, "[Liebig's was] solely for our benefit."[14]

Liebig's had sent representatives to Kenya as far back as 1922 to research the possibilities of setting up a meat processing plant. They returned again in 1926 following the passage of the Crop Production and Livestock Ordinance. Three years later the company acquired the report of an agricultural commission chaired by Sir Daniel Hall that focused in large part on Machakos. Hall recommended the construction of a meat factory ("*now* or very soon" – emphasis in original) for the disposal of stock from the reserves.[15] Finally in 1937, Liebig's again returned to Kenya, this time with a formal invitation from the government in hand. The government had promised to fully assist and cooperate with the company, and so Liebig's built a new factory on the outskirts of Nairobi (where the Kenya Meat Commission stands today). The factory was capable of converting tens of thousands of cattle into meat products, providing a much-needed boost to Kenya's economy. But within months of commencing operations, Liebig's was in financial trouble: It simply could not afford to purchase cattle at the high prices of the open market, and thus required the government's aid.[16]

A MARCH AND A "SIT-IN"

In late 1937, the government began the preparatory stages of its destocking plan. Officials and experts began a cattle census in northern Machakos. Each location was "assessed": Officials counted the number of cattle in it, and then determined the number that location could feasibly "carry." Thus in Matungulu, for instance, a count revealed 27,000 head of cattle in the location. Officials deemed 4,500 (or approximately 16 percent) the quota of cattle that the land could support, and thus needed to remove 84 percent. Each cattle owner therefore – at least in theory – had to "sell" (for a set price of approximately one-quarter of market value) 84 percent of his cattle. The proportion he was allowed to keep would be branded to

---

[13] Kanogo, "Kenya and the Depression"; Lonsdale, "Depression."
[14] Interview 53, Nairobi, September 12, 2006.
[15] Kenya, *Agricultural Commission*, 8, 28–32.
[16] *East African Standard*, "Council Debates Liebig's: Official Reply to Charge of Cavalier Treatment," April 22, 1939.

show they were officially "spared." The removal of cattle began on the Yatta Plateau – a grazing area to the northeast of the Machakos reserve, and designated for use by the Kamba – in September 1937. Officials cut the number of cattle from 50,000 to 12,000. During the several months that followed, colonial officials, accompanied by government soldiers, removed 21,000 head from Matungulu and Kangundo locations.[17] Farmers were shocked as soldiers herded away their animals. In Matungulu, sub-headman and future leader of the destocking protest Kavula Muli remembered, "I had 27 cows and 12 bulls ... The number branded were five and I had to sell the rest ... [my cattle] weren't thin so I knew that I had enough land for them."[18]

Resistance to the destocking appeared through the UMA, which was created just months prior to the commencement of destocking. It was led by Samuel Muindi, who served as president, Simeon Kioko (as secretary), Elijah Kavulu, and Isaac Mwalonzi. All were from Ngelani, were educated at Kamuthanga mission school, owned a few cattle themselves, and had spent time living in Nairobi. The destocking was a political issue to which the fledgling organization immediately attached, and it used the moment to try to catapult itself to the fore as the voice of "the Kamba." It began by protesting the destocking in Matungulu and Kangundo by writing directly to the Colonial Office in London. On March 1, 1938, the UMA sent a telegram to the colonial secretary, Ormsby-Gore: "We representative Wakamba tribe strongly protest stop Kenya Government forced our cattle sold without our consent stop beg no action be taken immediately our petition follows Kenya government notified." Two months later came a second, in similar vein: "Kenya government sent 47 askaris (soldiers) and one European Smith with firearms collecting over 500 and shooting unhealth [sic] cattle."[19] The telegrams had great effect in London, where the newly appointed colonial secretary – Malcolm Macdonald – faced some hostile questioning in his first days in office.[20]

Officials were greatly concerned that Kamba political isolation was broken. With the commencement of the cattle removal, the UMA immediately began working with the KCA. The two sets of leaders described the close, shared history of Kamba and Kikuyu, a nod, perhaps, toward

---

[17] KNA, DC/MKS/1/1/27, Machakos District Annual Report, 1938.
[18] JNP, Interview with Kavula Muli, Matungulu, December 12, 1973.
[19] TNA, CO 533/492/1, UMA to Colonial Office, March 1 and May 3, 1938.
[20] See, for instance, Great Britain, *House of Commons Debates*, Vol. 336, Cols. 403–404, May 18, 1938. Fay Gadsden provides a summary of the way Kamba leaders and their advocates pressed their cause in British news sources. Gadsden, "Further Notes."

the flexibility of identity in nineteenth-century Kenya. Muindi – who was married to a Kikuyu woman – together with Ndolo and Ngea published a piece expressing their grievances in *Muigwithania*, the KCA newsletter, beginning "Akamba and Wakikuyu are of the same race," and ending with a plea for assistance.[21] George Ndegwa – the secretary of the KCA – cabled Jomo Kenyatta in London on behalf of the Kamba, describing their plight as well as that of the Kikuyu, who were themselves upset about the closure of Mukui independent school.[22] And the UMA and KCA took joint action: As one official described, "It was significant that the subversive organisation [the UMA] was sufficiently powerful to effect an absolutely simultaneous act of defiance by the burning of trash lines both in Ukambani and Kikuyu starting on the same day and almost at the same hour." The official entitled his handwritten letter, "Combination of tribes to defeat the policy of Govt."[23]

Interviewees today are quick to stress the links between the UMA and KCA that existed at the time. Simeon Mwalonzi – the son of Isaac – specifically remembered that, "the Kikuyu started the Kamba in politics."[24] When I interviewed Muindi's daughter in 2004, she described meetings between Muindi and Kenyatta, and even claimed that Muindi first gave Kenyatta his name: Kenyatta apparently wore a thick belt called a *kĩnyata* in Kikamba.[25] Another woman explained to me that Muindi had commenced the fight for independence, then when he died, Kenyatta took over the mantle.[26] Kamba claim that they, too, had supported Harry Thuku in 1922 – though there is little evidence of it – although the UMA leaders seem to have done so.[27] The effort to draw the Kamba into this nationalist framework is likely in part related to an importance in postcolonial Kenya of demonstrating having "fought for freedom" from colonial rule. Yet the two groups certainly had common interests: Concerns about land were of utmost importance for both.

[21] KNA, DC/MKS/10B/15/1, Muindi, Ndolo, and Ngea to the President, KCA, July 1938. This letter reveals that a copy of its contents was published in *Muigwithania* 1, 2 (1938), 15–16.
[22] KNA, DC/MKS/10B/15/1, Ndegwa to Kenyatta, May 3, 1938.
[23] KNA, DC/MKS.4/9, Machakos District Political Record Book, Vol. VII (1930–1938), Enclosure: "Combination of Tribes to Defeat the Policy of Govt," 1938.
[24] Interview with Simeon Mwalonzi, Ngelani, July 7, 2004.
[25] Interview with Scholastica Maingi, Ngelani, July 21, 2004. It is unlikely that Kenyatta and Muindi actually met at this time, as Kenyatta was in Great Britain.
[26] Interview 11, Ngelani, July 16, 2004.
[27] JNP, Interview with Isaac Mwalonzi, Ngelani, January 17, 1974.

Jomo Kenyatta engineered much of the poor publicity about the colonial government in Kenya that appeared in Britain. He wrote articles for the *New Statesman and Nation* – a magazine in which he had published articles since the early 1930s – as well as other local media. He also wrote several letters to the *Manchester Guardian*, a left-wing newspaper that was often critical of the British government. Kenyatta described the destocking situation many times, referring to the administration's "semi-Fascist, dictatorial methods," and pointing out that such behavior was to be expected: After all, he argued, in Kenya Europeans had stolen land which belonged to Africans, including the Kamba.[28]

By late June, the focus of the destocking program had turned to Iveti. Iveti location lay to the south of Matungulu and to the southwest of Kangundo, and shared a border with both. Iveti – and specifically Ngelani sub-location – was also the heartland of the UMA. Its leaders lived there, as do their sons and daughters today. In Iveti, the government had ordered elders to assist in the counting and branding of livestock, yet they had met with stiff resistance. The government had set the date of July 7 by which the process had to commence, yet the date passed without any sign of compliance. Thus the very next morning a force of 116 – including 40 Kenya Police, 66 Tribal Police, and 10 Scouts, all led by the district commissioner, A. N. Bailward – mustered at 4 a.m. Three-quarters of the force descended on Ngelani sub-location from different directions, while the remainder took up flanking positions to prevent either men or cattle from escaping. The force removed 2,500 head of cattle, shooting those that appeared too weak to herd away.[29]

One result of the cattle confiscations in Ngelani was that more and more men and women joined the UMA. UMA leaders and their colleagues recruited widely throughout Machakos and into Kitui, raising support. Many paid subscription fees to the organization – the amounts varied – but these sums rapidly added up to a sizable total as the basis of protest spread.[30] The government had anticipated that the removal of cattle "would induce the natives to claim their cattle and receive them back

---

[28] *Manchester Guardian*, "Kenya Natives and Their Cattle: The Destocking Sales," (Kenyatta to the Editor), August 11, 1938. See also *New Statesman and Nation*, "Correspondence," June 25, 1938 or *Manchester Guardian*, "Forced Sales in Kenya: Government Methods," (Kenyatta to the Editor), July 2, 1938. There was even debate in government circles about whether Kenyatta should be prevented from raising the destocking issue in public. Savage, "Jomo Kenyatta."

[29] KNA, DC/MKS/10B/15/1, "Iveti Destocking Sweep: Operation Orders," July 5, 1938.

[30] Interview 5, Ngelani, July 10, 2004.

reduced by the obvious culls and with the quota branded." Yet to the surprise of officials, there was no sign of concession to their wishes. The government filed legal suit against all the cattle owners, yet they refused to even identify their cattle, let alone claim them. The government responded by strengthening destocking regulations, with the provision that unclaimed cattle could be sold within twenty-eight days, yet to no avail.[31]

On July 30, 1938, the Nairobi correspondent of *The Times* of London filed an extraordinary story: "Between 2,000 and 3,000 natives, including women and babies, have arrived in Nairobi." Within days of the Kenya legislature verifying the seizure of the cattle as legal, thousands of men, women, and children gathered from the hills around Ngelani and Mitaboni and left their homes, headed for Nairobi. UMA leaders made the decision to march after holding open meetings in which several thousand of their supporters participated. Though the government had confiscated few cattle from Mitaboni, the inhabitants there went in solidarity with their comrades. "They are our people," one man explained, "if theirs [their cattle] were taken, then they [the British] would then come and take those we had here." Each family in the area sent at least one representative on the march. Many homesteads were left almost deserted, with just one person remaining behind to stand guard.[32]

Today, interviewees in Machakos speak fervently about the march to Nairobi. Women, in particular, recall that many babies were born as they traveled. Elizabeth Kioko – the wife of Simeon – remembered, "We moved from here, and went to Nairobi on foot ... and women gave birth as we followed our cattle." She described how they faced the hardships of caring for the newborn babies together with the men and children.[33] Considering the fact that the majority of the march took place within twenty-four hours, it is extremely unlikely that many babies were born, yet the fact that this is the abiding memory of the march reflects its nature as something of an odyssey. The response of another woman when asked, "How many Kamba went to Nairobi?" reflects this: "There were many. I don't know the number, but when we saw an antelope some distance away, we could encircle it and catch it. We were that many!"[34]

The path that the marchers took west to Nairobi held particular significance. It was the old route that men and women had taken to sell

[31] KNA, DC/MKS/3/6, Handing Over Report. Bailward to Brumage, 1938.
[32] Interview 16, Mitaboni, July 21, 2004.
[33] Interview with Elizabeth Simeon Kioko, Mitaboni, July 5, 2005.
[34] Interview 12, Ngelani, July 17, 2004.

food in the city in the early years of the twentieth century. On those journeys, they had slept in the open air, often in danger from lions and leopards that roamed the plains in the past. They had relied on their talent as hunters with bow and arrow to procure antelope for food (hence the added significance of the antelope reference above). The marchers followed in the footsteps of older ancestors too – along precisely the same route – for the benefit of what they came to view for perhaps the first time as the entire Kamba population, in much the same way that their predecessors had traveled for the benefit of their extended families.

The marchers began arriving in Nairobi on the night of July 27 – with the last groups joining on the morning of July 28 – and they set up camp near the racecourse at Kariakor (modern day Eastleigh). The journey was a total distance of more than forty miles. The group marched across the plains to the city instead of through the town of Athi River in order to avoid the police. Most walked, and those unable to do so rode in lorries hired by the UMA. In Nairobi, the leaders of the march demanded an audience with the governor, but Brooke-Popham refused their entreaties, despite reportedly riding past them on several occasions on his way to play polo.[35] Brooke-Popham believed that to meet with the marchers would set a bad precedent, and would undermine the authority of those chiefs and headmen in the reserve who had attempted to support the government's destocking program. As he later explained, "The tactics they [the marchers] have been so misguided to adopt can serve no good purpose and will have no effect on the Government's policy."[36]

Yet the protestors showed little sign of moving, and each day their supporters arrived in Kariakor, bringing food and supplies. Finally, with the government facing particularly bad publicity in the British press (the disturbance even appeared on a radio transmission of *Empire News*), as well as the colonial secretary subject to frequent attacks in the House of Commons, Brooke-Popham was forced to concede to the UMA's demands by promising to hold a *baraza* (public meeting) in Machakos.[37] The marchers returned home buoyed by their success. "It has been an anxious time," wrote Brooke-Popham to Macdonald, believing that the worst was over.[38]

[35] TNA, CO 533/506/4, St. Barbe Baker to Macdonald, January 9, 1939.
[36] *East African Standard*, "Squat Strike Sequel," September 30, 1938.
[37] TNA, CO 533/506/4, *Empire News*: Transmission IVa, August 16, 1938. For the colonial secretary's difficulties see, for instance, Great Britain, *House of Commons Debates*, Vol. 338, Cols. 364–365, July 6, 1938 or Vol. 338, Cols. 2183–2184, July 20, 1938.
[38] TNA, CO 533/506/4, Brooke-Popham to Macdonald, August 18, 1938.

When the governor finally arrived in Machakos on August 25, it was clear that he no longer underestimated his opponents. His tone was conciliatory, though patronizing: "[W]hen your child has broken an arm or a leg you take him to the doctor. Do you think that the doctor is wrong because he hurts your child in putting the limb straight? No ... it will prevent him from being maimed for life ... This is the position of Government."[39] In this way, Brooke-Popham explained the necessity of destocking as being for the overall benefit of the Kamba. At the baraza Muindi handed Brooke-Popham an eight-page letter explaining why the government should return their cattle. The letter argued that the responsibility for soil erosion rested on the government, not Kamba. Muindi had a point: Ukambani had received almost no benefit from the millions of shillings paid in tax over the preceding three decades. In addition, the residents of Machakos and Kitui could not expand to new lands to reduce overcrowding – as they might have done in the past – due to the restrictions of the reserve system.[40]

Brooke-Popham was now certain that Muindi was the ringleader of the disturbances. Therefore on September 17, Muindi was arrested, and deported to Lamu after a speedy trial.[41] But despite his removal, resistance continued in the Machakos reserve. Officials collected less Hut and Poll Tax in 1938 than in any year since 1922.[42] Villagers uprooted terracing markers and refused to dig terraces. On more than one occasion the government brought the 2,500 confiscated cattle back to the reserve and asked their owners to claim them, but all refused. Finally, the government had no choice but to capitulate, and returned the cattle. The Liebig's factory closed its doors (temporarily, as it turned out). On December 2 – to praise from newspapers in Britain – the government made the following announcement: "Destocking by compulsory culling [will] be postponed for an indefinite period ... the 2,500 head of cattle from Mitaboni [will] be returned unconditionally to their owners ... [and] an intensive reconditioning campaign ... [will] be instituted."[43]

[39] TNA, CO 533/493/21, Transcript of Speech of Brooke-Popham at Baraza, August 25, 1938.
[40] Myrick, "Colonial Initiatives," 5–6.
[41] Arthur Creech Jones, the future colonial secretary, took up Muindi's case in Parliament. Great Britain, *House of Commons Debates*, Vol. 342, Cols. 413–414, November 30, 1938.
[42] KNA, DC/MKS/1/1/27, Machakos District Annual Report, 1938.
[43] Settlers were enraged. *East African Standard*, "Council Debates Liebig's: Official Reply to Charge of Cavalier Treatment," April 22, 1939.

The protest – a blend of an organized, peaceful demonstration with physical resistance – was an unqualified success.

UNDERSTANDING THE "ĨVINDA YA NG'OMBE" (TIME OF CATTLE)

Despite contemporary recollections and scholarship, a careful analysis of the destocking episode reveals that it was far more than a government versus Kamba "battle over cattle." There is little doubt, however, that cattle did take on a new level of significance from the late 1920s onward. A variety of men – young and old – argued that to be a "Kamba" was to possess cattle. A series of proverbs about their importance appeared. One stated, "Scratch a Kikuyu and you will find a *githaka* [a Kikuyu word, correctly *gĩthaka*, and variously meaning a forest, thicket, or "virgin land"] but scratch an Mkamba and you will find an *Ng'ombe* [cow]."[44] Another asserted, "*Nyamu itungaa ithaumyo ni nzeo mbee wa ila itatungaa ithaumyo*" – "the animal that chews its cud is better than the animal that does not chew its cud."[45] In their 1939 dictionary, AIM missionaries stated that *indo* – which had always meant either "cattle" or "things," depending on the context – now had just one meaning: cattle.[46]

The famine of Nzalukanje had reduced the number of cattle in the Machakos reserve by fully one-third (60,000 head) as men sold animals to buy grain.[47] As noted in Chapter 3, many animals went to Kikuyu areas, but a large number went to wealthy men in Machakos. These men were in position to easily support themselves and their families during the famine, and took advantage of depressed economic conditions to buy cattle cheaply from those in desperate straits. They built large herds as poorer families found themselves either without cattle at all, or with one or two scrawny beasts.

Chiefs and elders had long stressed the centrality of cattle in their communities. They owned vast herds, and therefore the more important the ownership of cattle, the more authority they possessed. They had been notably successful in cementing cattle as an inviolate part of the payment

[44] KNA, DC/MKS.1/1/22, Machakos District Annual Report, 1929. I am grateful to Frederick Iraki for his assistance with the Kikuyu translation.

[45] Farnsworth, *Kamba Grammar*, 50.

[46] AIMLCU, *Kikamba–English Dictionary*, 37. Compare to Rhoad's translation of John (for example, Rhoad (trans.), *Yoana*, 12 (John 4:12)) or the vocabularies of Hinde or Krapf.

[47] KNA, DC/MKS.1/1/22, Machakos District Annual Report, 1930.

of brideprice. Typical brideprice during the 1930s included between thirty
and forty goats (perhaps as many as sixty), assorted items such as honey,
blankets, foodstuffs, and beer, as well as two cows and either one bullock
or one ox, and possibly both.[48] In Kitui, the payment was higher, at eight
cows and one bullock, according to evidence presented to the Kenya Land
Commission.[49] Though the number of cattle thus required for marriage in
Machakos was low, the payment of brideprice could not happen without
the beasts; the only possible exception was in times when famine struck
the land *after* the families had agreed upon the terms of marriage. Officials had periodically tried to remove the requirement that cattle be
included in brideprice, suggesting cash as a substitute, but chiefs and
headmen had steadfastly refused to be swayed.[50]

The most telling elite expression of cattle's significance came from a
prominent chief named James Mutua. Mutua was an eloquent man, and
had visited Britain in April 1931 to give evidence in front of the Joint
Committee on Closer Union in East Africa, along with Ezekiel Apindi and
Chief Koinange wa Mbiyu. There, he had largely represented himself as
an African – versus a Kamba – though he did discourse on the importance
of cattle among Kamba peoples.[51] He was one of the few figures from
Ukambani who was actually named in the evidence of the KLC in the
early 1930s (see below), and his testimony was transcribed instead of
being summarized, a rarity. His voice was a powerful and influential one:
"[C]attle are the natives' bank," he explained, "If a man is poor [i.e.,
without cattle] it is very bad." He brought up long-past history, and
explained the riches in cattle that Kamba had once enjoyed. Another
man giving evidence to the Commission referred to people from Kitui as
"baboons," because they climbed trees to tend their beehives. He considered this a poor type of work, unworthy of respect.[52]

By the 1930s, then, all generations shared a common interest in cattle.
Young, married men had struggled to build up their herds following the
Depression, particularly in crowded areas like Matungulu, Kangundo,
and Iveti. Destocking brought the threat of losing those animals. For
unmarried men, life was a constant effort to buy several beasts, upon
which the possibility of marriage depended. Without a wife, a man – as

[48] Multiple interviews, Machakos and Kitui, 2004–2006.
[49] Kenya, *Kenya Land Commission: Evidence*, Vol. II, 1338.
[50] See, for instance, KNA, DC/MKS/5/1/3, Minute 10/38, "Dowries in Relation to Destock-
      ing," May 5–7, 1938.
[51] Great Britain, *Joint Committee on Closer Union*, Vol. II, 399–423.
[52] Kenya, *Kenya Land Commission: Evidence*, Vol. II, 1290, 1335–1342.

today – was seen as something "less" than a full adult. And for the older generation, their herds of cattle were essential for the maintenance of social status. As one man explained, "Someone who had few cattle had no honor and pride as far as other people were concerned." These men were part of that generation that had served during the First World War, and many had gained high status as a result of their fighting exploits, which was maintained through the cattle they had bought and now owned: "Having more cattle visible made you famous, a big man," the same man noted.[53]

At every stage, though, the ĩvinda ya ng'ombe was just as much about land as it was about cattle. Cattle and land were inextricably linked: Possession of cattle is, after all, fruitless if one has no access to land on which to graze them. The "land question" received immense, intense study during the early 1930s from the KLC. Under the watchful eye of Morris Carter, the Commission analyzed which parts of the country were in use by Africans and Europeans, and studied the claims put forth by various groups about their rights to land. It was an enormous task, and evidence from the Commission's work – together with its final report – ran to several thousand pages bound in four weighty volumes. The many pages of African testimonies recorded are some of the most useful sources for learning about colonial Kenya.

The KLC foreshadowed issues that became important in 1938, and demonstrated the centrality of the land issue. Isaac Mwalonzi, one of the leaders of the UMA, put it most clearly when discussing the origins of his organization: "We got the idea of forming this association ... to organise our own party to fight for our land and not for cattle then [,] as the business of cattle hadn't begun at that time."[54] The KLC heard statements from 187 Kamba. The majority was from Iveti, the most populated location in Ukambani (with 25,668 residents), and where the destocking protest began. Unlike in Kikuyuland, the testimonies recorded were – in the main – utterly formulaic; for instance:

____ states that he was born in ____ Location, that he lived for ____ years on the commonage, whence he had ____ agricultural *shambas* [farms] and ____ head of cattle. That he was removed thence by ____, District Commissioner, and now resides at ____. That he now owns ____ head of cattle and has not sufficient land available for his agricultural requirements.[55]

---

[53] Interview 4, Mutituni, July 9, 2004.
[54] JNP, Interview with Isaac Mwalonzi, Ngelani, January 17, 1974.
[55] Sample evidence from Kenya, *Kenya Land Commission: Evidence*, Vol. II, 1358.

Perhaps the most important issue raised by the KLC concerned individual land ownership. This system was practically unknown in the early 1920s, but a decade later was common in the northern half of Machakos. Many families without the knowledge or education to secure title to land found themselves grazing their cattle on *weũ* (common land or wilderness) to which anyone had access. But by the 1930s, weũ had all but ceased to exist in parts of northern Machakos, as wealthier landowners consolidated even tiny parcels of land. As far south as Kiteta and Mbooni, officials reported that almost no weũ remained.[56] In Iveti, the KLC reported that, "little or no agricultural land is available for acquisition under native custom." The Commission noted that one of the dangers with individualized land tenure was that those familiar with the system would end up being "land grabbers" and taking all the land; others would remain with nothing.[57] In contrast to weũ, privately held land owned by an individual was called *ng'ũndũ*, and the part of the ng'ũndũ on which a man grazed his cattle was *kĩsesi*. In 1947, H. E. Lambert noted that the term kĩsesi had "glamour" – because "it implies the ownership of cattle."[58]

The Machakos Local Native Council (LNC) – the top representative body of African community members, and mostly comprised of chiefs – further increased pressure on the land by passing a resolution in 1938 that required landowners to grow hedges to separate their farms from others', thus making it abundantly clear who owned what land and restricting the possibilities of communal farming. This was a profound shock to many, but provided a great advantage to educated Christians and the chiefs and prominent men of the LNC, who had long known about and understood the process. It is clear that those who were educated fared particularly well during the shift to individual land tenure.

The role of Christians in Machakos had become increasingly important over the preceding decade. Large Christian communities were concentrated in areas surrounding towns like Iveti, Ngelani, Kangundo, and Mbooni. They had established themselves as a fairly wealthy class, and had benefitted from their education that allowed them to keep accounts and records, and gain jobs in European employment. Boys and girls tried

---

[56] KNA, DC/MKS.4/10, Memorandum on Kamba Land Tenure and Grazing Rights in Relation to the Problems of Soil Erosion, *c.* 1933.

[57] Kenya, *Kenya Land Commission: Evidence*, Vol. II, 1312, 1443.

[58] Lambert, "Land Tenure," 143.

everything they could to receive education, as schools were never built quickly enough to keep up with demand. Some asked those who could read and write to teach them, and thus tried to glean what knowledge they could informally.[59]

From as early as the 1920s, missionaries had encouraged their charges to utilize land more effectively. This involved two major changes: first, using a plough to till the soil, and second, gaining permanent rights to land. One man remembered that Kamba did not believe land had any value until missionaries explained it to them: After that, they began formally demarcating their land, and buying up various pieces when they could afford it.[60] Thus when one man described how many of those who marched to Nairobi in 1938 "knew how to use ploughs," he meant that they were educated and Christian.[61] Officials concurred: They believed that 85 percent of Protestants in Machakos were members of the UMA by 1939.[62]

Chiefs, headmen, and members of the LNC conceived of land in a similar way to Ukambani's Christians. Indeed, separating the two groups is not possible: Some proportion of educated Christians had garnered positions in the administration by the 1930s. People called these men *asomi* (readers), and in some cases, directly translated "chief" as *muandĩkwa* (writer).[63] In April 1936, these chiefs and headmen gained the authority to order households to plant sisal hedges around their land (formalized by the Machakos LNC in 1938 – see above). In addition, they could even close land to grazing if they believed it was "severely eroded."[64]

These men acted to consolidate a position of strength. Mwinzi Mala, for instance, was a member of the Machakos LNC. Realizing how things were changing, he had bought land: 135 acres in southern Machakos, for which he paid 600 shillings.[65] Zachayo Ngao's story was similar: He was educated at Mbooni at Rhoad's mission, and later attended a government school in Kiteta. "Education helped me a great deal," he remembered, "as I was able to read and write letters. It also led me to be acquainted with

[59] Interview 36, Mulala, July 25, 2005.
[60] JNP, Interview with Elijah Mutambuuki, Tala, July 1, 1973.
[61] JNP, Interview with Kavula Muli, Matungulu, December 12, 1973.
[62] KNA, DC/MKS/1/1/28, Machakos District Annual Report, 1939.
[63] Whiteley and Muli, *Practical Introduction*, 15.
[64] KNA, DC/MKS/12/2/2, Minutes of the Machakos Reconditioning Committee, June 15, 1936.
[65] JNP, Interview with Mwinzi Mala, Tawa, November 2, 1974.

the land adjudication people when they came here."[66] Paolo Musau was a headman during the 1930s in Iveti, and as a result, he too bought land. This put him in a strong position, but not those without land: "Land [was] the main source of discontent among the people," he explained.[67]

Thus a two-tier system appeared during the 1930s. On one level, there were the "more well-to-do ... committed to market production, acquiring new land by purchase, and linked ... to the influential figures in local government, church and school."[68] These people bought up large parcels of land. They were aided by overcrowding in densely populated areas: If a man owned two acres, it was subdivided among his sons at his death. Small parcels of land therefore quickly became so tiny that they could not be farmed profitably. The lower classes eked out a living, grazing their few animals where they could.

The UMA leaders and their contemporaries thus faced a problem: They had little to no chance of gaining land, nor owning the cattle that would permit marriage. In addition, they resided in Nairobi, so it was difficult to stake any claim to land back at home. And here, Rhoad's influence appeared again. By the 1930s, Rhoad had left the AIM, and established his own, non-denominational missionary society called the Gospel Furthering Fellowship. All the UMA leaders were members of Rhoad's mission, and were educated by him at one point or another. One interviewee called the UMA leaders Rhoad's "friends," and Rhoad commonly preached at the Kamuthanga school they all attended.[69] Rhoad took the Kamba side during the destocking episode, believing they were unfairly treated.

UMA leaders knew that their chances of drumming up support would be seriously limited if they focused their protest on land; after all, affluent, prominent men in their communities were perfectly happy with the land situation. But the removal of cattle threatened everyone: Across

---

[66] JNP, Interview with Zachayo Ngao, Kiteta, November 2, 1974. Proverbs linked Christians' economic success to their social practices, especially the avoidance of teeth-chipping and ear-piercing. A man at Mbooni remembered one popular saying: "You continue eating *githeri* [Swahili: a meal of maize and beans] until you cross the bridge." As he explained, the proverb meant that with unaltered teeth, you could eat much faster than you could when your teeth had been chipped. He emphasized that one might even eat the share of those who could not eat so quickly. Interview 149, Mbooni, May 16, 2012.

[67] JNP, Interview with Paolo Musau, Tala, June 30, 1973.

[68] Munro, *Colonial Rule*, 204.

[69] JNP, Interview with Elijah Mbondu, Tala, November 26, 1973; Interview with Isaac Mwalonzi, Ngelani, January 17, 1974.

religious lines, geographical lines, and class lines, communities in Machakos (with a few supporters from Kitui) came together. Young and old, male and female, struck a social bargain based on protesting the removal of cattle.

UMA petitions reflected the focus on cattle. When leaders wrote to the Colonial Office in the first half of 1938, they described the threat to their animals, and detailed the horror felt by Kamba about the loss of their cattle. They argued that cattle ownership had always been a part of Kamba life: "[W]ith us cattle represent our wealth ... that form of wealth is bound up with all traditions of the past and is ... part and parcel of our social system," read one petition.[70] In a letter to the Kikuyu *Muigwithania*, Muindi recalled ancient history to explain the Kamba connection to the beasts: "Formerly our fathers used to go to war and lose their lives for the sake of cattle."[71] To recall Dorothy Uswii's words: Kamba were "given cattle by God."[72]

But once the government returned the 2,500 cattle, the glue that had unified Ukambani's disparate communities dissolved, and a shift in the nature of protest took place: Activism transformed from encompassing men and women of all ages throughout the region to one centered on educated young men – and to some extent women – from northern Machakos, and particularly Ngelani and Iveti. The return of the cattle – but more importantly the removal of the threat of destocking – secured the social statuses of the middle-aged and older men. In southern Machakos and Kitui, any opposition to the government quickly ended as a result of this.

Youthful leaders therefore turned back to the issue that had concerned them all along: land. They wrote four petitions to the Colonial Office between February and August 1939; three complained about sisal planting – for land demarcation – and one asked for Muindi's release. Claiming membership of 8,000 in their organization, they took and administered oaths of solidarity to resist government interference. All over northern Machakos, young men and women began pulling up the pegs that marked areas on their farms for future terracing (a part of the reconditioning campaign), placed by agricultural officers and their assistants. The senior agricultural officer moved his post from Nyeri (in central Kikuyuland) to Machakos to try to improve the success of

[70] KNA, DC/MKS/10B/15/1, UMA to Colonial Office, May 3, 1938.
[71] KNA, DC/MKS/10B/15/1, Muindi to the Editor, *Muigwithania*, c. April 1938.
[72] Interview 12 (pseudonym), Ngelani, July 17, 2004.

reconditioning work, and the government added an extra district officer in Machakos – a fourth – in an attempt to achieve calm.[73]

Women were greatly threatened by the loss of land and played a central role in this part of the protest. With the exception of widows, women had little legal right to own land, although experts from Lambert to the Australian anthropologist W. E. H. Stanner confessed that land tenure throughout Ukambani was an extremely confusing subject, and practices varied widely.[74] But as Heidi Gengenbach has shown in colonial Mozambique, women's legal access to land meant little; they had *expectations* to be able to cultivate land, irrespective of title deed.[75] These expectations were in fact formally enshrined in customary law in 1951: If a husband failed to provide land for his wife to cultivate, she had the right to divorce him.[76]

For many of these women, the ability to win respect was tied to the land, and they acted to protect their access to it. Women earned honor for raising productive gardens, and the results of their labors – which ranged from beans to maize and more – fed their families on a daily basis (meat was more of a luxury item that most might consume once a week, or on special occasions). As explained in Chapter 3, many women represented a vision of community in which the sustenance of the family was paramount; without land, they could play little role in achieving this.

Young women were also motivated to act because they would be unable to get married if their potential husbands could not procure land and cattle. Their only option, in that scenario, was to marry an older man, and district reports are clear that this was rarely a promising option: As early as 1921, women in Kitui commonly divorced older husbands when they became aware of the colony's divorce laws.[77] In Machakos a decade later, the district commissioner noted that women usually chose their own husbands, and the greatly disliked chiefs and headmen were rarely attractive.[78]

Thus women were intimately invested in the continuation of the protest, and female informants remember their contribution clearly. One explained, "It was women who uprooted the stakes when the marking

[73] KNA, DC/MKS/1/1/28, Machakos District Annual Report, 1939. See also Spencer, "Notes."
[74] KNA, W. E. H. Stanner, *The Kitui Kamba: A Critical Study of British Administration* (unpublished typescript, *c.* 1940); Lambert, "Land Tenure."
[75] Gengenbach, "I'll Bury You."   [76] Penwill, *Kamba Customary Law*, 18.
[77] KNA, DC/KTI/1/1.2, Kitui District Annual Report, 1921.
[78] KNA, DC/MKS/1/1/24, Machakos District Annual Report, 1931.

FIGURE 6: A typical hillside in the hills of central Machakos: Forests cover the hill's flat top, and terraces run through the farms below. (Photo: Author.)

for the terraces was done."[79] Many women were sent to jail in Machakos. They remember that during the judicial process, any time a woman was asked her name, she replied, *Isyo wa Mũũnda*, meaning "food from the farm" in Kikamba![80]

Female desires and expectations were reflected in proverbs and sayings of the period. When Emma Farnsworth published her *Kamba Grammar*, she produced several of them. Common, everyday phrases included, "There are many young women in my garden. They are cultivating." When it came to disapproval of women, it related to their abilities in farming: "That woman's millet is not good," went one, or "That young woman's digging stick is short."[81]

By the 1930s, male assertions about cattle ownership were juxtaposed against women's role in the gardens and fields. It became an undeniably important part of masculine identity to own cattle, and people looked down upon men who cultivated the land. The district commissioner of

[79] Interview 11, Ngelani, July 16, 2004.　　[80] Interview 2, Ngelani, July 8, 2004.
[81] Farnsworth, *Kamba Grammar*, 136–138.

Machakos noted as early as 1926 that young men considered anything
related to agriculture "women's work," and refused to do it.[82] Some
informants also use these notions to describe why Kamba did not respect
Kikuyu during the early part of the twentieth century; back then, they
explain, several thousand Kikuyu worked as agricultural laborers in
Ukambani. One informant said that Kamba never respected Kikuyu
because they did not possess cattle, and instead did "women's work."[83]
Thus during the destocking process, gendered lines were evident between
male and female occupations: While women gave their names to British
officials as Isyo wa Mũũnda, men did the same, but called themselves
Kasaũ wa Ng'ombe – "calf of the cow."[84]

MARTIAL MEN

As the youth fought for change, their attacks were aimed at two targets.
The first was chiefs and headmen, elders, and LNC councillors, most of
whom had failed to capably lead their communities. The second was the
British administration in Kenya, which had implemented the hated
destocking program and land policies. Young UMA leaders – all of whom
were past or present soldiers or policemen – first used the status they
possessed as brave men to gain followers, evoking a long tradition of
honor for such men in their villages. They then broadened their attacks,
and flung the Kamba martial reputation at the government, knowing the
threat it implied with war in Europe around the corner.

UMA challenges to the authority of their purported leaders surfaced as
soon as destocking commenced. Many "senior" men owned large herds of
cattle, had assisted with the organization of cattle quotas, and were then
often unofficially "exempted" from destocking culls through their own
machinations. UMA leaders specifically attacked them in their petitions
and letters, and rejected the possibility that such men could lead them.[85]
At a baraza held by the district commissioner of Machakos on June 29,
1938, Muindi and his colleagues exhorted people to ignore the instructions of their elders.[86] Six weeks later, the UMA organized its own
large, illegal baraza at Tala market, two weeks before Brooke-Popham

[82] KNA, DC/MKS.1/1/15, Machakos District Annual Report, 1926.
[83] Interview 3, Ngelani, July 9, 2004.   [84] Interview 7, Ngelani, July 13, 2004.
[85] KNA, PC/CP.13/4/1, UMA to Brooke-Popham, September 11, 1939; TNA, CO 533/492/
21, Petition of Samuel Muindi, August 25, 1938.
[86] TNA, CO 533/492/1, Criminal Case No. 104 of 1938: *Rex vs. Samuel Mwindi* [sic],
Evidence of A. N. Bailward.

was due to arrive. After the meeting – with anti-government fervor high –
a mob forced a chief called Josiah and another government employee to
close several shops they owned. Women actually seized Josiah and pulled
his shoes off.[87] The next day a district officer named Captain Grant – who
in an odd twist of fate lost his life eight years later when he tried to
confiscate a bullock from a young, armed Maasai – came to Tala to arrest
the perpetrators of the actions against Josiah. Another mob gathered and
forcibly freed the men Grant had arrested. Josiah's life was saved only
when Grant whisked him away to Machakos in a Land Rover, out of
reach of the baying crowd.[88]

A week later, the atmosphere of the orderly march to Nairobi was
again thrown into sharp relief. Muindi called another illegal baraza,
which 3,000 people attended. There, he had assembled two elderly men
from Kangundo, two from Iveti, two from Matungulu, and two from
Mwala – the four locations of northern Machakos – for the purpose of
cursing those who worked for the government. When Grant arrived at the
baraza, the elders cursed his translator, Ndambuki wa Matolo. Matolo
described the incident in court the following month: "They did not like
me as I had come to upset their meeting. Samuel [Muindi] said, 'curses on
them. May their huts be burnt and their food be spoilt and also their
children and cattle.'" Muindi's chosen elders continued to publicly curse
other chiefs and headmen. One soil conservation headman named Uku
removed his government-issued badge and returned it to a district official
in fear. The men responsible for the curses refused to remove them days
later at the personal request of the district commissioner.[89]

The chiefs, headmen, and at least some proportion of elders no longer
fulfilled their roles as mediators, balancing the requirements of the colonial
government with those of the people. Colin Newbury characterizes the
relationship between a chief and his people as one between a "patron" and
"client" – and now it had slipped into a framework where persons with
authority functioned as simple "collaborators," foregoing the interests
of their people for personal benefit.[90] One observer recalled, "Those …
who had refused to go to Nairobi – when the others returned, they
were socially excluded by people. People refused them."[91]

[87] JNP, Interview with Kavula Muli, Matungulu, December 12, 1973.
[88] KNA, DC/MKS/1/1/27, Machakos District Annual Report, 1938.
[89] TNA, CO 533/492/1, Criminal Case No. 104 of 1938: *Rex vs. Samuel Mwindi* [sic],
Evidence of Ndambuki wa Matolo.
[90] Newbury, *Patrons.*   [91] Interview 7, Ngelani, July 13, 2004.

These government employees had enriched themselves at others' expense, and gained wealth solely through their abilities to gather resources and obey the government's bidding. They stood in stark contrast to the young UMA leaders, who had demonstrated bravery in conflict, traveled widely, were highly educated, and were respected for these attributes. All UMA leaders were former police or soldiers: Kavula Muli had served in the police, and Isaac Mwalonzi and Petro Maingi – another leader later arrested – in the KAR (which Kioko later joined). Muindi had served in the Kenya Police for four years. As Newman notes, "The fact that he was a policeman is well known by people in the area he came from who attributed his bravery to this."[92]

One of the central figures in the protest was a sergeant major in the KAR called Nduba Mwatu, who had gained his rank in the First World War, and had also worked as a policeman (sergeant major was the highest rank attainable by an African). On a list of "non-cooperators and agitators," he was second only to Muindi.[93] Mwatu recognized the importance that UMA leaders show "bravery" in their interactions with the government. "[You] should not try and run away," he advised them, evoking a long history of warriors and askaris who were honored for their courage in dangerous situations. In this way, UMA leaders claimed the moral authority to lead their people, and guard their interests: These sorts of claims would certainly have resonated powerfully with a large proportion of villagers.

Mwatu himself was one of the first to protest the destocking. Soldiers had removed some of his cattle, a fact he only discovered when he returned home on leave from the army. He had complained vociferously. It was Mwatu who was responsible for directing the marchers to Nairobi across the Athi Plains instead of along the main road, where the police could have easily stopped them.[94] The fact that he was a sergeant major was cause for great concern among officials due to the influence he wielded; as one noted, "[H]is position as Sgt. Major gave him *heshima* [honor or respect] with the people."[95] Mwatu's influence was central in instigating widespread anger in the KAR and police about destocking. Many had sided with the UMA in 1938, their livelihoods also under

[92] Newman, *Ukamba Members Association*, 5.
[93] KNA, DC/MKS.4/9, Machakos District Political Record Book, Vol. VII (1930–1938), Enclosure: "Destocking: Notable Non-Cooperators and Agitators," November 15, 1938.
[94] JNP, Interview with Nduba Mwatu, Ngelani, August 31, 1974.
[95] KNA, DC/MKS.4/9, Machakos District Political Record Book, Vol. VII (1930–1938), Enclosure: "Destocking: Notable Non-Cooperators and Agitators," November 15, 1938.

threat from the cattle removal. The KAR had held meetings to collect money for the UMA in Nairobi and Mombasa, and the Tribal Police were "openly sympathetic" to the cause.[96]

The threat carried by these young soldiers and policemen was cause for great concern among British officials and administrators. For the destocking protest and resultant opposition to terracing and other government programs came at a crucial moment. The Italian forces of Benito Mussolini had invaded Abyssinia in 1935, defeating Haile Selassie's men with poisoned gas and armored cars, and bringing a new, foreign military presence to East Africa. In Europe, British politicians and civilians alike were nervous of Adolf Hitler's powerful Third Reich. With such enemies on the horizon, the service of every African soldier would be vital. This was especially true of the Kamba who, by 1938, were considered the premier martial race of East Africa. Kamba soldiers comprised 23.2 percent of KAR units, more than any other ethnic group, and 25.2 percent of the Kenya Police, with the Luo the next most numerous at 11.2 percent.[97] British concern – bordering on paranoia – was made abundantly clear in 1940, when the UMA leaders were tried in court. Prosecutors demonstrated an obsession with the possibility that some Kamba soldiers and police had taken an "anti-government" oath, and had links with German or Italian agents.[98]

UMA leaders framed their protest against British policies in terms of Kamba military service, fully aware of the strong hand they held. They played on their reputation as a "loyal" people and members of a martial race to warn of potential consequences if their demands were not met. In a letter to the colonial secretary, Elijah Kavulu wrote, "Unless you bring him [Muindi] back no co-operation can be expected between Wakamba and the District Administration ... We recall ... the great war of 1914–18 ... our blood was shed for this Government." After further detailing the past military service Kamba had undertaken, Kavulu looked forward and offered a warning: "We cannot think how Govt will get Wakamba ready if the war occurs once more."[99]

[96] KNA, DC/MKS/10B/6/1, "Collection of Intelligence: Kenya," January 24, 1938.

[97] Kenya, *Kenya Police Annual Report, 1938*, 3; Parsons, *African Rank-and-File*, 68.

[98] TNA, CO 533/523/6, Transcript of Evidence taken at Sittings of the Advisory Committee, July 17 and 18, 1940. For a fuller description of the trial – including details like the "well thumbed phrase book of English into German obviously much used," and "short sketch of the life of Adolf Hitler" – see Osborne, "Changing Kamba," 118–119.

[99] TNA, CO 533/506/4, Kavulu to Macdonald, April 4, 1939.

The UMA also used tactics that were less directly threatening. Most petitions recalled the military support Kamba had offered Britain to try to sway the government's decisions. They expressly noted Kamba "loyalty," a term British propagandists would later use to try to dissuade Kamba from joining Mau Mau during the 1950s. One petition of 1940 stated: "[W]e never thought that we should curse our Government or oppose [it] . . . We think that in the whole country of Kenya there is no other tribe which does the service for their King in the Kings African Rifles or Kenya Police in great number as Akamba tribe [*sic*]."[100]

Similarly, when UMA leaders defended themselves in court in 1940, they cited Kamba military service to aid their defense. They pointed out that Kamba had always proved themselves loyal subjects. Kavula Muli asked Louis Leakey – who was translating – rhetorically, "Did we do anything in the last war?" Isaac Mwalonzi and others raised the issue of the war fund, a voluntary account into which people could make donations to aid the war effort, noting that the UMA had made significant contributions.[101]

THE MOMBASA STRIKES

The UMA is often remembered as an organization that appeared with some fanfare in 1938, and then disappeared without trace after the destocking incident, subsumed by the more visible and larger KCA, then Kenya African Union. But in actuality, the UMA was very active in 1939 and 1940, and its influence seems to have spread far from central Kenya to Mombasa. In his authoritative work on the Mombasa strikes of 1939, Frederick Cooper notes that almost nothing is known about how they were organized.[102] Yet the government of Kenya certainly believed the UMA played a role there. This perception gave UMA leaders (and others later) a stronger hand in exerting pressure on the administration.

A wave of strikes began in the port city in late July 1939. The workers' major grievances related to low wages and poor housing conditions. The British government was particularly concerned by these strikes, as they seemed to follow a worrying trend that began in the West Indies in 1935. London viewed Mombasa – along with Dar es Salaam, which was also in

---

[100] TNA, CO 533/518/7, Petition of UMA to Macdonald, April 17, 1940.
[101] TNA, CO 533/523/6, Transcript of Evidence taken at Sittings of the Advisory Committee, July 30 and 31, 1940.
[102] Cooper, *African Waterfront*, 48–50.

the grip of strikes – as a port that would have tremendous tactical and logistical significance in the war, and its smooth functioning was essential. The failure of the 1938 Munich Agreement – in which Germany would make no further territorial acquisitions in Europe, in exchange for the Sudetenland – was guaranteed by the invasion of Czechoslovakia in March 1939. Thus though Britain was still months away from an official declaration of war, it was clear that "appeasement" had failed. Britain was preparing for the worst.

There were approximately 2,000 Kamba among the "upcountry" workers in Mombasa at the time, who periodically came to the port to work on short contracts lasting several months (the number was not high compared to other groups: 5,000 to 6,000 Luo, for instance, lived there). But the numbers did not reflect the Kamba impact; the official government report on the strikes drew particular attention to their role. It noted, "[It] is very significant that the strike[s] ... coincided closely with ... political agitation in the Teita[103] Reserve, proved to have been fostered by the Kikuyu Central Association. Teita and Kamba labourers employed by the Municipality were among the first to go on strike." The KCA, UMA, and Teita Hills Association – all of which were soon proscribed together – were closely linked during the destocking episode of 1938, as well as the disturbances that followed that year and in 1939. The author of the report also believed that railway workers were heavily involved in organizing the strikes, which included a large proportion of Kamba, who were believed to have the technical aptitude for such work. Even once the strikes were over, trouble continued (although at a lower level) in 1940. Again, an official noted that, "In cases where numbers of natives have given trouble they have generally been Wakamba."[104] As late as 1947, following another strike, suspicions were raised that the UMA might have played a part.[105]

The Special Branch and Criminal Investigation Department (CID) had carefully tracked the activities of African political parties in the months before the strikes. At that time, Brooke-Popham wrote to Macdonald in the Colonial Office. He noted that, "[T]he African agitator is guided by certain Indians who, profiting by experience in their own country, are expert in propaganda and agitation generally." Brooke-Popham's words

---

[103] During the colonial era "Taita" was typically rendered "Teita."
[104] Kenya, *Labour Conditions in Mombasa*; KNA, DC/MSA/1/4, Labour Department Annual Report, 1940 (Enclosure in Mombasa District Annual Report, 1940).
[105] TNA, CO 533/543/2, Mitchell to Creech Jones, January 20, 1947.

gained a ring of truth two weeks later when the connection between Ukambani and Mombasa became apparent.[106]

That connection was likely through a Punjabi Indian named Isher Dass. Dass had arrived in Kenya in 1927, and immediately began working as secretary of the East African Indian National Congress (EAINC). Dass – a powerful speaker and Marxist – quickly established himself as a thorn in the side of the colonial government. Until 1933, Dass was the leading advocate for non-cooperation between the Indian community and government, before he entered the Legislative Council in 1934. There, he became the de facto spokesman for Indian and African grievances.

Dass had travelled to London with Kenyatta in 1929 to promote African interests, and was a staunch advocate for Africans during the KLC. His style of representation led one scholar to describe him as "young, bold, outspoken, rash and stubborn," as a "violent communist," "evil genius," and "effective and copious speaker of the tub-thumping variety."[107] Thus when the UMA began its resistance to the government in 1938, it found him a willing ally. In 1938, Dass helped mediate between the protestors and colonial government in Nairobi during the "sit-in," and pressed the Kamba case variously to the provincial commissioner of Ukamba Province, chief native commissioner, and chief of police. He helped Muindi write a letter of protest to Brooke-Popham, and indeed delivered it to the governor himself. He stirred up trouble following Muindi's arrest, something he tried to have overturned on several occasions.[108] Perhaps his greatest contribution came on August 17, when he read aloud Muindi's petition in the Legislative Council chamber, as part of a long, impassioned speech in the defense of the Kamba position.[109]

Nor was Dass the only Indian advocate for the UMA. The EAINC passed a resolution officially confirming its support for the Kamba, and backed their cause in the press.[110] The UMA received legal representation from an Indian called Madan (most likely Chunilal Madan, the future chief justice), and another called Amin, who brought lamps, wood, and

---

[106] TNA, CO 533/506/7, Brooke-Popham to Macdonald, July 26, 1939.

[107] Gregory, *Quest*, 41–43.

[108] On Muindi's arrest see, for instance, Kenya, *Legislative Council Debates*, Vol. 7, 1st session, June 6, 1939, 322–323.

[109] Kenya, *Legislative Council Debates*, Vol. 5, 2nd session, August 17, 1938, 226–242.

[110] KNA, Papers of the East African Indian National Congress, Reel 8, Honorary Secretary of the East African Indian National Congress to Governor, August 15, 1938.

charcoal to the Kamba protest camp in Nairobi.[111] It is important to note that cooperation between members of Kenya's Indian community and African groups in central Kenya was nothing new: Harry Thuku had a close political alliance with Indians during the early 1920s, most prominently Manilal Desai. Dass's relationship with the UMA in 1939 was likely similar to that between Desai and Thuku's EAA in the early 1920s.

By early 1939, the Indian-run Labour Trade Union of East Africa (LTUEA) – founded three years earlier by Makhan Singh – was working closely with the UMA and KCA. It strongly backed the strikers in Mombasa in July and August, holding meetings in support of them. While some scholars (and indeed the principal labour officer in Nairobi, Percy de Vere Allen) suggest that the LTUEA organized the strikes, Singh himself does not, simply stating that it supported them.[112] It is unclear whether Dass was a member of the LTUEA, but he was a long-time supporter of African and indeed workers' rights, from at least 1931 in Kenya. In addition to assisting the UMA, he had supported African rights following the KLC; assisted Jesse Kariuki on a political expedition to Nyanza; and warned the government that it could not ignore the voice of Africans for long without difficulty. He also gave several speeches in support of the LTUEA.[113] Given his background and character, it is distinctly likely that Dass was connected to the labor agitation in Mombasa in August 1939.

At the same time, Dass paid several visits to Machakos. The superintendent of the Special Branch and CID noted that, "He [Dass] was seen proceeding towards Machakos at the time of the Mombasa strike. His conversation en route gave the impression that he desired to interest the Akamba in the prevailing labour unrest."[114] Once the Second World War began the following month, however, Dass made an abrupt about-turn; he changed his position to one in support of the government, taking the post of director of Indian manpower. Any connection to the strikes and Kamba involvement disappeared with his murder by three Sikhs three years later. Thus tantalizing evidence exists that connects the KCA, the UMA, and the mysterious origins of the crucial Mombasa strikes, yet no

---

[111] JNP, Interview with Isaac Mwalonzi, Ngelani, January 17, 1974. This was possibly Shivbhai Amin, a lawyer and Gujarati Muslim, who became president of the EAINC in 1946.
[112] KNA, AG/8/119, Evidence of Percy de Vere Allen, September 18, 1939.
[113] Mangat, *History*, 168–171; Singh, *History*, 66–95.
[114] KNA, DC/MKS/10B/15/1, Report of the Superintendent, Special Branch and Criminal Investigation Department, "Re: Akamba Activities," August 1939.

conclusive proof; however, the fact that the government believed such a connection existed was the most important factor in its assessment.[115]

CONCLUSION

The march to Nairobi was a unique event in Britain's African colonies. It was the only instance where men, women, and children from one ethnic group united to issue a successful challenge to British rule in non-violent fashion. Yet the episode was always more than a disagreement over cattle, and only ostensibly "anti-colonial." It was, in actuality, a contest that highlighted tensions in Ukambani's communities over existing systems of authority and questions of respect and honor, which pulled in old and young, male and female, and Christian and non-Christian.

That the Kamba were a "loyal" and "martial" people was cause for immense concern among British officials with war imminent, especially as protest continued into 1939 and spread as far as Mombasa. Young leaders used the Kamba history of martial service as a tool to pressure the government and try to sway its decision making, as they did to claim authority in their own battle against chiefs, headmen, and elders at home (something that continued for the remainder of the colonial period). In this process, the young men were outlining a version of Kamba ethnic identity based on the notion of martial honor.

By the late 1940s, the chiefs, headmen, and councillors of old were gone, dismissed by the voting populace of Ukambani whenever possible. They were replaced by a cadre of young, former soldiers, almost all of whom were Christian and educated.

[115] The colonial government was also concerned that Dass had "befriended" prominent African Americans, including Ralph Bunche. Horne, *Mau Mau in Harlem?*, 63.

Chapter 5

War and demobilization

People were woken up by KAR, and they knew now that they should do business and educate their children. Their eyes were opened.[1]

> God save our gracious Queen,
> Long live our noble Queen,
> God save the Queen!
> Send her victorious,
> Happy and glorious,
> Long to reign over us;
> God save the Queen!

The tiny village of Kathaana – near Mitaboni – felt like an odd location to witness a loud, powerful rendition of the British national anthem, but that did not stop the aging KAR veteran. Arms rigid by his sides, chest pumping, and bellowing in a voice that would have pleased the Duke of Wellington, the former sergeant proudly demonstrated his pride in fighting for Britain during the Second World War.[2] The sergeant's sentiments are not unusual among war veterans in Ukambani. They describe their loyalty to the Union Jack, and fond memories of their time in uniform.

But contemporary memories are at odds with the askaris' reactions when they returned to the reserves after the war. British officials hoped that the men would quietly go back to their farms to till the soil and tend their cattle, but they had no such desires. The askaris had seen far corners of the world; fought with and killed European troops; attacked Japanese

---

[1] Interview 12, Ngelani, July 17, 2004.　　[2] Interview 19, Mitaboni, July 24, 2004.

jungle positions; learned how to read and write; and been exposed to a host of new political ideas. They formed organizations to represent their interests, and acted to set themselves firmly at the center of their communities.

On one level, the veterans were frustrated with the colonial administration: They believed British officials had failed to adequately compensate them for the sacrifices they had made during the war. But their crosshairs were even more firmly fixed on the existing chiefs, headmen, and councillors, whose "easy tyranny" had caused untold stresses and problems in the villages of Ukambani over the previous twenty years. The younger, educated, former askaris emphatically rejected the corrupt old guard, and instituted a strikingly successful transfer of power, taking over their positions. Their victory was impressive; a range of young firebrands in other regions of the colony attempted to force similar transitions, but none had the same degree of success.

The war years – and those that followed – saw for the first time the development of a widespread sense of ethnic identification in Ukambani. It was inspired in large part by the men from all over Machakos and Kitui who came together in army camps abroad, where they lived and socialized together. They spoke and wrote in Kikamba, sang about Kamba bravery, cited "tribe" to explain their exploits, and received praise from British officers based on their ethnic reputation. When they returned to the villages, these veterans had great influence in inspiring people to think of themselves as "Kamba," and as possessing a shared history based around martial service that stretched back to the nineteenth century and beyond.

The veterans' efforts to create the history of the tribe in this fashion were possible due to the levels of respect and authority they had garnered in their communities based on their wartime service. When they returned home, the veterans were lauded as heroes, particularly because they had sent remittances to support their families during the difficult war years. By undertaking a dangerous occupation that required specialized martial skill, bravery, knowledge of the wider world, and for the benefit of those at home, they had demonstrated virtues that had a longer history in many communities in Ukambani. This is why their efforts to create the Kamba tribe in this form were successful: They *resonated* with many people living in the region.

Veterans quickly realized, too, that they had won a position of strength from which they could successfully exert pressure upon the colonial administration. They were aware of the power implicit in the Kamba martial reputation, and pressed the administration for educational facilities, new markets, permits to run businesses, and drivers' licenses, based on their loyal service. They neatly equated "Kambaness" with soldiering (something that was clearly gendered), aware that – in Lonsdale's words – "External ethnicity was the form of the politics of access to the state."[3] In this, they were successful into the 1950s, when women – in particular – came to challenge their assertions.

[handwritten marginalia: Ethnicity as access to the state]

RECRUITMENT AND SERVICE

During the final weeks of 1940, Arthur Creech Jones – a member of Parliament in Britain, "friend" to the UMA, and constant source of annoyance to the Conservative Colonial Office – submitted a written question to the undersecretary of state for the colonies, George Hall. He asked what facilities (such as pensions or health services) the government planned to provide for "conscripted natives" from Kenya who performed military service for Britain during the war. Hall brushed off the question, responding that there were no such plans. As he explained, "[N]o provision for pensions is proposed, since it is expected that the work should be done in back areas and for short periods only."[4] As in the First World War, however, African soldiers quickly proved invaluable; moreover, the definition of "back areas" was severely stretched in the following years, as African soldiers in the KAR saw service in Abyssinia, Madagascar, and Burma, and were based temporarily in India, Ceylon (Sri Lanka), and Mauritius.[5]

By the time Creech Jones wrote to Hall, the KAR was already involved in the defense of northern Kenya from Italian incursions. With this threat, and in particular the potential for attacks on the Sudan, Britain needed African manpower. The War Cabinet initially believed that the majority of Africans would provide non-combatant support. This support would come in two forms: first, providing logistical assistance for regular military units in Africa, and second, as labor in the colonies. The latter assignment would ensure high levels of production in industries deemed important for the war effort. While products like flax, maize, and sisal had clearly applicable uses in war, other products such as coffee and pyrethrum

---

[3] Lonsdale, "Moral Economy," 330.
[4] Great Britain, *House of Commons Debates*, Vol. 367, Col. 1240, December 18, 1940.
[5] For more details on the operations carried out by the KAR, see Moyse-Bartlett, *King's African Rifles*.

(a plant that produces a natural insecticide) brought in essential foreign exchange.[6] By the end of 1942, over 12,000 Africans in Kenya served in this fashion, and the number rose to 18,000 by the end of 1944.[7]

But as the war stretched Allied resources, the War Cabinet's carefully laid plans fell by the wayside, and African soldiers were required to participate in fighting both on and off the continent. The main force in East Africa was the KAR, which expanded from 6 to 43 battalions. Britain called up more than 300,000 men from East Africa for military service, which included close to 100,000 from Kenya. The KAR was supported by the East Africa Pioneers, plus a variety of other forces including the East Africa Army Medical Corps (EAAMC), East Africa Army Service Corps (EAASC), East Africa Military Labour Service (EAMLS), and Signals.[8]

As the war began, British officials quickly moved to recruit Kamba soldiers. In 1938, the KAR counted only 1,087 in its ranks, 23.2 percent of whom were Kamba, and 25.1 percent Kalenjin. By 1942, however – following the expansion – the number of Kamba rose to 1,713 out of 5,636, or 30.4 percent of the total (followed by the Luo at 23.8 percent). By 1945, combining figures for the KAR together with other military units, 14,389 Kamba were in military service, providing 20.2 percent of Kenya's recruits overall. Though a slightly higher number of Luo than Kamba served, this was a reflection of the fact that the Kamba population was significantly lower than the Luo. In 1945, 19.4 percent of all Kamba "able-bodied males" were in military service; the Luo followed a distant second with 16.6 percent.[9]

The Kenya Police was also important in the war effort, and was involved from the conflict's earliest days in the defense of northern Kenya. The size of the police force more than doubled between 1938 and 1945, increasing from 1,906 to 4,525: 25.2 percent of the police were Kamba (1,144 men), followed by the Luo at 13 percent.[10] Recruiting officers' desire to sign up Kamba as police and soldiers led the officer-in-charge of the Jinja Training Centre – the main KAR training complex, in Uganda – to point out that the supply of Kamba men was "not inexhaustible."[11]

---

[6] Great Britain, *Colonial Office Annual Report, 1946*, 3.

[7] Killingray, "Labour Mobilisation," 84.

[8] Parsons, *African Rank-and-File*, 25–35. For a wide-ranging analysis of the colonies' participation in twentieth-century British wars, see Jackson, *Distant Drums*.

[9] Parsons, *African Rank-and-File*, 65–79.

[10] Kenya, *Kenya Police Annual Report, 1945*, 3.

[11] KNA, ARC (MD) 4/5/136, Fox to PC Rift Valley, December 14, 1940.

This was perhaps a frustrated reaction to exhortations such as "Please do not repeat not reduce Kamba draft," a request received there in October 1940.[12]

In addition to serving in the KAR and police, the Kamba comprised 46.3 percent of the Signals (followed by the "KEM" – Kikuyu, Embu, and Meru – at 19.3 percent).[13] From the time of Ukambani's earliest administrators, Kamba had earned the reputation as being a "technically minded" people.[14] Such was the degree to which administrators believed this stereotype that in the 1920s – when other ethnic groups received more formal education – they emphasized technical training in Ukambani. The Machakos School was the only technical school in Kenya, and in the 1920s and 1930s ran classes such as telephone and telegraph operation, rather than those of a more standard academic nature.[15] Thus with the outbreak of war, officers descended upon the Machakos School to recruit its senior students. Stephen Savono Maveke's experience was representative of this: In his final years at the school, Maveke had received training in semaphore, Morse code, and radio operation. Along with his classmates, he was also a scout, and this was the medium through which he received a great deal of his instruction. British officers visited the school during his final year in 1939, and recruited him for the Signals. Maveke finally left the military in 1947, having served in Somaliland and Abyssinia, reaching as far as Asmara, the capital of Eritrea.[16]

In order to meet its large manpower needs, Britain pressed hard to find volunteers for service, but still required conscript labor, though not at the level of the First World War. Conscript labor was especially prominent in the EAMLS, the Second World War's version of the Carrier Corps whose work – though not as back-breaking and poorly paid, due to the presence of vehicles – was nevertheless hard. Initially, chiefs gathered informal quotas of men at the request of district officials, but in Kenya – from October 1940 onward – the government imposed Compulsory Service Regulations to formalize the system and provide the legal backing for conscription. Conscript labor was also commonly used for industries in the colonies deemed vital for the war effort. Officials procured this through the Defence (African Labour for Essential

---

[12] KNA, ARC (MD) 4/5/136, KAR Depot to Jinja Training Centre, October 13, 1940.
[13] Parsons, *African Rank-and-File*, 71.
[14] See, for instance, Hobley, *From Chartered Company*, 163.
[15] Munro, *Colonial Rule*, 159–161.
[16] Interview with Stephen Savono Maveke, Tala, November 14, 2006.

Undertakings) regulations in 1942, which created an Essential Undertakings Board with the ability to determine which industries were entitled to this labor.[17] Settlers owned the majority of businesses that served these industries, thus causing concern in government that they might take advantage of African workers.

In Ukambani, however, conscription was rare, and it is only in parts of northern Machakos where veterans recall being forced to serve. This was, of course, the area in which men and women resisted the colonial administration between 1938 and 1940 (the government maintained a levy force in Iveti until 1941).[18] One European settler called A. A. Slatter, an assistant inspector in the Kenya Police who lived in Ngelani, was involved in putting down the destocking protest, and had a role in recruiting Kamba for the war. One veteran recalled, "There were Kambas who had refused to go to war, who didn't want to die ... you were going to death [in the war]. When we refused, he [Slatter] beat us so hard. Oh no, we said, we better go to the war rather than dying here." Men and women in northern Machakos nicknamed Slatter *King-ethũ* – "the destructive one."[19]

There were several reasons for the lack of conscription in Ukambani. First, men had great incentives to join up, and few therefore required coercion. Second, and connected to this fact, was that as members of a martial race with technical know-how, Kamba were typically assigned to the KAR, Signals, or EAASC. These were prestigious and better-paid jobs for which men volunteered and conscription was unnecessary. Finally, from a military perspective, conscripting men who comprised the majority of Kenya's soldiers would have been a bad decision, especially as some amount of protest from the UMA continued into 1940, and the memory of destocking was so fresh.

A web of interlinked financial issues explain in part why men voluntarily enlisted to join the forces. As described in Chapter 4, financial security was becoming more and more difficult to achieve as a result of land pressure, especially in northern Machakos and central Kitui. The amount of land in the reserves had barely changed between the time they were initially gazetted (a process finalized in 1910) and the Second World War. Yet during that period, the population had risen by a factor of approximately two-and-a-half: In 1911, the population of Machakos

[17] Killingray, "Labour Mobilisation," 71–90.
[18] KNA, DC/MKS/1/1/28, Machakos District Annual Report, 1941.
[19] Interview 4, Mutituni, July 9, 2004; Interview 28, Mbooni, July 25, 2005.

(including Kikumbulyu) was 135,714 and Kitui, 86,649; the census of 1948 counted 356,545 in Machakos and 210,788 in Kitui.[20] Officials had also implemented stricter and stricter regulation on overflow grazing for cattle, further tightening the system, and the rains failed several times during the war period, adding further difficulties.

Young men were entirely dependent on their fathers and relatives for the cattle that would enable them to marry, and many families simply could not afford to spare these animals, particularly those with several sons. In some areas, elders and chiefs informed youth that they could not actually *own* cattle, and that all the beasts, according to Kamba "custom," belonged to their fathers.[21] An apparent increase in levels of brideprice was also evident in many parts of the reserves. This meant that many young men joined the army to earn enough money to return home and marry – and thereby attain full adulthood – at which point dependence on their families would be lessened. (These desires, indeed, were shared by youth in many areas of the colony.[22]) Even for those who were already married, it became so difficult to maintain a family in such conditions that husbands joined the forces. One pastor explained, "I discovered [due to lack of money] that I could not keep a wife, and in 1942 we had our first child. So I decided to enter the army."[23] Military service provided a salary that was almost impossible to achieve in the regular labor market, for the first time in the colonial period. While men in the EAMLS received low wages, the jobs that Kamba could procure were well paid. In 1941, for instance, a corporal in the EAMLS received 32 Sh (shillings) per month, whereas a man of the same rank in the KAR earned 48 Sh; in Signals, 55 Sh; and in the EAASC, 90 Sh per month.[24]

For young men, the ability to earn higher wages – and buy cattle with those wages – would provide a rise in social status and prestige on their return home. Many men believed that they might easily attract girls and potential wives through their service, and the idea of traveling to a foreign country and serving in the army was attractive for the adventurous youth. Many former soldiers recall the impression that a brand new uniform with shiny buttons created amongst onlookers. One said, "When those

[20] Kenya, *African Population*, 3; KNA, DC/KTI/1/1.1, Kitui District Annual Report, 1910–1911; KNA, DC/MKS.1/1/2, Machakos District Annual Report, 1910–1911.
[21] KNA, DC/KTI/7/5, "Visit of Akamba Chiefs to Gilgil," September 3, 1942.
[22] Waller, "Rebellious Youth," especially 87–92.
[23] Interview 73, Mulango, December 1, 2006.
[24] Parsons, *African Rank-and-File*, 88–89.

who were in the army came on leave, everyone saw their boots and raincoats and wanted to join!"[25] The boots, in particular, were a mark of status in communities where many went barefoot, or wore roughly hewn shoes. Another man who did not join the KAR remembered, "I personally loved the job of KAR, because the soldiers were clean. When they paraded, we used to think KAR was a good job ... it appeared a beautiful thing, which was praised, especially the uniforms they used to wear."[26] Memories of poor clothing and a lack of footwear – as had existed in the First World War – were quickly forgotten: This was a new war where those who fought received far better food and equipment. Their living conditions, indeed, were often far better than those for people who remained in the reserves.

Among the youth, there was a palpable sense of excitement about joining the army. The younger generation now had a chance to prove itself in a way that previous generations had, and earn the rewards that came from such service. Thus the district commissioner of Machakos was delighted to write that, "In spite of anti-Government agitation on the part of the Association [the UMA] ... thousands of Akamba clamoured to join the military forces on the outbreak of war in September [1939] ... whole battalions ... could still be secured here at any time."[27]

WAR AND "TRIBE"

During the preceding decades, various groups ranging from chiefs to the youthful leaders of the UMA had claimed to represent "the Kamba." Their efforts were attempts to utilize the weight conveyed by the notion of tribe to win or cement positions of authority. In acting in this fashion, these groups represented a world in which ethnicity was the primary method of self-identification, fully aware that it was the most advantageous way to negotiate with the colonial state, and hopefully make gains in their home communities.

These men, however, shared little in common with the majority of men and women living in central and eastern Kenya. The beekeeper from Ngomeni or cattle-herder from Mbitini little thought of the world around him or herself in such broad terms, and local systems of organization still guided everyday life. But the experience of serving in the Second World War was one of several catalysts that produced a sea change in the

[25] Interview 13, Mutituni, July 17, 2004.   [26] Interview 73, Mulango, December 1, 2006.
[27] KNA, DC/MKS/1/1/27, Machakos District Annual Report, 1939.

outlook of Ukambani's residents. Ethnic distinction was heightened, and many learned a new "tribal" affiliation, forged in the highlands of Abyssinia and jungles of Burma.

On one level, this new outlook seems difficult to reconcile with the memoirs of former askaris. The two most famous accounts – written by the Bugandan sergeant major, Robert Kakembo, and soon-to-be Mau Mau general, Waruhiu Itote – both describe how African soldiers built tight bonds with one another in foreign lands, based on their common experience as *Africans*. They were united by the different treatment they received compared to British and Indian soldiers, most clearly manifested in lower pay scales. In both authors' accounts, the salience of tribe or ethnicity is minimized.[28] This approach is also reflected in the research of the foremost scholars on the African soldiery, who stress the role of the military in influencing men to view themselves primarily as members of a privileged caste, versus part of an ethnic group.[29]

But others dissent. In her wide-ranging *Ethnic Soldiers*, Cynthia Enloe notes that a variety of state and "national" militaries have attempted to break down ethnic attachments among their troops, but have struggled to do so. She argues that the military system has, in fact, often strengthened and accentuated ethnic difference.[30] In the Kenya case, O. J. E. Shiroya interviewed a variety of former askaris during his own research. His subjects claimed that the British aimed to highlight tribal differences in soldierly life, causing "ethnic animosities."[31] While it seems unlikely that British officers ever deliberately fostered ethnic tensions – surely a potential disaster for a fighting force – ethnic distinction did exist, and the military system often emphasized and accentuated it.

Battalions were never comprised of one ethnic group. In addition, no formal regulations stipulated that members of one ethnic group had to sleep and live together. Yet in many cases, the latter occurred: Faced with an unfamiliar environment, soldiers frequently spent time with men with whom they had a language and cultural background in common. The effect of war and danger likely increased the desire to make these associations. Thus when Gerald Hanley – a war correspondent and novelist

---

[28] Itote, *"Mau Mau" General*, 9–10; Kakembo, *African Soldier Speaks*, 13, 28.

[29] Brands, "Wartime Recruiting Practices"; Killingray, *Fighting for Britain*; Parsons, *African Rank-and-File*.

[30] Enloe, *Ethnic Soldiers*.

[31] Shiroya, *Kenya and World War II*, 62–63. See also Schleh, "Post-service Careers," especially 198–207.

attached to the 14th Army – asked two Kamba men who had raided a Japanese position whether they were tired, they explained their exploits in ethnic terms: "No, *effendi* [sir/master]. We are not tired. We are Wakambas."[32]

Military leisure time was especially related to ethnic definition. One of the most popular events during the month was the *ngoma* (dance), usually held at the weekend. British officers recall that the *ngoma* frequently became a competition between different ethnic groups as to which could dance better. Patrick Barnes, based in Lusaka during the war, remembered, "Once a month there was a 'dance night' and I was expected to stand my company a brew of rice wine." He continued to note that for the dances, the soldiers always separated into tribal groups, in this case three: the Ngoni, Yao, and Nguru.[33] Another pointed out that "each tribe held its own dance and they would go on tirelessly stamping and posturing all night."[34] Decades later, officers could remember which ethnic groups' dances were slow, and which faster and more active. Major William Cockcraft said, "The Luos ... used to do a very sedate kind of dance rather like a waltz, and the Acholis always used to laugh at this because theirs was a very sort of warlike kind of dance."[35] Thus when Major General Charles "Fluffy" Fowkes, the commanding officer of the 11th Division in Burma, visited his troops on New Year's Day 1944, he was "entertained by distinctly tribal football competitions and displays of Akamba dancing."[36]

Another important leisure pursuit was writing letters to family back at home. Only a small minority of soldiers were sufficiently able writers to construct these missives, thus men from Machakos and Kitui came together to prepare letters in Kikamba, as well as to share news from the reserves. This gathering was certainly a daily occurrence: On one day in 1942, for example, district officials in Machakos had to sort through 1,514 individual letters for distribution to the villages.[37] In their letters,

[32] Hanley, *Monsoon Victory*, 62.

[33] RHL, Mss. Afr. s. 1715 (8), Papers of the King's African Rifles, University of Oxford Records Development Project, Written Memorandum of Patrick Barnes, March 28, 1981.

[34] RHL, Mss. Afr. s. 1715 (57), Papers of the King's African Rifles, University of Oxford Records Development Project, Written Memorandum of Brigadier G. H. Cree, July 16, 1979.

[35] Archives of the Imperial War Museum [hereafter IWM], Oral History 3935/1, Interview with Major William Cockcraft, September 25, 1978.

[36] Lewis, *Empire State-Building*, 192.

[37] KNA, DC/MKS/1/1/28, Machakos District Annual Report, 1942.

soldiers reflected their concern about the semi-drought conditions in Ukambani, but especially about their cattle. It was significant that the Second World War followed hard on the heels of the destocking episode of 1938. The story of the destocking and resultant protest was told and retold in army camps throughout northeastern Africa and southeast Asia. Rumors constantly circulated that a destocking would again take place now that the soldiers had left Ukambani, and many letters written by inhabitants of the reserves to serving soldiers communicated that in fact, one was occurring. The government had to publish articles in newssheets like *Askari* and *Pamoja* to dispel such rumors.[38]

The issue of language is especially important, as language is often an ethnic marker. KAR soldiers spoke "KiKAR," a "kitchen" version of Swahili. Parsons argues that having this language in common distinguished soldiers from the majority of those at home, but it seems unlikely that many Kamba soldiers of the rank-and-file ever became fluent in the language, though they could pass repetitive (and required) tests. There are several reasons for this assertion. First, Kamba were little educated compared to the other peoples of Kenya. In 1937, approximately 1,500 students attended school in Machakos (around 5 percent of school-age boys), and fewer than 1,000 in Kitui. They therefore had little academic background to help them pick up the Swahili-based KiKAR.[39] That few Kamba spoke Swahili or English when they arrived for service is supported by the testimony of British officers. As Major Haigh – who served in Abyssinia and Burma with the KAR – noted, "The Wakamba ... spoke absolutely no Swahili when they came in."[40] Second, and related, was that the education soldiers were promised via the army often never materialized, especially in the chaos of theaters of war. Thus while long-serving Kamba soldiers spoke Swahili, the majority who joined up at the beginning of the war had little chance to become competent, outside learning basic commands. Finally, most Kamba veterans from the Second World War do not speak Swahili today. Alone, this would be relatively insignificant, due to the effect of time on the memory; but combined with the evidence here, it is telling. Thus the primary medium for communication among Kamba, at

[38] KNA, DC/MKS/16/7, Thorp to East Africa Command Headquarters, March 12, 1945.
[39] School figures are calculated from attendance records given in district annual reports. KNA, DC/KTI/1/1.4, Kitui District Annual Report, 1937; DC/MKS/1/1/27, Machakos District Annual Report, 1937.
[40] RHL, Mss. Afr. s. 1715 (122), Papers of the King's African Rifles, University of Oxford Records Development Project, Major E. G. C. Haigh, Interview with William Beaver, March and April 1980.

least, was their "tribal" language, which served to reinforce difference. Some number of marching songs therefore also contained ethnic themes:

Solo: The people of Nairobi live in comfort,
           The people of Kisumu are dying of hunger,
           The people on the farms like to eat too much,
           Except the Wakamba!
Chorus: Out of the way, we are coming!
           The Kamba boys.[41]

One soldier summed up that, "If the soldiers were Luos, they would speak in the Luo language, the same with other tribes. But, when it came to matters of work, nobody was supposed to speak in another tongue. When soldiers were socializing after work, they used to share in the mother tongue."[42]

British officers emphasized ethnic lines. British KAR veterans interviewed by the Oxford Records Development Project in the late 1970s and early 1980s – whenever they responded to questions about "tribe" – were quick to allude to the fighting abilities of Kamba, frequently in contrast to the Kikuyu. One pointed out that, "Certain tribes ... were not recruited. The main one being the Wakikuyu. This tribe was suspected of being disloyal."[43] (It is important to remember, of course, that later statements such as these came after the Kikuyu-focused violence of Mau Mau during the 1950s.) Another went so far as to call the Kamba "almost a military tribe."[44] These sorts of statements precisely mirror the views of many Kamba veterans.

African chiefs also drew attention to "tribal" qualities when they visited the troops, encouraging soldiers to consider themselves part of this wider conglomerate. On several occasions, war officials brought prominent chiefs to the front lines, to speak to soldiers from their own ethnic groups, and boost morale. Thus Chief Kasina wa Ndoo visited and spoke to Kamba troops on several occasions, and Chief Amoth did the same for the Luo. Amoth, in particular, frequently raised supposedly tribal qualities to encourage his men: "When the Luo have set their hands to [a task], they do not drop until the job is finished," he told them.[45]

---

[41] Extract from "Kamba Porters' Song." Clayton, *Communication*, 50.
[42] Interview 49, Nzambani, March 13, 2011.
[43] RHL, Mss. Afr. s. 1715 (163), Papers of the King's African Rifles, University of Oxford Records Development Project, Written Memorandum of Colonel Thomas Leahy, July 24, 1979.
[44] IWM, Oral History 10257/1, Interview with Frank Wilson, July 19, 1979.
[45] KNA, ARC (MD) 4/5/37, "Visit of Government Officials and African Chiefs from the East African Territories," March 10, 1943.

Kamba in the army camps and at home drew connections between the war and the more distant past. This is especially clear in interviews today; veterans argue that military service reflected "traditional" Kamba values, for instance in the perceived similarities between Kamba dances and army parade songs. One informant recalled, "When Kambas were taken for training by Europeans, they learned very fast. Kamba traditional dances had similarities to army parade songs. The beats and rhythm were more or less the same." Others specifically recall that the most common time and location for recruitment to the army was at these dances – which recruiting officers visited to procure men – thereby linking older Kamba practices with this more modern military service.[46]

These connections appear clearly through the term *mwĩna*, a word used to describe someone brave, fearless, and skilled in war, or a "sharp-shooter." A *muthiani* in the nineteenth century was often described as such because he could kill an elephant with one arrow, and had his position of prestige based in part on his shooting abilities. Informants use the same term to describe "ideal" men during the two world wars, whose skills with the bow and arrow transferred over to the rifle. As one man noted, "Kambas could not miss, whenever they shot their arrows. The techniques needed to aim a gun were the same Kambas knew from shooting their arrows." One ex-soldier proudly informed me that the Kamba were the only ones who could help the British in a time of such need. He stated that the Kamba skills in "shooting without missing" were prized at the time.[47] The returning soldiers were in the process of creating a historical narrative of the Kamba tribe that they would use to suit their own interests, a process that continues today (see below and Epilogue).

THE RETURN OF THE ASKARIS

That African soldiers might present political problems on their return to the reserves was a possibility British military officials had discussed as early as 1940. But the pressures of war meant that they had implemented few solid plans as demobilization approached. The civil director of demobilization, for instance, was only appointed in May 1945 in East Africa. Aware of their lack of preparation, officials tried to postpone the return of

[46] Interview 39, Mulala, July 26, 2005; Interview 84, Ikutha, June 22, 2009; Interview 86, Kanziku, June 23, 2009.
[47] Interview 15, Ngelani, July 21, 2004; Interview 86, Kanziku, June 23, 2009; Interview 118, Kiomo, July 1, 2009.

troops to the colonies, offering extra inducements to soldiers to remain in service, in order to gain more time to organize themselves.[48]

The bulk of demobilization took place in 1945 and 1946. On his exit from the service, each askari had an interview arranged by the principal civil dispersal officer, received his wartime gratuity, and was given a booklet detailing how he might access future training and a pension (though the latter never materialized). Officials pinned their hopes on the idea that soldiers would simply return to the reserves and continue farming, as they had before the war. The lack of preparation was visibly demonstrated in the official paperwork when officials listed the kinds of jobs demobilized soldiers might do after the war. For European soldiers, the list numbered 100 occupations, neatly arranged in alphabetical order from accountants to wardens of prisons. For African soldiers, however, the list numbered only 28 items; after the fourteenth, it devolved into a random collection of occupations thrown together in no apparent order, as its author seemingly struggled for ideas and wrote down anything that came to mind (including "Flour Machinery workers").[49]

At the commencement of demobilization, almost 15,000 Kamba were in the military. In 1945 and 1946, slightly more than 10,000 received discharges, with the final men returning in early 1947. Soldiers traveled home on free transport provided for them, continuing their journeys to the villages on lorries that happened to be passing the right way. They returned with high hopes and flush with cash. Many remember a period of celebration that ensued, as families everywhere ignored the recent poor harvests, and slaughtered animals for their returning members. The moment was a break in an otherwise difficult year.

One man I interviewed in 2006 perfectly represented the type of experiences veterans remember following the war. I met Kitung'u Ngumi in Wikililye sub-location, a small outpost several miles downhill from Kitui Town, where several churches of different denominations sit within several hundred yards of one another. I spoke with Ngumi in his "office" – a small, concrete structure behind a shopping center, with a red, padlocked door that he carefully opened and resecured after our discussion. Ngumi was in his eighties, and seemed somewhat confused as we began our conversation; but when it came to his experiences in the war, the cloud lifted and his memories were clear and precise. Ngumi had reached

---

[48] KNA, ARC (MD) 4/5/80 (22), Chief Secretary to Governor's Conference to Chief Secretary, Nairobi (Secret), June 26, 1945.

[49] Kenya, *Progress Report on Demobilization*, 1–3. See also Shiroya, *African Politics*, 1–19.

the rank of corporal, following his three years' service from 1943 to 1946, and it was testament to his abilities that he received training as a parachutist.[50]

Ngumi had sent home remittances while he was away in Ceylon and Burma, with which his brother had bought six goats and four head of cattle. In 1946, he came home, but the money soon ran out:

When I returned from the war, I came and stayed at home. I found it impossible to stay here. I sold all the cows which my brother had bought, and I drank all the money away with my brother. When the money was gone, I boarded a vehicle here and went to look for a job in Mombasa.

Now used to the cash economy and all that wages could bring, many former soldiers departed for Mombasa (if from southern Kitui) or Nairobi (if from Machakos or northern Kitui) to try to find work. Many men believed themselves "above" working on the land, which was, in any case, in short supply in many areas. Ex-soldiers point out that they were more concerned with the fact that they could not find jobs.

Like Ngumi, most initially tried to make a home in the reserves. But they found themselves frustrated; they came to feel that their commanding officers in the army had duped them by falsely promising that they would return to top jobs and great financial rewards. Many wanted to set up businesses working as lorry drivers or taxi owners, putting to use skills they had learned in the army; others wanted to establish shops and begin trading. Ngumi put it best when he looked around his shamba and, shaking his head, explained that it was, "impossible to stay here." He did not mean that there were particular economic or social problems; but as a man who had traveled far and wide, and had interacted with all manner of people, he simply could not adjust to the quiet life of the reserves, so headed east to find his fortune.

When applying for a job, a former askari had to show his certificate of service to any prospective employer. Thus when Ngumi arrived in Mombasa, he brought the all-important document with him. With trembling hands, he showed me the folded paper, which he still carries in the inside pocket of his jacket. It was quickly apparent why he was proud of the document: "In spite of his youth [he] has made an excellent NCO (non-commissioned officer)," it began. "[He] is most reliable and trustworthy and in every way recommended for civilian employment. [He] is

---

[50] Information presented here about Kitung'u Ngumi (pseudonym) is from Interview 71, Mulango, November 30, 2006.

honest and of temperate habits." The Class A Release meant that he was an attractive candidate for employers. He applied for a job at Kilindini Harbour and was immediately accepted ahead of eight other candidates. He then moved to Nairobi and easily found a job as a watchman for British American Tobacco, and later at the Kenya Development Cooperative Union.

For those who had served with distinction, it was easy to find unskilled jobs. But few Kamba askaris were well educated, and therefore lost out to Kikuyu in the race for the better-paid jobs as clerks or scribes. This was cause for great anger; Kikuyu beat out Kamba as a result of their levels of education, and the skills they had learned in the *non-fighting* units of the military, which were more applicable to civilian employment. Thus men began to feel that anything they had learned during their tenure of service was somewhat useless. Most former soldiers took jobs that did not pay as well as the army. Some reenlisted in the KAR, unable to adapt to life in the reserves.

The soldiers, therefore, were fundamentally dissatisfied, and showed their anger. In 1945 and 1946, they organized and encouraged people to resist government reconditioning measures in the Machakos reserve. People took oaths to bond themselves together, and pulled out terracing markers. In 1946, they even laid down in front of tractors sent by the government to work on their land for free. Veterans railed against the reserve boundaries that – they argued – unfairly benefited European settlers. The district commissioner was forced to refer to specific sections of the Kenya Land Commission to try to calm their anger.[51]

The livestock levy was a particular bone of contention. Much to the consternation of officials, the war had required a large amount of livestock to feed troops in East Africa. The government therefore had little choice but to impose a livestock levy in the colony. In Ukambani – coming so soon after the destocking incident – this was an issue that required careful handling. The levy was organized by officers assigned to the Livestock Control Board. Instead of forcing Africans to sell cattle for low prices as they had in 1938, however, the officers competed with other buyers (such as Kikuyu) in open sales, thereby assuring that Kamba received a fair price for their animals. The government was also careful to exempt any soldiers and police from the levy, in an effort to minimize

---

[51] KNA, DC/MKS/1/1/30, Machakos District Annual Report, 1946; KNA, DC/MKS/5/1/4, Minute 56/46, "Machakos District Boundaries and Necessity for Additional Land," July 25–27, 1946.

potential problems. The number of cattle sold in Kitui was high – 5,181 in 1944 – but in Machakos it remained low, especially as a result of famine. In 1944, the quota for required cattle sales for Machakos was set at only 400 head, compared to 4,800 in Kitui.[52]

Kamba believed that the levy should have ended with the culmination of the war, but it continued through 1946. In June, the district commissioner of Machakos toured his district, and wrote a worried letter to his provincial commissioner:

[The tour] made me uneasy ... Practically the only topic at these barazas was food – flour and the meat levy ... [the] recent cut in flour has left the people very hungry ... all the more reason to stop the meat levy ... during the coming months, there well may be some real hunger, and my impression ... is that the tribe are not going to stand for it – by which I mean that riots in some form or other will come before real hunger. Such riots might develop any time now.

The impact of former soldiers was clearly uppermost in the district commissioner's mind:

Thousands of ex-askaris have now been demobilized, after quite a lot of rosy promises have been made to them about their life after demobilization ... STOP THE MEAT LEVY ... To summarize: warning is given to you that political outbreaks may occur at any moment.[53]

Soldiers formed political groups to represent their interests and grievances, as well as to address their various social concerns, especially to do with women and the youth (see Chapter 6). Each organization tried to position itself as the foremost representative of Kamba interests. One of the most notable was the *Ikunda ya Mbaa Lili*, the "Knot of the Bond of the Lili Clan." The Ikunda was formed by soldiers serving in southeast Asia, and when they returned to the reserves, they began collecting money. The group aimed to further "Kamba solidarity," and provide welfare and education for former soldiers and their families. It gathered vast donations in the two years following the war, as soldiers had returned to the reserves wealthy. It spent the extraordinary sum of £400 to buy a 16mm film projector and a generator to provide it with power, with enough money left over to send two needy students to Fort Hare in South Africa to study. Three-quarters of the funds for the projector were garnered from the filming of *King Solomon's Mines*, H. Rider Haggard's

---

[52] KNA, DC/KTI/1/1/5, Kitui District Annual Report, 1944; KNA, DC/MKS/16/7, "Livestock Census," August 15, 1944.

[53] KNA, DC/MKS/10B/17/1, DC Machakos to PC Central Province, June 5, 1946.

epic tale of adventure featuring the dashing (but self-deprecating) Allan Quatermain, which was filmed in Iveti by Metro-Goldwyn-Mayer.[54]

The colonial administration watched the Ikunda warily, as it did the Akamba Union, which appeared at the same time. The two groups were closely linked: The general secretary of the Akamba Union was also the treasurer of the Ikunda ya Mbaa Lili.[55] Both organizations claimed that "development" and "education" were their aims, and thus the government believed it had to ostensibly encourage their existence. But intelligence experts were cautious: One high-ranking official believed that the UMA was operating behind the scenes in both cases. Another attended the first meeting of the Akamba Union, to which the district commissioner of Machakos had been invited to give a speech. All seemed to go well, but – he commented darkly – "One has ... no clear knowledge of the proceedings after ... [his] departure."[56]

The government was right to be suspicious, something that was confirmed to me by a broadly grinning Philip Muinde, one of the Akamba Union's founding members. A short, wiry man, Muinde's razor-sharp mind and quick intelligence are still abundantly in evidence today. He was one of the first boys from Ukambani to attend the prestigious Alliance High School in Kikuyuland in the 1930s, where he schooled with many of Kenya's future political elites. Muinde explained that the Akamba Union did indeed have links to the UMA, but worked even more closely with the Kenya African Union (KAU), the colony's first genuine pan-ethnic political organization. Nor, despite its statements to the contrary, was the Akamba Union willing to work hand-in-hand with the government in the careful, measured "progress" of development and education desired by the latter. Muinde – together with other highly educated Union members – established a series of independent schools without "permission," in the same manner as two generations of Kikuyu in Central Province. Though they were poorly funded and teachers little qualified, it did nothing to dampen the enthusiasm possessed by those who attended them. Muinde recounts that the role he played in this educational expansion led to his dismissal from his position of councillor in the Kitui LNC.[57]

---

[54] KNA, DC/MKS/2/1/1, Machakos District Intelligence Reports, April 1948 and December 1949.

[55] KNA, MAA/2/122, "Extract from Kenya Colony Intelligence and Security Summary," June 1945.

[56] KNA, DC/MKS/2/1/1, Machakos District Intelligence Report, April 1945.

[57] Interview with Philip Muinde, Changwithia, July 24, 2006.

The Akamba Union constantly provoked colonial ire by acting beyond its claimed interests in education and development. It quickly settled into the well-ploughed furrow initially dug by the UMA, making the land issue a cornerstone of its agenda. The Union joined forces with the KAU to send teams to Kitui to advise people about land. They explained questions of land law to illiterate farmers, and helped them hire lawyers to contest the verdicts of native tribunals.[58] Nor was the Akamba Union afraid to issue its complaints directly to the Colonial Office, as the UMA had: It described how the land Kamba possessed was insufficient, and the product of incorrectly drawn colonial boundaries in the early twentieth century. Twice, the Union mentioned that cattle – the "wealth" of the Kamba – had to be maintained.[59]

In 1946, Arthur Creech Jones – by then the undersecretary of state for the colonies – visited Kenya and had an audience with the Akamba Union. As a supporter of the UMA, he likely expected a warm welcome, but was disappointed. Union leaders stressed powerfully – perhaps even angrily – that the Kamba did not have enough land. In an effort to bolster their claim to be the representatives of "the Kamba," they presented Creech Jones with a bow and arrows, the "traditional" weapons. In a fascinating blend of the old and new, leaders asked Creech Jones to use the weapons to "shoot the Colour-Bar" – the colony's racialist organizing principle and root of their problems. The following year, with apparently little change forthcoming, Union members wrote to Creech Jones and asked him to return the weapons as he had apparently "missed" his target.[60] *what an insult*

A NEW CADRE OF LEADERS

"People were woken up by KAR, and they knew now that they should do business and educate their children. Their eyes were opened." Having concluded her explanation, Dorothy Uswii sat back on her stool and spread her hands, opening her own eyes wide to emphasize her point.[61] Her reaction was a typical response to questions about the soldiers' return home after the war. She was describing a sea change that swept

[58] KNA, DC/KTI/1/1/5, Kitui District Annual Report, 1950.
[59] TNA, CO 533/561/15, Petition of Akamba Union to Dugdale, April 1951.
[60] KNA, DC/MKS/2/1/1, Machakos District Intelligence Reports, August 1946 and November 1947.
[61] Interview 12 (pseudonym), Ngelani, July 17, 2004.

through Ukambani, led by the men of the army, who from 1946 and 1947 onward would come to express themselves through their high positions in the colony's formal power structure.

The events of the war had profoundly affected African soldiers. They had experienced new and different circumstances in almost every possible way: psychologically, geographically, and personally, and formed relationships with Americans, Europeans, Indians, South Africans, and West Africans. The war opened their eyes to the different treatment Africans received compared to other peoples. Some had begun to question the validity of colonial rule itself. The wife of Paul Ngei – the man who would become Ukambani's most powerful politician – recalled that her husband became conversant with the works of Mahatma Gandhi in Burma.[62] Another man perhaps explained it best when he said: "Soldiers began to get clever while they were away. But before they went away they hadn't known how to speak to whites [but now they did]." He meant this metaphorically, but also literally: Some had learned to speak English well after years of serving with British officers.[63]

When these men returned to the reserves they emphatically rejected the authority of the existing chiefs and headmen. Their return rang the death-knell for the majority of these men; most were poorly educated, were complicit in any number of corrupt legal or other transactions, and had failed to earn respect in their communities. As Muinde put it, "Chiefs supported the government because they liked their cushy jobs. But they were hostile to the people."[64] These chiefs stood in striking contrast to the returning soldiers. "Soldiers were very much respected because they had seen a foreign land," one lady recalled, "They had survived the war when nobody knew if they would be seen again."[65] These men had traveled far from home, and explored a world that was unknown to those they had left behind; they had served bravely in martial capacities; some had learned to read and write; many had become Christian; and all returned flush with money, which they had used to buy cattle to demonstrate their high statuses. In short, everyone – whether young or old, Christian or not, male or female – could respect these men.

The veterans had also sent remittances home to support their families while they were abroad. With the exception of 1942, either the short or

[62] Interview with Emma Muloko Paul Ngei, Kanzalu, October 23, 2006.
[63] Interview 29, Kitundu, July 13, 2005.
[64] Interview with Philip Muinde, Changwithia, July 24, 2006.
[65] Interview 109, Mwingi, June 29, 2009.

long rains had failed each year between 1939 and 1945, resulting in food
shortages. In the villages, families viewed the absent soldiers as directly
responsible for their survival. Today, it is difficult to find a wife or child
who does not express happiness that a husband or father served abroad
during the war, as many families were entirely dependent on these partial
wages to sustain themselves. The district commissioner of Machakos
noted that without these payments, "[The] Wakamba would have become
a tribe of paupers." In 1944, for instance, administrators paid out
£160,000 of remittances to families in Machakos, and people there spent
£125,000 on food.[66] As in the First World War, the exploits of these
soldiers were lauded at home; these men represented a long history of
masculine service in the communities of the region.

Various authors have described how veterans of the Second World
War rarely headed political organizations or anti-colonial movements in
the post-war era.[67] While this is largely correct, it is not to say that they
did not hold power. In Ukambani, they found themselves in positions of
tremendous strength, as they replaced incumbent chiefs, headmen, and
LNC councillors in the colony's formal power structure. By 1950, the
Ikunda ya Mbaa Lili and Akamba Union had stagnated and practically
disappeared; they had catapulted former askaris into positions of power
as chiefs and councillors, and were therefore of little more use. The
African Brotherhood Church (ABC; see Chapter 6) – with few askaris
as members – was the only organization to remain relevant outside the
colony's governing system.

This transformation in leadership was never more evident than at the
LNC elections in Machakos in 1947 (in the LNC's last year before it was
renamed the African District Council (ADC)). The LNC was comprised of
prominent community members, the majority of whom were chiefs. District officials nominated some of the councillors, but the African population voted for the majority. In 1947, not one single incumbent councillor
retained his place, with the exception of several of the nominated
members. All the newly elected men were relatively young; six were
former soldiers, and of the other three, one was the secretary of the
Akamba Union, one a schoolteacher for the AIM, and the other a clerk
at the Public Works Department in Nairobi.[68] In Kitui's LNC elections in
1946, a similar transition occurred: Four of the seventeen elected members

---

[66] KNA, DC/MKS/1/1/28, Machakos District Annual Report, 1944.
[67] Killingray, *Fighting for Britain*, 222; Parsons, *African Rank-and-File*, 260.
[68] KNA, DC/MKS/2/1/1, Machakos District Intelligence Report, February 1947.

were veterans, and here the government even banned chiefs from serving on the LNC.[69] The message was clear: Veterans were dominating the region's most powerful councils, backed by youthful, educated, and for lack of a better word, "modern" men.

But while voters had a voice in electing councillors, they had no say in the appointment of chiefs (something against which the Akamba Union protested vociferously).[70] But here, Kamba and British interests merged: The colonial administration – and indeed Colonial Office – believed soldiers were the vehicles that would drive its new agenda for Africa forward (see Chapter 6). They were the ones on whom the new policies of development and welfare would rely, who would help transform "swords into ploughshares." Officials were glad to appoint former soldiers as chiefs, and did so, for the same reason that they appointed ex-askaris as "supernumerary headmen" to assist in demobilization in 1945: They were the only ones everyone listened to.[71]

Interestingly, those long-serving councillors who were able to maintain their positions were also veterans: Chiefs Kasina wa Ndoo, Uku Mukima, and Kalavoto Seke had served during the First World War, and were both Christian and educated, and therefore acceptable to the people. Kasina, a squat, portly man who became Ukambani's most powerful chief, is a fascinating case; whenever he walked around his home area, he wore his medals, along with a military helmet. This was likely an effort to benefit from the authority a strong military career conveyed, and showed the level of respect attached to such service.[72]

The position of the incoming councillors and chiefs was therefore one of extraordinary power. In Kikuyu areas, chiefs were frequently points of contestation against the colonial regime, whereas in Ukambani, they were not. Men like Simeon Kioko and James Mwanthi had attacked the government during the destocking protest as leading lights of the UMA, but now fitted into the colony's formal power structure, with the backing of both Kamba and Briton.

This position of strength was bolstered by a weakened administration in the post-war years. The "thin white line" – a reference to the tiny

[69] KNA, DC/KTI/1/1/5, Kitui District Annual Report, 1946.
[70] TNA, CO 533/561/15, Petition of Akamba Union to Dugdale, April 1951.
[71] KNA, DC/MKS/1/4, Tomkinson to DCs Central Province, August 24, 1945.
[72] Interviews 123 and 124, Mwingi, July 1, 2009. In an interesting parallel, former KAR sergeant major Washington Asamba Lusuli appeared in a court case during the 1950s wearing his medal of honor and "war veteran's badge." He won his case against a civilian. Amutabi, "Power and Influence," 211.

FIGURE 7: Chief Kasina talks with Governor Renison at Migwani, 1960. Note the artificial hands (see Chapter 7). KNA: 967.6203 KEN [993077]. Reproduced here with permission from the Kenya National Archives.

numbers of administrators in the colonies – numbered fewer than 200 in Kenya after the war, and these men were under strict instructions to ensure the profitability of the colony's economy; uprisings and discontent were intolerable due to the economic problems they caused. There was also little stability among administrative staff: Six different district commissioners served in Machakos between 1944 and 1953, as well as another seven in Kitui. Thus these Kamba leaders had immense power to shape policy.

Chiefs and councillors phrased their requests from the government in terms of Kamba military service, aware of their pivotal role in mediating between the people and the government. Following the end of the war, the chiefs' major forum for voicing their concerns was LNC meetings, attended by district officials. In one such meeting, Chief Jonathan Kala said:

It was generally known and recognised that the Akamba are, and always have been … a law-abiding tribe … and for that reason they find it impossible to understand the Government's present attitude of refusing to help them in their present trouble … The Akamba had played their full share in the 1914–1918 war … In 1939 … the Akamba once again showed their loyalty and had more than fulfilled every demand made upon them throughout the years of war. They were now passing through a period of exceptional drought and famine and they asked for assistance.[73]

James Mwanthi, the vibrant leader of opposition to the government for several decades before 1940, made a variety of similar requests. Mwanthi's statements appear more than any other chief's or councillor's in the Machakos LNC minutes, always demanding education or facilities for Kamba, and focusing on those who had fought in the war. In one such minute, he asked for, "[E]very possible help … [for] ex-soldiers, many of whom … would be progressive and of great help in the effort to advance the district."[74] In this, he tied Kamba military service to the new government agenda of development and "progress" in the colony.

But other chiefs did not speak from such confident and assured positions. Though Chief Uku Mukima was long-serving and seemingly respected, he was neither one of the younger generation, nor had a proven track record of supporting Kamba interests like Mwanthi. During the destocking protests, UMA supporters had attacked several shops he owned.[75] Several of his requests are terser, and perhaps – though reading too much into recorded minutes is dangerous – reflect nervousness. Mukima warned that, "[I]mmediate attention should be given to the applications by ex-soldiers for shops and lorries as otherwise they would become discontented."[76] On one level this could perhaps imply a threat to the government – but the threat was more pointedly to Mukima's position than anything else. For chiefs were beholden to their constituents: A failure to appease the common soldier in the reserves in 1946 or 1947 would cause certain problems in a location.

Even more politically marginal discontents seized upon the institution of Kamba military service to issue threats. Joseph Munyao – a senior clerk

[73] KNA, DC/MKS/5/1/3, Minutes of a Meeting of the Machakos LNC, Comment of Jonathan Kala, August 13–15, 1945.
[74] KNA, DC/MKS/5/1/3, Minute 111/45, "Assistance for Returned Ex-Soldiers," December 10–13, 1945.
[75] Munro, *Colonial Rule*, 234.
[76] KNA, DC/MKS/5/1/3, Minute 111/45, "Assistance for Returned Ex-Soldiers," December 10–13, 1945.

working in the district commissioner's office in Machakos – was the topic of an anonymous threatening letter, addressed to "The Councillors" of the Machakos LNC. The letter cited the well-known Kamba history of warfare with Maasai peoples to make its point: "Why then J. Munyao thinks that a European is his own brother? ... We wish to make out the number of Europeans who are at present possessing cattle ... the European is the second Masai." This letter, like another written by "180 Wakamba members" of 5 KAR, or others from assorted lance corporals and signalmen, sought to hit hard because it was ostensibly from Kamba soldiers serving abroad. The administration took great pains to learn who had written the letters: They typically came from within Kenya, and were signed with fictitious names and serial numbers.[77]

One term appears throughout field interviews and in archival documents from the later colonial period, in practically any sentence about Kamba military service: "loyalty." It was the word British officials used in speeches throughout Machakos and Kitui to praise Kamba and try to assuage discontent, and it is the word Kamba use today to describe why the British wanted them to serve in the armed forces, or to explain why they made good soldiers.

The question of Kamba "loyalty" was one with which I had struggled since the first few weeks I spent in Kenya in 2004. Back then, one of my first interviews was with a former corporal in the KAR called Philip Kyalo.[78] I can still remember the setting clearly: We sat near the bottom of a several-acre, terraced shamba, spread across a hillside. A variety of women worked while we spoke, periodically coming close to listen, out of curiosity. It was clear that while not wealthy, Kyalo was providing for a number of people in his extended family; perhaps twenty of them were present that day.

Perhaps the strongest memory I have from meeting Kyalo was a sense of injustice. Kyalo had gladly volunteered to join the KAR, and had served with distinction. But as he explained, Kamba did not receive recompense for their *loyalty*. After the First World War, he said, blacks received blankets, while whites received land. It was a similar story after the Second World War. The *loyalty* that Kamba had demonstrated,

---

[77] KNA, DC/MKS/10B/17/1, Anonymous to Munyao, December 1945; "Political Unrest – Ukamba Reserve," November 19, 1945.

[78] All information presented here about Philip Kyalo (pseudonym) is from Interview 8, Ngelani, July 13, 2004.

argued Kyalo, justified reward. When I left that afternoon, Kyalo asked me whether I could write to the Ministry of Defence in London to ask about the pension he believed he was owed. I promised that I would, knowing it would be a pointless letter. Sure enough, several weeks later, I receive a smart missive from the ministry, informing me that unfortunately any payments or pensions were now the responsibility of the government of Kenya.

Interviewees constantly raise the "loyalty" to which Kyalo referred. People recount how the British valued this quality in Kamba soldiers. They often express a sense of gratitude and pride that the British chose the Kamba to go to war in large numbers, and many refer to a close relationship between the British and Kamba. One informant recalled, "We wanted them [the soldiers] to go and see how the war was going. There was no 'white' and 'Kamba' – they were one."[79] Another explained, "Kamba wanted to go and fight, and did so willingly. The reason is because the whites took care of them."[80]

The issue of "loyalty" raises the specter of "collaboration." Did Kamba soldiers somehow act against "African" interests and on the side of the colonizer? This was an important question in the 1960s when Kenya became independent, and is still today. How, too, should we understand interview testimonies – and there are many – that fondly recall the interactions between Kamba and Briton? Chief Kasina perfectly exemplifies these awkward topics. He was a man who became immensely powerful and wealthy under British rule; he flew the Union Jack over his house, and always wore his military uniform, helmet emblazoned with the Union Jack; and in the words of one of his sons, retired in 1963 from government service because, "He didn't want to serve an African government. He was very much British . . . even after his death he was entirely British."[81]

In the conclusion to her *Worries of the Heart*, Kenda Mutongi explores a similar issue. How, she wondered, could she explain the series of interviews and conversations she had with elderly Maragoli men and women in western Kenya who praised the colonial system? She wanted to find them angry and critical of the British, but never came across that reaction, something she was at a loss to understand.[82]

[79] Interview 27, Mbooni, July 12, 2005.
[80] Interview with Elizabeth Simeon Kioko, Mitaboni, July 5, 2005.
[81] Interview 125, Mwingi Town, July 2, 2009.
[82] Mutongi, *Worries*, 193–198. Jennifer Cole's work provides a starting point for understanding the complexities of contemporary memories of the colonial encounter. Cole, *Forget Colonialism?*

loyalty & collaboration

Though it makes for uncomfortable reading, it is important to recognize that many Kamba *did* benefit from their association with the British. Askaris won great rewards for their service, from their abilities to pressure the colonial government and local leaders based on this loyalty (see especially Chapter 6). Martial service was a window to benefits, both individually and collectively.

But it is a mistake to view "loyalty" as something that only connected the British and Kamba. The latter had their own understandings of the notion. People today use the Kikamba word ĩwi to mean "loyalty," the same word they use to mean "obedient." But early biblical translations reveal that ĩwi and its derivatives meant either "hear" or "obey" before the 1940s. When Jesus' disciples saw evil spirits obeying his Word, for instance, missionaries rendered nĩmeũmwĩwa – "they obey him."[83] Any number of examples reflect the meaning of "hearing" as well.[84] Thus the missionaries of the AIM rendered ĩwa "to hear; to feel; to obey" in 1939.[85]

The transformation of ĩwi to mean "loyal" – a positive quality, versus the more subservient "obedient" – came around the time of the Second World War.[86] By traveling far away and undertaking martial service to sustain their communities, Kamba soldiers connected themselves to a set of values that had a long history. These values came to be represented through the idea of ĩwi that linked military service to the similar occupations of the athiani in the distant past.[87] Thus when soldiers celebrated their "loyalty," it was not some sycophantic attraction to the colonial power, but is better read as an evocation of an important part of the martial tradition with deep roots that had great resonance for them.

[83] Rhoad (trans.), *Maliko*, 5 (Mark 1:27). Consider also *Na no kũmwĩw'a* ("It should obey you"). Rhoad (trans.), *Luka*, 69 (Luke 17:6). This translation was likely rendered during the 1920s, though a more precise date is difficult to ascertain.

[84] Consider, for instance, *Ũla wĩwaa ndeto yakwa* ("He that heareth my word"). Rhoad (trans.), *Yoana*, 16 (John 5:24).

[85] AIMLCU, *Kikamba–English Dictionary*, 35.

[86] Unfortunately, it is difficult to pin down the word's altered meaning more precisely. The King James Bible – most commonly used by AIM missionaries – does not include the word "loyal" or "loyalty" in its English version, with the exception of a verse in 2 Maccabees. Because 2 Maccabees is part of the Apocrypha, missionaries did not translate it in their complete Kikamba Bible of 1956. Nor did John Mbiti translate the word in his short vocabulary of 1958. Africa Inland Mission (trans.), *Maandĩko Matheu ma Ngai* (The Bible); Mbiti, *English–Kamba Vocabulary*.

[87] One British educationalist was rather taken by this, and was at a loss to explain how the Kamba – as a "tribe" – seemed "possessed by a desire to get out into the world." Larby, *Kamba*, 24.

This was, moreover, an effort to center the notion of īwi at the heart of Kamba life, and pin Kamba ethnic identity around male virtues related to soldiering. Veterans were largely successful in this during the 1940s, but loyalty was, of course, no uncontested notion. Men and women in Kamba communities had argued about the sorts of qualities that were worthy of honor since the nineteenth century. Neither groups like the ABC nor the women of Ukambani's villages were willing to allow these men to possess a monopoly on virtue. Though the soldiers were able to drive themselves and their version of "Kambaness" to the fore during the decade, they met a challenge soon after.

CONCLUSION

The Second World War saw the transformation of the African soldier from the barefoot porter dressed in rags of the early twentieth century, into a highly trained, professional soldier noted for his bravery. At the forefront of this conversion were Kamba soldiers. Having served with distinction, they returned to their homes and took on leading roles in their communities. The experience of war, and life in army camps, inspired soldiers to articulate a "Kamba" ethnic identity, based on their experiences as soldiers.

Soldiers were successful in winning honor and respect from their own communities because their occupations and experiences reflected a series of virtues and values that had a long history among many peoples in the region. For these reasons, their efforts to take on the leadership mantle of the "tribe" worked, and their influence was rarely challenged during the 1940s. To British officials, though, the veterans' portrayal of Kamba ethnic identity was far simpler: They argued that the Kamba were a loyal, fighting people, who deserved respect and good treatment as a result. The contested web of values that underwrote their authority was hidden in negotiation with the colonial state.

But the winds of change were sweeping through the region: The Ukambani of the late 1940s was a vastly different world than that just a decade earlier. Veterans fought to maintain control on two fronts: Domestically, they had to contend with social developments to keep their communities in order – especially by reining in "loose" women – and more broadly, they continued to pressure the colonial government for greater and greater benefits.

Chapter 6

Controlling development

I would be grateful ... Sir, if you would assure the [Kamba] Chiefs ...
that I, and my superiors, are unreservedly apologetic for this breach of
manners.[1]

The town of Kanziku is tucked away in southeastern Kitui, close to the
Tsavo East National Park, Kenya's largest game reserve. When I visited in
2009, life was hard for the people living there. Water from the majority of
the boreholes in the area had developed a salty taste, and food was scarce.
The only available sustenance in the town was goat's head soup, so
Catholic Relief Services was sending in a truck filled with supplies most
days. The truck usually arrived between noon and 4 p.m., meaning that a
crowd started to appear outside the district officer's building in the late
morning, and slowly expanded throughout the day until the vehicle
arrived. I was ready to leave Kanziku when Saturday came.

You have one shot at leaving Kanziku every day, because there is only
one bus. It leaves Mtito Andei – on the Mombasa Road – in the early
hours of the morning, and arrives in Nairobi sometime around noon,
having wound its way around the various hamlets and villages of southern Kitui. After filling up in Nairobi, it makes the return journey back to
Mtito. Consequently, I sleep restlessly until the sound of honking and a
roaring, overworked engine wakes me. The bus storms into town, strung-
up chickens swinging wildly from the exterior. It is far past full: There are
perhaps forty seats, and at least seventy people inside, not to mention
luggage. The passenger door in the miraculously empty cab swings open.

[1] KNA, DC/KTI/7/5, Holt to DC Kitui, January 12, 1945.

"*Mūsūngū* [European], come on!" beckons a toothy grin. Seeing the look of bemusement on my face, he continues: "I saw you come on Monday, so I've been saving a seat for you all week to go back to Nairobi!"

The fact that Kanziku is directly connected to Nairobi at all is testament to an extraordinary explosion in road building that took place during the 1930s and 1940s. Even the most far-flung parts of Kenya were brought into contact with the colony's capital. Buses and taxis plied the routes between Ukambani, Nairobi, and Kikuyuland on a daily basis, causing a revolution in the daily lives of Kamba, and indeed many others in the colony. This transformation was one of a series of changes that swept through Ukambani: Schools opened, markets popped up all over the region, and social life underwent a radical shift. A visitor to Ukambani in 1930 would barely have recognized the countryside twenty years later.

These changes threatened the control of Ukambani's male leaders. Using Kamba "custom" and "tradition" to justify their actions, they attempted to restrict the rights of women and the youth. Women, in particular, they said needed to be reined in to avoid a descent into moral degeneracy. But women fought back against their efforts: Many had started successful businesses during the war years, and rejected these male visions of social order.

The changes in Kamba life were exacerbated by a polar shift in colonial policy. The Second World War, combined with the situation "on the ground" in Africa, provided the stimuli for a total rethinking of Britain's approach to colonial governance. The new effort included programs of "development," "welfare," and later "community development," all of which were attempts to provide evidence for Britain's trusteeship in Africa, and assuage pressure from the United States and the Soviet Union, as well as intellectuals in Africa, India, and the Caribbean, that decolonization proceed forthwith. The change also reflected a belief that the prewar system of administration was ineffective. Most visibly, this had been demonstrated by labor disturbances throughout the empire. In Africa, this included a major series of strikes on the Rhodesian Copperbelt in 1935, and four years later on the docks of Dar es Salaam and Mombasa. Further strikes in Mombasa in 1942 and 1945, as well as on the railway system of the Gold Coast and among Nigerian cocoa farmers, compounded the issue.

But these new development programs reflected more than just an altered style of rule; in actuality, they were methods of imperial control, based on the politics of ethnicity. In Kenya, the Kamba were their primary focus. Since 1945, officials had implemented stopgap measures in

Ukambani to try to ensure political calm (including creating open stock auctions, government programs to purchase cattle infected with bovine pleuro-pneumonia, and cutting the tax rate).[2] Now, the bulk of funding from the new development programs was aimed at Kamba areas. Officials needed to both calm discontent in the reserves and ensure that Kamba continued to sign up for service in the army and police.[3] Ex-soldiers and chiefs pressed for benefits from the government, evoking the loyalty they had demonstrated during the war, and arguing that the Kamba deserved reward for their service.

CHANGES IN EVERYDAY LIFE

Perhaps nowhere represented the "new Ukambani" better than a market-place in the late 1930s. Stanner visited a variety of them at this time, and described a typical scene:

The first people come to the market while the cattle are still being watered about nine o'clock in the morning but some are still arriving in the early afternoon ... The market at its peak presents an animated scene. Buyers and sellers crowd densely together; dust rises in clouds, there is constant movement, and the hum of voices, the busy stream of goods passing in and out, and the ripe smell of garden produce add their effects ... The roads and paths ... are filled even after sundown, with returning market-goers.

The Mui market ... and the Tiva market ... are the principal cattle selling markets. Secret sales of cattle outside the official markets, to evade the sales-tax of 50 cents, are common, and possibly as many are sold in this way as are recorded in the market places ... The principal commodities marketed ... are millets, sorghum, maize, cassava, pulses, sweet potatoes, sugar-cane ... milk, ghee, honey and meat; goats, sheep, and cattle; tobacco in the form of pressed leaf and snuff; prepared foods, e.g. porridges, stews, and relishes ... raw materials, e.g. red ochre, fibres ... a few articles of homecraft, e.g. stools, leather straps, woven baskets, earthen pots, bead and wire finery, splits calabashes ... bows, arrows, tweezers, etc.

---

[2] In Machakos, the rate dropped from 13 Sh in 1945 to 9 Sh in 1946, and stayed at that level until 1948. In Kitui, the rate decreased from 10 Sh to 9 Sh. KNA, ARC (MD) 4/5/80 (22), "Circular: Hut Tax Exemption," August 1945; KNA, DC/MKS/19/2, "Rates of Native Poll Tax," 1951.

[3] Officials continually demanded more Kamba recruits for forces ranging from the KAR to the Somalia Gendarmerie. KNA, ARC (MD) 4/5/65 (21), "Recruiting – EA Command," October 31 or November 1, 1946; Barkas to PCs Nyeri, Nyanza, Rift Valley, Nakuru, Northern Frontier District, Isiolo, "EAC Recruiting Scheme," March 24, 1947; Acting Chief Secretary, Nairobi to Civil Affairs Agent, Headquarters of the East Africa Command, May 20, 1947.

The market was a cacophony of gossiping, haggling, shouting, and general raucousness.[4] Kamba, Kikuyu, Indians, Tharaka, and more attended the larger markets, bringing their goods from all over the colony. In most marketplaces, a radio or two blared away, informing buyers and sellers of the latest news from Europe or around the colony. Sometimes, an information room was situated adjacent to the market, filled with maps showing the progress of the war in Europe, or by the early 1940s, the movements of KAR battalions in Burma. Late in the afternoon, a mobile cinema unit might arrive with great fanfare, and begin setting up for the evening's show when hundreds – if not thousands – would gather excitedly.

Marketplaces were built all over Ukambani during the late 1930s, and the following decade more opened every year. While most men and women walked to market – often traveling for more than two or three hours on foot to attend – some used the new network of roads that appeared during the 1940s. In Kitui, the transformation during the decade was emphatic, and perhaps more striking than in Machakos: Bridleways – paths used for foot or horse traffic – were replaced by graded roads (though tarmac was a rarity). Men and women took advantage of the buses that worked these routes, moving their goods from place to place, in much the same way as they do today.

Kamba remember the decade as one in which the world seemed to get bigger: Nairobi and Mombasa were no longer vaguely defined places to the "west" or "east," but were now part of the everyday worldview. Simeon Mwalonzi explained how people started leaving in large numbers to find work in Nairobi; Kamba called them *andũ Ilovi* ("Nairobi people"). They would stay there for a month or so, then come home for a weekend to "plan for what needed to be done [there]."[5] Those from Machakos and northern Kitui typically headed to Nairobi, and those from southern Kitui to Mombasa, as a journey of three to five days became a matter of hours. The reserves were flush with new ideas and products from the cities. As one man explained, people would "go to see the way things were done at the coast and bring those ideas back to their home area to do there."[6]

This participation in the wider world contributed to a greater sense of ethnic awareness. When Kamba moved to Nairobi, for instance, colonial

---

[4] Stanner, "Kitui Kamba Market," 127–130.
[5] Interview with Simeon Mwalonzi, Ngelani, July 7, 2004.
[6] Interview 3, Ngelani, July 9, 2004.

regulations decreed that they had to possess a kipande. The system had existed for more than two decades, but before the 1930s, few had left the reserves in search of work, and therefore had never applied for such documents. Now, as they flooded into Nairobi and Mombasa, each was legally identified as "Kamba." The majority moved into neighborhoods in the cities with friends and relatives from their home areas.

A hardening of ethnic lines was evident in an outpouring of antagonism against Kikuyu (and to some extent, Indians) during the 1940s. In Machakos, much of this was inspired by LNC councillors. Aware of the scarcity of land in the reserve, the LNC passed a regulation that no Kikuyu was permitted to own land in the Machakos reserve.[7] Members of Kamba communities had to choose whether they were Kamba, Kikuyu, Tharaka, or anything else, an occasionally complicated process for those who had migrated following famine – or for some other reason – during the previous decade or two. Councillors also decreed that no Kikuyus were allowed to sell their wares in marketplaces in Machakos.[8]

But there were also interesting moments of disagreement between people living in Machakos and those in Kitui. Before the 1940s, relatively little travel took place between the two areas. Kitui people, laughed one man from Machakos, "were said to be a little stupid. Because their language and their accents were somehow different."[9] But his nervous laughter concealed a sense of trepidation: Men and women from Machakos traveled to Kitui if they needed powerful witchcraft.

British officials believed that bringing Machakos and Kitui into closer contact could only be a positive thing; because the tribe was "loyal," it could form a powerful, unified bloc. From the late 1940s onward, therefore, officials gathered LNC councillors from the two districts to joint annual meetings where they discussed "tribal issues." The meeting's location alternated each year between Machakos and Kitui.

Members of the Machakos LNC, too, thought this a good idea. They expressed that because people from both districts were part of "a community of origin and interests," they should, therefore, be able to move freely throughout Ukambani, and live in whichever district they chose.[10] This was actually a rather cunning move by the Machakos councillors;

[7] KNA, DC/MKS/5/1/3, Minute 8/43, "Kikuyu Living in Kamba Native Lands," June 30, 1943.

[8] KNA, DC/MKS/5/1/3, Minute 8/40, "Kikuyu Traders," January 25, 1940.

[9] Interview 8, Ngelani, June 13, 2004.

[10] KNA, DC/MKS/5/1/3, Minutes of a Meeting of the Machakos LNC, August 2–4, 1938.

with land in scarce supply in the reserves there, they sought to open the door to wider migration into Kitui for landless people in their locations. They did this by citing the tribe's history, knowing the influence such a statement would have on officials. In Kitui, councillors were angered by what they saw as an effort by the Machakos LNC to take their land. They were fully aware that a number of Machakos Kamba had entered Kitui since the war's end in search of grazing territory. They passed a regulation that no man from Machakos could claim land in Kitui unless his grandfather was born there.[11]

At other points, too, disagreements appeared between the two districts. In 1946, Machakos veterans called for a ceremony to reconcile any differences between the Kamba and the government. Kitui councillors "rejected with scorn" the need for such a ceremony, adding that the Machakos veterans' wish was "inapplicable to Kitui."[12] But these moments of disagreement quickly disappeared by the 1950s. One of my older informants put it best: "People of Kitui were termed as bad, but they turned out to be just normal Kambas ... We realized that everyone had become one people [after the war]."[13]

Perhaps the greatest transformations that took place in Kamba life were related to the rise of education. Returning soldiers were at the forefront of this movement. Their absolute belief in the value of education is abundantly clear in interviews: They are quick to demonstrate that they can write their names, which they do in careful block capitals on scraps of paper, recalling how they were taught to do so while serving in the army. Annual reports of the district commissioners in both Machakos and Kitui reveal that soldiers constantly demanded new schools. In 1945, after all, schools facilities could handle only 12 percent of children in Machakos, and just 3 percent in Kitui.[14]

The clearest reflection of this change was visible in the education of girls. During the 1930s, people had sneered at girls who went to school. They had viewed them as prostitutes – at worst – or a pointless financial drain (incurring cost for the payment of school fees), at best. Educated girls were typically Christian as well; this meant that they were likely uncircumcised, and therefore not truly "adults" in the estimation of

---

[11] KNA, DC/KTI/1/1/8, Kitui District Annual Report, 1951.
[12] KNA, DC/KTI/1/1/5, Kitui District Annual Report, 1946.
[13] Interview 6, Ngelani, July 12, 2004.
[14] KNA, PC/CP/4/3/2, Central Province Annual Report, 1945.

many. Girls with sharpened teeth and pierced ears had giggled at them on their way to the popular dances from which Christians were banned.

By the 1940s, however, these girls were no longer looked down upon, but rather lauded for the education they had received. Even the institution of brideprice – so historically resistant to tampering – underwent a revolution. Before the war, an educated girl could command no higher brideprice than one who was uneducated. Now, however, she was highly valued. Fathers began to view fees they paid for their daughters' educations as something of an investment, as the girls became greatly desired as wives in their communities. One lady remembered the change well: "We were respected because of the education we had received," she explained, translating respect as taía, the word used to mean "honor" for warriors and soldiers.[15] Another man put it more simply: "Those who refused to send their daughters to school died."[16]

Most began to view education as a catapult to financial security; going to school was, after all, a route to a better job with better pay. Those who went to school during the 1940s ensured that without fail, all their children attended too. In interviews with the children of UMA leaders, the high levels of education attained by the succeeding generation is striking: Some are pilots, others businessmen; some live in the United States, some in India, and all are gainfully employed, at the very least.

Relatively few boys and girls from Ukambani attended school during the 1930s, but those who did were, by the following decade, frequently rich, and leaders of their communities. George Nthenge represents this group perfectly. His father was one of the earliest Christians in Mumbuni, and had ensured that Nthenge attended the best schools in Ukambani (including the Roman Catholic mission school at Kabaa), and even another in Tabora (in Tanganyika). Having worked for the government during the late 1940s, Nthenge began a curio business. He received a license from the government to hawk his products at the Stanley Hotel in Nairobi, and eventually employed forty or fifty people at his own curio factory. He exported his products to Britain and the United States, and as an educated man, became extremely popular with Europeans. Nthenge attributed his ability to get letters of credit in Nairobi to his competence in English: He says that the government always recommended him to European businessmen because he could speak the language so well. Nthenge achieved such success that while still in his twenties, he bought a large

[15] Interview 148, Mbooni, May 16, 2012.   [16] Interview 13, Mutituni, July 17, 2004.

American Studebaker in which he drove around the streets of the capital. This platform allowed Nthenge to become one of Ukambani's most prominent politicians: He entered the Legislative Council in 1960.[17]

These changes in Kamba life were clearly reflected in the two instructional grammars published in Kikamba around the time. Emma Farnsworth's grammar – written under the auspices of the AIM – was first published in 1952. The majority of the work, however, was done in the late 1930s and early 1940s, before her eyesight began to fail. Farnsworth's sample sentences included phrases like, "That young man has thirteen arrows," and "There are many young women in my garden. They are cultivating."[18] The sentences evoked an old world that was barely recognizable by the late 1940s. In contrast, W. H. Whiteley and Matthew Muli's *Practical Introduction to Kikamba* – that appeared ten years later – described a modern world, into which even politics had crept. "Last week the bus drivers stopped work, refused to drive the buses and asked for higher wages," ran one sentence. Another was, "Some of my friends went to the meeting, listened to the speaker and then went to the cinema."[19]

The spread of education and Christianity seemed to herald the end of a series of older "traditions." In interviews, subjects typically juxtapose the rise of education against the ending of these older practices. One such change came for the long-established thome (see Chapter 2). In the mornings and evenings a father typically sat at thome and made a fire. Several generations of senior men from the father's family or clan attended these gatherings. They ate food cooked by the man's wife or the women of his group, and invited members of the younger generation to attend, whom they then advised. The senior men taught the boys how to fight, behave properly, and respect their elders, amongst other things. Women rarely attended, but a similar gathering often occurred in the home itself at the same time, where the women would impart similarly relevant knowledge to girls. The reaction of one informant when asked about the ending of thome was typical: He explained that it happened due to the increase in the number of children attending school. Because children began going to school early in the morning and had to do homework in the evenings – times when thome typically took place – the institution died out.[20]

---

[17] Interview with George Nthenge, Mumbuni, November 16, 2006.
[18] Farnsworth, *Kamba Grammar*, 137–138.
[19] Whiteley and Muli, *Practical Introduction*, 76.
[20] Interview 36, Mulala, July 25, 2005.

Teeth-chipping was another long-standing practice that suffered the same fate. In 1949, the Machakos LNC passed a resolution formally discouraging the practice.[21] One lady recalled that she began attending dances in January 1952. Her older brother and sister both had had their teeth altered, but her parents did not permit her to do so; they had begun attending church on Sundays, and she a mission school. She could not decide whether religion or education spurred such a change in practices, but said that it was likely a combination of the two.[22]

In interviews, it is rare to come across negative reactions to older practices; more likely, the subject shakes his or her head, and wears an expression of bewilderment. One man, who attended a Christian school during the early 1940s, remembered his bemusement when his father left a pot of honey on an altar in the woods near his home, as an offering to some spirits. His father returned to the shrine several days later, and was happy to find an empty vessel. "Of course, bees had eaten it," the man told me, before discoursing on the "pointlessness" of such actions. He viewed the brewing of traditional alcohol as a similarly bad idea: "Those who drink traditional [-ly brewed] beer live in rags," he said, before citing Leviticus: "Do not take wine or strong drink, lest you die."[23]

While education increased in value, the importance of cattle declined. The number of cattle in the reserves was lower following the war than at any point since the beginning of the century. The difficult war years meant that many villagers had slaughtered the beasts for food. By 1949, the district commissioner of Kitui likely took great satisfaction in writing that the "cattle complex" in Kitui "has so far diminished that nearly 1800 cattle offered for slaughter had to be turned away for lack of buyers."[24] By 1951, Kitui exported more cattle than any other district in the colony.[25] Kamba spent their extra money on school fees and new types of goods. The decline in cattle's importance was also related to the spread of Christianity: Christian missionaries had tried for years to have cattle removed as part of brideprice, with notable success among their charges, who simply invested their funds in other businesses. As more became Christian, the importance of cattle for brideprice payments decreased.[26]

[21] KNA, DC/MKS/5/3/1, Minute 121/49, "Native Tribunals – Recording of Kamba Customary Law," October 26–28, 1949.
[22] Interview 55, Miu, October 19, 2006.
[23] Interview 46, Mulala, August 3, 2005; Leviticus 10:9.
[24] KNA, DC/KTI/1/1/5, Kitui District Annual Report, 1949.
[25] KNA, DC/KTI/1/1/8, Kitui District Annual Report, 1951.
[26] AIM, Box 6, File 16, Downing to Nixon, April 15, 1943.

MEN AND WOMEN

The new schools, marketplaces, and transport networks <u>permitted</u> <u>women a far greater level of autonomy</u>. It began during the war years; with thousands of men absent, women had seized the chance to establish themselves, doing business that men might have previously undertaken. Many women achieved a degree of financial independence that they were loath to sacrifice when the men returned from war. This new world precipitated a contest between men and women that lasted for much of the 1940s and 1950s.

Kamba men had departed the reserves in large numbers in the war's first years. They took on roles as soldiers, police, prison guards, and ratings in the Kenya Royal Navy Volunteer Reserve. More served as conscripted laborers, wage laborers, and squatters on European farms, meaning that the adult male population in Machakos and Kitui was extremely low. In Kalama, in central Machakos, 85 percent of young men had left the district.[27] Women – already burdened with the work of the home and farm – frequently turned to trading, taking advantage of the new marketplaces.

In her comprehensive study of trading in Nairobi, Claire Robertson shows <u>how women won great success as traders during the war</u>.[28] They proved adept at sidestepping colonial trading regulations that sought to restrict their freedoms. Kamba women traders were prominent in this, and an extensive black market in goods operated to and from Ukambani. Women from Machakos journeyed by foot or on buses to the neighborhoods of Pumwani and Shauri Moyo – in Nairobi's Eastlands – on a daily basis, and sold vegetables and charcoal.[29] The variety of trading ranged widely: In some cases, women sold produce in the cities that they grew on their farms; in others, they bought products in bulk and divided them into smaller amounts for resale wherever they could turn a profit in the capital's markets. The products ranged from dry staples, to potatoes, to bananas, beans, and more.[30] A variety of markets operated in the reserves,

---

[27] KNA, DC/MKS/8/10, Annual Report of the Machakos Social Welfare Organisation, 1950.
[28] Robertson, *Trouble*. It is important to note that women had begun to dominate trading in Kitui in the years leading up to the war. Stanner made a count of men and women attending market on one day in late 1938 or early 1939, and recorded that 618 of the 874 people there were women; they did approximately three-quarters of the selling that day, and more than half the buying. KNA, W. E. H. Stanner, *The Kitui Kamba: A Critical Study of British Administration* (unpublished typescript, *c.* 1940), 64–65.
[29] White, *Comforts*, 153.   [30] Robertson, *Trouble*, 102–145.

too, where peoples arrived from outside Ukambani to trade. When Stanner visited one in Kitui in 1938 or 1939, he noted that no gender segregation existed, so women interacted – and "flirted," in his words – with men from all parts of the colony.[31]

When drought struck Ukambani between 1942 and 1945, many families in Ukambani only survived by buying illegal maize from Kikuyu areas. Roads between Ukambani and the market towns of Murang'a and Nyeri had "thousands" of travelers *each day* between 1942 and 1945, the majority of whom must have been women, as most men were absent. In some cases, they paid seven times the government's fixed price for food, using remittances from the front lines.[32]

Kamba women also worked in a range of other occupations. Some became prostitutes in Nairobi, where they might even earn enough to buy houses to rent to other working women. Others brewed beer, and still more worked as domestic servants or *ayahs* (nurses) for European or Indian families.[33] Other women spread out from their homes to preach the Gospel to the alei, and some to work for private companies like East Africa Tobacco. These occupations troubled a range of male actors, from returning soldiers, to church leaders, to colonial officials, to community elders. Their joint efforts to resolve this "problem" constituted a massive assault on female autonomy.

While former soldiers were great believers in education, trading, and transport, the presence of these new developments in the sphere of women was worrying. Veterans were threatened by the new, more prominent roles women had taken on in their absence. Soldiers' status – whether they sat on the LNC or were simply participants in village life – was based on their service in the war, and the community-sustaining remittances they had sent home. When they returned, they were comparatively wealthy; but as they felt the financial bite several months later, they found themselves unable to support their families, and consequently, their prestige suffered. For the first time, they were often dependent on their wives' income and business networks.

Veterans expressed their concern about declining moral standards in their communities and positioned themselves as the guardians of "proper" standards of behavior. They expressed fear that women in their

---

[31] KNA, W. E. H. Stanner, *The Kitui Kamba: A Critical Study of British Administration* (unpublished typescript, *c.* 1940), 127.

[32] Anderson and Throup, "Africans and Agricultural Production," 338.

[33] White, *Comforts.*

communities would travel outside their home areas (and especially to Nairobi) – either under their own volition or taken by strange men – where, they said, the women would most likely become prostitutes. This story was typical of Kenya in the post-war era: Matthew Carotenuto and Kenda Mutongi have revealed similar happenings in western Kenya, notably including the forcible "repatriation" of women to the rural areas.[34] Their pronouncements found receptive ears among colonial officials, who feared what the appearance of the "modern world" might do to Africans. Missionaries, too, shared their concern. Emma Farnsworth – who seemed to cut a rather sad figure after her husband's death in 1944 – believed that mission girls in Kangundo were dressing and cutting their hair in inappropriate fashion. "Some of our women felt any 'laws' ... to be a curtailing of their liberty," she fumed.[35]

Ex-soldiers formed a variety of groups to try to "reestablish" male control in Ukambani. One was the Young Akamba Union, a group in which members bonded themselves together by taking oaths of solidarity.[36] Another was the Kĩng'ole Warriors, in which Stephen Savono Maveke (see Chapter 3) participated as a young man. Described by one newspaper as "dreaded," the group aimed to bring back "traditional" rules in the post-war era. The name came from the *kĩng'ole* system that existed in the nineteenth century and before. In kĩng'ole – described as "lynch-law" by one scholar – a person who had used witchcraft to cause death, or had stolen property repeatedly, was killed by a mob of young men.[37] While the reconstituted group did not carry out such actions, its members deliberately used the older name to recall this fearsome and "traditional" reputation.[38] Other veterans acted less formally; in Masii, they stationed themselves on the roads in and out of town to prevent women and the youth from traveling.[39]

The Akamba Union had similar aims: In order to gain LNC permission to open branches in Machakos in 1944, it expressed that it would stamp out the incidence of Kamba women traveling to Nairobi to become

[34] Carotenuto, "Repatriation"; Carotenuto, "*Riwruok E Teko*," especially 61–66; Mutongi, *Worries*, 139–159.

[35] AIM, Box 8, File 4, Emma Farnsworth to Davis, April 18, 1948.

[36] KNA, DC/MKS/5/1/4, Minute 18/47, "Young Akamba Union," March 25–29, 1947.

[37] Lindblom, *Akamba*, 176–180.

[38] Interview with Stephen Savono Maveke, Tala, November 14, 2006; *Kenya Times*, "Meet the Ukambani Paramount Chief," March 7, 1997.

[39] KNA, DC/MKS/8/10, Annual Report on Social Welfare Activities, 1949.

prostitutes. But it was the voices of LNC councillors that carried the most weight. It was they who enforced the formal regulations to restrict female autonomy. During the war, councillors had acted to ban "girls" – fourteen or younger – from traveling to Nairobi.[40] After the war, they passed a new bevy of legislation. In 1946, the Machakos LNC decreed that a woman could only leave the district on public transport if her husband or a male relative accompanied her. If she wished to travel without them, she needed to have a pass signed by her chief.[41] Three years later, the rule was tightened: Women could no longer leave their *locations* without male assent, or they faced being "prosecuted by Kamba Law and Custom."[42] In Kitui, the ADC went so far as to erect physical barriers on the two major roads out of the district, in order to stop vehicles and confirm that women were not leaving without appropriate permissions.[43] In Machakos, the LNC banned women from acquiring purchasers' licenses that permitted them to buy goods in Nairobi or Thika, thus removing their need to travel there.[44]

These concerns about women demonstrated by ex-soldiers and members of the Akamba Union were shared by a multitude of men in various communities throughout the colony – and East Africa – during the postwar era. As they sought to mold ethnic communities, therefore, they did so based on what they considered an appropriate set of standards of behavior. In building these "morally conservative patriotisms," Peterson argues, men "came to feel themselves responsible for women to whom they were not directly related."[45]

In Ukambani, former chiefs and elders played an important role in this process as they tried to restrict female autonomy and control the youth, all the while challenging the efforts of young, "modern" men to position themselves at the heart of their communities. They used "tradition" and "custom" to lend authenticity to their project, an effort that one official

[40] KNA, DC/MKS/5/1/3, Minutes of a Meeting of the Machakos LNC, December 14–15, 1944.
[41] KNA, DC/MKS/5/1/4, Minute 17/47, March 25–29, 1947.
[42] KNA, DC/MKS/5/3/1, Minute 81/49, "Kamba Women Wandering About," July 27–29, 1949.
[43] KNA, PDA/EMB/1/218, Minute 115/1951, "Passes for Wakamba Women Leaving the District," December 11–14, 1951.
[44] KNA, DC/MKS/5/1/5, Minute 79/48, "Issue of Purchaser's Licences to Women," July 6–9, 1948.
[45] Peterson, *Ethnic Patriotism*, 4.

neatly described as the "back to Methusalah" approach.[46] The elders'
side was strengthened by new British ideas about "local government":
Officials sought to bring back "traditional" institutions as a way to
provide stability in communities throughout Kenya. Elders used these
newly reconstituted councils to try to seize power.

In the years before British rule, village councils held political authority.
The councils were socio-religious in nature, and two levels of elders held
positions of authority. But with the advent of British rule, the councils fell
into disuse. During the mid to late 1940s, administrators – desiring closer
control, and believing that older institutions had great value – altered the
existing system of administration in Ukambani (and indeed most of
Kenya) to bring older councils back. The system of chief and sub-chief –
who were in charge of locations and sub-locations, respectively – was
modified to include larger and more numerous bodies of authority. In
1947 in Machakos, as a result, the government re-created ũtũi – or
village – councils, staffed by ũtũi elders. The following year, it added
sectional and locational councils to advise the chiefs, and the LNC fit
above them. In Kitui, the government also reintroduced locational councils, with thome elders ranking above ũtũi elders.[47]

The re-creation of older institutions was an effort to give increased
authority to a more widespread government machine. The government
gave locational councils responsibility for promulgating social welfare,
and their power increased year by year. The significance of the motũi was
especially great as it recalled the precolonial past: In the days before
British rule, hunting and trading parties were organized using this system,
and thus the "new" ũtũi system recalled these older occupations. By 1958,
the locational councils in Machakos financed the development of
markets, paid the leaders of women's clubs, and improved water supplies
in towns. In fact, administrators saw them as the future of the district
more so than the ADC. Yet the re-creation of these powerful councils had
one important difference from those of the precolonial past: They no
longer included women.[48]

Another institution that gained renewed power during the late 1940s
was the system of clans. Though clans had existed throughout the colonial period, they had been reduced to simply assisting with the payment of

[46] KNA, DC/MKS/1/1/30, Machakos District Annual Report, 1950.
[47] KNA, DC/MKS/18/8, Minute 24/49, "Social Policy – Discussion Paper," October 4,
1949; Tignor, "Colonial Chiefs," 358.
[48] KNA, DC/MKS/1/1/34, Machakos District Annual Report, 1958.

school fees for their members, or providing for the infirm or elderly. But the colonial administration viewed the increase in the power of the clan in the late 1940s as extremely beneficial. Thus in 1946, for instance, Kitui chiefs were expressly told to listen to the advice of clan and ūtūi elders.

From the government perspective, the "informal" clan system could provide social services of sorts (a "social insurance" policy), assist with welfare activities (including soil conservation), and add to the control over women and the youth, thus reducing the moral dangers of prostitution and drunkenness. In addition, it was free: Clan support cost the administration nothing. The clan had the legitimacy of an institution that had existed in the distant past, and appeared to provide the administration with recourse to traditional values, therefore ostensibly creating stability.

Clan elders pressed their members hard for subscription fees (despite government objections), and passed regulations, such as "No one may despise old customs," to hammer home their authority.[49] In 1948, a colony-wide report specifically noted that Machakos (and to a lesser extent, Kitui) was the only part of Kenya where clan authority was increasing: By 1950, one official noted that, "Loyalty to the clan remains so strong that members are often too terrified of the consequences ... not to pay the dues demanded."[50] The executive officers of both individual clans as well as ūtūi councils took the title mūthiani to evoke older forms of prestige.[51]

The clan's strength especially increased following the creation of the new, unified Clan Council in 1949. Such was the rapid increase in clan authority that the administration was concerned that it might infringe on the authority of the ADC. In one of its earliest meetings in 1950, the council left no doubts as to its aims: "To strengthen the Akamba customary laws which prohibit the youth and women from drinking intoxicating liquors, thus furthering the Government's intentions of curbing out this trend of affairs."[52]

Elders acted strongly to restrict the freedom of movement of young men. Many had left the reserves after the war to find work as migrant

---

[49] KNA, DC/MKS/15/2, "The E-ombe Security," *c.* 1946.

[50] Kenya, *African Affairs, 1948,* 21; KNA, PDA/EMB/1/218, Minute 75/1946, "Mbai and Utui Elders – More Power and Authority," June 25–26, 1946.

[51] KNA, DC/MKS/1/1/30, Machakos District Annual Report, 1948.

[52] KNA, DC/MKS/8/12, "Report on the Clans Meeting," January 28, 1950; KNA, PDA/EMB/9, Minutes of a Meeting of the Finance and General Purposes Committee of the Kitui ADC, July 18, 1960.

laborers, something that threatened elders' control: With money from Nairobi, young men could reshape social ordering back at home. Elders banned boys under the age of fourteen from attending markets in Machakos.[53] Some traveled to Nairobi and Mombasa to round up young men and bring them home, and others ensured the roads in and out of the districts were guarded.[54] Elders were especially concerned with the consumption of alcohol, and in 1949 in Machakos, imposed mandatory imprisonment (without the option of a fine) for any man under the age of thirty caught drinking.[55]

Clan elders also received the power to legislate about women's rights in marriage through their claimed positions as mediators in their communities. Around 1950, the right of women to take recourse to the courts in cases of spousal dispute was cut: Women were "discouraged" from filing suits in the courts or tribunals, and instead had to present their cases to clan elders. The latter argued that this was the "proper place for [resolving] domestic quarrels."[56]

Elders increased their level of influence through managing soil conservation. In Kitui after the war, thome and ūtūi elders became responsible for running these programs, and not the LNCs/ADCs or chiefs.[57] Though both men and women were expected to dig terraces, in almost all areas, women performed the majority of this work, and it was frequently on the personal shambas of the elders. On safari in Kibaoni in August 1947, for instance, F. J. Hart found 249 men and 609 women digging terraces.[58] In Kiteta, A. D. Shirreff counted 122 women and 16 men.[59] These figures were typical of those in other areas. But the program was not without controversy: In Matungulu, husbands argued that elders had no authority to order their wives to work, saying that only they could do so. "Who did women belong to?" they rhetorically asked a district officer.[60] This sort of debate was common throughout the decade: men arguing over which of them had the right to control women.

[53] KNA, DC/MKS/5/1/5, Minute 113/48, "Children to be Stopped from Attending Markets," September 28–30, 1948.
[54] KNA, PDA/EMB/1/218, Minute 54/1951, "Prevention of Women Travelling," August 7–10, 1951.
[55] KNA, DC/MKS/2/1/1, Machakos District Intelligence Report, November 1949.
[56] KNA, PDA/EMB/1/218, Minute 50/1951, "Litigation By Women," August 7–10, 1951.
[57] KNA, MW/8/26, Department of Agriculture Annual Report, Kitui District, 1947; KNA, DC/KTI/1/1/5, Kitui District Annual Report, 1949.
[58] KNA, DC/MKS/8/5, F. J. Hart, Safari Report: Kibaoni, August 11–12, 1947.
[59] KNA, DC/MKS/8/5, A. D. Shirreff, Safari Report: Kiteta, September 8–12, 1947.
[60] KNA, DC/MKS/8/5, Safari Report: Matungulu, July 18, 1947.

These sorts of restrictions on women's actions are reflected in a rather striking set of contemporary recollections about the period. Interviewees recall the sort of vitriol that was aimed at women who traveled outside their home areas. One elderly gentleman told me – pausing for the right words, not wanting to offend the visitor to his home – that women who left their villages were known as "women of the railway line," that is to say, prostitutes.[61] Some women shake their heads and refuse to accept the possibility that any woman from their home areas left for the towns, such was the stigma attached to such behavior. "Women were not allowed to go to Nairobi at all," one lady told me.[62] Proverbs reflected these ideas: *Mwĩĩtu wa kwĩyĩta ndaĩawa* ran one, cited in Emma Farnsworth's grammar: "A young woman who hangs herself is not wept over."[63] Farnsworth's translation was not literal, and careful readers will notice the term *ndaĩa* cropping up again: The actual translation is, "A woman who hangs herself has no honor." Real women, the proverb suggested, should know how to act in an "appropriate" manner.

These efforts were especially significant because the government – assisted by experts from the School of Oriental and African Studies in London – was in the process of recording up-to-date versions of customary laws. Many were more severe than those that preceded them. In one case in Machakos, for instance, elders decreed that: "It is an offence for a person of a lower age-group e.g. a KIUISI (youth) to abuse a person of a higher age-group e.g. a MUTUMIA (elder). The offence consists of using abusive or insulting language [emphases in original]." The fine was a maximum of 100 shillings – only a little lower than the fine of 150 shillings for kidnapping a married woman from her husband![64]

This assault on female liberties seems comprehensive from the archival documents, and to some extent, contemporary interviews. And perhaps the mid to late 1940s was a time in which men were winning the contest between the sexes. But women still demonstrated an ability to move outside these formal restrictions, and during the following decade, they came to gain the upper hand over the men who supposedly controlled them (see Chapter 7). Moreover, they had their own versions of what they considered virtuous behavior in their communities.

[61] Interview 36, Mulala, July 25, 2005. [62] Interview 11, Ngelani, July 16, 2004.
[63] Farnsworth, *Kamba Grammar*, 22.
[64] KNA, DC/MKS/15/2, "Restatement of Customary Criminal Offences," *c.* 1961.

A central part of the discourse between men and women circulated around the primary soldierly virtue of ĩwi (loyalty). Soldiers' claims to authority were based on the notion that as brave fighters who had traveled the world – and whose remittances had provided for their extended families – they were worthy of honor and therefore positions of leadership. They suggested that "proper" women should, too, be ĩwi – using the word's original meaning, "obedient." They said that, "proper women did not go to the market, which is like a bar" and "did not like going to ... towns."[65] They were arguing that the notion of ĩwi should represent someone who possessed virtue, whether male or female.[66]

But many women rejected the notion that any index of respectability or honor could be wholly centered on male-based or male-determined virtues. At the core of the value system that had existed for decades was the stipulation that those who sustained their home communities were deemed worthy of honor. If this did not take place, then martial service, and the bravery and specialized knowledge it entailed, were irrelevant. Some proportion of women felt that soldiers had abdicated their responsibilities by leaving for so many years, while their families struggled: The rains, after all, were poor during the years of war. In some cases, the remittances soldiers had sent were insufficient. Sara Waigo – a widow in her late twenties – decided to move to Nairobi to start a new life. As she explained, "Don't think if someone was helping me in my home I could have left it."[67] If the husbands could not provide financial support, then they had no claims to authority over women.

Nairobi and Mombasa provided safe havens for women seeking to win – or maintain – their independence. Waigo, for instance, moved to Nairobi and established herself as a prostitute, where she made a living better than she might have in the reserves.[68] Moving to the cities and setting up a business – or working as a prostitute – was relatively common among Kamba women, as Luise White shows in her classic study. In Nairobi, women had far greater freedoms, despite occasional efforts by district authorities to send them home. These women rejected the authority of men who sought to control them; many, indeed, had moved to the cities to avoid abusive husbands. One woman said, "Why wouldn't anybody want to trade and earn a little money?! And buy a good dress. If you waited

[65] Interview 24, Mitaboni, July 5, 2005.
[66] Clan elders, too, brought up the term, calling their members to be *loyal* to the clan, to gain assent for their decrees. KNA, DC/MKS/15/2, "The E-ombe Security," *c.* 1946.
[67] White, *Comforts*, 156.   [68] White, *Comforts*, 156.

for your husband, a herdsman, where would you get that money?"[69] One prostitute told her clients that jealousy or possessiveness was inappropriate: "I would tell them that they had not paid my bridewealth, I was not married to them, they could not feel jealous," she explained.[70] In this process, women were arguing that the maintenance of families was the core of what it was to be honorable. The interviewee above – who dismissed as an option waiting for money from her husband – explained that the money went to support her children. She contrasted her experience with women that remained "at home": "*Our* children are not hungry."[71]

It is important to note, though, that the relations between men and women were not always fractious. In some instances, women supported men in their city-based businesses.[72] A number of interviewees explain that if women went alone to Nairobi or Mombasa, then it was deemed inappropriate; but if they went to visit their husbands – or assist them in their businesses – then that was something else entirely. As one old lady put it: "It was a good thing as they were doing it [traveling to Nairobi] for the benefit of those at home."[73]

Some of these interviewees explain the absence of men from the reserves in terms that avoid attaching blame to them. They frequently explain the gender imbalance in terms of independent biological occurrences, or as the workings of the natural order of things. (The imbalance in sex ratios must have been striking: In Machakos in 1948, the ratio of women to men was almost 3:2.[74]) Thus for Dorothy Uswii – the "wizened relic" who appeared in Chapter 4 – the discrepancy could not be explained: It was simply that far more girls were being born than boys.[75] For another woman, this was "the work of nature," alone.[76]

Running through – and complicating – these relations between old and young, male and female, and veterans and civilians in the post-war era were Ukambani's ever-expanding Christian communities. Throughout East Africa, Christian revivalists[77] challenged conservative male visions

---

[69] Robertson, *Trouble*, 107.   [70] White, *Comforts*, 171.
[71] Robertson, *Trouble*, 107.   [72] Robertson, *Trouble*, 102–145.
[73] Interview 9, Ngelani, July 14, 2004.
[74] KNA, DC/MKS/1/1/30, Machakos District Annual Report, 1948.
[75] Interview 12 (pseudonym), Ngelani, July 17, 2004.
[76] Interview 20, Mitaboni, July 27, 2004.
[77] A revival was a spiritual event during which a congregation or church in decline could experience a divinely inspired renewal. The notion was prominent among struggling AIM churches during the 1930s and 1940s.

of ethnic patriotism, earning the reputation as people who were "displaced, unattached, and uncommitted to their natal communities," and whose public confessions of sin and wordy preaching to all and sundry were viewed as inappropriate.[78] In Ukambani, a genuine revivalist movement is difficult to identify, but Christian groups certainly promulgated their own visions of community, honor, and virtue that challenged these efforts to create ethnic patriotisms. They rejected custom and tradition as the cultural material from which "Kamba" might be created, as well as its place in constituting the framework for neo-traditional rule in Ukambani.

Christianity directly threatened the status of elders in their communities. Many elders held their wealth in cattle, something they argued was worthy of respect, and core cultural material for making "Kamba." But cattle were practically insignificant for Christians. After 1945 – and even earlier in some places – Christians no longer paid brideprice in cattle, meaning that they had no need to subscribe to the authority of elders who controlled many of the beasts. Elders harangued government officials about such matters, always playing on "tradition" to lend authority to their words: "Why does the Government change the Akamba original customs due to a Report brought to it (Govt) by a few religious people; who do not represent the Akamba's point of view?" asked one complainant.[79]

Marriage was, of course, the central social institution for gaining adulthood. And Christian marriage – or "marrying in light," as interviewees describe it – required neither meetings nor discussion between senior community and family members to arrange the union. Instead, young men and women were married in their churches by a priest, often in cities like Nairobi and Mombasa, and not in the villages. Many came home already married and simply informed their families what had taken place. In this process, these Christians were undermining the supposed cultural basis of marriage, rejecting the requirement for cattle and the advice of their elders in forging worthy unions.

In Ukambani, the most prominent order of Christians to appear was the African Brotherhood Church (ABC).[80] It emerged indirectly from the AIM, and was the brainchild of the 29-year-old Simeon Mulandi. By the

---

[78] Peterson, *Ethnic Patriotism*, 4.
[79] KNA, DC/MKS/8/12, Clans Memorandum to DC Machakos, *c.* 1949.
[80] The ABC was initially called the Akamba Christian Union and then Akamba Christian Brotherhood before it settled on its final moniker.

time Mulandi founded the ABC in 1943, he was already a well-known evangelist, having earned his spurs first preaching for the Salvation Army, and then for Rhoad's Gospel Furthering Fellowship (GFF), where he was the primary African pastor. Rhoad was a strong believer in African-run churches, and it seems, initially encouraged Mulandi to establish his own organization: In its first years, the ABC's official mailing address was Rhoad's post office box.[81] But the union between Mulandi and Rhoad did not last: In early 1945, Mulandi split the ABC from Rhoad's GFF. It seems that Mulandi had been working behind Rhoad's back for some time, as he quietly built a following of 1,000 people. Rhoad felt betrayed; he said to Mulandi, "I gave you my sheep to tend, but instead of taking care of them, you stole them."[82]

Within weeks, Mulandi began ordaining ABC priests, and carrying out baptisms, sweeping large numbers of Christians – and others – into his organization. His willingness to baptize was one of the main factors in driving men and women from the AIM (and Catholic missions) into ABC hands. When I carried out interviews in Mbooni, I noticed that a significant proportion of highly devout Christians were baptized ten or even twenty years after they began attending Sunday School and Church.[83] Dipping into the AIM Archives in Nairobi helped explain this gap. Documents revealed how difficult it was for Africans to gain baptism there. Members commonly had to wait four years for the ceremony, and any "backsliding" along the way (such as drinking alcohol or marrying a second wife) extended this period. Moreover, the AIM had drawn hard lines between itself and the GFF and ABC, refusing to recognize catechism classes carried out by the other two churches, and insisting that its members do their full courses of instruction in AIM facilities.[84]

Like many religious movements in East Africa, the ABC seemed – often – to reject tribal affiliation, and instead encouraged its followers to think of themselves as part of a wider community of believers. In this, Mulandi's efforts contrasted those of former soldiers and elders who were

[81] KNA, MAA/2/122, "Extract from Kenya Colony Intelligence and Security Summary," February 1945.
[82] Sandgren, "Kamba Christianity," 174.
[83] Interviews 148–151, Mbooni, May 16, 2012.
[84] The difficulty Africans faced in procuring baptism was an issue about which Rhoad and Mulandi had agreed during the latter's days with the GFF. AIM, Box 5, File 10, Rhoad to Nixon, January 1, 1942; Box 15, File 4, Minutes of the Ukamba Regional Council, September 30, 1949.

attempting to harness the power of "tribe." Mulandi's broad approach was clear in his thinking as he prepared to launch the ABC. At the organizational meeting before the church was publicly founded, Mulandi and his friends pored over one verse from the Acts of the Apostles. It read, "[God] hath made of one blood all nations ... That they should seek the Lord."[85] The motto Mulandi chose for his church was similar: "Go ... make disciples of the nations."[86] Mulandi's background had prepared him for this breadth of thinking: He had learned his trade in the cosmopolitan Nairobi with Rhoad, and had always preached the majority of his sermons in Swahili.

Yet Mulandi's movement is difficult to characterize: It also had strong "political" goals, and shifted to claim "tribal" status when it suited. One colonial official had referred to the ABC as a "quasi religious movement," which was in fact a fairly apt description.[87] Mulandi was a member of the UMA during the late 1930s, as were his fellow leaders, Goana Nzioka and Paolo Kavuo. Though Mulandi was born in Mukaa, he had lived in Ngelani during his formative years, and founded the ABC at the site where the UMA leaders were arrested in 1940.[88] Moreover, the ABC's constitution made no bones about speaking for Christians alone: It stated that the group was for "all Kamba who are not Christians too," and periodically spoke as an authority on "the Kamba."[89]

The ABC's agenda shared much with the Ikunda ya Mbaa Lili and Akamba Union regarding the importance of education. The ABC had carried out a program of unauthorized school building, recruiting widely to find teachers to work in its new facilities. The ABC's position on education directly contrasted that of the AIM: The AIM had built relatively few schools, in part due to a lack of funding, but also because it resolutely believed that it should "preach not teach." The ABC, on the other hand, used every tactic in the book to increase the number of its schools: One was to gain government authorization for a church – which was relatively simple – and then alter the application to include a school

---

[85] Acts 17:26–27.

[86] Anonymous, "African Brotherhood Church," 145–149. The motto is from St. Matthew's Gospel (28:19) and is Christ's great exhortation to his followers that they should spread the Word.

[87] KNA, DC/MKS/2/1/1, Machakos District Intelligence Report, September 1947.

[88] Information on the early activities of the ABC is drawn in part from Sandgren, "Kamba Christianity."

[89] KNA, MAA/2/122, Director of Intelligence and Security to Chief Secretary, Nairobi, Enclosure: "African Brotherhood Church Rules and Regulations," April 14, 1945.

either in addition to – or in place of – the original church.[90] ABC schools popped up all over Machakos – and to a lesser extent Kitui – setting the stage for a movement that would become more and more influential, especially during the 1950s.

The ABC also differed from many revivalist movements that appeared at the time by attacking women's autonomy. At the organization's founding, Mulandi explained that the ABC aimed to "maintain morals, particularly among Akamba women coming here [to Nairobi]."[91] It is frustratingly difficult to know to what degree this was a tactic to win permission to start a church or to genuinely restrict women's rights: It seems, after all, that female ABC followers traveled between Nairobi and the Kamba reserves to preach. But the statement was telling in reflecting Mulandi's ability to switch between the broad and narrow as it best suited his interests.

Like Christians of other denominations, Mulandi's church espoused a different version of honor beyond the possession of cattle, soldierly virtues related to ĩwi, or notions of community outside Christ. His followers gathered together in churches on Sundays bonded by their religious beliefs to support fellow congregants. They largely avoided polygyny, and married only fellow-Christians: Having multiple wives was acceptable if one converted after marrying them, but taking more than one post-baptism was not permitted. Unlike the AIM, converts could consume alcohol. And they respected education with a passion: Mulandi's converts strove to build schools as quickly as possible, and honored those who became learned.

DEVELOPMENT AND WELFARE FOR AFRICA

As this contest took place, colonial policy was undergoing an enormous reworking, which would have a tremendous impact on Ukambani. The most prominent voice in this process was that of Lord Malcolm Hailey, an administrator who had done the majority of his service in India. Hailey published his influential *Survey* in 1938, and together with his writings and speeches of the early 1940s, argued that Britain required a new approach to colonial administration. The new watchwords for colonial governance were "local government."[92]

---

[90] KNA, DC/MKS/5/1/4, Minutes of a Meeting of the Machakos LNC, July 25–27, 1946.
[91] KNA, MAA/2/122, Colchester to Officer-in-Charge, CID Nairobi, July 12, 1943.
[92] Hailey, *African Survey*.

In this era, the Colonial Office's approach to administration on the ground changed. In the prewar years, it had remained somewhat aloof from the colonies, typically serving them in a supervisory – and advisory – capacity. Now, however, it became more interventionist, instigating intricate, large-scale, multi-year projects in the colonies, relying on the advice of metropolitan experts more than men in the field.[93]

Several scholars have provided blow-by-blow accounts of these new methods, most prominently David Morgan, whose "official history" must stand as the foremost work on the subject.[94] From the Africanist perspective, Frederick Cooper's opus *Decolonization and African Society* has led the way. But though scholarly analyses of these programs and their workings have become more intricate and nuanced in recent years, they have ignored the crucial relationship between ethnicity and the new development programs.[95] In Kenya, they were heavily weighted toward the Kamba, as a result of their position as East Africa's premier martial race. By the 1950s, if not before, it was abundantly clear that development programs were a carefully deployed method of imperial control. But Kamba leaders also proved adept at manipulating the programs on their own terms.

Officials viewed Machakos as a test case for this new approach to colonial administration. This was for two main reasons; first, the district was one of the most eroded in the colony, and had received a significant amount of attention from colonial experts over the previous fifteen years. It was one that encompassed all the major difficulties faced by other regions; if Machakos could be "fixed," then anywhere could. Machakos was therefore constantly in the "limelight," noted one official, and was the location for all kinds of pilot schemes and experiments.[96]

Second, the district was inhabited by large numbers of demobilized soldiers. As noted in Chapter 5, veterans had led resistance to the government after 1945, and were certainly a potential source of conflict. But officials viewed the ex-soldiers' role as a dual one: They also believed that they could provide the impetus to drive Africa forward. Officials thought ex-soldiers could most effectively transfer metropolitan initiatives to the general population. This was no imposition: They had come back from

[93] Havinden and Meredith, *Colonial Development*, 218–225.
[94] Havinden and Meredith, *Colonial Development*; Lee and Petter, *Colonial Office*; Morgan, *Official History*; Pearce, *Turning Point*, especially 42–69, 132–161.
[95] See, for instance, van Beusekom, *Negotiating Development*, or Frederick Cooper's introduction to a special issue of the *Journal of Modern European History*. Cooper, "Writing the History of Development."
[96] KNA, DC/MKS/18/1, "Reconditioning Policy," May 1949.

their travels abroad fully convinced about the benefits of development, and in particular, the merits of education. Ukambani was thus the crucible where new notions of development, welfare, control, and social change mixed.

The most visible manifestation of the new colonial attention came through the Colonial Development and Welfare Act of 1940. The act provided funding totaling £5 million per year – for ten years – for projects related to development and welfare. It also allocated £500,000 per year for research into potential new projects.[97] Reflecting Britain's interests, the undersecretary of state for the colonies, Charles Jeffries, was quick to highlight that, "It was 'a matter of the highest political importance' ... that the government should demonstrate 'unassailable' justification for its claim that it acts as a beneficial trustee for its subject peoples.'"[98]

Yet the Second World War disrupted these plans, and in any case, the act was quickly forgotten when it was superseded by the new Colonial Development and Welfare Act of 1945, which dwarfed its predecessor. This act granted £120 million over ten years for the colonies, and would provide not for "a collection of individual projects," as had the previous one, but rather "integrated plans" that would fundamentally transform them. Kenya received £15.5 million of funding from the Act of 1945, £11 million of which was destined for the development of land, livestock, and water. While no statistics exist that delineate the amount of funding designated for African versus European land, the official report stated that "more than half" was for African land.[99] The largest chunk, and the only one for which specific figures broken down by region are available, was for African land development. Table 1 shows the amounts spent on the two most heavily funded provinces for the years between 1946 and 1955. Kamba areas received 38.9 percent of the entire colony's funding for land development. In addition, a list of Kenya's twenty-five major ("flagship") projects is revealing (the five most costly projects are shown in Table 2). At least three of the top five projects (Makueni, Machakos, and Emali-Tsavo) were for Kamba, and possibly four (Coast Hinterland

---

[97] Havinden and Meredith, *Colonial Development*, 218–225. New ideas of development and welfare for Africa were heavily influenced by metropolitan thinking. Pedersen, *Family, Dependence*.
[98] Lewis, *Empire State-Building*, 35.   [99] Kenya, *African Development*, 1.

TABLE 1

Southern Province		
Machakos		£713,648
Kitui		£63,907
Masai		£43,715
	Total	£821,270
Central Province		
Nyeri		£121,650
Fort Hall		£114,048
Kiambu		£75,447
Embu		£48,090
Meru		£6,184
Nanyuki		£15,841
	Total	£381,260
TOTAL FOR ALL PROVINCES:		£2,002,752

Source: Kenya, *African Land Development*, 229.

TABLE 2

Makueni Settlement	£189,000
Machakos Betterment	£110,800
Coast Hinterland Development	£58,700
Northern Province Grazing Control and Water	£55,100
Emali-Tsavo Development	£47,700
TOTAL FOR ALL 25 PROJECTS:	£794,700

Source: Kenya, *African Development*, 34–35.

Development).[100] Of the £794,700 spent on these individual schemes aimed at particular regions of the colony, a minimum of £393,400 went to Kamba areas (50.2 percent of the total) with a possible maximum of £452,100 (56.9 percent).[101] Kamba numbered 11.6 percent of Kenya's population.[102]

The post-war years also saw a transformation in educational services. In 1945, they were poor: In Machakos, facilities existed for the education

---

[100] In the 1950s, government development funding provided for the opening of new lands in the coastal hinterland for Kamba settlers (see below). It is unclear whether this was the case in the 1940s as well.

[101] The percentage of 50.2 is calculated from the figure £784,200, not £794,700. One expense of £10,500 for "Assistance to African farmers" is removed from this calculation because it is the only sum not tied to a specific region of the colony.

[102] Kenya, *African Population*, 6.

of only 12 percent of children. The district had 29 elementary schools (11 mission and 18 government), plus government primary schools at Machakos Town and Kangundo, and a Roman Catholic Mission primary school at Kabaa. Slightly more than 5,000 pupils attended school that year.[103] At Kitui in 1945, only 17 elementary schools were in operation and just one primary school, in Kitui Town: 2,224 pupils attended schools in 1946, with the number a little higher than in 1945, though hard figures do not exist for that year.[104] During the following six years, educational facilities in Kitui increased dramatically: By 1951, 46 primary schools operated (elementary and primary schools had now merged), with one secondary school, the Government African School in Kitui Town.[105] And in Machakos, the transformation was even more striking: By 1951, 3 teacher-training centers functioned, along with 1 secondary school, 7 junior secondary schools, and 135 primary schools.[106]

The vast amount of funding pumped into Ukambani is especially notable because the outlays seem to share little in common with development programs in practically all other parts of colonial Africa. The majority of large-scale colonial (and in fact post-colonial) development projects feature at least one of several facets: (1) They are carried out in areas of dense population (often urban) to maximize their impact; (2) they include mechanical constructions – that will benefit not only a large number of people but also the economy directly – such as dams, roads, or harbors;[107] (3) they feature the production of a crop or product that will sustain the economy, such as rice in French West Africa, or groundnuts in the infamous Tanganyikan scheme.[108] In contrast to these commonalities, the distribution in Ukambani took place in areas of low population density;[109] included few large infrastructural projects,

---

[103] KNA, DC/MKS/1/1/29, Machakos District Annual Report, 1945.

[104] KNA, DC/KTI/1/1/5, Kitui District Annual Reports, 1945 and 1946.

[105] KNA, DC/KTI/1/1/5, Kitui District Annual Report, 1951.

[106] KNA, DC/MKS/1/1/30, Machakos District Annual Report, 1951.

[107] Goldsworthy (ed.), *British Documents*, 172–175, referring to TNA, CO 537/7859, No. 1, "Colonial Development": Memorandum by United Kingdom Delegation to Commonwealth Economic Conference Preparatory Meeting of Officials, September 22, 1952.

[108] Iliffe, *Modern History of Tanganyika*, 440–442. On the centrality of economic concerns see, for instance, Hyam (ed.), *British Documents*, 94–95, referring to TNA, CO 927/1/2, Annex: Research Dept. Record of Discussion with Treasury, February 14, 1946.

[109] Machakos ranked 14th out of 30 districts in the colony in population density (64 people per square mile), and Kitui 22nd (16 people per square mile). (Northern Frontier Province – the only province not split into districts, because of low population – is

with certain exceptions; and would never produce anything approaching financial benefits for the colonial economy.

The "Makueni Scheme" best encompassed and represented the debate between Kamba leaders and colonial officials over development. One of the results of the Kenya Land Commission was that the government gave the Kamba the use of several new areas of land outside the reserves, the largest of which – by far – was Makueni, a region of southern Machakos. On paper this grant was immensely generous: Makueni was an area of more than 400,000 acres (over 625 square miles), but in practice the land was useless. Extensive bush coverage meant that the area was infested with tsetse fly, the vector for trypanosomiasis and sleeping sickness.[110]

In 1946, however, the government approved funds to allow initial settlement in Makueni, promising £189,000 over the following six years.[111] Colonial administrators viewed the Makueni Scheme as a model for rural land use in Kenya, and later copied its organization in Kako, Simba-Emali, and other places. The feeling amongst officials and agricultural experts was that if their new techniques made a dry part of Ukambani inhabitable, then they would work anywhere.

Officials carefully planned how they would establish the new settlers in Makueni. Before anyone was allowed to move onto the land, Chief Game Warden J. A. Hunter and his team culled more than 1,000 rhinoceros, at the cost of £67,000.[112] Officials then gazetted the entire area and began bush clearing. Settlement officers created model holdings, on which they tested everything from the amount of water needed per head of stock, to the amount of grazing land required for each type of animal. They drew up a strict set of points with which "permit holders" had to comply, known as the "Makueni Rules," an agreement each would have to physically sign. The Makueni Rules were strict regulations on settlement: They stated, for instance, that any permit holder was allowed only seven

---

excluded from these statistics.) These densities are especially low in comparison with districts like Kiambu (420 people per square mile), North Nyanza (236), or Nandi (128). Kenya, *African Land Development*, 220–221.

[110] Much of the information presented here about the Makueni Scheme is from the detailed description in KNA, DC/MKS/14/3/2, Machakos District Agricultural Gazetteer, 1959.

[111] In 1939, the first settlement took place in a tiny section of Makueni. Several families moved there, but the amount of bush clearing required was prohibitively high, and the onset of the Second World War prevented further progress. Kenya, *African Development*, 12.

[112] Shorter, *East African Societies*, 124.

head of cattle, with the option of five sheep or goats as a substitute for one cow, and that he must submit to all instructions of settlement officers regarding the branding, dipping, and inoculation of his cattle. Failure to adhere to these rules would result in the confiscation of his cattle, and possibly removal from the settlement.[113]

By March 1947, officials made offers of land in Makueni to forty families from Machakos. Each family had demonstrated "landlessness" to some degree; however, each offer was "categorically declined." People were unwilling to settle in Makueni because the LNC had refused to accept the Makueni Rules, objecting to the restrictions on settlement. Jomo Kenyatta – an oft-seen figure in Machakos at the time – supported the LNC in this venture, claiming that because Makueni was "part of the Akamba Native Land Unit only those rules that already applied in the Reserve should be used there." To the frustration of district officials, Kenyatta did this with the recently freed Samuel Muindi by his side, both acting in concert with the chiefs.[114] Near the end of the year, a member of the Legislative Council raised the issue with the speaker, Ferdinand Cavendish-Bentinck, asking him about the number of families settled in Makueni. In a rather waffling response, Cavendish-Bentinck detailed logistical plans for the scheme, before the member reminded him of the original question. Cavendish-Bentinck responded, "40 families have been registered and are *in process* [my emphasis] of being settled."[115] He was concealing the fact that not a single family was in residence. By December 31 of the year, only twelve families were settled, at the astronomical cost of £5,500 per family.[116]

On one level, chiefs and councillors objected to the promulgation of any rules whatsoever in the settlement. But they particularly disliked points six and seven of the Makueni Rules, which included the stipulation that unless a farmer grew certain crops requested by settlement officers, the government could uproot them without paying compensation. In addition, they refused to accept the insistence that permit holders in Makueni practice communal farming. Chiefs were also angry at the use of conscripted labor for bush clearing. As usual, they phrased their displeasure in terms of Kamba military service. One LNC minute attested

[113] KNA, DC/MKS/12/2/1, "Makueni Rules," and "Comments on Draft Rules," November 19, 1945.
[114] KNA, DC/MKS/1/1/30, Machakos District Annual Report, 1947.
[115] Kenya, *Legislative Council Debates*, Vol. 28, 4th session, November 3, 1947, 204–205.
[116] RHL, Mss. Afr. s. 1469/13, Papers of J. W. Balfour, Balfour to the Editor, *Baraza*, March 1, 1951.

that, "Councillors Simeon Kioko and Socius Mutiso considered that in view of the Wakamba war effort, it was wrong to conscript labourers for Makueni. They called it slavery."[117]

In the face of opposition from the chiefs, the government had little choice but to amend the Rules. It removed the obligation of participating in communal farming and ended the conscription of labor. All this was a measure of the respect and influence that Kamba leaders possessed both among British officials and their own people. Landless people had refused free land – already broken, which would soon feature dispensaries, schools, and churches – because settlement there did not have the chiefs' and councillors' blessing. The situation was extraordinary, and showed the ability of Kamba leaders to manipulate the hegemony of a weakened colonial state. Yet niggling debate over the Rules, combined with a desire to start the Makueni Scheme slowly, meant that by early 1950, only 100 families were settled, at the cost of £1,249 per family. The Makueni Scheme was eventually successful – so much money was thrown at it that the opposite was unthinkable – and was widely cited in London as an example that colonial development both worked and was beneficial for Africans.[118] Land regeneration in Machakos (the major part of which was Makueni) was, in fact, touted as the "greatest miracle in Africa," during the 1950s.[119]

CONCLUSION

By 1950, life in Ukambani had undergone a seismic shift. People did a roaring trade in new marketplaces, more and more children attended school and church, and a system of roads connected the reserves to one another, as well as Nairobi and Mombasa. A sense of ethnic ascription became more widespread in the villages, and many older practices such as teeth-chipping and thome disappeared, now dismissed as "backward" or "pointless."

Some older institutions, however, were resurrected on the terms of elders, who tried to bolster their positions in the face of powerful war

[117] KNA, DC/MKS/5/1/4, Minute 30/47, "Forced Labour – Indirect Servitude Suffered," March 25–29, 1947. See also KNA, DC/MKS/2/1/1, Machakos District Monthly Intelligence Reports, 1945–1950.
[118] See, for instance, Great Britain, *House of Commons Debates*, Vol. 450, Cols. 1181–1183, November 9, 1950 or Vol. 485, Col. 181W, March 14, 1951.
[119] KNA, MSS/120/4, Papers of Tom Askwith, Anthony Lavers, "Press Office Feature No. 439," June 1958.

veterans, chiefs, and Christian leaders. Determined not to lose their positions of strength to young, "modern" chiefs, they challenged them through a variety of administrative and clan councils. Common to most was a desire to subjugate women to male control, something deemed a splendid idea by the majority of colonial officials and missionaries. But women responded powerfully, especially in the cities of Nairobi and Mombasa. They maintained businesses and trading relationships they had established during the war, and argued that factors such as martial service or the possession of cattle only connoted respect if they contributed to the sustenance of communities.

Following the war, new methods of trusteeship – involving development and welfare – became the official approach to British rule in Africa. The new policies were implemented through the vehicle of ex-soldiers, recently returned from fighting abroad, who – it was hoped – would become shining examples of the new, modernized Africa. Yet there was more to these policies than simply new ideas about trusteeship: They formed a new aspect of imperial control, based on "tribe." Welfare, development, and education were areas of contestation between powerful Kamba leaders and the colonial administration, with Kamba leaders demonstrating an ability to pressure the government to provide development on terms they desired. As Lonsdale notes about the post-Second World War era, in an important article on political accountability, "those who prospered [from change] ... demanded the power with which to prosper more."[120]

The process of negotiation between Kamba leaders and the colonial state had its roots in the 1938 destocking protest, and fully developed in the post-war years. During the time of Mau Mau, however, the position of Kamba chiefs progressed from strength to strength, as the government desperately needed their assistance.

[120] Lonsdale, "Political Accountability," 153.

Chapter 7

Mau Mau

The Kamba occupy a key position in the general situation in this country.[1]

In 1952, the eyes of the world were drawn to Kenya; they rarely strayed for the remainder of the decade. The Mau Mau conflict captured the imagination of the world's intellectuals, academics, and the public at large, entering popular culture in places from New York to the Caribbean, provoking debate at every step. To many, it was a battle of "good" versus "evil"; the sides changed depending on your perspective. Was Mau Mau a battle between civilized colonialists and a savage, barbaric, dreadlocked enemy, or oppressed Africans struggling for freedom against an empire violently clinging to its past glory?

The reality, of course, was far more complex. Mau Mau was never a coherent, unified movement, but rather – in Lonsdale's words – a "manipulated monolith."[2] It was an uneasy alliance of a variety of peoples of different ages and genders mostly living in Kikuyuland, who never even used the term "Mau Mau" to describe their movement.[3] They fought as much amongst themselves in striving for a renewed, virtuous Kikuyu society as against the European visitors to their lands.

As central Kenya descended into conflict, British officials came to believe that the Kamba had a pivotal role to play. There were two possible

---

[1] KNA, DC/MKS/8/8, DC Machakos to Commissioner for Community Development, Nairobi, November 5, 1954.
[2] Lonsdale, "Moral Economy," 402.
[3] The origins of the name "Mau Mau" are unclear. Perhaps the most likely explanation relates to generational tensions in the insecure Kikuyu world that existed at the time. Lonsdale, "Authority, Gender," 59–60.

outcomes in the colonial imagination: Either the tribe would join Mau Mau, causing untold repercussions for ~~security in the colony, or Kamba serving in the army and police would provide the backbone of efforts to defeat the movement.~~ The British therefore undertook numerous propaganda programs designed to bolster Kamba loyalty to the government, and provided extended levels of development funding to dissuade sympathizers from joining Mau Mau. Though few officials realized it, the new programs played an important role in alleviating the sorts of social tensions that drove poor men and women in Kikuyuland into the movement.

Kamba chiefs responded to these British efforts with their own demands. They did so by playing on the Kamba reputation for "historic" loyalty to the government, and in many cases, enriched themselves tremendously. By placing loyalty at the center of Kamba ethnic identity in this fashion, chiefs were also trying to cement their own positions of authority; the honor they possessed, after all, was usually derived from martial service. This was an attempt to vanquish the women, youth, and Christians who challenged them. But they were ultimately unsuccessful: Women, in particular, fought for their own community-based visions of what should constitute "Kamba," and won new levels of respect and authority that would be manifested politically as Kenya neared independence.

MAU MAU AMONG THE KAMBA

In mid 1952, Mau Mau fighters in Kikuyuland instigated a wave of violence that swept through Nairobi and Central Province. The perpetrators "hamstrung" cattle, murdered Kikuyu loyal to the government at a rate of fifteen to twenty per week, and performed various acts of sabotage. With the murder of Senior Chief Waruhiu – a staunch "loyalist" – Governor Evelyn Baring had little choice but to declare a State of Emergency on October 20.

Kamba leaders comprised a small proportion of the Mau Mau hierarchy, and they were active with their Kikuyu peers long before the descent into violence that characterized the middle months of 1952. Attracting like-minded followers – who pledged their allegiance to the movement through an oath – was one of the most important activities in which they participated.[4] "Oathing" was controlled by radicals in

---

[4] Marshall Clough provides a useful introduction to the primary source material on the Mau Mau oath. Clough, *Mau Mau Memoirs*, 85–125.

the executive committee of the KAU Nairobi branch after 1951.[5] Paul
Ngei – assistant secretary of the KAU and later imprisoned with Jomo
Kenyatta as part of the "Kapenguria Six" – was one such member of the
committee. From as early as 1951, Ngei invited interested Kamba to
Kiburi House in Nairobi to take the oath. Other Nairobi-based Kamba
copied Ngei's actions.[6] They then returned to the reserves to spread the
word about the movement. Ngei's first wife – "an absolute Mau Mau," in
her own words – helped him try to recruit members back in Machakos.[7]

The movement found willing supporters in Nairobi. Thousands of
Africans had poured into the colony's capital since the end of the war in
search of work. This surge was especially notable among Kamba men,
who wanted to escape the dry conditions of the overcrowded reserves,
and had done so frequently against the wishes of their elders and chiefs.
In Nairobi, members of every ethnic group mixed freely, and thousands
of Kamba took the oath, some at their own wish, and others forced by
oathing teams made up of Kikuyu or Kamba leaders. Those few in
Nairobi who categorically refused to take the oath faced an uncertain
future, with violence a daily occurrence on the streets. One of these men,
living in the city in 1953, described how he ensured his family was ready
to depart for their home in Kitui at a moment's notice. He recalled the
threatening notes he received from Mau Mau: "X will come to fetch your
head on Wednesday, please be there!" read one.[8]

In the rural areas of Ukambani, however, Mau Mau did not enjoy the
same success. The KAU had realized the importance of winning Kamba
support there as early as 1951, especially because the majority of former
servicemen resided in the reserves. That year, Paul Ngei had toured
Machakos, giving speeches under the guise of the KAU and promoting
the role of Africans in politics. Other members of the KAU such as
Kenyatta and Fred Kubai also spoke in Machakos and Kitui. But on
the eve of the Emergency, the government acted to prevent the movement
of people between the Kamba reserves, Kikuyuland, and Nairobi.
On September 23, 1952, it passed a traffic amendment restricting the
passage of vehicles at night along the three major routes into Ukambani:
between Machakos and Nairobi, Thika and Machakos, and Thika and
Kitui.[9] The Kenya Police began night patrols in Machakos, and the

---

[5] Rosberg and Nottingham, *Myth*, 271.   [6] Corfield, *Historical Survey*, 203, 205.
[7] Interview with Emma Muloko Paul Ngei, Kanzalu, October 23, 2006.
[8] Interview with Philip Muinde, Changwithia, July 24, 2006.
[9] KNA, DC/MKS/26/2, Police Notice: Traffic (Amendment) Rules, 1952.

government increased the number of Tribal Police there. It also created a new West Ukamba division of the Kenya Police Reserve.[10]

The government was highly successful in creating a degree of isolation in Ukambani. The success of this tactic is clearly revealed in contemporary interviews carried out in the central parts of Machakos and Kitui. Mitaboni location – certainly no stranger to "political" activity – provides a neat example. Martha Ngandi, a member of the ABC, summed up the assertions of many when she described the major rumor that floated around at the time: that some Kamba had been forced to take a Mau Mau oath. Those in Mitaboni were scared of Mau Mau, she explained, but neither she nor those living around her ever actually came across someone who had directly participated in the conflict.[11]

It was the following year – after days of asking around – that I finally heard about someone in Mitaboni who was reputed to have been involved in Mau Mau. The referral came from Elizabeth Kioko, the wife of Chief Simeon, who described to me that Wambua Ndambuki (not his real name) was the "only person" in the area who had participated. Wambua lived far from Martha Ngandi's home, down the valley and on the other side of Mitaboni Town in wretched quarters. Elizabeth had, out of a sense of Christian duty, made a variety of efforts over the years to reintegrate him into the community from which he had been ostracized for his participation in Mau Mau.[12] Wambua was immediately uneasy when I came to speak with him: He was evasive, and made it clear that he would only consider speaking with me if I paid him a large sum of money for his trouble. Even our short conversation made it clear that he was unpopular in his community: Ultimately, I left without interviewing him.[13]

This kind of isolation in central Machakos was such that the district commissioner – J. K. R. Thorp – pleaded with the provincial commissioner of Central Province to hold a baraza in Machakos to convince prominent leaders there of the serious state of affairs in the colony. "Many Akamba find it hard really to believe that the situation in parts of the Colony ha[s] reached an almost indescribable degree of savagery and lawlessness," Thorp told the assembled men, to explain why he had brought his senior officer to address them.[14]

---

[10] KNA, DC/MKS/1/2/1, Central Province Annual Report, 1952.

[11] Interview 20 (pseudonym), Mitaboni, July 27, 2004.

[12] Interview with Elizabeth Simeon Kioko, Mitaboni, July 5, 2005.

[13] Meeting with Wambua Ndambuki (pseudonym), Mitaboni, July 9, 2005.

[14] KNA, DC/MKS/10B/14/1, Address by Thorp, October 30, 1952.

But as time passed, and the government did not achieve its anticipated victory, more Kamba became involved in the movement. They worried that the spoils of independence would pass them by if Mau Mau won, but they had not contributed to the physical struggle. Officials fretted that the security situation was likely much worse than it appeared. Hints seemed to suggest that more and more Kamba were joining Mau Mau: On one European farm – belonging to a Mrs. Davis-Evans – twenty oathed Kamba were discovered. The government then found out that several oathing groups comprised of young Kamba men were circulating throughout the reserves. When Kawa Musili was arrested, his confession was indicative of this new trend: "I wish to tell the Screening Team about 'Kwasya na Kwika.' a Mau Mau war Council [*sic*]. The following were the aims and objects of the council: 1. To fight to the end, 2. To administer Mau Mau oaths to all the Wakamba, 3. To subscribe money for furthering Mau Mau ends in Ukambani."[15] Chiefs – on whom the government was so reliant for maintaining stability – began receiving threats.

There was a strong connection between Mau Mau activity and the railway line. The government expected trouble in areas such as Kangundo – home of Paul Ngei – and Iveti, and therefore neglected places like Mbitini and Kilungu in the southwest, where Mau Mau took root. When I conducted interviews in this area in 2005 – having worked previously only in central Machakos – I was struck by the sea change in the way people discussed Mau Mau. Gone were any vague mentions of the movement or rumors of its existence: Here, people spoke passionately about their direct participation. One Kamba man from Kilungu gave evidence against Jomo Kenyatta at his trial in 1953: The people of his location told him he had "sold his country" to the British.[16]

One of the most impressive men I came across during my years in Ukambani lived close to the railway line, in the old Mbitini division, which has since been sub-divided. John Mutinda is from a village about an hour's walk from the bustling truck stop town of Emali, on the Mombasa Road.[17] He held the rank of senior colonel in Mau Mau. Mutinda claimed he was the highest-ranking Kamba involved in the war, although unconfirmed reports mention the existence of one or two

[15] TNA, WO 276/407, Intelligence Summary: April 23, 1955.

[16] TNA, CO 822/780, Infiltration of Mau Mau Into Tribes Other Than the Agikuyu (Secret), 1955.

[17] Information presented here about John Mutinda (pseudonym) is from Interview 46, Mulala, August 3, 2005.

Kamba generals. In 1967, former Mau Mau in Ukambani began political organizations to represent their interests: Mutinda was chosen to be chairman of the Freedom Fighters of Makueni.

There was something about Mutinda that commanded respect. It certainly was not his physical appearance: There at the gate of his home I saw a stick-thin man, wrinkled from head to toe, and dressed in a decaying sport coat with accompanying flat cap. He looked slightly confused, as though I had interrupted his evening's occupation of sitting close to a *jiko* (stove) and warming his hands. But his handshake was surprisingly firm. He introduced himself to me as "Malovoo." I had never heard the word before, so I enquired. He grinned, but said nothing, and instead gestured toward his house. He pulled ahead of me as we walked, and all of a sudden, bent down, grabbed a machete, and swung it with impressive force into a nearby tree stump. Seeing the look of surprise on my face, he laughed: "Malovoo means 'machetes,'" he explained, "I earned that name during the Mau Mau war."

Mutinda was a part of the Mau Mau leadership from 1950, and was captured in 1954. He was ultimately detained at Hola, the camp for the most notorious Mau Mau prisoners, where he stayed with nine other Kambas (including Ndutu Kilungu, a man who caused British officials many sleepless nights). Mutinda provided comprehensive and verifiable details about his detention in various camps in the colony, but politely refused to provide information about oaths he took – or the missions in which he participated, those he killed, or the names of those under his command – stating that he was still bound by the oath.

Men from areas like Mulala frequently received visits from Kikuyu Mau Mau. They stowed away on trains leaving Nairobi, and deposited themselves further down the line in Ukambani where they joined with sympathetic Kamba to perform oathing ceremonies. One informant remembered this process clearly: "The Kikuyu passed through Emali at night. They would alight and enter the neighboring Kamba areas, and then they mixed with the Kamba committees to give the oath, as the Kambas were the ones who spoke Kikamba. By dawn, they would return home."[18] The prevalence of this method of movement is clear from both my interviews and the Corfield Report. The latter details that in March 1954, security forces arrested a significant fighting group of Kamba Mau Mau, and that 10 of the 17 arrested were railway workers. Later

[18] Interview 41, Mulala, July 27, 2005.

that year, the government identified 253 known Kamba members of Mau Mau who were employed as railway workers, and began an operation to round them up.[19] The significance of the line is also suggested by the fact that Mau Mau made no attempt to sabotage it during the conflict.[20]

As 1953 drew to a close, one official wrote that, "The cancer is spreading."[21] District Officer John Nottingham told Major General Hinde that he believed the "vast majority" of Kamba in Nairobi had taken the oath.[22] Kamba now began to take a greater part in the physical struggle. Security forces intercepted a gang of fourteen Kamba and two Kikuyu in Nairobi, foiling its plan to pass through Konza to kill a chief in Ukambani. The government then learned that Waruhiu Itote – General China – had sent oath administrators from the forests of Mount Kenya to Kitui, to further recruit members to his force that already included a number of Kamba among its Kikuyu base. Nor was Itote's force unique: The government believed that at least one Kamba Mau Mau general was at the head of a battalion of over 1,000 Mau Mau in the Aberdares forests.[23] One Mau Mau major from Meru told me that a Kamba general named Kavyu ("knife") was in charge of his fighting unit, which operated in the forests around Mount Kenya. "In every fighting group of about thirty, there might be five or six Kambas," he noted.[24] Itote himself – during his 68-hour interrogation in January 1954 – warned, "There are very many Kamba in the Mau Mau. They will, in time, think the same way as the Kikuyu."[25]

Some exploited their status as non-"KEM" – Kikuyu, Embu, or Meru – to evade detection and provide logistical support, and some even pretended to belong to different "tribes," even if momentarily, as a tactic of war.[26] Those who assisted government enemies without actually bearing arms still faced extraordinary risk. As the New Emergency Regulations of May 1953 detailed:

[19] TNA, WO 276/407, Intelligence Summary: June 24–July 12, 1954.
[20] For an example of the use of the railway line in Mau Mau, see Wamweya, *Freedom Fighter*, 98.
[21] TNA, CO 822/780, Infiltration of Mau Mau Into Tribes Other Than the Agikuyu (Secret), 1955.
[22] RHL, Mss. Afr. s. 1580 (4), Papers of Sir W. R. Hinde, "Visit to MMIC – Kamba Section – DO [District Officer] Nottingham in Charge CPEC (S) Min. 579," December 13, 1955.
[23] TNA, CO 822/780, Infiltration of Mau Mau Into Tribes Other Than the Agikuyu (Secret), 1955.
[24] Interview 77, Kirimara, May 11, 2009.
[25] KNA, BB/1/210, Interrogation of Waruhiu s/o Itote (Alias) "General China," January 26, 1954.
[26] Itote, *"Mau Mau" General*, 54; Kabiro and Barnett, *Man in the Middle*, 46.

It is now an offence, punishable by death, to do, attempt or conspire to do any act likely to endanger life, assist terrorists or impede the operations of the security forces ... The death penalty will also be imposed on anyone who gives, sells, lends, lets out on hire or delivers possession of firearms, ammunition or explosives.[27]

One KAR veteran who worked as a driver for British American Tobacco during the 1950s described how despite the risks, his loyalties lay with Mau Mau. As a non-"KEM" with a reputable job, he could sometimes move around parts of Central Province in his employer's van. He recalled traveling to various places, including the Mau Forest, to deposit food and supplies with fighters there.[28] This type of Kamba contribution in Mau Mau also appears in the memoirs written by former Mau Mau fighters.[29] It is difficult to estimate the number of those who provided non-military assistance for Mau Mau, yet their impact was certainly significant, as was their support for the organization.

Yet the final months of 1954 – and the early ones of 1955 – saw a resurgent colonial military that finally ended Mau Mau's success. The movement's embryonic popularity in Ukambani waned. The British reestablished control in the colony that year, based on military victories in Central Province. In addition, the government's "screening teams" finally made their presence felt, helping to detect and excise Mau Mau among the Kamba. These teams included "loyal" chiefs, as well as European personnel with experience living or working with Kamba. In September 1953, a screening team had begun operating in Nairobi, and in February 1954, the government set up a Kamba screening center at the Mau Mau Investigation Centre in Embakasi, in a successful attempt to control the movement of Kamba workers between Nairobi and Ukambani.

THE PIPELINE

One part of the government's strategy to first gain and then maintain control in the colony was the imprisonment of hundreds of thousands of Africans in detention camps and enclosed villages. Officially, the camps were meant to "rehabilitate" the detainees; most importantly, they had to confess their Mau Mau oaths. Detainees then passed through a network

---

[27] KNA, DC/MKS/26/2, Press Office Handout No. 139, "New Emergency Regulations," May 18, 1953.
[28] Interview 3, Mutituni, July 9, 2004.
[29] Kabiro and Barnett, *Man in the Middle*, 55; Wachanga, *Swords of Kirinyaga*, 85; Wamweya, *Freedom Fighter*, 102.

of progressively less secure camps known as the "Pipeline." Once they had demonstrated that they no longer held Mau Mau sympathies, they were released to their home areas. Though Kikuyu made up the majority of Africans in the camps, the government also imprisoned a high number of Kamba.

In 1953 and 1954, Kamba Mau Mau were detained in the same camps as Kikuyu. But early in 1955, the government instituted a policy of "segregation" to keep the two apart, creating an entirely separate system of camps in Ukambani. In February 1955, Kathonzweni Works Camp opened, followed by Thwake Works Camp, and then Kaasya "Open" Camp in February 1956. After processing at Embakasi, screeners sent Kamba to one of these three camps. They sent "Hardcore" or "Dangerous" detainees (classified as "Z1" or "Z2") to Thwake; "Suspect" or "Y" detainees to Kathonzweni; and finally those on "Probation" – "X" detainees – to Kaasya.[30] Detainees moved through the Pipeline in sequence, before returning to their home villages under restriction orders.

It is difficult to produce an accurate estimate of the numbers of men and women who entered the Kamba Pipeline. Thwake remained open for only 8 months, during which time 206 prisoners were admitted. When the camp closed, prisoners were transferred to either Kathonzweni or Athi River detention camp. At the start of 1956, Kathonzweni had 427 detainees, which fell to 123 by the end of the year.[31] Although no hard numbers exist for Kaasya, by the end of 1957, 547 Kamba had passed through the Pipeline to the villages.[32] The total number incarcerated in the Kamba Pipeline thus appears lower than 1,000 individuals.

Yet from the available evidence it is clear that many Kamba Mau Mau – particularly the "hardcore" – never reached the Kamba Pipeline in the first place. Thwake was open for less than a year, and many Kamba Mau Mau remained in the detention camp at Athi River or in other camps spread around Kenya. John Mutinda, for instance, was detained for six years before his release in 1960. He carried out part of his sentence in a Nairobi prison, before his transfer to Langata Prison, and then finally to Hola, the location for "unrepentant" Mau Mau. He did not pass through the Kamba Pipeline at any point.[33] Others remained entirely outside the system in prisons or camps in Ukambani such as

[30] KNA, AB/4/97, Machakos Community Development Monthly Report, February 1958.
[31] KNA, AB/1/107, Annual Report: Kamba Pipeline, January 10, 1957.
[32] KNA, DC/MKS/1/1/33, Machakos District Annual Report, 1956.
[33] Interview 46 (pseudonym), Mulala, August 3, 2005.

Machakos, Yatta, Kangundo, Mbooni, or Kilome. The detention of others took place at the office of their local chief.

In mid 1954, the governor of Kenya estimated that 8,000 Kamba had taken the Mau Mau oath.[34] Documents declassified in 2006 – including assorted daily and weekly intelligence reports from 1954 and 1955 – reveal Kamba Mau Mau confessing their oaths at a rate of ten to twenty per report. Among other things, their confessions expose an extensive Kamba Mau Mau network in operation, including a committee at Ngong that specialized in making homemade guns.[35] It is frankly inconceivable that the government detained fewer than 1,000 Kamba Mau Mau given these statistics and the popularity of the movement, particularly considering that camps in the Kamba Pipeline opened so late. Perhaps 3,000 to 4,000 Kamba spent time in detention, although in the absence of firm data, this is an extremely speculative estimate.

Records concerning Kamba detainees are remarkable. A senior community development officer reported, "It has been stated by the Rehabilitation Staff of Athi River camp that the Kamba M.M. [Mau Mau] are as bad and often worse than the Kikuyu."[36] In addition, "Recent incidents indicate that the majority of these are still ardent supporters of Mau Mau ... 65 detainees ... are definitely hard-core and completely unrepentant."[37]

Caroline Elkins has extensively documented the level of mistreatment that took place in the detention camps.[38] My interviews uncovered similar stories from Kamba detainees. Most notorious was a European screening officer named Louvaine Dunman, known to Kamba as "Luvai" (meaning "disliked" or "ruthless," but also a Kikamba-ization of his English name). Dunman spoke Kikamba fluently, and was responsible for rounding up and interrogating suspected Kamba Mau Mau. He performed much of this work at the Mau Mau Investigation Centre at Embakasi. Stories of torture carried out by Dunman are still told in Ukambani today, hundreds of miles from that area.[39]

One Kamba man who was involved in an attack on a Captain McAusland was arrested and sent to the Athi River detention camp:

---

[34] TNA, CO 822/780, Acting Governor to Gorell Barnes, June 26, 1954.
[35] TNA, WO 276/407, Daily Intelligence Report: June 10–11, 1954.
[36] KNA, AB/1/107, Annual Report: Kamba Pipeline, January 10, 1957.
[37] KNA, AB/1/107, "Thwake Works Camp," July 26, 1956.
[38] Elkins, *Imperial Reckoning*.
[39] Dunman and his family were fortunate to survive several assassination attempts during the Emergency.

Inside the prison camp Mau Mau were terribly beaten on the allegation that they wanted to chase the whites away. We were beaten with rhinoceros whips. They used to remove the skin whenever they touched you. We were also beaten with sticks, and tied with rope to a vehicle and dragged along. Death [in this way] eventually happened to some Mau Mau. There was a lot of torture done by the African soldiers. The whites used to demonstrate to the black soldiers what to do. [One] was Luvai, who was married to a Kamba lady ... He used to show them how to torture us and order them to do the same ... We were tied by our testicles and then the veins were pinched.[40]

What is clear, however, is that in Kathonzweni and Kaasya – the final two camps of the Kamba Pipeline – detainees experienced almost no violence. They remembered clearing bushes and uprooting trees, but nothing more.[41] One informant specifically contrasted his time at Kathonzweni with that at Manyani detention camp; other detainees explained that Kamba guards treated them well in the Kamba Pipeline, as they were all from the same tribe.[42] Interestingly, informants also remember that they received better treatment from Kamba guards in detention camps in the remainder of the colony than they did from non-Kamba guards. Overall, it appears that the punishment inflicted on Kamba was neither as widespread nor severe as that inflicted upon Kikuyu detainees.

BRITISH CONCERN AND THE "DEVELOPMENT DEAL"

British military and civilian officials expended countless hours considering the potential outcome if large numbers of Kamba joined Mau Mau. Approximately 20,000 former servicemen inhabited the Kamba reserves, many of whom had served in the various theaters of the Second World War, as well as Malaya more recently. Governor Baring had noted the potentially decisive role of the Kamba in the conflict as early as 1952, in a top-secret telegram.[43] Perhaps the district commissioner of Machakos – D. J. Penwill – most clearly summarized British concern:

The Kamba occupy a key position in the general situation in this country. Mau Mau must not spread beyond the Kikuyu, Embu and Meru; if it were to do so, and, above all, if it were to spread to the Kamba, the consequences cannot be foreseen, but they would be extremely serious ... There is no doubt whatsoever that the Kamba could go into Mau Mau.[44]

[40] Interview 47, Emali, August 3, 2005.   [41] Interview 44, Mulala, July 14, 2005.
[42] Interview 45, Mulala, July 29, 2005.   [43] Corfield, *Historical Survey*, 274–275.
[44] KNA, DC/MKS/8/8, DC Machakos to Commissioner for Community Development, Nairobi, November 5, 1954.

Baring's anxiety, and that of the district commissioner, related chiefly to the potential difficulties that would ensue if a portion of Kamba serving in the police and army changed sides. Almost six battalions of the KAR were engaged in the Emergency, and in them, Kamba made up a high percentage of the fighting strength: By 1959, they comprised 36.3 percent of the KAR, followed by the Kalenjin at 25.8 percent.[45] While it appears unlikely that KAR soldiers ever provided assistance to Mau Mau – despite statements to the contrary in Mau Mau memoirs – Commander-in-Chief General Sir George Erskine was nevertheless well-aware of the pressure on them, and the "insidious propaganda" to which they were subjected.[46] In the Kenya Police, the numbers of Kamba were no less significant: In 1953, the force numbered 1,754 Kamba, with the Luo the next most populous group at 1,062.[47] Kamba service was therefore essential in the effort against Mau Mau, and as former Police Commissioner O'Rorke noted, "Police reliability is a very precarious thing."[48]

Colonial officials became progressively more concerned as the conflict persisted into 1954. In March, the colonial secretary – Oliver Lyttelton – arrived in Nairobi. In a meeting with Lyttelton, the provincial commissioner of the newly created Southern Province sounded caution. He noted that Mau Mau had not penetrated the Kamba to a critical extent, but that the situation "might change radically were the Emergency to continue for another year ... [It is] essential to do nothing to upset the Wakamba."[49] A crucial moment arrived with the commencement of Operation Anvil on April 24, 1954. Government forces swept through Nairobi, and soldiers forced Africans of all ethnic groups into the streets. They removed thousands of Kikuyu from the city, leaving a vacuum that Kamba filled: One official estimated that 40,000 arrived in the city around that time.[50] In 1953, Kamba made up 18.6 percent of Nairobi's population, and Kikuyu 46.5 percent. By 1956, the Kamba proportion had risen to 28 percent, and the Kikuyu dropped to 22 percent.[51]

---

[45] Parsons, *African Rank-and-File*, 95.
[46] TNA, WO 236/18, Report by General Sir George Erskine, "The Kenya Emergency, June 1953–May 1955," 39.
[47] Kenya, *Kenya Police Annual Report, 1953*, 4.
[48] RHL, Mss. Afr. s. 746, Papers of Sir Michael Blundell, Box 5, File 2, O'Rorke to Blundell, March 22, 1954.
[49] TNA, CO 822/822, Minutes of a Meeting between Lyttelton and PCs, March 1, 1954.
[50] KNA, DC/KTI.2/3, Kitui District Handing Over Report, 1954.
[51] Anderson, *Histories*, 352.

These concerns made Erskine "very much against training further Africans in mobile armed operations." He noted that, "What may be a loyal tribe today might easily become infected in the future and the risk is not worth while."[52] The *Daily Telegraph* hysterically stated that Mau Mau had "won" the Kamba.[53] British worries increased as a number of Kamba chiefs received anonymous, threatening letters claiming to represent the voices of "the [Kamba] askaris."[54]

The ultimate result of this panic was that British officials instituted a "deal of development" to reduce the possibilities of the Kamba joining Mau Mau.[55] This "deal" – providing development funding in exchange for political calm – had first appeared immediately following the Second World War; now, it occurred again, but at a far greater order of magnitude. It was an essential part of Baring's bifurcated approach to addressing the Mau Mau problem: While the forests of Central Province shook with the ordinance of Harvard and Lancaster bombers, the government offered "moderate" Africans tremendous incentives not to join the guerrilla organization.[56]

Initially, however, Baring was unsuccessful in his efforts to procure funding from London. The British government's finances were in dire condition, and development projects little merited budgetary attention. But as Mau Mau won victories in the forests of Central Province during 1952, Baring – thoroughly convinced of his approach – hounded the exchequer for grants of money. London dallied for almost eighteen months, then conceded in 1954 when faced with the serious situation in Kenya. The exchequer released the funds on the condition that they form part of the "grand strategy" against Mau Mau.[57]

[52] RHL, Mss. Afr. s. 746, Papers of Sir Michael Blundell, Box 5, File 2, Memorandum on Some of the Points Raised with HE [His Excellency] the Acting Governor by Mr. Humphrey Slade and Other Elected Members, June 15, 1954.
[53] *Daily Telegraph*, "Kenya Fears Mau Mau Has Won New Tribe," May 14, 1954. See also the following articles from *The Times*: "Mau Mau Breaks New Ground," May 11, 1954; "Infiltration by Mau Mau: Oath Ceremonies in Kamba Tribe," June 2, 1954; "Final Warning to Kamba Terrorists," June 21, 1954; "Mau Mau Among the Wakamba," July 3, 1954.
[54] TNA, CO 822/780, Infiltration of Mau Mau Into Tribes Other Than the Agikuyu (Secret), 1955.
[55] A preliminary effort to resolve some of the complexities of what follows below appeared in 2010, but its approach steered too closely to archival documents and too far from the internal dynamics among Kamba that were important at the time. Osborne, "Kamba and Mau Mau."
[56] Lonsdale, "Constructing Mau Mau."
[57] Douglas-Home, *Evelyn Baring*, 263; *East African Standard*, "Elected Members Welcome Minister," October 24, 1952.

Once the decision was made, the money quickly arrived in the form
of the Swynnerton Plan. Described by one expert as the "most comprehensive of all the post-war colonial development schemes," the five-year
Swynnerton Plan aimed to raise the level of production of land across the
colony by implementing new agricultural techniques and programs.[58]
Various scholars of Kenya – including Daniel Branch, Keith Sorrenson,
and Anne Thurston – have identified how those loyal to the government
garnered benefits (ranging from land security to voting rights) from the
Swynnerton Plan.[59] But neither these scholars nor others have questioned
precisely how this funding was distributed, nor extended their analysis
beyond Kikuyu areas, and have therefore missed the crucially important
point that the majority of funds seem to have been spent not in *Kikuyu*
but *Kamba* areas.

The largest provision in the Plan was £2,740,770 for "Betterment,
Settlement and Ranching Schemes." Approximately one-third of this
amount was designated for non-district specific schemes, such as "Tsetse
survey and control" or "African livestock marketing." Of the remaining
two-thirds, the government made provision for a vast £940,000
(or 53 percent of the total) for schemes to benefit Kamba, leaving
£834,390 for the rest of the colony.[60]

Colonial Office correspondence emphatically confirms the links
between development funding and political control. A working party
assigned to study colonial development outlays during the mid 1950s
stated that Kenya's development and welfare funding would have been
cut down to the bare bones, but this had proved impossible due to the
"political disturbances."[61] Officials deemed development essential to
avoid "East Africa and probably Central Africa drift[ing] into chaos,"
wrote the assistant undersecretary of state.[62] As late as 1956, the colonial
secretary – then Alan Lennox-Boyd – informed the chancellor of the
exchequer that it was "not ... practicable" to carry out an anticipated

---

Thurston, *Intensification*, 1.
Branch, *Defeating Mau Mau*, 121–122, 174; Branch, "Loyalists"; Sorrenson, *Land
Reform*, 113–134, 166–167, 201; Thurston, *Intensification*.
Swynnerton, *Plan*, 43–44. Swynnerton allocated Kwale Hinterland Development and
Shimba Hills Settlement – both in Coast Province and each costing £100,000 – for the
settlement of Kamba families.
Goldsworthy (ed.), *British Documents*, 207, 211, referring to TNA, T 229/865, Note by
Bristow on the Report of the Colonial Development and Welfare Working Party, August
21, 1954.
Goldsworthy (ed.), *British Documents*, 225, referring to TNA, CO 1025/82, Nos. 22,
22B, 22C, Minute by Gorell Barnes, September 16, 1955.

reduction of funding to Kenya, as it was vital to "nip in the bud" trouble in areas outside Central Province where "growing disaffection" had begun to appear.[63]

This use of development funding was demonstrated even more clearly with the creation of "Emergency Expenditure Funds." The government authorized various departments in the colony to spend this additional money for the fight against Mau Mau. One of the most prominent was the African Land Development Board (ALDEV). In addition to receiving funds from the Swynnerton Plan, ALDEV received extra money to provide physical development projects – such as dams or boreholes – for those who were loyal to the government. Benefits from the program – entitled "Reward Projects for Loyal Tribes" – were published throughout the colony, in an attempt to persuade any people harboring Mau Mau sympathies to fall into line.[64] Kitui was one of the early recipients of the grants, receiving £10,000 for the "improvement of water supplies," something extremely valuable in such an arid area.[65]

One of the most complex ALDEV projects was the building of the Yatta Furrow, which commenced in 1953. The Furrow took the majority of the decade to complete, at the extraordinary cost of £300,000, and was built by Mau Mau detainees. The forty-mile-long "lifeline" brought water from the Thika river to dry parts of northwestern Kitui, as well as parts of North Yatta (the latter area was initially designated as a Kikuyu area, but had recently become overflow grazing land for Kamba from Machakos).[66] These areas now became viable for farmers and livestock owners.

Officials continually devised and publicized new schemes to demonstrate the rewards that might be expected for loyal service (this went a long way toward satisfying the European settlers, whose leader – Michael Blundell – had suggested, "For the non-Kikuyu, a short-term Development Plan thoroughly boosted by Information Services").[67] Out of a series of six pilot schemes established in 1954 for the colony,

---

[63] Goldsworthy (ed.), *British Documents*, 315, referring to TNA, CO T 220/498, Lennox-Boyd to Macmillan, May 12, 1956.

[64] KNA, PC/NKU/2/1/51, Baron to Executive Officer, ALDEV, February 16, 1954; Minute 28/53, "Reward Projects for Loyal Tribes," October 1, 1953.

[65] TNA, WO 236/17, Press Office Handout No. 1295, "Kenya Emergency Report by the War Council," broadcast October 20, 1954.

[66] Tiffen, Mortimore and Gichuki, *More People*, 210.

[67] RHL, Mss. Afr. s. 1580 (1), Papers of Sir W. R. Hinde, "Suggestions by Brigadier Orr and Mr. Blundell," January 7, 1954.

three were for Kamba areas. They included a loan to the Machakos ADC to develop the sisal industry, a 16,000-acre farm for Kamba settlement, and a grant for water management in Kitui. Machakos also received the adult literacy scheme first ("in consideration of their loyalty"), a rural training school (for intermediate education), and a teacher training school for women ("Before the Emergency, it was ... [for] Kikuyu country ... it has now been decided to transfer it to Machakos"). The administration made a great effort to show how the Emergency was actually helping the Kamba, in contrast to their neighbors, especially in Kikamba radio-broadcasts from February 1954.[68] When the colonial secretary, Oliver Lyttelton, visited Kitui in March 1954, he described to thousands of Kamba how "much of the £11,000,000 which Britain is making available to Kenya [from the Colonial Development and Welfare Act of 1945, soon bolstered by Swynnerton funding] ... will go to develop the Wakamba's land ... he was satisfied that the investment would be a sound one."[69] One press handout provided recent results from the Kenya African Primary Examinations in Kamba and Kikuyu areas. In the former, it showed that the pass rate between 1952 and 1953 had increased by 46 percent, and in the latter, dropped by 18 percent. Officials were fully aware of the Kamba desire for education, and suggested that the Kamba were now pulling ahead of the Kikuyu.[70]

This effort to separate Kamba from Kikuyu appeared in every realm of life. Kikuyu workers were removed from Ukambani, and, as noted above, restrictions imposed on travel between Ukambani and Kikuyu-land or Nairobi. In September 1953, Machakos and Kitui were removed from Central Province – which the Kamba shared with the Kikuyu – and placed into the new Southern Province.[71] Social changes, too, appeared. Kamba and Kikuyu had long intermarried, but such unions were now banned.[72] Concerned officials even removed sick Kikuyu from hospitals in Machakos, believing that there was a possibility that they might "infect" Kamba with Mau Mau ideas. As one official noted, these actions were to, "Ensure and maintain the cooperation of the

---

[68] TNA, WO 236/17, Press Office Handout No. 1295, "Kenya Emergency Report by the War Council," broadcast October 20, 1954.

[69] KNA, AHC/8/173, Press Office: Department of Information Handout, March 1954.

[70] TNA, WO 236/17, Press Office Handout No. 1295, "Kenya Emergency Report by the War Council," broadcast October 20, 1954.

[71] KNA, PC/SP.1.1.1, Southern Province Annual Report, 1953.

[72] KNA, DC/MKS/16/5, Deputy Assistant Adjutant and Quartermaster General, 70th (East Africa) Infantry Brigade to DC Machakos, January 13, 1956.

loyal tribes ... [And] the Kamba, forming 40 percent of the armed forces, are by far the most important."[73]

Alongside physical development came social welfare, known after 1950 as "community development." One of the most important social welfare programs was homecrafts. In homecrafts classes, African women received instruction in basic hygiene, sewing, baby care, and the like. The concept of homecrafts existed informally from the late 1940s, but by the time of Mau Mau, officials recognized it as an important part of the struggle against the movement in which women would participate. "Social welfare is very important in combatting Mau Mau and we should not let this matter rest," commented one official at the Colonial Office.[74]

The government believed that homecrafts would help provide for a "proper" family life – based, of course, on the British ideal of the nuclear family – which could help to prevent the spread of Mau Mau. This reflected the notion that Mau Mau was backward and anti-progress, and was thus in direct opposition to programs such as homecrafts. The link was explicitly clear in government propaganda. One pamphlet stated: "THE GOVERNMENT PROVIDES CLASSES TO TEACH YOU SEWING AND HOMECRAFT: THE MAU MAU WOULD HAVE YOU LIVE IN SKINS FOREVER"; another, "THE GOVERNMENT PROVIDES EDUCATION FOR YOUR CHILDREN. THE MAU MAU ARE TRYING TO STOP EDUCATION" [emphases in originals]. The government dispersed thousands of pamphlets by air in both Kikamba and English during Mau Mau.[75]

Christian missions bolstered the government agenda. The AIM highlighted precisely the same divide in its publicity. The cover of a 1953 edition of *Inland Africa* – the organization's mouthpiece – featured a young woman leaning over a microscope. The caption noted, "The sacrificing of animals and other heathen rites that were presided over by the old witch doctors used to be the standard way to ascertain the cause of illness. This young African nurse in a mission hospital is making tests by means of a modern microscope."[76]

Archival sources reflect a genuine and powerful belief in the value of homecrafts in fighting against Mau Mau. To cite just one example: As the political situation worsened in 1954, the district commissioner of Machakos wrote:

---

[73] KNA, DC/MKS/10/3, "Internee Camp – Athi River," May 21, 1953.
[74] TNA, CO 822/674, Hall to Rogers, April 4, 1953.
[75] KNA, AHC/9/86, Anti-Mau Mau Pamphlets, *c.* 1954.
[76] *Inland Africa* 37, 6 (1953), cover page.

[I have a] very strong case for a full-time Women's Homecrafts Worker here, on Emergency grounds ... Mau Mau must not spread ... It is absolutely essential to carry the women with the men ... I would readily offer a reduction in establishment of one Police Officer in exchange for one Women's Homecrafts Officer.[77]

Changes wrought by the Swynnerton Plan – and its predecessor – played an important role in assuaging a variety of social concerns that catalyzed Mau Mau's growth in Kikuyu areas. There, as Lonsdale argues in a seminal essay, a variety of interrelated social tensions existed that related to civic virtue, gender relations, "proper" behavior, and economics. For thousands of Kikuyu poor, the road to adulthood was blocked: They had no access to land – so vital in Kikuyu society – and simply no possibility of attaining wealth and status, and rising up through Kenya's class structure. In many communities, elites (in large part, the future "loyalists") had become wealthy at the expense of those who struggled by. The former had gained large plots of land while the poor had had to sacrifice their rights to property ownership.[78]

The concerns that inspired Kikuyu men and women to join Mau Mau were little present in Ukambani. On one level, this was related to the possession – or use of – farming or grazing land. The vast Makueni Scheme was only one of a series of gifts of land given to residents of the Kamba reserves. Other areas included parts of the Kwale hinterland, Shimba Hills, Kako-Emali, Machakos Crown land, the Yatta Plateau, and the 16,000-acre "farm," excised from the eastern fringe of the White Highlands. These additions permitted a significant number of men and women to provide an acceptable standard of living for their families through farming or livestock ownership. These new areas of land – and a range of programs that gave assistance in matters ranging from fertilizer use to irrigation – were a huge relief for thousands of Kamba living in difficult regions. As one chief commented about the Yatta Furrow, "We cannot begin to understand what wealth will be brought to us by this canal ... This the Government has done for us."[79]

Unlike those living in poverty in Kikuyuland, the Kamba poor had avenues open for bettering themselves and winning respect in their communities. First, they could join the armed forces, that traditional venue for achievement. The desire for more and more Kamba recruits rarely

[77] KNA, DC/MKS/8/8, DC Machakos to Commissioner for Community Development, Nairobi, November 5, 1954.
[78] Lonsdale, "Moral Economy."   [79] Huxley, *New Earth*, 184–187.

dropped during the 1940s and 1950s. Officials undertook constant recruiting campaigns for the KAR, Kenya Police, and other assorted bodies (including the Somalia Gendarmerie), meaning that young men always had the opportunity to earn a decent wage and gain honor. Second, men or women could join the schools that popped up all over Ukambani during the late 1940s, and especially in the 1950s. Employers during the 1950s were quick to give jobs to those Kamba who succeeded in school due to bans on employing Kikuyu.

These efforts in the reserves went some distance toward relieving worries felt by Kamba men, who could use their financial successes to buy land, farm, and marry. And they provided vast benefits for Kamba women, who used the opportunities brought by development to make great gains (see below). Colonial officials' correspondence features a quite extraordinary attention to detail regarding development in Ukambani: One outlined the overall aim to provide "an economic holding for every Kamba family" – something that was a far cry from the situation in Kikuyuland.[80] Reading colonial files, one is struck by a determination to take on and solve even difficulties facing individuals: It seems as though officials wanted to make Ukambani "work" where they had failed in Kikuyuland.

Officials attempted to bring the same level of attention to Kamba living in Nairobi, especially after men and women from Machakos – in particular – poured into the city to replace Kikuyu forced out by Operation Anvil. But the situation here was far more chaotic and unmanageable. Officials made sporadic efforts to organize groups of chiefs to bring women and young men back to the reserves, without much impact, and at one point tried to group all Kamba together in the neighborhood of Ziwani, with a similar lack of success.[81]

Officials frequently complained that Kamba laborers were "inefficient," but the truth was that they were simply unwilling to accept poor working conditions or wages. Kamba workers had an enormous advantage post-Anvil, as members of a tribe with a reputation for "loyalty." For comparative elites – like George Nthenge (see Chapter 6) – the business opportunities were enormous. But great potential existed for the poor, too. Kamba had an "Emergency created monopoly" when it came to unskilled labor, and men and women found that their services were in

[80] KNA, AB/4/32, Southern Province Annual Report, 1954.
[81] Prins, "Uneasy Alliance," 88 n. 217, referring to KNA, MAA/7/112, Officer-in-Charge, Nairobi to Secretary for African Affairs, February 2, 1954.

steep demand.[82] One official reported that, "Any Kamba *toto* [child] can look superior and flick a grain of dust from his shorts at any offer under 70 Sh/a month."[83] Considering that a serviceman in the KAR earned 48 Sh a month during the Second World War, this was well-paid work (even accounting for inflation), especially as much of it was unskilled.

CONTESTING "LOYALTY" AND CHIEFSHIP

At the heart of the discourse between Kamba and Briton – and between Kamba men and women – was the notion of "loyalty." It was the arena in which British propaganda sought to control Kamba opinion, where chiefs pressed for benefits from the state, and women fought for autonomy from men who sought to control them.

From the British perspective, the approach was simple: Implement a wide array of tools to remind Kamba soldiers of their "historic" loyalty to the Crown, and connect this service to a longer history of warfare. A significant manifestation of this new concern came through a series of prominent visitors to Ukambani. On March 2, 1953, Governor Baring gave an important speech near Machakos Town, during a three-day tour of the district he carried out with his wife, Lady Mary. As Baring arrived with the acting chief native commissioner, provincial commissioner, and district commissioner of Machakos, events meant to evoke Kamba loyalty and recall their military service took place. A detachment of Kenya Police and Tribal Police formed a Guard of Honor, and the band of the Lancashire Fusiliers played the Royal Salute. The dignitaries sat on a brightly decorated dais, adjacent to a flagpole bearing the Union Jack, and the ensuing speeches boomed out over loudspeakers to the 12,000 Kamba assembled there. In his speech, Baring described the horrors that Mau Mau had wreaked in Kikuyuland. He then noted:

Compare this with the state of your own country … You have refused to be diverted from peaceful pursuits into a campaign of violence. On the contrary following the famous traditions of your people, traditions of service, traditions of courage in both the Army and the Police, very many of you have joined in the struggle to restore security and prosperity to Kenya.[84]

---

[82] KNA, DC/MKS/1/1/33, Machakos District Annual Report, 1956. Interestingly, the one place that had difficulties procuring Kamba labor was the Kenya Meat Commission, formerly Liebig's.

[83] KNA, DC/MKS/1/1/32, Machakos District Annual Report, 1954.

[84] *Daily Chronicle*, "His Excellency the Governor's Speech at Baraza," March 3, 1953.

FIGURE 8: Governor Baring meets askaris of 3 KAR engaged in the battle against Mau Mau. KNA: 967.6203 DEP [991201]. Reproduced here with permission from the Kenya National Archives.

Baring's visit was unexceptional. During 1954 as Mau Mau raged, Baring, Lyttelton, and Field Marshal Sir John Harding – a veritable "who's who" of British colonial statesmen – all visited Kitui to congratulate the Kamba for their "loyal support." The *East African Standard* covered Lyttelton's visit and speech:

[H]e brought the Queen's greetings to the Wakamba people, [and] told them that in England he heard regularly from the governor about the help given by the Wakamba ... He assured them that just as the two world wars had ended in victory, so would the struggle against Mau Mau.[85]

Two years later, Princess Margaret – third in line to the throne – visited Machakos. She held a baraza at the Machakos Sports Club in front of 20,000 men and women from all parts of Ukambani, and inspected a Guard of Honor put on by 23 KAR. She was also entertained by a play set in the distant past in which Kamba men took on and defeated Maasai warriors. The district commissioner approved the "discipline and obvious

[85] *East African Standard*, "Mr. Lyttelton Praises Kamba Loyalty," March 12, 1954.

FIGURE 9: Princess Margaret receives flowers from Ndinda Kioko – the daughter of a prominent chief – at Machakos, 1956. KNA: 394.4 KEN [964521]. Reproduced here with permission from the Kenya National Archives.

pride in the bearing of the ex-servicemen." Princess Margaret then gave a speech: "I am particularly glad to be able to visit Machakos during my short stay in Kenya," she said. "Her Majesty [Queen Elizabeth II] knows well that the Akamba of both Machakos and Kitui have a long record of faithful and brave service to the Crown ... They have served with great distinction in the Army and the Police."[86]

This effort was backed by a surge of propaganda. Information rooms, community halls, and schools were all in the remit of the African

---

[86] KNA, DC/MKS/1/1/33, Machakos District Annual Report, 1956.

Information Services (which became the Department of Information in 1954), the activities of which peaked during the years of Mau Mau. By 1956, at the end of the Mau Mau episode, government radio programs in Kikamba consistently reached over 192,000 people across Ukambani, and mobile cinema vans broadcast programs to 58,000 that year.[87] The vans, in particular, drew large crowds wherever they went. "Cinema then was a miracle, almost," recalled one man who was in charge of the van for a period, "[It was] popular with all the people including seniors."[88] In this regard, Ukambani was exceptional: Charles Ambler has shown how there was no noticeable spike in mobile cinema use elsewhere in the colony.[89]

More traditional forms of propaganda such as pamphlets and newsletters supported film and radio programs. The most significant publication was *Akamba*, created by the Department of Information, which grew from two pages to sixteen during the 1950s. Its circulation peaked in 1956 at 350,000 copies distributed throughout Machakos and Kitui.[90] (The population in Ukambani at the time was between 750,000 and 800,000; roughly half this number were children, and of the adults [anyone older than sixteen], fewer than half were literate.[91]) *Akamba* linked welfare and development with the emphasis on loyalty. It typically contained photographs of Kamba soldiers and police on the cover, and featured biographical articles about loyal Kamba chiefs. Four of the first five issues made a tremendous fuss about the visit of Princess Margaret in 1956, with double-page photographic spreads and numerous articles.[92]

To some degree, British propaganda about Kamba loyalty (ĩwi) likely resonated with veterans, police, and chiefs, and certainly, ĩwi had come to describe an important virtue among men at the time of the Second World War. But the notion primarily stood to benefit Kamba chiefs, who possessed it based on their military service. Chiefs utilized the notion to "sell" a clear martial ethnic identity to British officials: that of a race of soldiers whose traditions of loyal service ranged far back into the past. (They had been largely successful in this in the years following the Second

---

[87] KNA, DC/MKS/1/1/33, Machakos District Annual Report, 1956.
[88] Interview with George Nthenge, Mumbuni, November 16, 2006.
[89] Ambler, "Projecting." I am grateful to Charles Ambler for sharing an advance copy of this chapter with me.
[90] KNA, DC/MKS/1/1/33, Machakos District Annual Report, 1956.
[91] The census of 1948 listed 611,725 Kamba and the census of 1962, 933,219. Kenya, *African Population*, 6; Kenya, *Population Census, 1962*, Vol. I, 28–29, 45.
[92] See, for instance, "Princess Margaret Kusingia Ndeto Masaku," *Akamba* 1, 5 (1956), 6.

World War: Norman Larby's semi-anthropological work *The Kamba* – which formed part of the *Peoples of Kenya* series, published around the time of the war – waxed lyrical about the long history of Kamba soldiering, drawing a direct trajectory from nineteenth-century conflicts against the Maasai to the First and Second World Wars, to explain how the Kamba became East Africa's premier soldiers.[93]) This identity was, of course, gendered. Chiefs constantly raised the idea of "loyalty" and martial service to both British and African audiences to increase their personal statuses and prestige, as well as to procure benefits for themselves and their constituents.[94]

This theme is clear in the minutes of LNC/ADC meetings, in interviews with ex-soldiers, and indeed in higher profile speeches. It was also common for chiefs to draw Kamba against Kikuyu to demonstrate the distinction between the two peoples, and emphasize the soldierly qualities of the former. When Chief Simeon Kioko of Mitaboni – vice president of the Machakos ADC – responded to Baring's speech (above), he shouted: "We utterly condemn the evils of Mau Mau and those Kikuyu who have torn their tribe apart ... We, the Kamba ... are a fighting people ... But we do not want war in our country." Kioko continued by professing loyalty to the government.[95] Similarly in 1954, Chief Kasina gave a speech at the African Agricultural Show in Kitui, in front of several important visitors and thousands of Kamba. The *East African Standard*'s correspondent summarized: "[Kasina] gave an assurance that Mau Mau would never be allowed to spread to the Kitui or Machakos district, but said ... If the Kamba had had educational facilities like the Kikuyu ... they would have made better use of them." Linking military service to the martial history of the Kamba, Kasina presented Governor Baring and Oliver Lyttelton – the colonial secretary – with gifts of bows and arrows.[96]

These ideas were also prominent in meetings of the Akamba Association (AA), an organization created by the administration in 1954 to "unite the Kamba as a tribe." It was established to form a bulwark against Mau Mau, as well as to provide social facilities for Kamba, especially those working in Nairobi and Mombasa. The administration brought in loyal chiefs to assist in its running: Joseph Mutiso was

[93] Larby, *Kamba*, 3, 25.
[94] "Loyalty" was a route to gains for any veteran. Any government employee (such as a soldier) with five years' service could vote, or a serving soldier of *any* experience who had won a military decoration. Branch, "Loyalists"; Coutts, *Report of the Commissioner.*
[95] *East African Standard*, "Akamba Reject Mau Mau," March 3, 1953.
[96] *East African Standard*, "Mr. Lyttelton Praises Kamba Loyalty," March 12, 1954.

president, an ADC member based in Kangundo; Kasina was second-in-command, with Chief Jonathan Nzioka of Kangundo serving as secretary, and Chief Uku Mukima of Matungulu as treasurer. At one such meeting on January 15, 1955, for instance, practically every single speaker referenced Kamba loyalty, and most included a nod to Kamba military service.[97]

Such occasions must have been striking. European observers noted that any time war veterans collected for a ceremony of even minor significance, they wore their medals and army uniforms. Frank Wilson – who served in the Far East during the war, and was later a district officer in Kitui – remembered, "Whenever there was a gathering of Kamba, there were all the medals of the First World War and the recent war on display on every chest," due to the respect and legitimacy such demonstrations conveyed.[98]

When the colonial secretary, Alan Lennox-Boyd, visited Kenya in 1957, Kamba chiefs presented him with a petition. It stated, "[We] most loyally wish to welcome you to Kenya and most dutifully reaffirm the loyalty of the Akamba people to Her Majesty the Queen Elizabeth II." The petition listed a series of demands related to land and improved education. It ended by requesting assurances that "[t]he Wakamba will be respected by the government of the United Kingdom for their loyalty."[99]

Deriving honor and advantage from notions of "loyalty" was not, however, the sole preserve of elites. Non-elite Kamba, too, could win the respect that came from martial service, and it was easily accessible because the British called for more and more Kamba men to fight against Mau Mau during the 1950s. Many genuinely and powerfully believed in the value of these virtues. A distinct body of oral testimony suggests that it was simply anathema for Kamba to join Mau Mau, as they were "loyal." One man informed me that "not a single one" of the Kamba joined Mau Mau.[100] Another agreed: "A Kamba simply *cannot* be a Mau Mau," he explained to me, shaking his head.[101]

Many Kamba use nativist terminology in explaining this phenomenon. Ngala Mwendwa, a member of Parliament during the 1960s and 1970s and from Kitui, was one of them. In 2005, the jovial Ngala and I had a series of

[97] KNA, MV/1/18, "Akamba Association Meetings (Secret)," January 15, 1955.
[98] IWM, Oral History 10257/1, Interview with Frank Wilson, July 19, 1978.
[99] KNA, MAC/KEN/31/4, "A Memorandum of the Akamba to be Presented to the Hon'ble Lennox-Boyd, MP," 1957.
[100] Interview 8, Ngelani, July 13, 2004.   [101] Interview 10, Tala, October 25, 2006.

discussions over the course of a week in Kitui Town's fanciest teashop. Unlike the majority of Kamba politicians I tried to meet, Ngala was happy to arrange times for us to speak. Carrying a thin cane, Ngala would bang it hard against the floor from his seated position in order to hammer home his points. He explained that Kamba were "naturally" a loyal people. This loyalty, he continued, was part of the "inborn culture" of the tribe.[102]

This information is, on one level, tricky to utilize: Without doubt, the past half-century of ethnic contestation has played into this recounting. Some post-modern scholars would hold that these words can inform the historian about the present, but reveal little about the past. But the prevalence and consistency of these testimonies makes them difficult to dismiss. Kamba had a long history of martial service: It had often been a dangerous and honored route to financial gains, and a central part of community sustenance. As Kamba men died in Central Province fighting against Mau Mau, resolve hardened against the forest fighters. One chief summed up the feelings of many when he pointed out: "We could not support Mau Mau if the police were in danger from them."[103]

Chiefs had an extraordinary opportunity to solidify their positions – and indeed make vast gains – during Mau Mau. In some cases, this was legally sanctioned: They were allowed to prohibit any "act or conduct" that could cause a "breach of the peace," and officials noted that they enforced this law at a record level.[104] Chiefs used the moment to act against a resurgent Akamba Union, the organization staffed by younger, educated men who threatened their leadership in Machakos, in particular. Playing on a government fear of "political organizations" during the early 1950s, leading chiefs resolved that the AA (that they controlled) should "take over" all the Akamba Union's property in Nairobi. Their suggestion received rapid government backing.[105] The Akamba Union ceased to exist as any kind of meaningful group, and was soon replaced by the New Akamba Union.

In Kitui, chiefs and elders exerted powerful pressure on communities of Christians. The more conservative Kitui had been far less affected by the rise in education and political awareness: Daily newspapers, for

---

[102] Interview with Ngala Mwendwa, Kitui Town, August 9, 2006.
[103] Interview 49, Nzambani, August 4, 2005.
[104] KNA, DC/MKS/7/2, Evans to PCs, March 4, 1953. Tribunal returns are contained in this file.
[105] KNA, MV/1/18, "Akamba Association Meetings (Secret)," January 15, 1955.

instance, only arrived in Kitui after 1955 with the construction of the Machakos to Kitui road.[106] Chiefs and elders had frequently criticized Christians as they sought to build ethnic patriotisms in the post-war era (see Chapter 6), and argued that the freedoms brought by education were "un-Kamba" or against "custom." From their perspective, problems crystallized around the ABC. In 1952, the KAU had formed links with this new African-run church, and the two groups together clamored for independent schools, following the Kikuyu example, and opposed mission schools and churches. But this largely innocuous approach was transformed by an apparent Mau Mau oathing ceremony at Kathithymaa School near Ngelani. Chief Uku Mukima – a staunch loyalist – was on hand and tried to prevent it from taking place.

This – it seems – was the only incident involving Mau Mau and the ABC, but chiefs and elders in Kitui quickly tarred the ABC with the Mau Mau brush. Within weeks, the ABC was known as the "Mau Mau Church." Officials summarily denied any and all permits for the ABC to build new churches, and indeed closed all existing churches in Kitui until 1960. It seems missionaries – already angered by an African church that had won success independent from the missions – encouraged this portrayal.[107] It is worth noting that their approach was mirrored by district officials: When government reports described "Mau Mau raids" in Kitui, they are difficult to credit; more likely, these were plain robberies recast in imagined dreadlocks.[108] Perhaps the clearest example of such a tactic concerned an attack on Chief Kasina in 1953 (see below), one the administration publicized as a "terrorist" action, but which had nothing whatsoever to do with Mau Mau.[109]

Close alliance with the colonial administration was a route to financial and other material gains. Chief Kalavoto, for instance, received a large parcel of land belonging to the ADC when he retired in 1955, something described as a "gift" for his "good service."[110] Chiefs therefore had strong personal reasons to ensure that Mau Mau did not spread. The government rarely challenged their decisions during Mau Mau, due to their essential role in maintaining stability in Ukambani.

[106] KNA, DC/KTI/1/1/12, Kitui District Annual Report, 1955.
[107] KNA, DC/KTI/1/1/12, Kitui District Annual Report, 1955; Sandgren, "Kamba Christianity," 187–188.
[108] KNA, DC/MKS/1/2/1, Central Province Annual Report, 1952.
[109] KNA, MAA/2/122, Hickson-Mahoney to PC Southern Province, February 28, 1958.
[110] KNA, CS/1/14/84, Minutes of a Meeting of the Machakos ADC, November 16–18, 1955.

Reports and interviews demonstrate that Kasina – an invaluable resource of the administration – was corrupt. One man I interviewed explained that, "Kasina would never allow anyone else to have anything better than him," and said that he stole land and animals from local farmers as it suited him. Kasina often parceled out some of this land to his wives. Extensive interviews in Mwingi suggest that this behavior was responsible for a brutal attack in 1953 that left Kasina without hands, and almost caused his death. One of Kasina's nephews was supposedly responsible, acting out of frustration at Kasina's thefts.[111] Once Mau Mau was over, people complained to the government that Kasina had appropriated land and property that did not belong to him. Yet the administration would not question chiefly authority: Kasina – and other chiefs – were invaluable and largely unsupervised resources for the government.[112]

New development schemes also provided chiefs with the opportunity to make gains. District officers asked them to provide suitable candidates for settlement in Makueni, for instance, and it was not uncommon for potential settlers to offer bribes and favors to ensure that chiefs added their names to the list. The colonial administration also asked trusted chiefs for the names of those under suspicion of sympathizing with Mau Mau. In some cases, it appears that chiefs labeled their personal enemies "Mau Mau," knowing that they would be arrested. Ngala Mwendwa remembered that, "[Kasina] didn't like me. So he reported my being in Mau Mau to the DC and the DC sent the DO to arrest me."[113] Some chiefs made these accusations in an effort to attain a disputed piece of land, something which was easy to do once a person was in detention. Detention, indeed, often took place at the office of the chief, who was later in charge of the "restriction orders" once the person was released.

WOMEN AND VIRTUE

The simplified equation of honor with the male-centered îwi was, however, anathema to thousands of women in Ukambani, who challenged the idea. They rejected the suggestion that men had a monopoly on honor and respect, or that they alone could delineate the ways in which women earned those attributes. By the 1950s, women had come to view themselves as the guardians of their communities, and fulfilling what they

[111] Interview 75, Kitui Town, March 12, 2008; Interview 109, Thaana, June 29, 2009.
[112] KNA, MV/14/12, Complaints against Chiefs, c. 1966.
[113] Interview with Ngala Mwendwa, Kitui Town, August 9, 2006.

argued was "Kamba": sustaining their communities and extended families. They, after all, were the ones who remained at home and cared for sons, daughters, and grandparents, and moreover, brought in significant wages. [Today, many interviewees describe how Kamba communities have always had more egalitarian gender relations than Kenya's other ethnic groups; they contrast themselves to those who view women as only important for cooking and raising children.] The roots of this transformation lie in the 1950s, and built upon women's arguments about community values from the 1940s.

Women's success was built upon hard-won networks of trade and business forged during the 1940s. In the following decade, this base received an enormous boost from programs brought by the Swynnerton Plan and its predecessor. Development and welfare funding provided significant monies for programs designed to increase women's abilities to look after their families and earn additional income. Colonial officials were motivated in large part by the belief that without steady income, women would likely travel to Nairobi and become prostitutes.

The importance of these programs was powerfully brought home to me in 2006. That year, I interviewed a lady on her small farm near Mulango. She did not speak a word of English or Swahili. In English, I asked Mwendwa – my research assistant – to translate a question into Kikamba for me: "Would you please ask this lady, was she ever involved in welfare groups?" I asked. Before he could speak, she clapped her hands, recognizing one of the few English words she knew: "Welfare! Welfare!" she shouted, smiling. She then launched into a description about how an instructor from the Jeanes School in Kabete trained her to make wedding dresses, and how much she "loved" these classes.[114] This sort of reaction is common in Ukambani to questions about welfare: Women view it as responsible for producing great benefits and advantages for them (several villages, indeed, are actually named "Welfare").

Many of the new programs were courses for women run by district officials, and typically came under the heading of "homecrafts" (see above). Women from across Ukambani applied in significant numbers to join the courses, and in some cases, applicants clashed, such was their desire to join the programs.[115] Other programs were more specific: One called *Kūkilya Nthĩ wa Ukamba* ("Prosperity for Ukamba" but literally

Women's welfare

---

[114] Interview 70, Wikililye, November 30, 2006.
[115] KNA, AB/4/27, Extract on Community Development from Machakos District Annual Report, 1951.

meaning "digging the shallow soil of Ukamba") had "agriculture, veter-
inary and forestry work, health, hygiene, cooking and allied domestic
subjects" as its remit. Women who were selected left their homes for three
months, and moved to Machakos. They then returned to their villages to
establish clubs for other women.[116]

While officials thought that many of their development and welfare
ideas were slow starters, they noted that women's clubs were some of the
few that "flourish[ed]."[117] The clubs started during the late 1940s, but
after 1952 were often grouped together as *Maendeleo ya Wanawake*
("Women's Progress"). The government initially started these women's
groups, although Kamba women take such pride in their activities with
the groups that it is common to hear interviewees refuse to attribute
their origin to the government.[118] Activities ranged widely, from baby
care to study groups, establishing women's cooperatives, forming dancing
troupes, farming instruction, and instruction in making clothes.
Most meeting places had babycare facilities so women could leave their
children while attending meetings.[119]

Women created less formal groups too. At Kamuthanga village, a
group of friends clubbed together to buy land.[120] In Kathaana village,
female members of the Athanga clan formed a group to raise school
fees for their children.[121] This operated beyond the remit of the
male clan council. In Mitaboni, Martha Ngandi joined a group called
Kĩtũmi kya Kũthesya Mĩsyĩ ("The Reason for Cleaning Homes"), a social
club for women. They wove and sold baskets, and set up a station
at Mitaboni Town where they took turns to sell paraffin.[122] And in
Kibaoni, women organized themselves to carry water and firewood
to the marketplaces in exchange for food.[123] One lady expressed
the enjoyment that the women received working together in this fashion:
"We liked getting together and helping each other. We liked to gossip
with one another – we didn't want the men around for this!"[124]

---

[116] KNA, DC/MKS/8/10, Annual Report of the Machakos Social Welfare Organisation, 1950.
[117] KNA, AB/4/27, Extract on Community Development from Machakos District Annual
Report, 1951.
[118] Interview 17, Mitaboni, July 22, 2004.
[119] KNA, DC/MKS/1/1/30, Extract on Social Welfare from Machakos District Annual
Report, 1949.
[120] Interview 11, Ngelani, July 16, 2004.   [121] Interview 19, Mitaboni, July 24, 2004.
[122] Interview 20 (pseudonym), Mitaboni, July 27, 2004.
[123] KNA, DC/MKS/18/8, J. W. Balfour to DC Machakos, September 23, 1953.
[124] Interview 74, Mulango, December 1, 2006.

Manufacturing clothing was an excellent way for women to earn additional funds. One lady expressed this clearly to me when she brought out her old, black, and extraordinarily heavy Singer sewing machine, bought during the 1950s with money borrowed from a women's cooperative. She told me how she used to make clothes she then sold at the market. Her husband was angry, she recalled, but she used the proceeds from her work to pay for her children's school fees, and saved some in case there was anything else she needed that he would not pay for.[125]

Spinning provided a similar opportunity. At the Welfare Hall in Machakos, for instance – or the Royal British Legion Hall in Kitui – development funds covered the salary of a full-time spinning instructor. Women could come to learn the trade, and usually procure a loan to cover the cost of purchasing a spinning wheel. In a special radio broadcast, Julius Ngundo explained how women could succeed in this venture. A pound of sheep's wool cost 4 Sh, he explained. "Each of those ounces is worth Sh 1/- if it is well spun. You can see therefore that you have turned Sh 4 into Sh 12/- by spinning." A woman might spin a pound of wool in two or three evenings without difficulty, taking into account the time required to do other family duties, meaning that she could earn upward of 80 Sh per month in profit.[126] This was at least as good a wage as a man performing migrant labor could earn in Nairobi.

Development programs also blurred supposedly neat gender lines. Development and welfare officials created contests that pitted men and women against one another in events like needle threading, and took great delight when women won. They believed that they were closing the "gender gap" in this most "masculine" of societies. Interestingly, some aspects of women's programming seemed to challenge male occupations: Women's club teams marched together and wore uniforms, much like soldiers did.[127] Moreover, district officials began sending women to new livestock courses, training them in typically male occupations that women now took on in increasing numbers due to the "absence of most of the men folk from the Reserve," as one official put it. Such was the transformation that the district commissioner of Machakos noted men had begun farming, as one could now earn "respect" from the profession.[128]

---

[125] Interview 11, Ngelani, July 16, 2004.
[126] I am grateful to Maggie Casey and Barb Day for sharing their knowledge about spinning with me.
[127] KNA, DC/MKS/8/8, James Boninger, "New Ideas Help Kamba Women's Clubs," September 17, 1955.
[128] KNA, DC/MKS/1/1/32, Machakos District Annual Report, 1954.

These empowered women took action against their husbands if they felt themselves insufficiently supported. In Machakos, a number of women "dissolved" their marriages because they felt the amount of bride-price paid for them was insufficient.[129] In Kitui, women began filing legal suits against their husbands in the nzama.[130] District officials concluded that these women's organizations were "strong and progressive" and that "a move towards greater personal liberty [among Kamba women] is being made comparable with the development of the Nyanza tribes."[131]

By 1960, women had won themselves a practically unrestricted hand to engage in trading and their own businesses, especially with the ending of many formal restrictions in 1956.[132] More and more women were trained as teachers, and men away engaged in migrant labor or in the military came to rely on them for caring for the home, and the vital financial contributions they made.

Stories recorded during the 1950s demonstrate how highly women and their activities were respected, and how much the maintenance of the community sat at the core of Kamba life. In his *Akamba Stories*, John Mbiti – arguably the world's foremost authority on the Kamba – collected seventy-eight tales in different parts of Machakos and Kitui. He considered these stories the "mirror of life." The stories demonstrate that there was no such thing as a Kamba man without a woman. Based on all the stories he recorded – and many more he did not – Mbiti concluded that a young man could do no better in life than to marry a good wife, who should be "clean, industrious, generous, hospitable, sociable . . . *and able to look after the family properly* [my emphasis]." A young man would go through almost "any sacrifice" to achieve this, and without a wife by his side, was nothing.[133]

These stories inextricably link women to notions of community sustenance at the heart of society. Kamba stories rarely touch on wealth directly, or the experiences of men traveling for war or the hunt. The majority, in fact, primarily describe various happenings in the domestic realm. Women are at the center of almost all these stories. As Mbiti states, "The wife is perhaps the most important person in society. She is at the centre, and all relationships radiate from her. She

[129] KNA, DC/MKS/15/2, DC Machakos to PC Nyeri, June 7, 1949.
[130] KNA, PDA/EMB/1/218, Minutes of a Meeting of the Kitui ADC, August 7–10, 1951.
[131] KNA, DC/MKS/1/1/30, Extract on Social Welfare from Machakos District Annual Report, 1949.
[132] Robertson, *Trouble*, 108, 141.   [133] Mbiti, *Akamba Stories*, 5–6, 31.

is the link between life and death." Young men who did not marry had a responsibility that extended far beyond their own lives; such an action also caused the wider community to suffer. Mbiti labeled such actions as "suicidal ... [to] the nation," and explained that in Ukambani "the solidarity of the community depends so much on the contributions of each person."[134]

CONCLUSION

In 1954, Kenya's Minister of Finance E. A. Vasey described plans for development over the following three-and-a-half years. "[This is] Government's expression of what it believes to be the best pattern of development," he stated, then "refuted suggestions that the plan arose from the Emergency – it was continuation of previous work, and the history of the Colony had been one of steady development."[135] Vasey's bluster, however, little disguised the unmistakable links between development and political control.[136] Sir Roger Swynnerton, speaking seven years after Kenya's independence, perhaps felt that he could be more honest. When asked by an interviewer, "Would it be true to say that these Government proposals for African development [via his plan] were a direct result of the Mau Mau disturbances?" Swynnerton responded, "It would be absolutely true to say that."[137]

The "development deal" assuaged many social concerns felt by men and women in Ukambani. The Kamba poor had the ability to prosper in the 1950s in a way that their close cousins to the west did not. Groups ranging from chiefs to women fought to draw advantages from their positions: Chiefs tried to recenter military service as the defining manifestation of Kambaness, something that became abundantly clear as Kenya moved toward independence. But women disagreed, and fought for the right to receive honor in their villages. They soon took on a central role in political organization in the region.

---

[134] Mbiti, *Akamba Stories*, 27–32.

[135] TNA, CO 822/970, Extract from *Kenya Calling*, 1955.

[136] Something not lost on Oginga Odinga, who noted in his autobiography, "Agricultural policy was made to serve the political ends of the government." Odinga, *Not Yet Uhuru*, 125.

[137] RHL, Mss. Afr. s. 1426, Sir Roger Swynnerton, Interview with Geoffrey Masefield, November 5, 1970.

Chapter 8

Independence and beyond

There are only two important jobs which the Akamba have to do: one is to keep cattle; the other is to go into the Army.[1]

In Nyeri in late September 1961, Paul Ngei stood quietly on stage at a political rally in front of 120,000 Kikuyu supporters. Ngei – a squat man with a grating voice, and orator of quite remarkable skill – waited patiently as the crowd roared with wild anticipation. Few knew what Ngei might say: The self-styled "King of Ukambani" – known also as *Bwana Mashamba* ("Mr. Farms"), *Mũnyambo wa Kenya* ("The Lion of Kenya"), or "Cat with Nine Lives," depending on who you asked – had a flair for the dramatic, and took instruction from no one. His constant attacks against the colonial government and European settlers had led to his sanction from delivering radical speeches about land redistribution from white to black.

Ngei opened his speech by informing the crowd that the minister of defense had forbidden him from giving political speeches at the rally. Therefore, he said, "Let us pray":

African God who created this country to be for Africans, the trees, the grass and the cattle for milk for our children, we ask you today to see the European God and let him know that the African children want their farms back. Amen.

The crowd roared its support for the "Land Hymn," and continued to demand Ngei return to the stage for minutes after he had finished his performance.[2]

---

[1] Statement of Ngala Mwendwa. Parsons, *1964 Army Mutinies*, 86.
[2] *Nation*, "Ngei Leads 120,000 in the 'Land Hymn,'" September 25, 1961.

Ngei demonstrated extraordinary acumen to position himself as the leading figure in Ukambani following his release from detention, despite the fact that he held no formal political office in government before 1963. Like other Kamba leaders before him, he manipulated aspects of custom to ensure people voted for him by implementing traditional oathing practices. But his ability to move beyond the limitations of other leaders past and present came about from his fusion of the traditional with the modern: He also projected himself as a *Kenyan* politician who acted beyond the boundaries of tribe through his African People's Party (APP).

Neither Ngei nor Ngala Mwendwa of Kitui, though, could act independently of their constituents' desires. Women had long argued that to be "Kamba" was to support and maintain the family and community, and this notion seemed to resonate as Kenya approached independence. Male politicians had to demonstrate – at least on paper – that they would reflect these virtues in order to win their positions. No member of Parliament could win an election without women's votes; and moreover, women were beginning to play an increasingly direct role in politics.

For the man who would soon become Kenya's first president, Jomo Kenyatta, the high proportion of Kamba in the army represented a profound threat. By 1963, Kamba chiefs and leaders had spent almost two decades projecting military service as the defining tenet of being "Kamba." But they overplayed their hand as they "doubled down" on this essentialized version of Kamba ethnic identity and history that little reflected the increasingly cosmopolitan and diverse Ukambani. The seemingly powerful, martial, ethnic bloc was worrying for the first president of the new nation, who was aware of this *damnosa hereditas* – the curse of a soldiery whose ethnic proportions (inherited from colonial times) little reflected the make-up of the country.[3] The role of Kamba actors in the army unrest at Lanet in 1964, as well as a coup plot in 1971, led Kenyatta to reorder the army, removing the high numbers of Kamba and replacing them with Kikuyu. Thus by the early 1970s, the ability of the Kamba to maintain an advantageous position in the country was fast disappearing; as the main route to government benefits was removed, the area became a backwater with little public spending on education or development.

For young men, military service remained an important avenue to prestige and financial gain. A series of conflicts against the Maasai during the 1950s and early 1960s showed the continuing importance of martial service

[3] As Kirk-Greene put it, Africa had "clasped the Indian asp to its bosom." Kirk-Greene, "*Damnosa Hereditas*," 398.

in affirming what it was to be a Kamba man: Officials pronounced over and over how Kamba viewed the Maasai raids as an affront to their "manliness." But the military role for the youth was disappearing slowly; not only were Kamba restricted from joining the army, but more and more took on roles outside the military as education levels increased and Kamba became more in tune with national politics. By the 1960s, respect and honor was widely accepted as being available to all who looked after their dependents and communities, irrespective of occupation or career trajectory.

THE ROAD TO "UHURU" [INDEPENDENCE]

From the early 1950s onward, the British government came under strong pressure to grant independence to its colonies. Ever-louder voices within Africa clamored for "freedom," especially those associated with the Pan-Africanist movement, and they were backed by similarly vociferous supporters abroad. The words and actions of the United States and Soviet Union carried great weight and influence, as was amply demonstrated when the American threat to call in Britain's debt resulted in its humiliation in the Suez Crisis of 1956. The following year, Kwame Nkrumah's Ghana won its independence from London, and the roll toward independence for Africa had begun.

The upheaval caused by the Mau Mau revolt, as well as its subsequent repression, meant that the transition to independence in Kenya was never going to be a simple process. This was compounded by the problem of the large number of European settlers: They numbered approximately 80,000 by 1960, and possessed significant influence. One of the trickiest balancing acts British politicians had to accomplish was meeting African demands without being accused of abandoning the settlers. Yet it was clear that Britain could no longer afford to ignore African political and land rights, in either Kenya or the rest of its colonies.

By 1960, the African political voice in Kenya was represented by two parties: the Kenya African National Union (KANU) and Kenya African Democratic Union (KADU). As British, settler, and African politicians negotiated the process of independence, most visibly at two conferences at Lancaster House in London in 1960 and 1962, KANU and KADU struggled for political supremacy. KADU was the darling of British and settler politicians as a result of its *majimbo* (regional) agenda. It advocated a system in which each part of the country would have the ability to shape policy to a large degree, which settlers believed gave them a better chance of retaining their positions of privilege in the country.

But while KADU had the support of British politicians, KANU had Kenyatta. The man himself was an enigma: Sentenced to detention in northern Kenya following a sham trial in 1953, few had seen or heard from the man in almost a decade. No one knew whether he was senile or out of touch; the British saw him as a figure little more appealing than the devil, and settlers fretted about what he might do to them if he rose to power. By late 1960, KANU's main agenda was to procure Kenyatta's release. In early 1961, it handed a petition to the governor of the colony with more than one million signatures calling for Kenyatta's freedom, and on July 14, it was granted. With Kenyatta aboard, it was immediately apparent that KANU would lead Kenya to uhuru.

Kamba voters largely seemed to favor KANU before the 1961 elections. But the two-party competition was suddenly blown wide open when Paul Ngei announced the formation of the APP in November 1962. It was a crucial moment: KANU almost certainly needed a large number of votes from Ukambani to win a majority in the colony, and it had seemed that Ngei would be the man to deliver them.[4]

Few politicians in Kenya's colorful political history can match the personality and character of Paul Ngei. Every Kenyan can recount a story about the man, who was frequently seen in his wheelchair in Nairobi before his death in 2004. Most are related to women, drink, or a Mercedes-Benz he supposedly took from a dealership on University Avenue, telling the salesman to "send the bill to State House." What is less well known, however, is Ngei's role in Kenya's political history.[5]

Ngei's pedigree as a political leader was perhaps hinted at by his birth and upbringing. The grandson of the prophet Masaku, Ngei attended Machakos Boys Primary School, followed by the prestigious Alliance High School. He joined the KAR during the Second World War and served in the Abyssinia and Burma campaigns, before gaining a degree from Makerere College in Kampala. But what brought Ngei to national prominence was his role in Mau Mau, and subsequent detention.

Ngei joined the KAU in 1947, as the editor of its mouthpiece, *Sauti ya Mwafrika* ("The African Voice"). He received several promotions in quick succession, first to assistant secretary – and then assistant secretary-general – of the organization. By 1951, Ngei had taken the Mau Mau oath. But it was his arrest and imprisonment that caused his reputation to

[4] On the politics of independence, see Ochieng', "Independent Kenya" or Kyle, *Politics*.
[5] For more on Ngei, see Osborne, "Cat With Nine Lives."

explode. Ngei was detained in mid 1952 for threatening a witness in the trial of J. M. Kariuki, but was imprisoned together with the colony's most important African political figures at the end of the year following Governor Baring's declaration of a State of Emergency.[6] Ngei, together with Jomo Kenyatta, Fred Kubai, Bildad Kaggia, Kungu Karumba, and Achieng' Oneko, comprised the "Kapenguria Six." They were sent to prison in the frontier towns of Lokitaung and later Lodwar in northern Kenya's Turkana district.

It is vital to consider the long years of detention that Ngei spent with Kenyatta in order to understand the relationship between the two men at the time of independence and beyond. Today, members of Ngei's family are quick to describe the close bond that existed between the two men, but colonial documents and accounts reveal a quite different story.[7] In 1953, a district officer working at the prison in Lokitaung noted that, "Towards the end of the year the strain of each other's company was beginning to tell, and a noticeable tension arose between Kenyatta and Ngei ... Twice in my hearing harsh words were exchanged over trivial matters ... Ngei with a visible effort controlled his temper, but the impression remains that there is no love lost between them."[8] Following the Six's conviction, Kenyatta seemed to sink into depression. Leslie Whitehouse – "Jomo's Jailor," and a man who became friends with Kenyatta in later life – was concerned. Kenyatta became isolated, and was seemingly bullied by Ngei, who had "shouted at Kenyatta that he was a thief and had been nothing but an agricultural labourer in England."[9] Ngei, together with the other detainees (with one exception), even wrote a letter "denouncing Kenyatta as being on the side of the government."[10]

The fact of the matter was that Ngei – and indeed the other, younger members of the Six – had little to nothing in common with Kenyatta. Unlike them, Kenyatta was a part of the colony's conservative, landed African elite. He had married Grace Wanjiku, the daughter of Senior Chief Koinange and sister of Mbiyu Koinange, two of the most powerful men in Kiambu, and indeed Central Province. And the common ground Kenyatta shared with the majority of Mau Mau's supporters was smaller still. Thus when Kenyatta was released from jail, his message was one

[6] Kaggia, *Roots of Freedom*, 125.   [7] Interview 58, Kanzalu, October 23, 2006.
[8] KNA, DC/TURK/1/10, Lokitaung Sub-District Annual Report, 1953.
[9] Kenyatta lived in Britain for the majority of the period between 1931 and 1946, during which time he earned a doctorate in anthropology and wrote *Facing Mount Kenya*.
[10] Watkins, *Jomo's Jailor*, 183–189.

of reconciliation and maintenance of the status quo. He assured settlers that they had a place in Kenya's future.

Ngei, on the other hand, was a radical. Within a month of his release from detention in August 1961, Ngei had gained a large following, based in great part on the reputation he had earned as part of the Six. Yet unlike Kenyatta, he spoke publicly against Europeans in Kenya, and attacked multi-racialism. In front of 60,000 people at Nairobi's Doonholm Road Stadium he shouted unequivocally: "You must condemn those who give assurances to the Europeans that the land they hold is theirs ... You have never seen good relations between the dog and the cat. I am telling you they [European settlers] should be prepared to pack their baggage."[11] When Ngei spoke, people listened: One settler grudgingly recalled, "He had a very powerful way of talking ... [it was] his eyes ... when Ngei spoke everyone was silent. It was oratory."[12] Some Kamba moved onto European farms near Ol Donyo Sabuk, claiming Ngei gave them permission to settle there.[13]

Ngei sent Kenya's settlers, and indeed legislators in Britain, into fits of apoplexy. After the Doonholm Road speech, settler leader Michael Blundell met with Governor Renison to express his concern.[14] In the House of Lords, Lord Colyton implied that perhaps Ngei was expressing opinions that Kenyatta did not reject quite so strongly as it seemed, noting that Ngei "surely would not have been allowed to speak on so many occasions in the presence of Kenyatta and other leaders without permission."[15] Reginald Maudling, the colonial secretary, wondered whether Kenyatta, Odinga (see below), and Ngei – to whom he referred in a secret memorandum to the Cabinet as "men of violence with Communist contacts" – could perhaps be politically split from Tom Mboya, the Luo trade unionist he believed was more "moderate."[16]

It is more likely, however, that Ngei was just as much a political thorn in Kenyatta's side as he was to the British. At the stadium rally, Ngei and

---

[11] *East African Standard*, "Our Land Must Be Returned To Us, Mr. Kenyatta Tells Mass Rally," September 11, 1961.

[12] Interview 53, Nairobi, December 12, 2006.

[13] *East African Standard*, "Kamba Squatters Mark Out Plots on Thika Farms," September 4, 1961.

[14] *East African Standard*, "Mixed Reactions to Speeches at Weekend Rally," September 12, 1961.

[15] Great Britain, *House of Lords Debates*, Vol. 235, Cols. 84–87, November 1, 1961.

[16] TNA, CAB 129/108, Memorandum by Colonial Secretary, "Kenya" (Secret), February 6, 1962.

Kenyatta shared the same stage, and the latter could not denounce a former freedom fighter with such immense popularity. Ngei had earned the nickname "Bwana Mashamba" for his hard-hitting speeches about taking European-owned land and giving it to common Kenyans. As a result, Ngei had forced himself into the spotlight. In 1961, the four Kamba members of the Legislative Council, or "LegCo," (Henry Mulli, George Nthenge, Ngala Mwendwa, and Mwalimu Mati) could only hope to wield his level of influence.

The potential threat carried by Ngei was soon starkly demonstrated to Kenyatta. In January 1962, Ngei publicly challenged Kenyatta's right to lead KANU, a moment of such significance that it reached page three of *The New York Times*.[17] Then in November, upset by Mboya's faction in KANU that disputed his claim to lead the Kamba (preferring Henry Mulli), Ngei formed an opposition party called the APP. It was something that only a man with Ngei's personality could have done. Despite the fact that other Kamba leaders (such as J. D. Kali, James Muimi, or members of the LegCo) claimed influence among the people, those in Machakos and even a good proportion of those in Kitui overwhelmingly followed him. The danger for Kenyatta was that if the APP joined Ronald Ngala's KADU, the combination would pose a significant challenge to KANU. A secret Special Branch report – referring to Ngei as the "only Kamba leader of any stature" – stated that despite their assurances, the "defection caused KANU leaders greater worry than they cared to admit," and that KADU with the APP was a potentially victorious team.[18]

At the general election of 1963, the APP made good on its threat: It polled 104,548 votes for the lower house seats in Machakos, and KANU won only 6,935, sending a "shock wave" through the party.[19] Ngei's victory was even more impressive as KANU Minister of Works Mwinga Chokwe had threatened that "no roads would be built in Kamba country" if people voted for Ngei, and that Kamba at the coast risked being "dropped into the sea."[20] Though KANU's Ngala Mwendwa remained in control in Kitui, Ngei's popularity was spreading fast.

Ngei's rhetoric was matched with action. Around that time, Kenyatta came to speak at Tala market in northern Machakos under the aegis of KANU. APP members came to the meeting, and Kenyatta was jeered.

---

[17] *The New York Times*, "Kenyatta is Challenged," January 29, 1962.
[18] TNA, CO 822/3166, Special Branch Report, "The General Election – May 1963," May 6, 1963.
[19] Sanger and Nottingham, "Kenya General Election," 4–5.   [20] Kyle, *Politics*, 173.

He was forced to end his speech early, and finally had to flee Machakos, the windows of his car broken.[21] One of the few KANU supporters in the area recalled that a mob of APP members had kicked down his door, as they knew he was a member of KANU.[22] KANU supporters in northern Machakos wrote to Kenyatta imploring him for protection, because – they wrote – Ngei was arming groups of "youth wingers" to "exterminate" them, and was suggesting that Ukambani could secede from Kenya like Katanga had in the Congo.[23] As one woman noted, describing the hand signals used to demonstrate one's allegiance to a particular political party, "Jomo Kenyatta showed a finger, we replied with a fist."[24]

WINNING KAMBA VOTES

Ngei's successes may be attributed to a blend of the "traditional" and the "modern," and ranged from the ethnic to the national. His political platform via the APP was, of course, broad in scope: APP, after all, was the party that could catapult him to national prominence. The APP's constitution therefore spoke specifically to the "peoples of Kenya," describing them as "down trodden masses" who must be freed from the "colonial york [yoke]." But it also grandly tied Kenya's struggle to a pan-African one, and indeed to that of all oppressed peoples around the world. The APP promised to "[f]ight against colonialism and imperialism, tribalism, and such doctrines as apartheid."[25]

The APP's claim to battle tribalism was ironic, for Ngei knew very well that he needed to mobilize *ethnic* support to win prominence. Like chiefs before him, he played on custom to make gains. In 1963, he secretly undertook a large program of oathing in his home area of Kangundo (then a vast constituency known as "Machakos North" and also including Matungulu, Masii, and Tala). Ngei used the *kĩthĩtũ* oath to seal people's promise to vote for him.[26] It was not until 1983 that the oath was formally cleansed by Stephen Savono Maveke (see Chapter 3). Over

---

[21] John Nottingham, personal communication, 2005.
[22] Interview 5, Ngelani, July 10, 2004.
[23] KNA, MAC/KEN/36/8, KANU Members, Northern Division, Machakos to Kenyatta, June 22, 1963.
[24] Interview 11, Ngelani, July 16, 2004.
[25] KNA, DC/MSA/2/1/104, Constitution of the African People's Party, *c.* 1963.
[26] The powerful *kĩthĩtũ* oath had been used in many communities in Ukambani for more than 100 years, and was a way to ensure that people told the truth in disputes: If one lied after taking the oath, one could expect to die.

a plate of *mũthokoi* (de-husked maize, a Kamba staple), the stiff-backed 91-year-old recalled, "Ngei … [was] performing *kĩthitũ* to people in the years before 1983, to vote for him. That is why Ngei could not be defeated."[27]

These factors alone, though, could not win Ngei a clear majority of potential voters, and there are strong reasons to believe that his support of redistributive politics during the early 1960s was significant in drawing followers to his camp. This support became even more pronounced in 1966 when Ngei built close ties to Kenya's newly formed opposition party, the Kenya People's Union (KPU). The KPU – brainchild of Oginga Odinga, the Nyanza leader and Kenya's first vice president – favored a socialist system in which all people of the country shared in its land and benefits. While Ngei never formally joined the KPU, he was apparently less than one day away from doing so, and refused to campaign for KANU at certain points in 1966, spurring calls that he publicly reveal his relationship with the KPU.[28] It seems likely that the ever-adept Ngei was genuinely attracted to the KPU, but unwilling to sacrifice his position of power with KANU.

Ngei's sympathies with the KPU were mirrored by large numbers of Kamba. Machakos was one of the only parts of Kenya where the KPU had any degree of success in the 1966 "Little General Election." At the election, only nine KPU candidates won seats in Parliament: six from the stronghold of Nyanza, one from Busia (just to the northwest), and only two more in the entire colony, both of whom ran in Machakos.

KPU's political philosophy resonated in Ukambani, especially among women. The KPU emphasized the "need for communal activity," which contrasted KANU's approach that "stressed the need for hard work and individual effort."[29] For two decades women had argued that the maintenance of the community and extended family was the central Kamba virtue, and the roots of these ideas ran deeper still. Ngei's egalitarian streak therefore made him a highly attractive candidate for women in Ukambani, and their support gave him a practically unassailable position during the 1960s. It derived especially from the *Mbaĩ sya Eĩtu* ("Clans of Women"), an all-female political group that appeared in 1961. It was run by twenty "presidents" – all women aged over 55 – who were mostly market women with the money and power

---

[27] Interview with Stephen Savono Maveke, Tala, March 27, 2011. See also Mutiso, *Kenya*, 267.
[28] Mueller, "Political Parties," 238–242.   [29] Gertzel, *Politics*, 83–84.

that position conveyed. Ngei's mother was especially prominent in the group: One informant specifically remembered how she had united all women together, with each contributing 5 Sh for membership.[30] The group ensured that its members voted for the APP in 1963, and was also active in the 1969 elections. Women's influence was so great, in fact, that Gideon-Cyrus Mutiso states: "Many men tended to feel that politics had become such a women's affair that no self-respecting man should continue to be involved."[31] With women's votes, Ngei was practically unbeatable.

Ngei's efforts won him great support in Machakos, but not in Kitui, where Ngala Mwendwa held sway. A central part of the political struggle between the two was, of course, Kamba military service. Ngei's credentials were impeccable in this regard: He had won at least four decorations for his service in Abyssinia and Burma with the KAR.[32] As a result, Ngei had great influence among the rank-and-file of the army, something he used as a political tool in the upper echelons of government, and as a way to draw supporters to his camp.

Mwendwa's approach was more conservative. He did not have Ngei's military background: Mwendwa had spent the Second World War years completing his schooling, and then took a job teaching in Kitui immediately after the war's end. But – like George Nthenge, a Kamba member of the LegCo – he pushed hard for Kamba jobs in Kenya's soldiery, aware of the importance of the historic service Kamba had shown: For in that service lay a route to power that would be essential as independence approached, as Kamba were little represented in African political life compared to other ethnic groups. It was also a way for Mwendwa to win support among his constituents. Thus as he explained:

We are prepared to accept the Kikuyus and the Luos as teachers, but we ask them to accept the Akamba and Kalenjin as Army people … Whoever is the Prime Minister, we do not care from which tribe he comes; we ask him to be loyal to the Akamba and we shall defend him.[33]

---

[30] Interview 11, Ngelani, July 16, 2004.   [31] Mutiso, *Kenya*, 256–279.

[32] KNA, RR/9/15, *The Trial of Jomo Kenyatta and Five Others* (unpublished typescript, c. 1954), Vol. III, 1759–1760.

[33] Statement of Ngala Mwendwa. Parsons, *1964 Army Mutinies*, 86–87. The incoming district commissioner of Kitui – A. D. Galton-Fenzi – used precisely the same technique to win support from his charges in 1960, saying he would: "Do all he could to foster the tradition of the Kamba to provide the backbone of both the Armed Forces and Kenya Police in Kenya." KNA, DAO/MERU (without file reference), Box 1, Shelf 6524, Serial No. 7, Minutes of a Meeting of the Kitui ADC, November 8–9, 1960.

Mwendwa used the notion of Kamba loyalty to try to drive a wedge between the APP and his own supporters. In 1962, he said that the APP was "underground" and "against ... [the colonial] Government," unlike KANU. This was an extraordinary suggestion, and implied that it would be anathema for a Kamba to join Ngei's party because it would constitute disloyalty.[34]

But despite these easily anticipated debates about martial service, Mwendwa himself returns to the notion of community to explain politics at the time. Mwendwa argues that differing notions of desirable political behavior separated him from Ngei. He believes that people in Kitui saw Ngei as a "selfish" man – the worst possible label – and this was why Ngei's efforts did not resonate there. A military career meant nothing without a record of strong community advocacy and support, and Mwendwa believes that Ngei did not display this sort of leadership that was expected of men of high social status.

In contrast, even a short walk around Kitui Town today reveals the love that the people of Kitui have for Mwendwa, and the respect that they accord his values. Men and women here explain how Mwendwa has always been a genuine public servant and looked out for their interests. Unlike Ngei from the late 1960s onward – or many of Kenya's politicians today – Mwendwa has no fancy vehicles or houses, but lives a simple life and rarely visits Nairobi. People honor him by naming their children after him: As he himself succinctly explains, "Few people call their sons 'Ngei.' But if you asked for Ngalas or Mwendwas around here there are many."[35]

Ultimately, Ngei won the upper hand over Mwendwa in Machakos, but never in Kitui. Nor was he able to spread his political appeal far beyond the Kamba, leading one district official to even mislabel his file on the APP, "Akamba Peoples Party" instead of "African People's Party."[36] But despite the failure of APP, Ngei had proved his mettle: He had come head-to-head with Kenyatta in the public arena in a way that few others had before, or would after. Kenyatta went to extraordinary lengths to keep Ngei in line during his presidency, at one point even changing the constitution to allow him to remain in office.[37]

---

[34] KNA, MV/2/46, Kitui District Intelligence Summary, March–April 1964.
[35] Interview with Ngala Mwendwa, Kitui Town, August 9, 2006.
[36] The file is KNA, MAC/KEN/36/8, Kenya Political Associations: Akamba People's Party, 1963–1964.
[37] For more on Ngei's relationship with Kenyatta during this period, see Osborne, "Cat With Nine Lives," 203–204.

THE ARMY

Paul Ngei was especially dangerous to Kenyatta due to his connection
with the armed forces. Ngei was a KAR veteran and known to have close
associates in the military. As Kenya neared its independence, the army
little represented the country's ethnic composition. The policy of recruiting
heavily from martial races meant that in 1959, the KAR was comprised
of 36.3 percent Kamba and 25.8 percent Kalenjin.[38] As late as 1960,
a British recruiting handbook emphasized that from the "traditional and
well tried fighting tribes of Kenya ... we must turn to get our recruits." In
some months, so many Kamba volunteered for service that army officers
could afford to take as few as 5 out of every 200 potential recruits.[39] These
facts were not lost on Kenyatta, who was fully aware that many Kalenjin
had declared their support to KADU, and many Kamba (at least temporarily) to the APP: Therefore the bulk of Kenya's 5,000 soldiers – who
formed the Kenya Rifles after December 1963 – were not in line with
Kenyatta's KANU.

The threat of this potential source of instability was made abundantly
clear to Kenyatta in early 1964.[40] On the morning of January 20, askaris
from the Tanganyika Rifles stationed in Dar es Salaam rose in protest,
requesting better pay and quicker promotions. The protest spread to other
battalions in the country, and within a week, soldiers in both Uganda and
Kenya joined in. The focal point in Kenya was the barracks of the 11th
Battalion of the Kenya Rifles, stationed at Lanet near Nakuru in the Rift
Valley. There, soldiers went on strike, seizing weapons and ammunition
and taking over parts of the camp. Only after a confrontation with British
troops did they finally surrender after several hours of stalemate.

The presence of the British troops was in some ways fortuitous: As
the uprisings happened so soon after independence – approximately six
weeks – the 24th Brigade was still in Kenya. But in other ways, it was no
accident: British officers, in particular, had remained in the colony due to a
dearth of highly trained, long-serving African officers. The Africanization
of the army had started relatively late, thus Major General I. H. Freeland
was head of the Kenyan Army, and British officers occupied many of its

---

[38] Parsons, *African Rank-and-File*, 95.
[39] KNA, MSS/100/1, Guide to Recruiting and an Introduction to the KAR, November
17, 1960.
[40] The majority of the background detail presented in the following paragraphs is from
Parsons, *1964 Army Mutinies*.

highest ranks, as they did in Tanganyika and Uganda. This was in some ways a source of public embarrassment for Kenyatta, but privately it worked in his favor: He could count on British officers to be impartial and back the government, and it meant that Kamba and Kalenjin officers did not control the entire army.

While Kenyatta played down the significance of the army uprising in public, in private he was greatly alarmed. Odinga – one of the men close to the then-prime minister – noted that, "He seemed not to recover from the shock of the army mutiny and he seemed to be plagued by a fear that the government was not safe from internal revolution."[41] Kenyatta did not trust Odinga or Ngei: The latter's influence with the Kamba members of the Kenya Rifles was well known, and Kenyatta's British advisors even claimed that Ngei was personally involved in the uprising (something Parsons demonstrates was untrue). The threat of an army rebellion meant that Kenyatta began to change the ethnic balance in the soldiery, to increase the numbers of Kikuyu. (Odinga, too, was opposed to Kamba maintaining their prominent position in the armed forces.[42]) But this reordering could not happen overnight without causing great discontent.[43] Between 1963 and 1967, Kenya sent more officers for training in Britain than any other former British colony: 36 to Sandhurst and 132 to Eaton Hall and Mons Officer Cadets Schools. Kenyatta maintained a British officer as the head of the army and employed expatriate advisors for the majority of the 1960s to keep his hold on power secure while this "Kikuyuization" got underway.[44]

Kenyatta also expanded the General Service Unit (GSU) to further dilute the power of the army. Made up almost entirely of Kikuyu, the GSU was an elite paramilitary force armed with automatic weapons, described by one author as a "praetorian guard." It was created toward the end of the colonial period, and though supposedly for internal security, Kenyatta used the GSU to solidify his position against restless elements in Kenya (its commander was implicated in J. M. Kariuki's murder in 1975). In addition to the GSU, Defence Minister Njoroge Mungai arranged for members of the British Special Air Service to train an elite presidential bodyguard for Kenyatta's protection, comprised entirely of

---

[41] Odinga, *Not Yet Uhuru*, 281.   [42] Parsons, *1964 Army Mutinies*, 86.

[43] There is some suggestion that Kenyatta rescinded restrictions on hunting and ivory trading in Ukambani as compensation (though admittedly this seems somewhat unlikely). Campbell, *Charging Buffalo*, 143.

[44] Lee, *African Armies*, 126.

Kikuyu. Kenyatta also appointed Kikuyu to head the police, Criminal Investigation Department, and Special Branch by 1968.[45]

Toward the end of the decade, the president's plans were bearing fruit: In the late 1960s, the Kamba proportion in the army had dropped to 21.4 percent and the Kikuyu had risen to 13.1 percent (from 3.4 percent in 1959).[46] In the officer corps, the transformation was even more pronounced: In 1966, the Kikuyu proportion had risen to 22.7 percent. Among the army heads, Kenya's three battalions had the enforced breakdown of one Kikuyu, one Kamba, and one Nandi or Kipsigis.[47]

The process of Kikuyuization in the army, combined with Kenyatta's promotion of Kikuyu economic and political interests over the preceding decade, led to a coup attempt in 1971.[48] Kamba leaders played the central role in the bungled effort (which was known as a "Kamba coup" in some circles). The major figures were a Kamba member of Parliament, Gideon-Cyrus Mutiso, and the chief of the general staff (and therefore head of the Kenyan Army, having replaced a British officer in May 1969), Major General Juma "Joe" Ndolo. Mutiso, for his part, claimed that he was angry about Kamba who were forced to take oaths along with Kikuyu to support Kenyatta's presidency in 1969; Ndolo was possibly motivated by the same reason, but also by the increasing corruption he perceived in Kenyatta's government.

While lower-level figures were imprisoned for their roles in the conspiracy, Mutiso and Ndolo escaped serious punishment. Ndolo was permitted to retire, as was Kitili Mwendwa, the first African chief justice, who was meant to replace Kenyatta as president after the coup.[49] Deputy Chief of Staff Jackson Mulinge – also a Kamba – warned Kenyatta that to act too strongly against Ndolo would risk "a mutiny and spark a civil war" due to the respect Ndolo commanded among the rank-and-file.[50] When Vice President Daniel arap Moi explained the government's actions toward Ndolo, the language and reasoning reeked of the colonial martial

---

[45] By the 1970s, the GSU had 2,000 members – compared to approximately 7,500 in the army – and it could therefore provide a solution if some parts of the army became troublesome. Tamarkin, "Roots," 308.
[46] The 3.4 percent also included Embu and Meru. Parsons, *1964 Army Mutinies*, 175; Parsons, *African Rank-and-File*, 95.
[47] Lee, *African Armies*, 110.
[48] For more on the 1971 coup attempt, see Leys, *Underdevelopment*, 239–243.
[49] *East African Standard*, "Court Told of 'Revolt' Plot: Counsel Describes Wide Implications," July 19, 1972.
[50] *Nation*, "How Mulinge Saved Kenyatta from Coup," March 26, 2000.

races imperative, and evoked the government–Kamba relationship that had existed since the 1940s: Ndolo's "37 years of loyal service should be taken into account," Moi explained, "If he is allowed to retire he will henceforth be loyal and this is important since he is an important figure in the Kamba tribe."[51]

Such was the salience of ethnicity in Kenyan political life that during the conspirators' trial in 1972 in a Nairobi court, the member of Parliament for Kitui North, Mr. Mwengi-Nzelu, felt it necessary to appeal to the government. He asked the government to "clear the air by telling the country that this was 'only a minor' matter in which individuals were involved and not an organised matter involving all Kambas and Luo tribes." He continued to point out that, "All people in Ukambani and Nyanza now lived in fear that all members of the two tribes in high posts in the country would be arrested." He then, "appealed to the Government not to use the conspiracy to eliminate all Kambas and Luos in important positions."[52]

The coup gave Kenyatta renewed energy to continue excising Kamba officers and rank-and-file soldiers from the army. By the end of the 1970s, the Kamba proportion in the army had dropped to 12 percent and the Kikuyu had risen to 19 percent, conveniently reflecting Kenya's ethnic balance under the Kikuyu president. One of the few Kamba officers who remained was Mulinge, who took over from Ndolo following the coup attempt. With Kenyatta's death in 1978, Kenya's second president – Moi – undertook a similar program of ethnic cutting, increasing the numbers of his own ethnic group – the Kalenjin – in the army.

SOLDIERING, ETHNICITY, AND COMMUNITY

A series of clashes between Kamba and Maasai in the 1950s and early 1960s – about which district officials wrote copious reports – provide a useful point of entry for gauging the salience of martial service in Kamba

---

[51] Hornsby, *Kenya*, 229, referring to Norris to FCO, June 24, 1971. In a rather odd series of circumstances, four of the conspirators in the 1971 coup attempt died in car accidents. Air Force pilot Lawrence Mwanzia and businessman Daniel Nthiwa both perished in 1981, followed by Ndolo, and finally Mwendwa in 1985. Members of the Mwendwa family, as well as the former vice president Kalonzo Musyoka, have all cast doubt on the "accident." As one family member noted, "[T]he family is aware of the planned death that was meant to look like an accident." Anonymous, personal communication, February 3, 2011; *Nation*, "25 Years On, Kitili Mwendwa's Family Seeks Answer on his Death," September 11, 2010; *Nation*, "Coup Leaders Killed in Road Accidents," April 2, 2000.

[52] *East African Standard*, "Conspirators Condemned by Parliament," July 29, 1972.

life at the end of the colonial period. The most significant outbreak of
violence took place near Sultan Hamud – at a Kamba/Maasai border
area – during the first week of September 1960. Several people on each
side were killed, several thousand head of cattle raided, and a number of
homes burned. In the aftermath, a formal commission was established
under the chairmanship of Sir William Lindsay to hear testimony from
British officials and Kamba and Maasai leaders.

That the clashes were more than a simple scrap over cattle was made
abundantly clear on the Kamba side when they raised an "army" of 4,000
men to fight the Maasai. Lorries brought in men from Kitui to bolster the
force, and others walked for several days to join their compatriots.[53] One
district officer in Kajiado stated that the Kamba fighters contained a large
number of former KAR soldiers, and that they were organizing themselves
into "companies" in preparation for battle. He said that they "asked only
for an opportunity to fight it out with the Masai."[54] 7 KAR was brought
in to keep the peace, and 11 KAR sent into the reserves to carry out flag
marches.[55]

As expected, Kamba leaders phrased their displeasure at Maasai
actions in terms of their loyalty to the government, arguing that as the
people who made up the majority of the colony's police and soldiers, and
who obeyed the law, they deserved to receive government support. When
the district commissioner of Kitui, Hugh Galton-Fenzi, was asked by the
commission: "Did the question of the Kamba loyalty to the Government
ever crop up?" he replied, "Yes ... they maintain that the Kamba have
always been loyal to the Government – they form the background of the
Police and prisons, and K.A.R. and they have discussed that a lot."[56]

One of the most useful – though perhaps unconventional – sources for
understanding the Kamba reaction to the Maasai comes from the celebrated but troubled author Ernest Hemingway. Hemingway spent much
of 1953 and 1954 on safari with Kamba trackers and hunters, and the
long days and nights in camp provided him with ample time for discussion. His conclusion was that:

Their [Kamba] warriors had always fought in all of Britain's wars and the Masai
had never fought in any. The Masai had been coddled, preserved, treated with a

[53] KNA, CS/1/12/1, Sultan Hamud Disturbances: Diary of Events, September 1–7, 1960.
[54] KNA, CS/1/12/1, J. B. Deverell, "Masai/Kamba Affair," September 5, 1960.
[55] KNA, CS/1/12/1, Minutes of the Southern Province Security Committee, September
9, 1960.
[56] KNA, CS/1/12/10, Testimony of H. Galton-Fenzi, December 8, 1960.

fear that they should never have inspired ... The Wakamba hated the Masai as rich show-offs ... [In contrast] The Wakamba ... liked to fight, really fight, not Masai fight, which is, usually, a mass hysteria which cannot come off [i.e., take place] except under the influence of drugs.[57]

The pride felt by Kamba men about their military service reached deeper. British officers agreed in their testimonies that these men felt that their "manliness" was threatened by the Maasai incursions. As Maasai had described them in disrespectful terms – as "women" or *Iloongu* (Maasai: "a smelly thing"), a term used by Maasai even today – they requested the chance to be able to fight the Maasai and end the conflict once and for all.[58] As had occurred during the nineteenth century, the Maasai came under great pressure from the Kamba bows. At one point, the Maasai requested help from the government against Kamba incursions: "Masai Elders ... are appalled at the success of their [Kamba] tactics ... Stolen stock is recoverable only with the co-operation of the Kamba."[59] Officials, of course, gave speeches about Kamba loyalty in an effort to persuade them to lay down their arms.

To colonial officials, the clashes appeared to be a blend of modern and older practices: One district officer described them as "a reaction to the 19th century," and another noted that Kamba were removing their "modern dress" and reverting to older costume.[60] The moment is better understood, though, as an effort to recall older practices and mobilize a shared history to achieve contemporary legitimacy and success, a process described throughout this book.

The Kamba reaction to the series of conflicts with the Maasai reflected the hardening of ethnic lines that had taken place during the past decades. This process was magnified by happenings on the national political scene. The period between 1955 and 1960 had an important and lasting effect on Kenya's political culture. One of the techniques used by the colonial government to quell the spread of Mau Mau during the early 1950s was to ban all African political parties. The ban was partially rescinded in June 1955, after which point district political parties and associations were permitted, yet no

---

[57] Hemingway (ed.), *True at First Light*, 112.
[58] Interviews 139 and 140, Athi River, April 4, 2011; KNA, CS/1/12/1, Penwill to PC Central Province, "Masai-Kamba Border," May 20, 1953.
[59] KNA, CS/1/12/1, Masai/Kamba Disturbance, Sultan Hamud: Simba Area, May 15–19, 1953.
[60] KNA, CS/1/12/1, Penwill to PC Central Province, "Masai-Kamba Border," May 20, 1953.

organizations with national agendas were allowed until 1960. Thus African politicians (including those on the LegCo) came to be viewed as "ethnic spokesmen" for their people, as their popularity was initially built on an ethnic basis. Thus by the time KANU and KADU appeared, ethnic or tribal agendas and alliances already underwrote the political process.

In Ukambani, perhaps the most powerful expression of these ethnic lines came in the Regional Boundaries Commission (RBC). The RBC taskforce – appointed in July 1962 – was meant to determine the precise boundaries of Kenya's six regions (plus Nairobi). The commission's chairman submitted his report to the colonial secretary at the end of the year, having visited Kenya twice and heard testimony from several hundred delegates. In Ukambani, delegations from Machakos and Kitui joined together to provide a united front to the commission. The report noted that this was a "notable exception," for "[i]n the main major political parties organised themselves to present their views in accordance with party policy." Delegates absolutely refused to be placed in a district with the Maasai or Kikuyu. They claimed many of the European farms in Machakos, a large part of the Maasai land unit, and told commissioners that most of Thika was in fact Kamba land.

George Nthenge, the leader of the New Akamba Union (NAU), dismissed the Kikuyu as "not fighters" or soldiers in his submission, before discussing nineteenth-century Kamba warriors at length, specifically drawing attention to their use of the bow and arrow. Nthenge's statement worked on three levels: First, it rejected the Kikuyu claim to lands that he argued they did not merit, as they had never contributed to the colonial forces. Second, it was an effort to bring past history to bear on the present boundary-making situation. If Kamba warriors were as fierce as Nthenge and others claimed, then in the past they surely would have encroached far to the west into areas known in the 1960s as "Kikuyuland." And finally, by using the cultural material of the bow and arrow – a weapon used only by the Kamba in central Kenya – Nthenge tried to distinguish and set apart the Kamba from Kenya's other ethnic groups. NAU therefore submitted a demand that the Kamba receive their own district in independent Kenya. In response to these interviews with delegates, the commission recommended that the Kamba be removed from Southern Province – which they shared with the Maasai – and put into the new Eastern Province after 1963.[61]

---

[61] Kenya, *Regional Boundaries Commission*; KNA, GO/1/2/1, Kenya Regional Boundaries Commission, 1962: Record of the Oral Representations, Part I, especially 1–18.

Reading their testimonies, one is struck by the confidence expressed in the words of Kamba leaders. They had become used to receiving privileged treatment from the government, which they had enjoyed for several decades. But the Kamba position – based largely on their military reputation – had reached its zenith and would fall away in independent Kenya. And in any case, the simplified, external equation of Kamba ethnic identity with martial service little reflected changes in Ukambani.

By the 1950s, women's arguments about Kamba values had gained deeper and deeper traction. A majority of people in Machakos and Kitui deemed the sustenance of extended families and the wider community a primary virtue worthy of enormous respect. Women had driven this transformation through their positions as guardians of their communities, as men had come to realize that they were enormously reliant on women for everything from care of the home, to support in finances and business. This only increased after independence, when men could no longer access martial occupations in significant numbers due to Kenyatta's cuts.

Ngala Mwendwa strongly supported these notions in one of our discussions in the Kitui teashop. He recognized that women had historically played a vital role in Kamba communities during his lifetime. Women were not "kitchen only," he explained, as they were in other parts of the country. "We have no problem with women leading," he said, "We regard everyone as equal to everyone else." Mwendwa then tied this description into a discussion about the values that he considered important in Kamba communities. He spoke with pride as he explained how Kamba were reliable and trustworthy: Any hotel or restaurant could employ them without danger of them stealing, he explained. A lack of this kind of dependability was why people in Kitui had rejected Ngei's overtures, he said: A lack of trustworthiness and "selfish" behavior had no place in Kamba society, which had always been about looking after one's neighbor.[62]

The increasing influence exerted by women was reflected in the political arena as independence approached. At the LegCo elections in 1957, only 12 women out of 9,442 (0.12 percent) registered to vote.[63] But by 1958, 2 of 15 nominated members of the LegCo were women, and by the time of independence, Mutiso could describe politics as a "women's affair," and write that women had "great political influence."[64] This political

---

[62] Interview with Ngala Mwendwa, Kitui Town, August 9, 2006.
[63] KNA, DC/MKS/1/1/33, Machakos District Annual Report, 1956.
[64] Mutiso, *Kenya*, 266.

authority was in significant part due to female control over the *Harambee* ("pulling together") system advocated by Kenyatta for developing rural communities in Kenya. In northern and central Machakos – at least – it was almost entirely run by women, and a suitable fit based on their assertions about privileging community sustenance.[65]

These new roles for women reflected an Ukambani that had flourished during the 1950s. From village to village, soldiers and police certainly earned honor; but in practice, they had no monopoly on it. Other avenues to respect were open too. Development and welfare funding had caused the wood carving industry, schools, and women's organizations to expand, and agriculture had gone through something of a revolution: The productive farms that dotted Ukambani in the late 1950s were barely recognizable from those of twenty years earlier.[66] People could support their families in a way they could not before, and win honor for doing so.

[65] Interview with Emma Muloko Paul Ngei, Kanzalu, October 23, 2006; Throup and Hornsby, *Multi-Party Politics*, 506.

[66] For a full exposition of these changes – especially in agriculture – see Osborne, "Changing Kamba," 264–270.

Epilogue

And brewing inside this space, from fifty or so ethnic histories and angles, is Kenya – a thing still unclear ... disemboweling that which came before, remaking it. Sometimes moving. Sometimes not.[1]

As I sit writing these concluding words, Uhuru Kenyatta – Kenya's fourth president and son of the nation's founding father, Jomo – has just appointed his first cabinet. Contrary to widespread expectations, his springtime electoral victory over Raila Odinga was comprehensive. Happily, alarmingly "tribalist" rhetoric that appeared daily in the run-up to the vote caused barely any difficulties at election time. The specter of 2007 – when approximately 1,500 Kenyans died and perhaps half a million were displaced following the election – was banished, at least temporarily.

Kamba have been little involved in the "ethnic" violence that has characterized the past several decades of Kenya's political history. This absence of conflict is due – in at least some significant part – to the fact that the Kamba share no resource-rich lands with other ethnic groups (as do the Kikuyu and Kalenjin in the Rift Valley, for instance), nor have much of a share of the spoils of political office to fight over. But when explaining this absence of conflict, many Kamba assert that it is the long-standing attribute of "loyalty" that means that the tribe could not fight the government or other Kenyans. Thus the blogger Richard Mutungi, for instance, explains how the Kamba, "Have always been loyal to regimes in

---

[1] Wainaina, *One Day*, 132.

power," and to do anything else would be dishonorable.[2] In online discussion boards – a popular venue for young Kenyans to voice their political views – one commonly finds sentiments like, "Kambas are extremely loyal and devoted."[3] These sorts of sentiments have deep roots, and demonstrate how notions of historic "loyalty" are important and a source of pride. But now they are accessible to all (including men *and* women), and are no longer attached plainly to martial occupations.

In the political arena, candidates and their supporters are quick to draw on the Kamba past to score points from one another, especially during electoral periods. In his 2013 campaign, the foremost Kamba politician and Kenya's one-time vice president – Kalonzo Musyoka – attacked Kamba who had decided to vote for his opponents, Kenyatta and William Ruto. "[You are] traitors to the community," he shouted.[4] He was attempting to stir his Kamba audience, believing that the word "traitor" would resonate powerfully for a people who have historically attached such value to conceptions of loyalty.

Similarly, Charity Ngilu – currently cabinet secretary for Land, Housing, and Urban Development, and Kenya's joint-first female presidential candidate in 1997 – found herself in a difficult position in Machakos in late 2001. Ngilu – then a member of the National Party of Kenya – had been honored by a group of Kamba elders, who had presented her with a bow and arrows, thereby making her a "Kamba warrior." Yet the moment caused great controversy: Her opponent Mulu Mutisya, the Machakos KANU branch chairman, accused the elders of making a "blunder." She was said to have "abused the community by wielding a quiver full of arrows, a bows [*sic*] and arrow in the presence of men and 'breaking traditions.'" As opposition politicians stated, evoking the notion of gendered, martial service, Ngilu "was not fit to lead 'a field that had men capable of defending the community.'"[5]

This dated notion, though, finds little basis in truth. Kamba have been quick to elect women to positions of political prominence. Women like

[2] Richard Mutungi, "Kamba Community in Kenya Politics," accessed April 15, 2013, www.kenya-today.com/opinion/kamba-community-in-kenya-politics.
[3] Senior SSS, "The Kamba Community," accessed April 19, 2013, www.kenyanlist.com/kls-listing-show.php?id=121248.
[4] Mbuzi Mzee, "Kalonzo Tells Kamba to be Ready for a Run-Off and Calls Those Who Defected to Uhuru/Ruto Traitors," accessed March 28, 2013, www.mbuzimzee.blogspot.com/2013/03/kalonzo-tells-kamba-to-be-ready-for-run.html.
[5] *Nation*, "Kamba Elders to Discuss Ngilu," October 5, 2001; *Nation*, "Ngilu Made Kamba Warrior as NPK Prepares for Poll," October 16, 2001.

Ngilu, Nyiva Mwendwa (Kenya's first female cabinet minister), and Agnes Ndetei (formerly assistant minister for education), have all made significant contributions to Kenya's political life that men have historically dominated. Kamba consider that these women make excellent leaders because they put the needs of their communities first. It is common, indeed, to hear people refer to the young lawyer Kethi Kilonzo as a possible future president of the country.

Moreover, few would conceive of Kamba identity as simplistically "martial" (and therefore gendered) today. Walking through Ukambani, it is common to find many chiefs and assistant chiefs who are former soldiers. In many cases, they wear hats or badges from their days in the army. But their positions are usually the result of their abilities to support the needs of their communities, not as a simple result of their former occupations. Many of the assertions Kamba make about "loyalty" and "trust" reflect qualities people value today, and are typically the response to any enquiry about what it is to be "Kamba." People claim that their leaders must demonstrate these qualities, despite not infrequent examples that they do not.

In practically every interview I carried out in Ukambani between 2004 and 2012, I asked people about men and women who moved between tribes in the past. I never received one positive response to this question, nor, in fact, an admission that this had ever occurred. One woman summed it up best: "To change your tribe, you must have done something wrong."[6] This is, in many ways, a reflection of the ethnicized present.

But perhaps in Kamba history there is a lesson. Nineteenth-century communities accorded their leaders respect if – and only if – they demonstrated virtue. Those who did not merit honor were not accorded leadership positions. Some today argue that similar values should be a part of the political scene: in Mutungi's words, "The leaders are accountable to the party members and should consult them."[7] If Kenyans demand that their political candidates demonstrate genuinely *virtuous* behavior – irrespective of ethnic identity – then the political climate might indeed be shaken up.

[6] Interview 109, Mwingi, June 29, 2009.   [7] Mutungi, "Kamba Community."

Bibliography

Interviews

As I began research on this project in 2003, I quickly realized that oral interviews would be essential for reconstructing Kamba history, especially due to the dearth of available published sources. A significant amount of this book, therefore, is built from the testimony of more than 150 interviewees. The names of the locations where the interviews were conducted appear in the footnotes, and broader details about the interviews themselves appear below.

The majority of interview subjects were Kamba, but the remainder included Kikuyu, Embu, Meru, and Maasai, as well as European settlers and former district officials. Interviewees' testimonies are quoted anonymously in most cases in the text. In several instances, I have attached a pseudonym to an interviewee whose life history I have expanded upon to illustrate some broader point. Where this occurs, it is identified in the footnotes. Actual names are only used in cases where I received specific permission from the subject to use his or her words and name in this book, and still have an intact recording of that oral consent.

The collection of oral testimonies involved working with a research assistant, Mwendwa Musyimi. Mwendwa and I covered almost the entirety of Ukambani on foot, on the backs of bicycles ridden by their kindly and perspiring owners, and in crowded *matatus*. We used public transport to get to each and every interview, never once setting foot in a private vehicle. As much of Ukambani is hilly and has few roads, we commonly covered more than ten miles in a day on foot to reach remote villages. We slept in small "hotels" and in the homes of strangers.

This approach presented the opportunity to speak with many people along the road, in various shops, and in tiny teahouses. We gleaned much information and anecdotal evidence in this fashion. It was – and is – my belief that walking the routes to and from the markets with Kamba men and women earned us a level of acceptance in the communities we visited, which would not have been possible if we had arrived in a shiny four-wheel-drive vehicle. We found that people welcomed us into their homes to do interviews when they saw that we had acquired the same dark red dirt from the road that they accumulated each day.

Mwendwa and I carried out interviews in whatever language the subject felt most comfortable. This was typically Kikamba, as few of the older generations speak Swahili or English. In all interviews conducted in Kikamba, Mwendwa provided translation; while I conducted interviews in Swahili and English, my Kikamba language skills were not sufficient to adequately fulfill this charge, though I could comprehend portions of the conversations. Interviews were loosely based on a preprepared questionnaire, though they typically deviated instantly from its content and rarely returned. They usually followed a pattern where I began by asking, "Tell me about the time when you grew up" and then prompted the subject through the telling of his or her life story. I typically asked small points of detail or clarification during this recounting, and then returned to topics in which I was interested later in the interview.

I tape-recorded almost every interview, and both Mwendwa and I took copious notes. After we completed an interview, we discussed it in detail the same evening, and compared our written records. Where we found discrepancies, we returned to the tape to correct any errors. I then asked Mwendwa to relisten to the tape and remove an average of around ten quotes or perhaps several stories in which I was interested. He then transcribed the words in Swahili or Kikamba, and we discussed the most appropriate English translations that remained faithful to the original sense of the words.

All interview materials remain in my possession.

Interviews conducted by the author (the majority with the assistance of Mwendwa Musyimi)
Interviews 1–23. Dates: July 7–28, 2004
Locations: Ngelani, Mutituni, Mitaboni
District: Machakos
Sex ratio: 15 men, 8 women

Interviews 24–49. Dates: July 5–August 4, 2005
Locations: Mitaboni, Mbooni, Kitundu, Okia, Kee, Mulala, Emali, Nzambani
Districts: Machakos, Makueni
Sex ratio: 21 men, 5 women

Interviews 50–75. Dates: July 24–December 1, 2006
Locations: Changwithia, Kitui Town, Miu, Kanzalu, Tala, Kiima Kimwe, Yathui, Mumbuni, Mulango
Districts: Machakos, Kitui, Nairobi
Sex ratio: 17 men, 9 women

Interviews 76–137. Dates: May 11–July 4, 2009
Locations: Kirimara, Ngelani, Kiine, Kanziku, Ikutha, Simisi, Kiomo, Mwingi, Mivukoni, Tseikuru
Districts: Meru, Machakos, Kirinyaga, Kitui, Mwingi
Sex ratio: 34 men, 28 women

Interviews 138–142. Dates: April 4–11, 2011
Locations: Athi River, Mukaa
Districts: Kajiado, Makueni
Sex ratio: 5 men, 0 women

Interviews 143–152. Dates: May 14–16, 2012
Locations: Mukaa, Kabaa, Mbooni
Districts: Makueni, Machakos
Sex ratio: 8 men, 2 women

Interviews conducted by Jeremy Newman (with various translators)
David Kaindi, Mbooni, February 13, 1974
John Muiya Kivati, Tala, December 10, 1973
Mwinzi Mala, Tawa, November 2, 1974
Elijah Mbondu, Tala, November 26, 1973
Mary Muendi, Okia, March 5, 1974
Mukonzo, Kee, January 4, 1974
Kavula Muli, Matungulu, December 12, 1973
Paolo Musau, Tala, June 30, 1973
Elijah Mutambuuki, Tala, July 1, 1973
Isaac Mwalonzi, Ngelani, January 17, 1974
Nduba Mwatu, Ngelani, August 31, 1974
Ishmael Mwendwa, Tala, June 16, 1973
Zachayo Ngao, Kiteta, November 2, 1974

Archival Sources

The list below contains collections referenced in the book's text. In addition to the archives below, several files from the following collections were also consulted. In Kenya: the University of Nairobi Library and McMillan Library, both in Nairobi; and in the United Kingdom: the University of Nottingham Library, Nottingham; the British Library Newspaper Library, London; and the Liddell Hart Centre for Military Archives at King's College, London. Specific references for all files appear in the footnotes.

Kenya National Archives, Nairobi

AB – Community Development
AG – Attorney General
AHC – Office of Information/Press Office
ARC (MD) – Ministry of Defence
BB – Eastern Province, Embu
CS – Chief Secretary
DC/KTI and MV – District Commissioner, Kitui
DC/MKS – District Commissioner, Machakos
DC/MSA – District Commissioner, Mombasa
DC/TURK – District Commissioner, Turkana
MAA – Ministry of African Affairs
MAC/KEN – Murumbi Africana Collection
MSS/23 – Papers of T. H. R. Cashmore
MSS/100 – Papers of George Pearson
MSS/120 – Papers of Tom Askwith
MW – Ministry of Works
Papers of the East African Indian National Congress (microfilm), Reel 8
PC/CP – Provincial Commissioner, Central Province
PC/NKU – Provincial Commissioner, Nakuru
PC/SP – Provincial Commissioner, Southern Province
PDA/EMB – Provincial Director of Agriculture, Embu
TC – *Taveta Chronicle*

National Archives of the United Kingdom, London

CAB 129 – Cabinet Memoranda
CO 533 – Colonial Office: Kenya Original Correspondence
CO 822 – Colonial Office: East Africa Original Correspondence

WO 236 – War Office: Papers of General Sir George Erskine
WO 276 – War Office: East Africa Command Papers

*Bodleian Library of Commonwealth and African
Studies at Rhodes House, Oxford*

Mss. Afr. s. 54–57 – Papers of Francis George Hall
Mss. Afr. r. 143–148 – Papers of C. W. Hobley
Mss. Afr. s. 377–382 – Papers of John Ainsworth
Mss. Afr. s. 391 – Papers of J. A. Stuart Watt
Mss. Afr. s. 746 – Papers of Sir Michael Blundell
Mss. Afr. s. 755 – Papers of Colin Maher
Mss. Afr. s. 771 – Papers of Robert Foran
Mss. Afr. s. 1120 – Papers of Sir Robert Brooke-Popham
Mss. Afr. s. 1426 – Interview with Sir Roger Swynnerton
Mss. Afr. s. 1469 – Papers of J. W. Balfour
Mss. Afr. s. 1580 – Papers of Sir W. R. Hinde
Mss. Afr. s. 1715 – Papers of the King's African Rifles
Mss. Brit. Emp. s. 22 – Papers of the Anti-Slavery Society

Africa Inland Mission Archives, Nairobi

Box 2 – Correspondence of Elwood Davis
Box 3 – Correspondence of Lee Downing
Box 4 – Correspondence of W. J. Guilding
Box 5 – Correspondence of George Rhoad
Box 6 – Correspondence of Harmon Nixon
Box 8 – Correspondence of LeRoy and Emma Farnsworth
Box 10 – Mission Station Reports and Statistics
Box 15 – Regional Church Councils

*Billy Graham Center Archives and Wheaton College
Archives and Special Collections, Wheaton, IL*

BGC 81 – Africa Inland Mission, International
SC/165 – Diary of Gordon Rhoad

Church Missionary Society Archives, Birmingham, UK

CA5M2 – Mission Book, 1846–1856
CA5O16 – Original Papers, 1841–1880

Imperial War Museum, London

Oral History 3935 – Major William Cockcraft, September 25, 1978
Oral History 10257 – Frank Wilson, July 19, 1978

Government Publications

Corfield, F. D. *Historical Survey of the Origins and Growth of Mau Mau.* London: H. M. Stationary Office, 1960.
Coutts, W. F. *Report of the Commissioner Appointed to Enquire into Methods for the Selection of African Representatives to the Legislative Council.* Nairobi: Government Printer, 1956.
Great Britain. *Colonial Office Annual Report: Kenya: 1946.* London: H. M. Stationary Office, 1948.
Joint Committee on Closer Union in East Africa, Vol. II. London: H. M. Stationary Office, 1931.
Kenya: Report of the Regional Boundaries Commission. London: H. M. Stationary Office, 1962.
Papers Relating to the Mombasa Railway Survey and Uganda. Parliamentary Papers: Africa No. 4, May 1892.
Parliamentary Debates, House of Commons, 1917-1951. London: H. M. Stationary Office, 1918–1952.
Parliamentary Debates, House of Lords, 1961. London: H. M. Stationary Office, 1962.
Kenya, Colony and Protectorate of. *African Affairs Department Annual Report, 1948.* Nairobi: Government Printer, 1950.
African Development in Kenya, 1946–1955: Land, Livestock and Water. Nairobi: Government Printer, 1953.
African Land Development in Kenya, 1946–1955. Nairobi: Published by the Ministry of Agriculture, Animal Husbandry and Water Resources, 1956.
African Population of Kenya Colony and Protectorate: Geographical and Tribal Studies. Nairobi: East African Statistical Department, 1950.
Kenya Land Commission: Evidence, Vol. II. Nairobi: Government Printer, 1933.
Kenya Police Annual Reports, 1938–1953. Nairobi: Government Printer, 1939–1954.
Legislative Council Debates, 1938–1947. Nairobi: Government Printer, 1939–1948.
Progress Report on Demobilization No. 3, June 1945. Nairobi: Government Printer, 1946.
Report of the Agricultural Commission. Nairobi: Government Printer, 1929.
Report of the Commission of Inquiry Appointed to Examine the Labour Conditions in Mombasa. Nairobi: Government Printer, 1939.
Report of the Meat and Live Stock Inquiry Committee. Nairobi: Government Printer, 1937.

Kenya, Republic of. *Kenya Population Census, 1962*, Vol. I. Nairobi: Ministry of Economic Planning and Development, 1964–1966.

Swynnerton, Roger. *A Plan to Intensify the Development of African Agriculture in Kenya.* Nairobi: Government Printer, 1954.

Other Periodicals and Newspapers

Akamba
Daily Chronicle
Daily Telegraph (London)
East African Standard
Hearing and Doing
Inland Africa
Kenya Times
Manchester Guardian
Nation
New Statesman and Nation
The New York Times
The Times (London)

Personal Communications

Dick Cashmore, various, 2011–2012
Jeremiah Kitunda, February 15, 2008; various, 2011
John Nottingham, various, 2005–2012

Websites

Mutungi, Richard. "Kamba Community in Kenya Politics." Accessed April 15, 2013. www.kenya-today.com/opinion/kamba-community-in-kenya-politics.

Mzee, Mbuzi. "Kalonzo Tells Kamba to be Ready for a Run-Off and Calls Those Who Defected to Uhuru/Ruto Traitors." Accessed March 28, 2013. www.mbuzimzee.blogspot.com/2013/03/kalonzo-tells-kamba-to-be-ready-for-run.html.

SSS, Senior. "The Kamba Community." Accessed April 19, 2013. www.kenyan-list.com/kls-listing-show.php?id=121248.

Kikamba Vocabularies, Dictionaries, and Grammars

Africa Inland Mission Language Committee in Ukamba. *A Kikamba–English Dictionary*, 3rd edition. Nairobi: The Literacy Centre of Kenya for Afrolit Association, 1970 [1939].

Bleek, Wilhelm. *A Comparative Grammar of South African Languages.* London: Trübner, 1862.

Farnsworth, Emma. *Kamba Grammar.* Nairobi: Published under the Auspices of the Africa Inland Mission, 1957.

Hinde, Hildegarde. *Vocabularies of the Kamba and Kikuyu Languages.* Cambridge: The University Press, 1904.

Krapf, Johann. *Vocabulary of Six East-African Languages: Kisuaheli, Kinika, Kikamba, Kipokomo, Kihiau, Kigalla.* Tübingen, Germany: L. F. Fues, 1850.

Last, J. T. *Grammar of the Kamba Language, Eastern Equatorial Africa.* London: Society for Promoting Christian Knowledge, 1885.

Polyglotta Africana Orientalis. London: Society for Promoting Christian Knowledge, 1885.

Mbiti, John. *English–Kamba Vocabulary.* Nairobi: Kenya Literature Bureau, 1958.

Mwau, John. *Kikamba Dictionary.* Nairobi: J. H. Mwau, 2006.

Shaw, Archibald. *A Pocket Vocabulary of the Ki-swahili, Ki-nyika, Ki-taita, and Ki-kamba Languages.* London: Society for Promoting Christian Knowledge, 1885.

Whiteley, Wilfred and Matthew Muli. *Practical Introduction to Kikamba.* London: Oxford University Press, 1962.

Biblical Translations in Kikamba

Africa Inland Mission, with Aaron Kasyoki and Jeremiah Kyeva, trans. *Maandĩko Matheu ma Ngai metawa Mbivilia nĩmo Ũtianĩo Mũkũũ na Ũtianĩo Mweũ* (The Bible). London: British and Foreign Bible Society, 1956.

Brutzer, Ernst, trans. *Meka ma Atume* (Acts of the Apostles). London: British and Foreign Bible Society, 1904.

Krapf, Johann, trans. *Evangelio ta Yunaolete Malkosi* (St. Mark's Gospel). Tübingen, Germany: L. F. Fues, 1850.

Pfitzinger, H., trans. *Mataio* (St. Matthew's Gospel). London: British and Foreign Bible Society, 1909.

Rhoad, George, trans. *Maliko* (St. Mark's Gospel). London: British and Foreign Bible Society, 1915.

Yoana (St. John's Gospel). London: British and Foreign Bible Society, 1916.

Rhoad, George and Africa Inland Mission, trans. *Ũtianĩo Mweũ wa Mwĩaĩi na Mutangĩĩ waitũ Yesũ Klĩsto* (New Testament). London: British and Foreign Bible Society, 1920.

Rhoad, George et al., trans. *Luka* (St. Luke's Gospel). Nairobi: Bible Society in East Africa, 1966 [?1926].

Unpublished Theses and Papers

Cummings, Robert. "Aspects of Human Porterage with Special Reference to the Akamba of Kenya: Towards an Economic History, 1820–1920." PhD dissertation, University of California, Los Angeles, 1975.

Grignon, François. "Le politicien entrepreneur et son terroir: Paul Ngei à Kangundo (Kenya), 1945–1990." PhD dissertation, Université Montesquieu-Bordeaux IV, 1997.

Herskovits, Melville. "The Cattle Complex in East Africa." PhD dissertation, Columbia University, 1923.

Jackson, Kennell. "An Ethnohistorical Study of the Oral Traditions of the Akamba of Kenya." PhD dissertation, University of California, Los Angeles, 1972.

Mueller, Susanne. "Political Parties in Kenya: Patterns of Opposition and Dissent, 1919–1969." PhD dissertation, Princeton University, 1972.

Onneweer, Maarten. "Redeeming Ukamba Word and World, 1893–1905." Unpublished paper, 2007.

Osborne, Myles. "Changing Kamba, Making Kenya, c. 1880–1964." PhD dissertation, Harvard University, 2008.

Prins, Martine. "Uneasy Alliance: Machakos District: Political Developments in a Framework of Collaboration, 1938–69." PhD dissertation, Rijksuniversiteit Leiden, 1997.

Schleh, Eugene. "Post-service Careers of African World War Two Veterans: British East and West Africa with Particular Reference to Ghana and Uganda." PhD dissertation, Yale University, 1968.

Waller, Richard. "The Lords of East Africa: The Maasai in the Mid-Nineteenth Century, c. 1840–1885." PhD dissertation, Cambridge University, 1978.

Books and Articles

Ainsworth, John. "On a Journey from Machako's to Kitwyi." *Geographical Journal* 7 (1896): 406–412.

Allman, Jean. "Be(com)ing Asante, Be(com)ing Akan: Thoughts on Gender, Identity and the Colonial Encounter." In *Ethnicity in Ghana: The Limits of Invention*, edited by Carola Lentz and Paul Nugent, 97–118. Basingstoke, UK: Macmillan Press, 2000.

Alpers, Edward. *Ivory and Slaves: Changing Patterns of International Trade in East Central Africa to the Later Nineteenth Century*. Berkeley: University of California Press, 1975.

Ambler, Charles. *Kenyan Communities in the Age of Imperialism: The Central Region in the Late Nineteenth Century*. New Haven, CT: Yale University Press, 1988.

"Population Movement, Social Formation and Exchange: Central Kenya in the Nineteenth Century." *International Journal of African Historical Studies* 18 (1985): 201–222.

"Projecting the Modern Colonial State: Mobile Cinema in Kenya." In *Film and the End of Empire*, edited by Lee Grieveson and Colin MacCabe, 197–224. London: Palgrave Macmillan, 2011.

"'What Is The World Going To Come To?' Prophecy and Colonialism in Central Kenya." In *Revealing Prophets: Prophecy in East African History*, edited by David Anderson and Douglas Johnson, 221–239. London: James Currey, 1995.

Amutabi, Maurice. "Power and Influence of African Court Clerks and Translators in Colonial Kenya: The Case of Khwisero Native (African) Court, 1946–1956." In *Intermediaries, Interpreters, and Clerks: African Employees in the Making of Colonial Africa*, edited by Benjamin Lawrance, Emily

Osborn, and Richard Roberts, 202–219. Madison: University of Wisconsin Press, 2006.

Anderson, David. "Depression, Dust Bowl, Demography, and Drought: The Colonial State and Soil Conservation in East Africa during the 1930s." *African Affairs* 83 (1984): 321–343.

Histories of the Hanged: The Dirty War in Kenya and the End of Empire. New York: W. W. Norton, 2005.

Anderson, David and David Throup. "Africans and Agricultural Production in Colonial Kenya: The Myth of the War as a Watershed." *Journal of African History* 26 (1985): 327–345.

Anderson, Dick. *We Felt Like Grasshoppers: The Story of the Africa Inland Mission.* Nottingham, UK: Crossway Books, 1994.

Anonymous. "The African Brotherhood Church." *Ecumenical Review* 24 (1972): 145–159.

Arkell-Hardwick, Alfred. *Ivory Trader: The Record of an Expedition Through Kikuyu to Galla-land in East Equatorial Africa.* London: Longmans, Green & Co., 1903.

Atieno Odhiambo, E. S. *The Paradox of Collaboration and Other Essays.* Nairobi: East African Literature Bureau, 1974.

Atkinson, Ronald. *The Roots of Ethnicity: The Origins of the Acholi of Uganda before 1800.* Philadelphia: University of Pennsylvania Press, 1994.

Barlow, Arthur. *Tentative Studies in Kikuyu Grammar and Idiom.* London: Printed for the Foreign Mission Committee of the Church of Scotland and the Society for Promoting Christian Knowledge by W. Blackwood, 1914.

Barth, Fredrik. *Ethnic Groups and Their Boundaries: The Social Organization of Culture Difference.* Boston, MA: Little, Brown, 1969.

Beachey, R. W. "The East African Ivory Trade in the Nineteenth Century." *Journal of African History* 8 (1967): 269–290.

Beecher, Leonard and Gladys Beecher. *Kikuyu–English Dictionary.* Nairobi: Church Missionary Society Bookshop, 1938.

Benson, T. G. *Kikuyu–English Dictionary.* Oxford: Clarendon Press, 1964.

Berman, Bruce. *The Dialectic of Domination: Control, Crisis, and the Colonial State in Kenya, 1895–1963.* Athens: Ohio University Press, 1990.

Berry, Sara. *No Condition is Permanent: The Social Dynamics of Agrarian Change in Sub-Saharan Africa.* Madison: University of Wisconsin Press, 1993.

Boteler, Thomas. *Narrative of a Voyage of Discovery to Africa and Arabia,* Vol. II. London: R. Bentley, 1835.

Branch, Daniel. *Defeating Mau Mau, Creating Kenya: Counterinsurgency, Civil War, and Decolonization.* Cambridge: Cambridge University Press, 2009.

"Loyalists, Mau Mau, and Elections in Kenya: The First Triumph of the System, 1957–1958." *Africa Today* 53 (2006): 27–50.

Brands, Hal. "Wartime Recruiting Practices, Martial Identity and Post-World War II Demobilisation in Colonial Kenya." *Journal of African History* 46 (2005): 103–125.

Bravman, Bill. *Making Ethnic Ways: Communities and Their Transformation in Taita, Kenya, 1800–1950.* Portsmouth, NH: Heinemann, 1998.

Brubaker, Rogers and Frederick Cooper. "Beyond 'Identity.'" *Theory and Society* 29 (2000): 1–47.

Burton, Antoinette. *At the Heart of the Empire: Indians and the Colonial Encounter in Late-Victorian Britain.* Berkeley: University of California Press, 1998.

Burton, Richard. *Zanzibar: City, Island, and Coast,* Vol. II. London: Tinsley Brothers, 1872.

Burton, Richard and John Speke. "A Coasting Voyage from Mombasa to the Pangani River." *Journal of the Royal Geographical Society of London* 28 (1858): 188–226.

Campbell, Guy. *The Charging Buffalo: A History of the Kenya Regiment.* London: Cooper in Association with Secker and Warburg, 1986.

Caplan, Lionel. *Warrior Gentleman: "Gurkhas" in the Western Imagination.* Providence, RI: Berghahn Books, 1995.

Carotenuto, Matthew. "Repatriation in Colonial Kenya: African Institutions and Gendered Violence." *International Journal of African Historical Studies* 45 (2012): 9–28.

"*Riwruok E Teko*: Cultivating Identity in Colonial and Postcolonial Kenya." *Africa Today* 53 (2006): 53–73.

Chanler, William. *Through Jungle and Desert: Travels in Eastern Africa.* New York: Macmillan, 1896.

Chanock, Martin. *Law, Custom and Social Order: The Colonial Experience in Malawi and Zambia.* Cambridge: Cambridge University Press, 1985.

Church Missionary Society. *Proceedings of the Church Missionary Society for Africa and the East.* London: The Society, 1906.

Clayton, Anthony. *Communication for New Loyalties: African Soldiers' Songs.* Athens: Ohio Center for International Studies, 1978.

Clayton, Anthony and David Killingray. *Khaki and Blue: Military and Police in British Colonial Africa.* Athens: Ohio Center for International Studies, 1989.

Clough, Marshall. *Mau Mau Memoirs: History, Memory, and Politics.* Boulder, CO: Lynne Rienner Publishers, 1998.

Cole, Jennifer. *Forget Colonialism? Sacrifice and the Art of Memory in Madagascar.* Berkeley: University of California Press, 2001.

Cooper, Frederick. *Decolonization and African Society: The Labor Question in French and British Africa.* Cambridge: Cambridge University Press, 1996.

On the African Waterfront: Urban Disorder and the Transformation of Work in Colonial Mombasa. New Haven, CT: Yale University Press, 1987.

"Writing the History of Development." *Journal of Modern European History* 10 (2010): 5–23.

Cummings, Robert. "The Early Development of Akamba Local Trade History, *c.* 1780–1820." *Kenya Historical Review* 4 (1976): 85–110.

Decle, Lionel. *Three Years in Savage Africa.* London: Methuen & Co., 1898.

de Luna, Kathryn. "Hunting Reputations: Talent, Individuals, and Community in Precolonial South Africa." *Journal of African History* 53 (2012): 279–299.

Dirks, Nicholas. *Castes of Mind: Colonialism and the Making of Modern India.* Princeton, NJ: Princeton University Press, 2001.

Douglas-Home, Charles. *Evelyn Baring: The Last Proconsul.* London: Collins, 1978.

Dundas, Charles. "History of Kitui." *Journal of the Royal Anthropological Institute of Great Britain and Ireland* 43 (1913): 480–549.

———. "Native Laws of Some Bantu Tribes of East Africa." *Journal of the Royal Anthropological Institute of Great Britain and Ireland* 51 (1921): 217–278.

———. "The Organisation of Laws of Some Bantu Tribes in East Africa." *Journal of the Royal Anthropological Institute of Great Britain and Ireland* 45 (1915): 234–306.

Echenberg, Myron. *Colonial Conscripts: The Tirailleurs Sénégalais in French West Africa, 1857–1960.* Portsmouth, NH: Heinemann, 1991.

Eliot, Charles. *The East Africa Protectorate.* London: E. Arnold, 1905.

Elkins, Caroline. *Imperial Reckoning: The Untold Story of Britain's Gulag in Kenya.* New York: Henry Holt, 2005.

Emery, Lieutenant. "Short Account of Mombas and the Neighbouring Coast of Africa." *Journal of the Royal Geographical Society of London* 3 (1833): 280–283.

Enloe, Cynthia. *Ethnic Soldiers: State Security in Divided Societies.* Athens: University of Georgia Press, 1980.

Falola, Toyin and Paul Lovejoy, eds. *Pawnship in Africa: Debt Bondage in Historical Perspective.* Boulder, CO: Westview Press, 1994.

Ford, John. *The Role of the Trypanosomiases in African Ecology: A Study of the Tsetse Fly Problem.* Oxford: Clarendon Press, 1971.

Fox, Richard. *Lions of the Punjab: Culture in the Making.* Berkeley: University of California Press, 1985.

Gadsden, Fay. "Further Notes on the Kamba Destocking Controversy of 1938." *International Journal of African Historical Studies* 7 (1974): 681–687.

Galaty, John. "Maasai Expansion and the New East African Pastoralism." In *Being Maasai: Ethnicity & Identity in East Africa,* edited by Thomas Spear and Richard Waller, 61–86. London: James Currey, 1993.

Gengenbach, Heidi. "'I'll Bury You in the Border!': Women's Land Struggles in Post-War Facazisse (Magude District), Mozambique." *Journal of Southern African Studies* 24 (1998): 7–36.

Gertzel, Cherry. *The Politics of Independent Kenya, 1963–8.* Evanston, IL: Northwestern University Press, 1970.

Glassman, Jonathon. *Feasts and Riot: Revelry, Rebellion, and Popular Consciousness on the Swahili Coast, 1856–1888.* Portsmouth, NH: Heinemann, 1995.

Goldsmith, F. H., ed. *John Ainsworth, Pioneer Kenya Administrator, 1864–1946.* London: Macmillan, 1959.

Goldsworthy, David, ed. *British Documents on the End of Empire,* Series A, Vol. III: *The Conservative Government and the End of Empire, 1951–1957,* Part III: *Economic and Social Policies.* London: H. M. Stationary Office, 1994.

Greene, Sandra. *Gender, Ethnicity, and Social Change on the Upper Slave Coast: A History of the Anlo-Ewe.* London: James Currey, 1996.

Gregory, Robert. *Quest for Equality: Asian Politics in East Africa, 1900–1967.* Hyderabad, India: Orient Longman, 1993.

Guillain, Charles. *Documents sur l'histoire, la géographie et le commerce de l'Afrique Orientale*, Vol. II. Paris: A. Bertrand, 1856.

Guyer, Jane and Samuel Eno Belinga. "Wealth in People as Wealth in Knowledge: Accumulation and Composition in Equatorial Africa." *Journal of African History* 36 (1995): 91–120.

Hailey, Malcolm. *An African Survey: A Study of Problems Arising in Africa South of the Sahara*. London: Oxford University Press, 1938.

Hanley, Gerald. *Monsoon Victory*. London: Collins, 1946.

Havinden, Michael and David Meredith. *Colonial Development: Britain and its Tropical Colonies, 1850–1960*. London: Routledge, 1993.

Hemingway, Patrick, ed. *True at First Light* by Ernest Hemingway. New York: Scribner, 1999.

Hildebrandt, J. M. "Ethnographische notizen über Wakamba und ihre nachbaren." *Zeitschrift fur Ethnologie* 10 (1878): 347–406.

Hill, Martin. *The Harambee Movement in Kenya: Self-Help, Development, and Education among the Kamba of Kitui District*. London: Athlone Press, 1991.

Hill, Shelagh. *Early Memories of Settlers in Machakos, Kenya*. Sherborne, UK: Shelagh Hill, 2006.

Hobley, Charles. *Bantu Beliefs and Magic: With Particular Reference to the Kikuyu and Kamba Tribes of Kenya*. London: H. F. & G. Witherby, 1922.

Ethnology of A-Kamba and Other East African Tribes. Cambridge: The University Press, 1910.

Kenya: From Chartered Company to Crown Colony. London: H. F. & G. Witherby, 1929.

Hodges, Geoffrey. *The Carrier Corps: Military Labour in the East African Campaign, 1914–1918*. Westport, CT: Greenwood Press, 1986.

"Military Labour in East Africa and its Impact on Kenya." In *Africa and the First World War*, edited by Melvin Page, 137–151. New York: St. Martin's Press, 1987.

Höhnel, Ludwig v. *Discovery of Lakes Rudolf and Stephanie*, 2 vols. London: Cass, 1968 [1894].

Horne, Gerald. *Mau Mau in Harlem? The U.S. and the Liberation of Kenya*. New York: Palgrave Macmillan, 2009.

Hornsby, Charles. *Kenya: A History Since Independence*. London: I. B. Tauris, 2013.

Hunter, J. A. *Hunter*. New York: Harper and Brothers, 1952.

Huxley, Elspeth. *A New Earth: An Experiment in Colonialism*. London: Chatto & Windus, 1960.

Red Strangers: A Novel. London: Harper, 1939.

Hyam, Ronald, ed. *British Documents on the End of Empire*, Series A, Vol. II: *The Labour Government and the End of Empire, 1945–1951*, Part IV: *Race Relations and the Commonwealth*. London: H. M. Stationary Office, 1992.

Iliffe, John. *A Modern History of Tanganyika*. Cambridge: Cambridge University Press, 1979.

Honour in African History. Cambridge: Cambridge University Press, 2005.

The African Poor: A History. Cambridge: Cambridge University Press, 1987.

Isaacman, Allen and Barbara Isaacman. *Slavery and Beyond: The Making of Men and Chikunda Ethnic Identities in the Unstable World of South-Central Africa, 1750–1920*. Portsmouth, NH: Heinemann, 2004.

Itote, Waruhiu. *"Mau Mau" General*. Nairobi: East African Publishing House, 1967.

Jackson, Ashley. *Distant Drums: The Role of the Colonies in British Imperial Warfare*. Brighton, UK: Sussex Academic Press, 2010.

Jackson, Frederick. *Early Days in East Africa*. London: E. Arnold, 1930.

Jackson, Kennell. "The Dimensions of Kamba Pre-Colonial History." In *Kenya Before 1900*, edited by Bethwell Ogot, 174–261. Nairobi: East African Publishing House, 1976.

Kabiro, Ngugi and Donald Barnett. *Man in the Middle: The Story of Ngugi Kabiro*. Richmond, BC: Liberation Support Movement, 1973.

Kaggia, Bildad. *Roots of Freedom, 1921–1963: The Autobiography of Bildad Kaggia*. Nairobi: East African Publishing House, 1975.

Kakembo, Robert. *An African Soldier Speaks*. London: Livingstone Press, 1946.

Kanogo, Tabitha. "Kenya and the Depression, 1929–1939." In *A Modern History of Kenya, 1895–1980*, edited by William Ochieng', 112–143. Nairobi: Evans Brothers, 1989.

Squatters and the Roots of Mau Mau, 1905–1963. London: James Currey, 1987.

Kenyatta, Jomo. *Facing Mount Kenya*. Nairobi: Heinemann, 1971 [1938].

Kiewiet Hemphill, Marie de. "The British Sphere, 1884–94." In *History of East Africa*, Vol. I, edited by Roland Oliver and Gervase Mathew, 390–432. Oxford: Clarendon Press, 1963.

Killingray, David. "Labour Exploitation for Military Campaigns in British Colonial Africa, 1870–1945." *Journal of Contemporary History* 24 (1989): 483–501.

"Labour Mobilisation in British Colonial Africa for the War Effort, 1939–46." In *Africa and the Second World War*, edited by David Killingray and Richard Rathbone, 68–96. Basingstoke, UK: Macmillan, 1986.

"The Idea of a British Imperial African Army." *Journal of African History* 20 (1979): 421–436.

Killingray, David with Martin Plaut. *Fighting for Britain: African Soldiers in the Second World War*. Woodbridge, UK: James Currey, 2010.

Kimambo, Isaria. "The Economic History of the Kamba, 1850–1950." *Hadith* 2 (1970): 79–103.

Kimilu, David. *Mũkamba wa Wo*. Kampala: East African Literature Bureau, 1962.

Kirk-Greene, Anthony. "'*Damnosa Hereditas*': Ethnic Ranking and the Martial Races Imperative in Africa." *Ethnic and Racial Studies* 3 (1980): 393–412.

"The Thin White Line: The Size of the British Colonial Service in Africa." *African Affairs* 79 (1980): 25–44.

Kitching, Gavin. *Class and Economic Change in Kenya: The Making of an African Petite Bourgeoisie, 1905–1970*. New Haven, CT: Yale University Press, 1980.

Kjekshus, Helge. *Ecology Control and Economic Development in East African History: The Case of Tanganyika, 1850–1950*. London: James Currey, 1996 [1977].

Krapf, Johann. *Travels, Researches and Missionary Labours in East Africa*. London: Frank Cass & Co., 1968 [1860].

Kyle, Keith. *The Politics of the Independence of Kenya*. Basingstoke, UK: Macmillan, 1999.

Lal, K., ed. *Trial of Balwant Rai and Others*. Leicester, UK: Taleaga, 1984.

Lambert, H. E. "Land Tenure Among the Kamba." *African Studies* 6 (1947): 131–147.

Lamphear, John. "The Kamba and the Northern Mrima Coast." In *Pre-Colonial African Trade: Essays on Trade in Central and Eastern Africa before 1900*, edited by Richard Gray and David Birmingham, 75–101. London: Oxford University Press, 1970.

Landau, Paul. *The Realm of the Word: Language, Gender, and Christianity in a Southern African Kingdom*. Portsmouth, NH: Heinemann, 1995.

Larby, Norman. *The Peoples of Kenya 8: The Kamba*. London: CMS Literature Society, 1944.

Lee, J. M. *African Armies and Civil Order*. New York: Published for the Institute for Strategic Studies by Praeger, 1969.

Lee, J. M. and Martin Petter. *The Colonial Office, War and Development Policy: Organisation and the Planning of a Metropolitan Initiative, 1939–1945*. London: Published for the Institute of Commonwealth Studies by M. T. Smith, 1982.

Lewis, Joanna. *Empire State-Building: War and Welfare in Kenya, 1925–52*. Oxford: James Currey, 2000.

Leys, Colin. *Underdevelopment in Kenya: The Political Economy of Neo-Colonialism, 1964–1971*. Berkeley: University of California Press, 1974.

Lindblom, Gerhard. *Kamba Folklore I: Tales of Animals*. Uppsala, Sweden: Appelbergs Boktryckeri Aktiebolag, 1928.

Kamba Folklore III: Riddles, Proverbs and Songs. Uppsala, Sweden: Appelbergs Boktryckeri Aktiebolag, 1934.

Notes on Kamba Grammar: With Two Appendices: Kamba Names of Persons, Places, Animals and Plants; Salutations. Uppsala, Sweden: Appelbergs Boktryckeri Aktiebolag, 1926.

The Akamba in British East Africa: An Ethnological Monograph. Uppsala, Sweden: K. W. Appelbergs, 1916.

Lindsay, Lisa and Stephan Miescher, eds. *Men and Masculinities in Modern Africa*. Portsmouth, NH: Heinemann, 2003.

Lloyd-Jones, William. *K.A.R.: Being an Unofficial Account of the Origin and Activities of the King's African Rifles*. London: Arrowsmith, 1926.

Lonsdale, John. "Authority, Gender & Violence: The War Within Mau Mau's Fight for Land & Freedom." In *Mau Mau and Nationhood: Arms, Authority & Narration*, edited by E. S. Atieno Odhiambo and John Lonsdale, 46–75. Oxford: James Currey, 2003.

"Constructing Mau Mau." *Transactions of the Royal Historical Society* 40 (1990): 239–260.

"Mau Maus of the Mind: Making Mau Mau and Remaking Kenya." *Journal of African History* 31 (1990): 393–421.

"Political Accountability in African History." In *Political Domination in Africa: Reflections on the Limits of Power*, edited by Patrick Chabal, 126–157. Cambridge: Cambridge University Press, 1986.

"The Conquest State, 1895–1904." In *A Modern History of Kenya, 1895–1980*, edited by William Ochieng', 6–34. Nairobi: Evans Brothers, 1989.

"The Depression and the Second World War in the Transformation of Kenya." In *Africa and the Second World War*, edited by David Killingray and Richard Rathbone, 97–142. New York: St. Martin's Press, 1986.

"The Moral Economy of Mau Mau: Wealth, Poverty & Civic Virtue in Kikuyu Political Thought." In *Unhappy Valley: Conflict in Kenya and Africa*, Vol. II, edited by Bruce Berman and John Lonsdale, 315–504. London: James Currey, 1992.

"When Did the Gusii (Or Any Other Group) Become a 'Tribe'?" *Kenya Historical Review* 5 (1977): 123–133.

Low, D. A. "The Northern Interior, 1840–84." In *History of East Africa*, Vol. I, edited by Roland Oliver and Gervase Mathew, 297–351. Oxford: Clarendon Press, 1963.

Lugard, Frederick. *The Rise of Our East African Empire: Early Efforts in Nyasaland and Uganda*, 3 vols. London: W. Blackwood and Sons, 1893.

Luongo, Katherine. "If You Can't Beat Them, Join Them: Government Cleansings of Witches and Mau Mau in 1950s Kenya." *History in Africa* 33 (2006): 451–471.

"Prophecy, Possession, and Politics: Negotiating the Supernatural in 20th Century Machakos." *International Journal of African Historical Studies* 45 (2012): 191–216.

Witchcraft and Colonial Rule in Kenya, 1900–1955. Cambridge: Cambridge University Press, 2011.

Lynch, Gabrielle. *I Say To You: Ethnic Politics and the Kalenjin in Kenya.* Chicago, IL: University of Chicago Press, 2011.

MacArthur, Julie. "The Making and Unmaking of African Languages: Oral Communities and Competitive Linguistic Work in Western Kenya." *Journal of African History* 53 (2012): 151–172.

Macdonald, James. *Soldiering and Surveying in British East Africa, 1891–1894.* London: E. Arnold, 1897.

MacMunn, George. *The Armies of India.* London: A. and C. Black, 1911.

Macpherson, Robert. *The Presbyterian Church in Kenya: An Account of the Origins and Growth of the Presbyterian Church of East Africa.* Nairobi: Presbyterian Church of East Africa, 1970.

MacQueen, James. "Notes on the Present State of Geography of Some Parts of Africa." *Journal of the Royal Geographical Society of London* 20 (1850): 235–252.

Mahone, Sloan. "The Psychology of Rebellion: Colonial Medical Responses to Dissent in British East Africa." *Journal of African History* 47 (2006): 241–258.

/ Mamdani, Mahmood. *Citizen and Subject: Contemporary Africa and the Legacy of Late Colonialism.* Princeton, NJ: Princeton University Press, 1996.
"Making Sense of Political Violence in Postcolonial Africa." *Identity, Culture and Politics* 3 (2002): 1–24.

Mangat, J. S. *A History of the Asians in East Africa, c. 1886–1945.* Oxford: Clarendon Press, 1969.

Mann, Gregory. *Native Sons: West African Veterans and France in the Twentieth Century.* Durham, NC: Duke University Press, 2006.

Marjomaa, Risto. "The Martial Spirit: Yao Soldiers in British Service in Nyasaland (Malawi), 1895–1939." *Journal of African History* 44 (2003): 413–432.

Matson, A. T. and Thomas Ofcansky. "A Bio-Bibliography of C. W. Hobley." *History in Africa* 8 (1981): 253–260.

Maxon, Robert. *John Ainsworth and the Making of Kenya.* Washington, DC: University Press of America, 1980.

Mbiti, John. *Akamba Stories.* Oxford: Clarendon Press, 1966.

Metcalf, Thomas. *Ideologies of the Raj.* Cambridge: Cambridge University Press, 1994.

Mettam, R. W. M. "A Short History of Rinderpest with Special Reference to Africa." *Uganda Journal* 5 (1937): 22–26.

Middleton, John. *The Central Tribes of the North-Eastern Bantu.* London: International African Institute, 1953.

Middleton, John and Greet Kershaw. *The Kikuyu and Kamba of Kenya.* London: International African Institute, 1965.

Moore, Henrietta and Megan Vaughan. *Cutting Down Trees: Gender, Nutrition, and Agricultural Change in Northern Zambia, 1890–1990.* Portsmouth, NH: Heinemann, 1994.

Morgan, David. *The Official History of Colonial Development,* 5 vols. London: Macmillan, 1980.

Mottahedeh, Roy. *Loyalty and Leadership in an Early Islamic Society.* Princeton, NJ: Princeton University Press, 1980.

Moyse-Bartlett, Hubert. *The King's African Rifles: A Study in the Military History of East and Central Africa, 1890–1945.* Aldershot, UK: Gale & Polden, 1956.

Mukherjee, Mithi. "Justice, War, and the Imperium: India and Britain in Edmund Burke's Prosecutorial Speeches in the Impeachment Trial of Warren Hastings." *Law and History Review* 23 (2005): 589–630.

Munro, J. Forbes. *Colonial Rule and the Kamba: Social Change in the Kenya Highlands, 1889–1939.* Oxford: Clarendon Press, 1975.

Muriuki, Godfrey. *A History of the Kikuyu, 1500–1900.* New York: Oxford University Press, 1974.

Murton, John. "Population Growth and Poverty in Machakos District, Kenya." *The Geographical Journal* 165 (1999): 37–46.

Muthiani, Joseph. *Akamba from Within: Egalitarianism in Social Relations.* New York: Exposition Press, 1973.

Mutiso, Gideon-Cyrus. *Kenya: Politics, Policy and Society.* Kampala: East African Literature Bureau, 1975.

Mutongi, Kenda. *Worries of the Heart: Widows, Family, and Community in Kenya*. Chicago, IL: University of Chicago Press, 2007.

Mwanzi, H. A. "African Initiatives and Resistance in East Africa, 1880–1914." In *UNESCO General History of Africa*, Vol. VII, edited by A. Adu Boahen, 72–82. London: James Currey, 1990.

Myrick, Bismarck. "Colonial Initiatives and Kamba Reaction in Machakos District: The Destocking Issue, 1930–1938." In *Three Aspects of Crisis in Colonial Kenya*, 1–26. Syracuse, NY: Maxwell School of Citizenship and Public Affairs, Syracuse University, 1975.

Newman, Jeremy. *The Ukamba Members Association*. Nairobi: Transafrica Publishers, 1974.

Njau, Rebeka and Gideon Mulaki. *Kenya Women Heroes and Their Mystical Power*. Nairobi: Risk Publications, 1984.

Nottingham, John. "Sorcery among the Akamba in Kenya." *Journal of African Administration* 11 (1959): 1–14.

Ochieng', William. "Independent Kenya, 1963–1980." In *A Modern History of Kenya, 1895–1980*, edited by William Ochieng', 202–218. Nairobi: Evans Brothers, 1989.

Odinga, Oginga. *Not Yet Uhuru: The Autobiography of Oginga Odinga*. London: Heinemann Educational Books, 1967.

Oldenquist, Andrew. "Loyalties." *Journal of Philosophy* 79 (1982): 173–193.

O'Leary, Michael. "Responses to Drought in Kitui District." *Disasters* 4 (1980): 315–327.

—— *The Kitui Akamba: Economic and Social Change in Semi-Arid Kenya*. Nairobi: Heinemann Educational Books, 1984.

Oliver, Roland. *The Missionary Factor in East Africa*. London: Longmans, 1952.

Omissi, David. *The Sepoy and the Raj: The Indian Army, 1860–1940*. Basingstoke, UK: Macmillan, 1994.

Osborne, Myles. "'The Cat With Nine Lives': Paul Ngei and the Making of Modern Kenya." *Journal of Eastern African Studies* 6 (2012): 196–210.

—— "The Jeremy Newman Papers." *History in Africa* 39 (2012): 355–359.

—— "The Kamba and Mau Mau: Ethnicity, Development, and Chiefship, 1952–1960." *International Journal of African Historical Studies* 43 (2010): 63–87.

Paice, Edward. *Tip and Run: The Untold Tragedy of the Great War in Africa*. London: Weidenfeld & Nicolson, 2007.

Parsons, Timothy. *The 1964 Army Mutinies and the Making of Modern East Africa*. Westport, CT: Praeger, 2003.

—— *The African Rank-and-File: Social Implications of Colonial Military Service in the King's African Rifles, 1902–1964*. Portsmouth, NH: Heinemann, 1999.

—— "'Wakamba Warriors Are Soldiers of the Queen': The Evolution of the Kamba as a Martial Race, 1890–1970." *Ethnohistory* 46 (1999): 671–701.

Pearce, R. D. *The Turning Point in Africa: British Colonial Policy, 1938–1948*. London: Frank Cass, 1982.

Pearson, Michael. *Port Cities and Intruders: The Swahili Coast, India, and Portugal in the Early Modern Era*. Baltimore, MD: The Johns Hopkins University Press, 1998.

Pedersen, Susan. *Family, Dependence, and the Origins of the Welfare State: Britain and France, 1914–1945.* Cambridge: Cambridge University Press, 1993.

Peers, Douglas. "Martial Races and South Asian Military Culture in the Victorian Indian Army." In *Military History of Modern India*, edited by Daniel Marston and Chandar Sundaram, 34–52. Westport, CT: Praeger, 2007.

Penwill, D. J. *Kamba Customary Law: Notes Taken in the Machakos District of Kenya Colony.* London: Macmillan, 1951.

Perham, Margery, ed. *The Diaries of Lord Lugard*, 3 vols. London: Faber and Faber, 1959–1963.

Peters, Karl. *New Light on Dark Africa: Being the Narrative of the German Emin Pasha Expedition.* London: Ward, Lock, and Co., 1891.

Peterson, Derek. *Creative Writing: Translation, Bookkeeping, and the Work of Imagination in Colonial Kenya.* Athens: Ohio University Press, 2004.

Ethnic Patriotism and the East African Revival: A History of Dissent, c. 1935–1972. Cambridge: Cambridge University Press, 2012.

Pigott, J. R. W. "Mr. J. R. W. Pigott's Journey to the Upper Tana, 1889." *Proceedings of the Royal Geographical Society and Monthly Record of Geography* 12 (1890): 129–136.

Raikes, Philip. *Livestock Policy and Development in East Africa.* Uppsala, Sweden: Scandinavian Institute for African Studies, 1981.

Ranger, Terence. "The Invention of Tradition in Colonial Africa." In *The Invention of Tradition*, edited by Eric Hobsbawm and Terence Ranger, 211–262. Cambridge: Cambridge University Press, 1983.

"The Invention of Tradition Revisited." In *Legitimacy and the State in Twentieth-Century Africa*, edited by Terence Ranger and Olufemi Vaughan, 62–111. Basingstoke, UK: Macmillan, 1993.

Ravenstein, E. G. "Messrs. Jackson and Gedge's Journey to Uganda via Masai-Land." *Proceedings of the Royal Geographical Society and Monthly Record of Geography* 13 (1891): 193–208.

"The Rev. R. M. Ormerod's Journeys on the Tana River." *Geographical Journal* 8 (1896): 283–290.

Richardson, Kenneth. *Garden of Miracles: A History of the Africa Inland Mission.* London: Published in Association with the Africa Inland Mission by P. Victory, 1968.

Rigby, C. P. "Mr. J. M. Hildebrandt on his Travels in East Africa." *Proceedings of the Royal Geographical Society of London* 22 (1877–1878): 446–453.

Robertson, Claire. "Gender and Trade Relations in Central Kenya in the Late Nineteenth Century." *International Journal of African Historical Studies* 30 (1997): 23–47.

Trouble Showed the Way: Women, Men, and Trade in the Nairobi Area. Bloomington: Indiana University Press, 1997.

Rosberg, Carl and John Nottingham. *The Myth of "Mau Mau": Nationalism in Kenya.* New York: Meridian, 1970 [1966].

Sandgren, David. "Kamba Christianity: From Africa Inland Mission to African Brotherhood Church." In *East African Expressions of Christianity*, edited by Thomas Spear and Isaria Kimambo, 169–195. Oxford: James Currey, 1999.

Sanger, Clyde and John Nottingham. "The Kenya General Election of 1963." *Journal of Modern African Studies* 2 (1964): 1–40.

Savage, Donald. "Jomo Kenyatta, Malcolm Macdonald and the Colonial Office, 1938–39: Some Documents from the P. R. O." *Canadian Journal of African Studies* 3 (1969): 615–632.

Savage, Donald and J. Forbes Munro. "Carrier Corps Recruitment in the British East Africa Protectorate, 1914–1918." *Journal of African History* 7 (1966): 313–342.

Shiroya, O. J. E. *African Politics in Colonial Kenya: Contribution of World War II Veterans, 1945–1960.* Nairobi: Educational Research and Publications, 1992. *Kenya and World War II: African Soldiers in the European War.* Nairobi: Kenya Literature Bureau, 1985.

Shorter, Aylward. *East African Societies.* Boston, MA: Routledge & Kegan Paul, Inc., 1974.

Shutt, Allison. "The Settlers' Cattle Complex: The Etiquette of Culling Cattle in Colonial Zimbabwe, 1938." *Journal of African History* 43 (2002): 263–286.

Singh, Makhan. *History of Kenya's Trade Union Movement to 1952.* Nairobi: East African Publishing House, 1969.

Sinha, Mrinalini. *Colonial Masculinity: The "Manly Englishman" and the "Effeminate Bengali" in the Late Nineteenth Century.* Manchester, UK: Manchester University Press, 1995.

Somba, John. *Akamba Mirror: Some Notable Events in the Machakos District of Kenya, 1889–1929 A.D.* Kijabe, Kenya: Kesho Publications, 1979.

Sorrenson, M. P. K. *Land Reform in the Kikuyu Country: A Study in Government Policy.* Nairobi: Oxford University Press, 1967.

Spear, Thomas. *Kenya's Past: An Introduction to Historical Method in Africa.* London: Longman, 1981.
"Neo-Traditionalism and the Limits of Invention in Colonial Africa." *Journal of African History* 44 (2003): 3–27.

Spencer, John. *The Kenya African Union.* Boston, MA: Routledge & Kegan Paul, Inc., 1985.

Spencer, Leon. "Notes on the Kamba Destocking Controversy of 1938." *International Journal of African Historical Studies* 4 (1972): 629–636.

Stanner, W. E. H. "The Kitui Kamba Market, 1938–39." *Ethnology* 8 (1969): 125–138.

Stapleton, Timothy. *African Police and Soldiers in Colonial Zimbabwe, 1923–80.* Rochester, NY: Rochester University Press, 2011.

Steinhart, Edward. *Black Poachers, White Hunters: A Social History of Hunting in Colonial Kenya.* Oxford: James Currey, 2006.
Conflict and Collaboration: The Kingdoms of Western Uganda, 1890–1907. Princeton, NJ: Princeton University Press, 1977.
"Elephant Hunting in Nineteenth-Century Kenya: Kamba Society and Ecology in Transformation." *International Journal of African Historical Studies* 33 (2000): 335–349.

Stone, Michael. "Organized Poaching in Kitui District: A Failure in District Authority, 1900 to 1960." *International Journal of African Historical Studies* 5 (1972): 436–452.

Streets, Heather. *Martial Races: The Military, Race and Masculinity in British Imperial Culture, 1857–1914.* Manchester, UK: Manchester University Press, 2004.

Struck, Bernhard. "Collections Towards a Bibliography of the Bantu Languages of British East Africa." *Journal of the Royal African Society* 6 (1907): 390–404.

Tamarkin, Mordechai. "The Roots of Political Stability in Kenya." *African Affairs* 77 (1978): 297–320.

Tate, H. R. "Notes on the Kikuyu and Kamba Tribes of British East Africa." *Journal of the Anthropological Institute of Great Britain and Ireland* 34 (1904): 130–148.

Thiong'o, Ngugi wa. *Weep Not, Child.* London: Heinemann, 1964.

Thomas, Lynn. *Politics of the Womb: Women, Reproduction, and the State in Kenya.* Berkeley: University of California Press, 2003.

Thornton, Richard. "Notes on a Journey to Kilima-ndjaro." *Journal of the Royal Geographical Society of London* 35 (1865): 15–21.

Throup, David and Charles Hornsby. *Multi-Party Politics in Kenya: The Kenyatta & Moi States & the Triumph of the System in the 1992 Election.* London: James Currey, 1998.

Thuku, Harry with Kenneth King. *An Autobiography.* Nairobi: Oxford University Press, 1970.

Thurston, Anne. *The Intensification of Smallholder Agriculture in Kenya: The Genesis and Implementation of the Swynnerton Plan.* Oxford: Oxford Development Records Project, 1984.

Tiffen, Mary, Michael Mortimore and Francis Gichuki. *More People, Less Erosion: Environmental Recovery in Kenya.* Chichester, UK: J. Wiley, 1994.

Tignor, Robert. "Colonial Chiefs in Chiefless Societies." *Journal of Modern African Studies* 9 (1971): 339–359.

"Kamba Political Protest: The Destocking Controversy of 1938." *African Historical Studies* 4 (1971): 237–251.

The Colonial Transformation of Kenya: The Kamba, Kikuyu, and Maasai from 1900 to 1939. Princeton, NJ: Princeton University Press, 1976.

Unomah, A. C. and J. B. Webster. "East Africa: The Expansion of Commerce." In *The Cambridge History of Africa*, Vol. V, edited by John Flint, 270–318. Cambridge: Cambridge University Press, 1976.

Vail, Leroy, ed. *The Creation of Tribalism in Southern Africa.* Berkeley: University of California Press, 1989.

van Beusekom, Monica. *Negotiating Development: African Farmers and Colonial Experts at the Office du Niger, 1920–1960.* Oxford: James Currey, 2002.

Wachanga, H. K. *The Swords of Kirinyaga: The Fight for Land and Freedom.* Kampala: East African Literature Bureau, 1975.

Wainaina, Binyavanga. *One Day I Will Write About This Place: A Memoir.* Minneapolis, MN: Graywolf Press, 2011.

Wakefield, T. and Keith Johnson. "Routes of Native Caravans from the Coast to the Interior of East Africa." *Journal of the Royal Geographical Society of London* 40 (1870): 303–339.

Waller, Richard. "Ecology, Migration, and Expansion in East Africa." *African Affairs* 84 (1985): 347–370.

"Economic and Social Relations in the Central Rift Valley: The Maa-Speakers and their Neighbours in the Nineteenth Century." *Hadith* 8 (1985): 83–151.

"Rebellious Youth in Colonial Africa." *Journal of African History* 47 (2006): 77–92.

Wamweya, Joram. *Freedom Fighter*. Nairobi: East African Publishing House, 1971.

Ward, H. F. and John Milligan. *Handbook of British East Africa*. London: S. Prade, 1912.

Watkins, Elizabeth. *Jomo's Jailor: Grand Warrior of Kenya: The Life of Leslie Whitehouse*. Watlington, UK: Britwell Books, 1996.

Watt, Rachel. *In the Heart of Savagedom: Reminiscences of Life and Adventure during a Quarter of a Century of Pioneering Missionary Labours in the Wilds of East Equatorial Africa*. London: Marshall, 1900.

White, Luise. *The Comforts of Home: Prostitution in Colonial Nairobi*. Chicago, IL: University of Chicago Press, 1990.

Widner, Jennifer. *The Rise of a Party-State in Kenya: From "Harambee!" to "Nyayo!"* Berkeley: University of California Press, 1992.

Wolf, James. "Asian and African Recruitment in the Kenya Police, 1920–1950." *International Journal of African Historical Studies* 6 (1973): 401–412.

Wolff, Richard. *The Economics of Colonialism: Britain and Kenya, 1870–1930*. New Haven, CT: Yale University Press, 1974.

Young, Crawford. "Nationalism, Ethnicity, and Class in Africa: A Retrospective." *Cahiers d'Etudes Africaines* 26 (1986): 421–495.

The African Colonial State in Comparative Perspective. New Haven, CT: Yale University Press, 1994.

Zeleza, Tiyambe. "The Establishment of Colonial Rule, 1905–1920." In *A Modern History of Kenya, 1895–1980*, edited by William Ochieng', 35–70. Nairobi: Evans Brothers, 1989.

Index

virtue (cont.)
community, 10, 12, 16, 162, 177–8, 193,
219, 224, 226, 243–4
hunters and warriors, 26–34, 79
Kikuyu, 40, 192
loyalty, 216
soldiers and police, 60–2, 77, 79, 101,
134, 152–3, 160
wealth, 67–8, 77
women, 13, 16, 79, 191, 193, 233–4
See also honor; women: virtue

Watt, Rachel, 45
Watt, Stuart, 45, 83
welfare, 162, 208, 220
See also community development;
development
Whitehouse, Leslie, 229
witchcraft, 165, 172

women, 78
clubs and organizations, 220–2
divorce, 122, 176, 223
freedoms restricted by male authority
c. 1945, 173–7, 191
maintaining autonomy, 80, 170–3,
177–9, 191, 220–3
Nairobi and Mombasa, 178–9
political role post-1960, 16, 233–4, 244,
247
virtue, 11, 80–1, 122, 162, 177–8,
191, 193, 219–24, 226, 233–4,
243–4
work, 81, 176
See also honor: women; virtue: women

Yatta Furrow, 206, 209
Yatta Plateau, 63, 109, 209
Young Akamba Union, 172

Made in the USA
San Bernardino, CA
13 June 2018